SEVILLE
& ANDALUSIA

EYEWITNESS TRAVEL GUIDES

SEVILLE
& ANDALUSIA

LONDON, NEW YORK,
MELBOURNE, MUNICH AND DELHI
www.dk.com

PROJECT EDITOR Anna Streiffert
ART EDITOR Robert Purnell
EDITORS Marcus Hardy, Jane Oliver
DESIGNERS Malcolm Parchment, Katie Peacock
PICTURE RESEARCH Monica Allende, Naomi Peck
DTP DESIGNERS Samantha Borland, Sarah Martin

MAIN CONTRIBUTORS
David Baird, Martin Symington, Nigel Tisdall

PHOTOGRAPHERS
Neil Lukas, John Miller, Linda Whitwam

ILLUSTRATORS
Richard Draper, Isidoro González-Adalid Cabezas
(Acanto Arquitectura y Urbanismo S.L.), Steven Gyapay,
Claire Littlejohn, Maltings, Chris Orr, John Woodcock

Reproduced by Colourscan (Singapore)
Printed and bound by L. Rex Printing Co. Ltd., China

First published in Great Britain in 1996
by Dorling Kindersley Limited
80 Strand, London WC2R 0RL
**Reprinted with revisions 1997, 1998, 1999, 2000,
2001, 2002, 2003, 2004, 2006**

Copyright 1996, 2006 © Dorling Kindersley Limited, London
A Penguin Company

A CIP CATALOGUE RECORD IS AVAILABLE FROM THE BRITISH LIBRARY.

ISBN 1-4053-1193-2
ISBN 9-7814-0531-1939

Previous pages: Torre del Oro in Seville by night

CONTENTS

Bible illustration in Moorish style
dating from the 10th century

INTRODUCING
SEVILLE AND
ANDALUSIA

Horse and carriage at Plaza de
España, Parque María Luisa

Zahara de la Sierra, one of Andalusia's traditional *pueblos blancos* (white towns)

Tiled street sign for Plaza de San Francisco, Estepona

Fritura de pescados

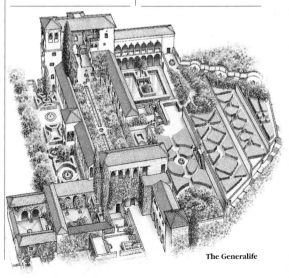

The Generalife

How to Use this Guide

THIS GUIDE HELPS you to get the most from your stay in Seville and Andalusia. It provides both expert recommendations and detailed practical information. *Introducing Seville and Andalusia* maps the region and sets it in its historical and cultural context. *Seville Area by Area* and

Andalusia Area by Area describe the important sights, with maps, pictures and detailed illustrations. Suggestions on what to eat and drink, accommodation, shopping and entertainment are in *Travellers' Needs*, and the *Survival Guide* has tips on everything from transport to using Spanish telephones.

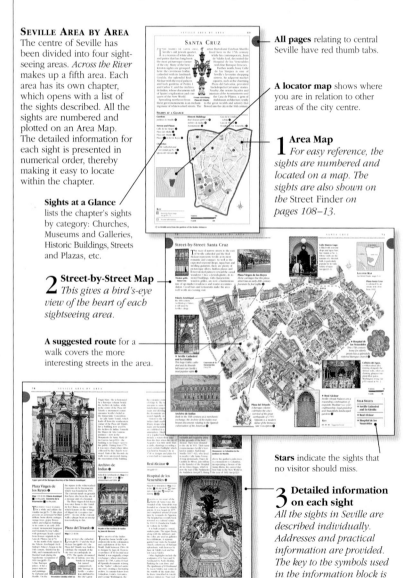

SEVILLE AREA BY AREA

The centre of Seville has been divided into four sight-seeing areas. *Across the River* makes up a fifth area. Each area has its own chapter, which opens with a list of the sights described. All the sights are numbered and plotted on an Area Map. The detailed information for each sight is presented in numerical order, thereby making it easy to locate within the chapter.

Sights at a Glance
lists the chapter's sights by category: Churches, Museums and Galleries, Historic Buildings, Streets and Plazas, etc.

2 Street-by-Street Map
This gives a bird's-eye view of the heart of each sightseeing area.

A suggested route for a walk covers the more interesting streets in the area.

All pages relating to central Seville have red thumb tabs.

A locator map shows where you are in relation to other areas of the city centre.

1 Area Map
For easy reference, the sights are numbered and located on a map. The sights are also shown on the Street Finder *on pages 108–13.*

Stars indicate the sights that no visitor should miss.

3 Detailed information on each sight
All the sights in Seville are described individually. Addresses and practical information are provided. The key to the symbols used in the information block is shown on the back flap.

1 Introduction
The landscape, history and character of each region is described here, showing how the area has developed over the centuries and what it offers the visitor today.

ANDALUSIA AREA BY AREA
In this book, Andalusia has been divided into four distinct regions, each of which has a separate chapter. The most interesting sights to visit have been numbered on a Pictorial Map.

Each area of Andalusia has colour-coded thumb tabs.

2 Pictorial Map
This shows the main road network and provides an illustrated overview of the whole region. All entries are numbered and there are also some useful tips on getting around the region by car, bus and train.

3 Detailed information on each entry
All the important towns and other places to visit are dealt with individually. They are listed in order, following the numbering given on the Pictorial Map. Within each town or city, there is detailed information on important buildings and other sights.

Features give information on topics of particular interest.

The Visitors' Checklist provides a summary of the practical information you need to plan your visit.

4 The top sights
These are given two or more full pages. Historic buildings are dissected to reveal their interiors; museums and galleries have colour-coded floorplans to help you locate the most interesting exhibits.

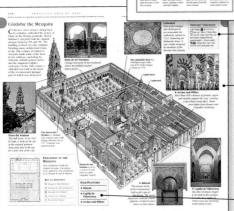

Stars indicate the best features and important works of art.

INTRODUCING
SEVILLE AND
ANDALUSIA

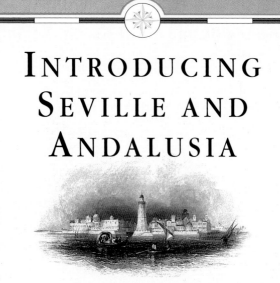

Putting Seville and Andalusia on the Map

A NDALUSIA IS SPAIN'S SOUTHERNMOST REGION, bordered by
Extremadura and Castilla-La Mancha to the north and
Murcia to the northwest. Its long coastline faces the Atlantic
to the west and the Mediterranean to the south and east. One
of Spain's largest regions, it covers an area of 87,267 sq km
(33,693 sq miles) and has a
population of 6.8 million.
Seville is the pro-
vince's capital.

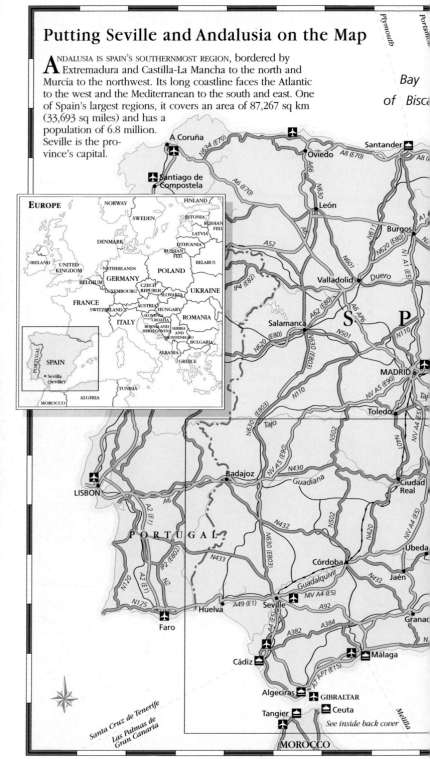

◁ **Painting of the Feria de Abril in Seville by Dominguez Becquer (1885)**

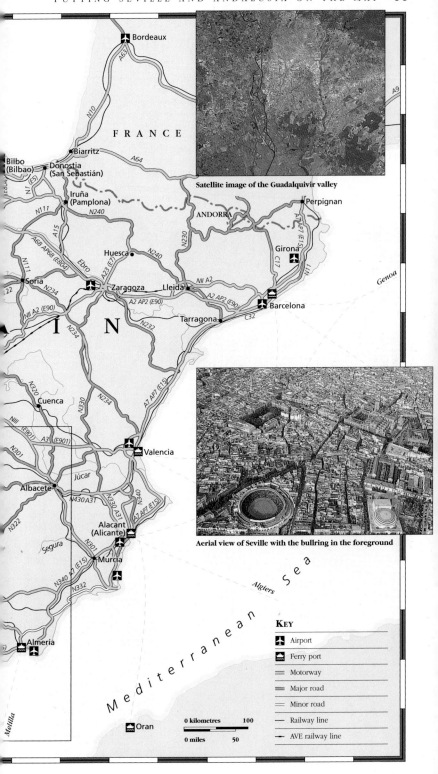

Satellite image of the Guadalquivir valley

Aerial view of Seville with the bullring in the foreground

KEY

✈	Airport
⛴	Ferry port
═	Motorway
━	Major road
─	Minor road
—	Railway line
⊶	AVE railway line

0 kilometres   100

0 miles   50

Seville City Centre and Greater Seville

Seville city centre is a compact maze of old, narrow streets, with most sights within walking distance. A couple of wide, busy avenues cut through the centre, dividing it into separate areas. This book focuses on these areas, starting with the historic neighbourhoods on each side of Avenida de la Constitución. To the west, along the river, is El Arenal with the Plaza de Toros; and to the east lies the old Jewish quarter of Santa Cruz, dominated by the massive cathedral and the Reales Alcázares. In the north lies La Macarena with its many churches, while the Parque María Luisa stretches out beyond the Universidad, south of the historic centre.

El Arenal: Teatro de la Maestranza and Torre del Oro

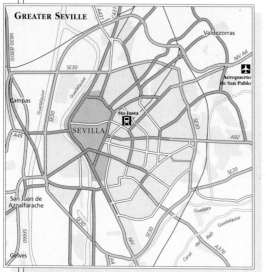

Greater Seville
West of the Guadalquivir river lies the site of Expo '92 and the picturesque Triana quarter. Sprawling industrial zones and modern residential areas surround the town centre.

Parque María Luisa: the Plaza de España, built for the 1929 Exposition

La Macarena: Sevillian façades with window grilles lining Calle Santa Clara

Santa Cruz: Horses and carriages at Plaza del Triunfo by the cathedral

KEY

▢	Major sight
▢	Seville city centre
▢	Built-up area
▢	Greater Seville
✈	Airport
▦	Railway station
▦	Bus terminus
▦	Coach terminus
▦	River boat boarding point
▦	Taxi rank
P	Parking
i	Tourist information
✚	Hospital with casualty unit
▣	Police station
✚	Church
✚	Convent or monastery
⊠	Post office
═	Motorway
═	Major road
=	Minor road
—	Railway
Ⓜ	Metro Station

0 metres   400

0 yards   400

Map labels

DON FADRIQUE
RESOLANA   ANDUEZA
CALLE MUÑOZ LEON
S JUAN DE LA RIBERA
BLANQUILLO
PACHECO Y NUÑEZ DEL PRADO
CALLE PERAL
ESCOBEROS
PARRAS
CALLE TORRES
PLAZA SAN GIL
PODER
ANTONIO SUSILLO
CALLE DE LA FERIA
CALLE DE   RELATOR
PLAZA DE PUMAREJO
LUMBRERAS
PERIS MENCHETA
CALLE CASTILLEJA STA MARIA
CALLE PARRAS
PLAZA DEL CRONISTA
RONDA DE CAPUCHINOS
GRAN
ALAMEDA DE HERCULES
CALLE SAN LUIS
PAZA GIRALDILLO
PLAZA DEL PELICANO
JESUS
CALLE TRAJANO   AMOR DE DIOS
SAAVEDRAS   CALLE   CASTELLAR
PLAZA EUROPA
PLAZA MALDONADOS
PLAZA SAN MARCOS
PL SANTA ISABEL
CALLE DE LA ENLADRILLADA
CALLE MARIA AUXILIADORA
CORTES
PL SAN MARTIN
S DE LA PALMA
CALLE TAVERA
JARDINES DE EL VALLE
SOL
REGINA
BUSTOS TAVERA
LA MACARENA
PL POZO SANTO
PLAZA ZURBARAN
CALLE GERONA
PEÑUELAS
CALLE
CALLE DE RECAREDO
PLAZA DE LA ENCARNACION
IMAGEN
PL DE LOS TERCEROS
PL PONCE DE LEON
ESCUELAS PIAS
LARAÑA
PEDRO
SAN ROMAN
SAN JERONIMO
CORDOBA
SAUREGUI
PL DOÑA CARMEN
MEJIAS
CALLE IMPERIAL
SIERPES
PLAZA DEL ALFALFA
CALLE AGUILAS
SAN ESTEBAN
PLAZA SALVADOR
VIRGENES
PL PILATOS
PL SAN AGUSTIN
PL DE SAN FRANCISCO
CORRAL DEL REY
SANTA CRUZ
SAN JOSE
PL DE LAS MERCEDARIAS
ARGOTE DE MOLINA
PL VIRGEN DE LOS REYES
PLAZA CURTIDORES
ALEMANES
SACIA DE NUESA
Giralda **Catedral**
PL DEL TRIUNFO
PLAZA SANTA CRUZ
PLAZA REFINADORES
JARDINES DE MURILLO
PL DOÑA ELVIRA
PLAZA ALFARO
ADOLFO RODRIGUEZ JURADO
NADER
Reales **Alcázares**
PL CONTRATACION
CALLE DE MENENDEZ PELAYO
PUERTA DE JEREZ
Puerta de **Jerez**
ALMTE LOBO
CALLE SAN FERNANDO
JARDINES DE CRISTINA
PALOS
PL DON JUAN DE AUSTRIA
AVENIDA DE CARLOS V
Prado de **San Sebastián**
LA FRONTERA
JARDINES DEL PRADO
AVENIDA DE PORTUGAL
JARDINES DE SAN TELMO
AVENIDA DE MARIA LUISA
PLAZA EJERCITO ESPAÑOL
DIEGO DE RIAÑO
AVENIDA REINA LUISA
AVDA RODRIGUEZ CASO
AVDA ISABEL LA CATOLICA
PARQUE MARÍA **LUISA**
GLORIETA DE LOS MARINEROS VOLUNTARIOS
PARQUE DE MARIA LUISA
AVENIDA DE HERNAN CORTES
PLAZA DE ESPAÑA
Puente del Generalísimo
GLORIETA COVADONGA
Guadalquivir
DELICIAS
AVENIDA DE PIZARRO
GLORIETA BUENOS AIRES
GLORIETA SANTIAGO MONTOTO
GLORIETA MEXICO
AVDA DE ERITAÑA
AVDA DE MOLINI
Puente de Alfonso XIII
AVDA DE ROMA

A PORTRAIT OF ANDALUSIA

*A*NDALUSIA IS WHERE *all Spain's stereotypes appear to have come together. Bullfighters, flamenco dancers, white villages and harsh* sierras *are all there in abundance. But they form only part of an intricate tapestry. Beneath the surface, expect to find many contradictions. Wherever you travel, particularly when you escape from the tourist-engulfed coast, you will come across the unexpected, whether it is a local* fiesta *or a breathtaking view.*

Until the 1950s Andalusia had changed scarcely at all since the middle of the 19th century, when the English traveller, Richard Ford, described it as "a land bottled for antiquarians" – almost a feudal society, with attendant rigid social strata.

A basket of newly-harvested olives

Today, four-lane highways stretch from horizon to horizon where not so long ago there were only dirt tracks. Children whose parents are illiterate play with computers and plan their university careers. Agriculture is still important, but there are also factories turning out cars and aircraft. As in most other European countries, the service industries, tourism especially, predominate. In 1991 they accounted for 63 per cent of the region's GNP as compared with 8.7 per cent for agriculture and fishing. Yet the seven million inhabitants of Andalusia retain their characteristic love of talk and folklore, their indifference to time and their abundant hospitality.

THE MOORISH LEGACY

The Andalusian character is complex because it reflects a complex history. Successive invaders, including the Phoenicians, Romans, Visigoths and Moors, have all left their indelible mark. Although the Christian rulers of Spain ejected both Jews and Moors

Musicians, singers and dancers continuing a flamenco tradition that dates from the 18th century *(see p26)*

◁ Bullfighters *(see pp24–5)* in traditional costumes, preparing for the *corrida*

from their kingdom, they could not remove their influences on the country – let alone on Andalusia. Look at the face of an Andalusian man or woman and you will catch a glimpse of North Africa. Centuries of Moorish occupation *(see pp44–5)* and the inevitable mingling of blood have created a race and culture different from any in Europe.

Sevillanos enjoying a pre-dinner drink and some tapas (see pp222–3)

As you travel around the region, you will find abundant physical evidence of the Moorish legacy: in the splendour of the Alhambra *(see pp186–7)* and the Mezquita *(see pp140–41)* in Córdoba, and in ruined fortresses and elaborate tilework. Workshops across the region still practise crafts handed down from great Moorish kingdoms. Many of the irrigation networks in use today follow those laid out by the Moors, who built *norias*

(waterwheels), *aljibes* (tanks for collecting the rain), *albercas* (cisterns), and *acequias* (irrigation channels).

As these words show, the Moors also left a strong linguistic legacy, not only of agricultural terms, but also of words for foods – *naranja* (orange), for example, and *aceituna* (olive).

Moorish influence may also account for Andalusians' love of poetry and fine language. It is no coincidence that Spain's finest poets, including among them Nobel prize winners, come from this region.

PEOPLE AND CULTURE

Sevillanos work hard to sustain their reputation for flamboyance and hedonism. A 13th-century Moorish commentator noted that they

Moorish-style stucco work

were "the most frivolous and most given to playing the fool". Living up to that image is a full-time occupation, but the visitor should not be deceived by the exuberant façade. One surprising aspect of both Seville and Andalusia is that although the society may appear open and extrovert, it is, in fact, one that also values privacy.

The Andalusian concept of time can also be perplexing. Progressive business types may try to adjust to the rigorous demands of Europe, but in general, northern Europeans' obsession with time is an object of mirth here. The moment is to be enjoyed and tomorrow will look after itself. A concert will often begin well after the advertised time, and lunch can feasibly take place at any time between 1pm and 4:30pm.

Penitents parading a monstrance, Semana Santa (see p36)

Barren, remote countryside, one of the many faces of Andalusia's varied landscape *(see pp18–19)*

Attitudes to women in Andalusia are changing, as elsewhere in western Europe, though southern Spain's tradition for *machismo* means that there is still some way to go. The number of women, for example, who work outside the home is still lower than in other countries of the West. Although many women have a job in their twenties, they still give up work when they marry in order to have children and look after the house.

Paradoxically, the mother is an almost sacred figure in Andalusia, where family ties are written in blood. Although new affluence and a steady movement to the cities is now beginning to erode old values, Andalusia remains a traditional rural society with a distinct emphasis on personal relationships.

Decorative tilework in the Palacio de Viana *(see p139)*

Sevillian lady in the traditional costume of the *feria (see p36)*

Catholicism is Spain's dominant religion, and adoration of the Virgin is a striking feature of Andalusia. Apart from a purely religious devotion, she is also subject to a peculiar admiration from the male population. A man who never attends Mass may be ecstatic about the Virgin of his local church; when she emerges from the church in procession, he feels fiercely possessive of her. If you try to think of the gorgeously robed figure as a pagan earth mother or fertility goddess, the phenomenon is much easier to understand.

As a society, Andalusia is unafraid of its emotions, which are almost always near the surface. There is no shame in the singing of a *saeta*, the "arrow" of praise launched at the Virgin in Semana Santa (Holy Week), nor is there any ambivalence in the matador's desire to kill his antagonist, the bull. The quintessence of this is flamenco; the pain and passion of its songs reflect not just the sufferings and yearnings of gypsies and the poor, but also Andalusia's soul.

Nun with convent jams

The Landscape of Andalusia

ᴇᴀᴄʜ ʏᴇᴀʀ, several million visitors are drawn to the high-rise resorts along Andalusia's Mediterranean coast. Away from these, however, are empty, windswept Atlantic shores and expansive areas of wetland wilderness. Inland there are rugged mountain ranges clothed with forests of pine, cork and wild olive. Also typical of the landscape are the undulating hills awash with vines, cereals and olive trees. Of Andalusia's total land area, some 17 per cent has been designated national parks or nature reserves in order to protect the region's unique abundance of animal and plant life.

Prickly pear, a native of the Americas

The fertile plains *of the Guadalquivir valley are watered by the river and have been the bread basket of Andalusia since Moorish times. Fields of cereals alternate with straight lines of citrus trees.*

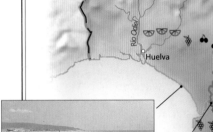

0 kilometres 50

0 miles 25

SIERRA DE ARACENA

Río Odiel

Huelva

Sevilla

Río Guadalquivir

Córdoba

S I E R R A M O

Río Genil

Embalse del Guadalhorce

Río Guadalete

Cádiz

SERRANÍA DE RONDA

Río Guadalhorce

Mála

The Atlantic beaches, *where pine trees grow behind the sand dunes, are less developed than the Mediterranean* costas. *Fishing fleets from Cádiz and Huelva operate offshore.*

The Río Guadalquivir runs through the wetlands of Coto Doñana (*see pp126–7*) before finally entering the Atlantic Ocean.

The Costa del Sol and the rest of the Mediterranean coast are mainly characterized by arid cliffs draped in bougainvillea and other subtropical shrubs. The beaches below are either pebbly or of greyish sand.

Kᴇʏ

☐	Desert
☐	Marshland
☐	Forest
☐	Cultivated land
♠	Olive groves
🍇	Vineyards
🍊	Citrus cultivation

Craggy mountains *around Ronda encompass the nature reserve of Sierra de Grazalema. The area is home to a diverse wildlife, including griffon vultures and three species of eagle, and a forest of the rare Spanish fir.*

Endless olive groves *give the landscape in the provinces of Córdoba and, in particular, Jaén a distinct, crisscrossed pattern. These long-living trees are of great importance to the local economy, for their oil (see p144) as well as their beautiful wood.*

Vast forests, mainly of Corsican pine, cover the craggy sierras of Cazorla, Segura and Las Villas *(see p152)* in one of Spain's largest nature reserves.

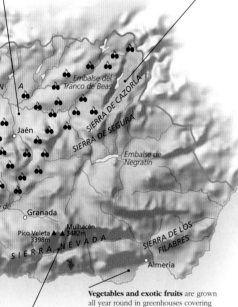

Vegetables and exotic fruits are grown all year round in greenhouses covering many hectares around El Ejido. The soil of Almería is otherwise unproductive.

***The Sierra Nevada**, Spain's highest mountain range, reaches 3,482 m (11,420 ft) at the peak of Mulhacén. Although only 40 km (25 miles) from the Mediterranean beaches, some areas are snow-capped all year round. The skiing season starts in December and lasts until spring. In summer the area is perfect for hiking and climbing.*

ANDALUSIAN WILDLIFE

Southern Spain is blessed with some of the richest and most varied flora and fauna in Europe, including some species which are unique to the area. The best time to appreciate this is in spring when wild flowers bloom and migratory birds stop en route from Africa to northern Europe.

***Cork oak** grows mainly in the province of Cádiz. Its prized bark is stripped every ten years.*

***The Cazorla violet**, which can only be found in Sierra de Cazorla (see p153), flowers in May.*

***A mouflon** is a nimble and agile wild sheep that was introduced to mountainous areas in the 1970s.*

***Flamingos** gather in great flocks in the wetlands of Coto Doñana and the Río Odiel delta in Huelva.*

Moorish Architecture

THE FIRST SIGNIFICANT PERIOD of Moorish architecture arrived with the Cordoban Caliphate. The Mezquita was extended lavishly during this period and possesses all the enduring features of the Moorish style: arches, stucco work and ornamental use of calligraphy. Later, the Almohads imported a purer Islamic style, which can be seen at La Giralda *(see p76)*. The Nasrids built the superbly crafted Alhambra in Granada, while the *mudéjares (see p22)* used their skill to create beautiful Moorish-style buildings such as the Palacio Pedro I, part of Seville's Reales Alcázares. *(See also pp44–7.)*

Reflections *in water combined with an overall play of light were central to Moorish architecture.*

Moorish domes *were often unadorned on the outside. Inside, however, an intricate lattice of stone ribs supported the dome's weight. Like this one in the Mezquita (see pp140–41), they were inlaid with multi-coloured mosaics featuring flower or animal motifs.*

Defensive walls

Moorish gardens were often arranged around gently rippling pools and channels.

DEVELOPMENT OF MOORISH ARCHITECTURE

Pre-Caliphal era 710–929		Caliphal era 929–1031		Almoravid and Almohad era 1091–1248	Nasrid era 1238–1492		
		1031–91 *Taifa* period *(see p44)*			c.1350 Alhambra palace		
700	800	900	1000	1100	1200	1300	1400
	785 Mezquita in Córdoba begun		1184 La Giralda in Seville begun		c.1350 Palacio Pedro I		
			936 Medina Azahara near Córdoba begun		Mudéjar era, after c.1215		

Azulejos *(see p74) were used for wall decorations. Patterns became increasingly geometric, as on these tiles in the Palacio Pedro I (p80).*

MOORISH ARCHES

The Moorish arch was developed from the horseshoe arch that the Visigoths used in the construction of churches. The Moors modified it and used it as the basis of great architectural endeavours, such as the Mezquita. Subsequent arches show more sophisticated ornamentation and the slow demise of the basic horseshoe shape.

Caliphal arch, Medina Azahara *(see p134)*

Almohad arch, Patio del Yeso *(see p81)*

Mudéjar arch, Salón de Embajadores *(see p81)*

Nasrid arch, the Alhambra *(see p187)*

MOORISH PALACE

The palaces of the Moors were designed with gracious living, culture and learning in mind. The imagined palace here shows how space, light, water and ornamentation were combined to harmonious effect.

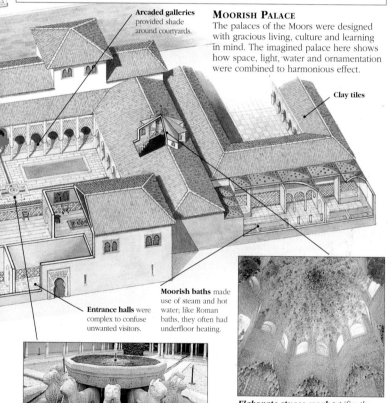

Arcaded galleries provided shade around courtyards.

Clay tiles

Entrance halls were complex to confuse unwanted visitors.

Moorish baths made use of steam and hot water; like Roman baths, they often had underfloor heating.

Elaborate stucco work *typifies the Nasrid style of architecture. The Sala de los Abencerrajes (see p187) in the Alhambra was built using only the simplest materials, but it is nevertheless widely regarded as one of the most outstanding monuments of the period of the Moorish occupation.*

Water *cooled the Moors' elegant courtyards and served a contemplative purpose. Often, as here in the Patio de los Leones (p187), water had to be pumped from a source far below.*

Post-Moorish Architecture

THE CHRISTIAN RECONQUEST was followed by the building of new churches and palaces, many by *mudéjares (see p46)*. Later, prejudice against the Moors grew as Christians began to assert their faith. Gothic styles from northern Europe filtered into Andalusia, though Mudéjar influences survived into the 18th century. In the 16th century, Andalusia was the centre of the Spanish Renaissance; and a uniquely Spanish interpretation of the Baroque emerged in the 18th century.

Mudéjar tower, Iglesia de Santa Ana *(see p184)*

THE RECONQUEST (MID-13TH TO LATE 15TH CENTURY)

Moorish craftsmen working on Christian buildings created a hybrid Christian Islamic style known as Mudéjar. Mid-13th-century churches, such as the ones built in Seville and Córdoba, show a varying degree of Moorish influence, but the Palacio Pedro I in the Reales Alcázares *(see pp80–81)* is almost exclusively Moorish in style. By the early 15th century, pure Gothic styles, which are best exemplified by Seville Cathedral *(see pp76–7)*, were widespread. After the fall of Granada in 1492 *(see p46)*, a late Gothic style, called Isabelline, developed.

Bell towers were often added later; this one is a Baroque addition.

Windows are framed by Islamic-style, marble columns.

The Iglesia de San Marcos
(see p88) *is a typical example of a Christian church built at the time of the Reconquest. Mudéjar features include the portal and minaret-like tower.*

Window openings become progressively narrower towards ground level.

Islamic-style decoration on the main entrance is characteristic of many Mudéjar churches.

Mudéjar portal, Nuestra Señora de la O *(see p158)*

Classical arches, a motif of the transitional Isabelline style, look forward to Renaissance architecture.

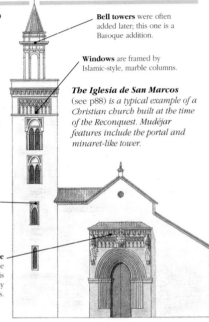

Gothic window, Seville Cathedral

Heavily worked stone reliefs, as decoration on façades of buildings, have their roots in the Gothic style.

The Palacio Jabalquinto
(see p148) *has a highly ornate façade. Its coats of arms and heraldic symbols, typical of Isabelline buildings, reveal a strong desire to establish a national style.*

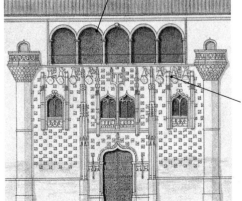

THE RENAISSANCE (16TH CENTURY)

Early Renaissance architecture was termed Plateresque because its fine detailing resembled ornate silver-work. (*Platero* means silversmith.) The façade of the Ayuntamiento *(see p72)* in Seville is the best example of Plateresque in Andalusia. A High Renaissance style is typified by the Palacio Carlos V. The end of the 16th century saw the rise of the austere Herreran style, named after Juan de Herrera, who drafted the initial plans of the Archivo de Indias *(see p78)*.

Plateresque detail on Seville's Ayuntamiento

Courtyard, with Herreran proportions, in the Archivo de Indias

Stone roundels were used as decoration; the central ones would bear the emperor's coat of arms.

Classical pediments adorn the windows.

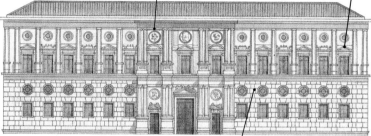

***The Palacio Carlos V**, begun in 1526, is located in the heart of the Alhambra* (see p187). *Its elegant, grandiose style reflects Carlos V's power as Holy Roman Emperor.*

Rusticated stonework gives the lower level a solid appearance.

BAROQUE (17TH AND 18TH CENTURIES)

Early Spanish Baroque tended to be austere. The 18th century, however, gave rise to the Churrigueresque, named after the Churriguera family of architects. Although the family's own style was fairly restrained, it had many flamboyant imitations. Priego de Córdoba *(see p146)* is a showcase of the Baroque; La Cartuja *(p183)* in Granada contains a Baroque sacristy.

Flamboyant, Baroque sacristy of La Cartuja, Granada

Palacio del Marqués de la Gomera, Osuna *(p129)*

Baroque pinnacles were carved individually from stone.

Repeated string courses define the church's storeys and contribute to the complex decoration of the façade.

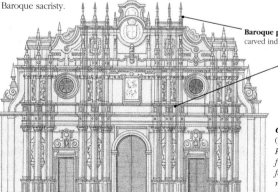

Guadix Cathedral
(see p190) *comprises a Renaissance building fronted by a Baroque façade. Such a combination of styles is very common in Andalusia.*

The Art of Bullfighting

Poster for a bullfight

BULLFIGHTING is a sacrificial ritual in which men (and some women) pit themselves against an animal bred for the ring. In this "authentic religious drama", as poet García Lorca described it, the spectator experiences vicariously the fear and exaltation of the matador. Some Spaniards oppose it on the grounds of cruelty, but it remains as popular as ever in Andalusia.

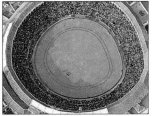

Maestranza Bullring, Seville
This is regarded, with Las Ventas in Madrid, as one of the top venues for bullfighting in Spain.

Bull Breeding
Well treated at the ranch, the toro bravo *(fighting bull) is bred specially for aggressiveness and courage.*

The matador wears a *traje de luces* (suit of light), a colourful silk outfit embroidered with gold sequins.

The passes are made with a *muleta*, a scarlet cape stiffened along one side.

FIESTA!

Bullfighting is an essential and highly popular part of many *fiestas* in Spain. An enthusiastic and very knowledge-able audience, often in traditional dress, fills the arenas from the start of the season in April until its end in October *(see pp36–37).*

Fiesta wear

THE BULLFIGHT

The *corrida* (bullfight) has three stages, called *tercios*. In the first one, the *tercio de varas*, the matador and *picadores* (horsemen with lances) are aided by *peones* (assistants). In the *tercio de banderillas*, *banderilleros* stick pairs of darts in the bull's back. In the *tercio de muleta* the matador makes a series of passes at the bull with a *muleta* (cape). He then executes the kill, the *estocada*, with a sword.

The matador *plays the bull with a* capa *(red cape) in the* tercio de varas *in order to gauge its intelligence and speed. Peones then draw it towards the* picadores.

Today, horses are heavily padded

Picadores *goad the bull with steel-pointed lances, testing its bravery as it charges their horses. The lances weaken the animal's shoulder muscles.*

THE BULLRING

The *corrida* audience sits in the *tendidos* (stalls) or in the *palcos* (balcony), where the *presidencia* (president's box) is. Opposite are the *puerta de cuadrillas,* through which the matador and team arrive, and the *arrastre de toros* (exit for bulls). Before entering the ring, the matadors wait in a corridor *(callejón)* behind the *barreras* and *burladeros* (ringside barriers). Horses are kept in the *patio de caballos* and the bulls wait in the *corrales.*

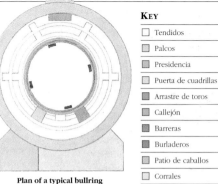

Plan of a typical bullring

KEY

☐ Tendidos
☐ Palcos
☐ Presidencia
☐ Puerta de cuadrillas
☐ Arrastre de toros
☐ Callejón
☐ Barreras
☐ Burladeros
☐ Patio de caballos
☐ Corrales

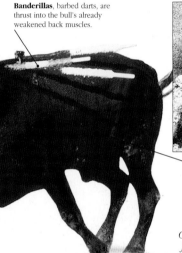

Banderillas, barbed darts, are thrust into the bull's already weakened back muscles.

Manolete

Regarded as one of the greatest matadors ever, Manolete was gored to death by the bull Islero at Linares, Jaén, in 1947.

The bull may go free if it shows courage – spectators wave white handkerchiefs, asking the *corrida* president to let it leave the ring alive.

Joselito

One of Spain's leading matadors, Joselito, is famous for his purist approach and for his flair with both the capa and the muleta.

The bull weighs about 500 kg (1,100 lb)

Banderilleros *enter to provoke the wounded bull in the* tercio de banderillas, *gauging its reaction to punishment by sticking pairs of banderillas in its back.*

The matador *makes passes with the cape in the* tercio de muleta, *then lowers it to make the bull bow its head, and thrusts in the sword for the kill.*

The estocada recibiendo *is a difficult kill which is rarely seen. The matador awaits the bull's charge rather than moving forwards to meet it.*

Flamenco, the Soul of Andalusia

Seville feria poster 1953

MORE THAN JUST A DANCE, flamenco is a forceful artistic expression of the sorrows and joys of life. Although it has interpreters all over Spain and even the world, it is a uniquely Andalusian art form, traditionally performed by gypsies. There are many styles of *cante* (song) from different parts of Andalusia, but no strict choreography – dancers improvise from basic movements, following the rhythm of the guitar and their feelings. Flamenco was neglected in the 1960s and '70s, but serious interest has once again returned. Recent years have seen a revival of traditional styles and the development of exciting new forms.

***Sevillanas**, a folk dance that is strongly influenced by flamenco, is danced by Andalusians in their bars and homes (see p230).*

At a *tablao* (flamenco club) there will be at least four people on stage, including the hand clapper.

***The origins of flamenco** are hard to trace. Gypsies may have been the main creators of the art, mixing their own Indian-influenced culture with existing Moorish and Andalusian folklore, and with Jewish and Christian music. There were gypsies in Andalusia by the early Middle Ages, but only in the 18th century did flamenco begin to develop into its present form.*

THE SPANISH GUITAR

The guitar has a major role in flamenco, traditionally accompanying the singer. The flamenco guitar developed from the modern classical guitar, which evolved in Spain in the 19th century. Flamenco guitars have a lighter, shallower construction and a thickened plate below the soundhole, used to tap rhythms. Today, flamenco guitarists often perform solo. One of the greatest, Paco de Lucía, began by accompanying singers and dancers, but made his debut as a soloist in 1968. His slick, inventive style, which combines traditional playing with Latin, jazz and rock elements, has influenced many musicians outside the realm of flamenco, such as the group Ketama, who play flamenco-blues.

Classical guitar

Paco de Lucía playing flamenco guitar

***Singing is an integral** part of flamenco and the singer often performs solo. Camarón de la Isla (1952–92), a gypsy born near Cádiz, is among the most famous contemporary* cantaores *(flamenco singers). He began as a singer of expressive* cante jondo *(literally, "deep songs"), from which he developed his own, rock-influenced style. He has inspired many singers.*

WHERE TO ENJOY FLAMENCO

Flamenco festivals pp32–7, p230
Flamenco guitar pp32–5, p230
Flamenco in Sacromonte p185
Flamenco singing pp32–5, p230
Flamenco tablaos p230
Flamenco dress p225

The proud yet graceful posture of the *bailaora* seems to suggest a restrained passion.

A harsh, vibrating voice is typical of the singer.

***La Chanca** is a* baila-ora *(female dancer) renowned for her fiery and forceful movements. Cristina Hoyos, another dancer famous for her personal style, leads her own flamenco dance company which received world-wide acclaim in the 1980s. Other international flamenco stars include Juana Amaya.*

Traditional polka-dot dress

***The bailaor** (male dancer) plays a less important role than the* bailaora. *However, many have achieved fame, including Antonio Canales. He has intro-duced a new beat through his original foot movements.*

THE FLAMENCO TABLAO

These days it is rare to come across spontaneous dancing at a *tablao,* but if dancers and singers are inspired, an impressive show usually results. Artists performing with *duende* ("magic spirit") will hear appreciative *olés* from the audience.

FLAMENCO RHYTHM

The unmistakable rhythm of flamenco is created by the guitar. Just as important, however, is the beat created by hand-clapping and by the dancer's feet in high-heeled shoes. The *baila-oras* may also beat a rhythm with castanets; Lucero Tena (born in 1939) became famous for her solos on castanets. Graceful hand movements are used to express the dancer's feelings of the moment – whether pain, sorrow or happiness. Like the movements of the rest of the body, they are not choreo-graphed, and the styles used vary from person to person.

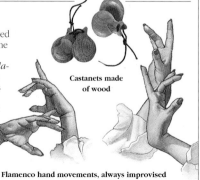

Castanets made of wood

Flamenco hand movements, always improvised

The Land of Sherry

THE PHOENICIANS INTRODUCED the vine to the Jerez region 3,000 years ago. Later, Greeks, then Romans, exported wine from these gentle hills bordering the Atlantic. However, the foundations of the modern sherry trade were laid by British merchants who settled here after the Reconquest *(see pp46–7)*. They discovered that the chalky soil, climate and local grapes produced fine wines, particularly if fortified with grape spirit.

González Byass logo

The connection persists today with companies such as John Harvey still in British ownership.

Preparing soil to catch the winter rain

Grapes thriving in the chalky soil near Jerez

SHERRY REGIONS

Sherry is produced at *bodegas*, or wineries, in the towns of Jerez de la Frontera, Sanlúcar de Barrameda and El Puerto de Santa María. It is also produced in smaller centres such as Rota and Chiclana de la Frontera.

SANLÚCAR DE BARRAMEDA

JEREZ DE LA FRONTERA

Rota

Rio Guadalete

EL PUERTO DE SANTA MARIA

CADIZ

Puerto Real

San Fernando

Chiclana de la Frontera

A471 · A480 · A491 · N IV · A4 AP4 (E5) · A382 · N IV A4 · A4 E5 · A381 · A393

KEY

- ☐ Sanlúcar de Barrameda
- ☐ Jerez de la Frontera
- ☐ El Puerto de Santa María
- — Delimited sherry-producing region

0 kilometres   10

0 miles   5

DIFFERENT TYPES OF SHERRY

Three months after pressing, and before the fortification process, all sherry is classified as one of five principal types.

Fino *is by far the favoured style in Andalusia. Dry, fresh, light and crisp, it is excellent as an apéritif or with tapas. It should always be served chilled.*

Manzanilla *is similar to fino, but comes exclusively from Sanlúcar. Light, dry and delicate, it has a highly distinctive, salty tang.*

Amontillado *is fino aged in the barrel. The "dying" flor (yeast) imparts a strong, earthy taste. Some brands are dry, others slightly sweetened.*

Oloroso *(which in Spanish means fragrant) is a full, ruddy-coloured sherry, with a rich, nutty aroma. It is sometimes sweetened.*

Cream *sherry is a full, dark, rich blend of oloroso with Pedro Ximénez grapes. As the sweetest type, it is often drunk as a dessert wine.*

HOW SHERRY IS MADE

Sherry is mixed from two principal grape varieties: Palomino, which produces a drier, more delicate sherry; and Pedro Ximénez, which is made into a fuller, sweeter sherry type.

Crusher and de-stemmer

Grape-drying is only required for Pedro Ximénez grapes. They are laid on esparto mats to shrivel in the sun, concentrating the sugar before they are pressed.

Grape-picking takes place during the first three weeks in September. Palomino grapes are taken as quickly as possible to the presses to ensure freshness.

Grape-pressing and de-stalking, in cylindrical stainless steel vats, is usually done at night to avoid the searing Andalusian heat.

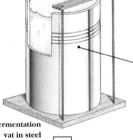

Fermentation vat in steel

Flor, a yeast, may form on the exposed surface of young wine in the fermentation vat, preventing oxidization and adding a delicate taste. If flor develops, the wine is a fino.

Fortification is the addition of pure grape spirit, raising the level of alcohol from around 11 per cent by volume to around 18 per cent for olorosos, and 15.5 per cent for finos.

The solera system

The youngest solera contains new wine.

Sherry for bottling is taken from the oldest solera at the bottom row.

The solera system assures that the qualities of a sherry remain constant. The wine from the youngest solera is mixed with the older below, taking on its character. The oldest solera contains a tiny proportion of very old wine.

The finished product

Beach Life and Leisure in Andalusia

Painted fishing boat, Costa del Sol

THANKS TO its subtropical climate with an average of 300 days' sunshine a year, the coastline of Andalusia – in particular the Costa del Sol – has become one of the most favoured playgrounds for those looking for fun and relaxation. In the 1950s, there was nothing more than a handful of fishing villages *(see p175)*. Now the area attracts several million tourists a year who are well catered for by the vast array of hotels and apartments along the coast. The varied coastline lends itself perfectly to the whole gamut of water sports *(see p232)*, while just inland golf courses have become a major feature of the landscape *(see p232)*. Some of the most popular golf courses are shown on this map, together with a selection of the beaches most worth a visit.

Sunbathing on one of Marbella's beaches, Costa del Sol

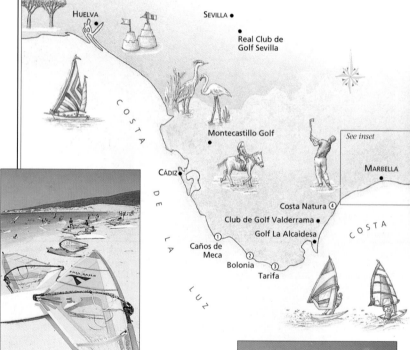

HUELVA

SEVILLA ●

● Real Club de Golf Sevilla

COSTA

● Montecastillo Golf

CÁDIZ ●

See inset

MARBELLA ●

Costa Natura ④

Club de Golf Valderrama ●

COSTA

①
Caños de Meca

Golf La Alcaidesa

DE LA

② Bolonia ③

Tarifa

LUZ

Costa de la Luz *in western Andalusia is a stretch of largely unspoiled beaches, refreshingly free from crowds and tower blocks. Atlantic winds make it a windsurfer's paradise.*

Costa Tropical *is punctuated by pretty coves, ideal for scuba diving. The water is warmer and clearer than on Costa de la Luz, while the sand is coarse and stony.*

| 0 kilometres | 50 |
| 0 miles | 25 |

ANDALUSIA'S BEST BEACHES

Caños de Meca ①
Charming white, sandy beach sheltered by cliffs and sand dunes.

Bolonia ②
Picturesque beach with Roman ruins close by.

Tarifa ③
Sweeping white sands, and winds and waves perfect for skilled windsurfers.

Costa Natura ④
Popular nudist beach just outside Estepona.

Babaloo Beach ⑤
Trendy spot just off Puerto Banús. Gym and jetskiing.

Victor's Beach ⑥
A classic Marbella beach for stylish barbecue parties.

Don Carlos ⑦
Perhaps Marbella's best beach, shared by the exclusive Don Carlos beach club.

Cabopino/Las Dunas ⑧
Nudist beach and sand dunes beside modern marina. Not too crowded.

Rincón de la Victoria ⑨
Nice unspoiled family beach area just east of Málaga.

La Herradura ⑩
A stony but picturesque bay west of Almuñécar.

Playa de los Genoveses ⑪
One of the unspoilt beaches between Cabo de Gata and the village of San José.

Playa Agua Amarga ⑫
Excellent sand beach in secluded fishing hamlet turned exclusive resort.

Costa de Almería is famous for its picturesque fishing villages, and rocky landscapes which come to life in the breathtaking sunsets. Beaches tend to have escaped overdevelopment, in particular those in the nature reserve of Cabo de Gata, such as San José, here.

Agua Amarga ⑫

Playa de los Genoveses ⑪

ALMERÍA

ALAGA ⑨
Rincón de la Victoria

La Herradura ⑩

COSTA TROPICAL

COSTA DE ALMERÍA

DEL SOL

COSTA DEL SOL

Apart from the crowds of holiday-makers, half a million foreign residents have chosen to live on the Costa del Sol. Complementing the luxury and high life of Marbella are a number of popular beaches and more than 30 of Europe's finest golf courses, including the prestigious Club de Golf Valderrama, host of the 1997 Ryder Cup tournament.

MÁLAGA ●

Club de Campo de Málaga ●

TORREMOLINOS

Golf Torrequebrado

Club Mijas Golf ●

La Cala Golf ●

Club de Golf Las Brisas ●

Club Dama de Noche ●

Guadalmina Golf ●

Monte Mayor ●
Golf

MARBELLA
⑥
Victor's
Beach

Golf Río Real ●
⑦ ● Marbella Golf

Don
Carlos

⑧
Cabopino and
Las Dunas

⑤
Babaloo
Beach

Player on the green at the high-profile Marbella Golf

ANDALUSIA THROUGH THE YEAR

ESTIVALS and cultural events fill Andalusia's calendar. Every town and village has an annual *feria* (fair) featuring parades, dancing, fairs, fireworks and bullfights. These are held from April to October throughout Andalusia. There are also numerous *fiestas*, all exuberant occasions when religious devotion mixes with *joie de vivre*. Spring is an ideal time to visit; the countryside is at its most beautiful, the climate is mild and *ferias* and *fiestas*

Poster for 1903 Seville *feria*

celebrate the ending of winter. Summer brings heat to the interior and crowds to the *costas*. Autumn is greeted with more *fiestas* and heralds the opening of music and theatre seasons. In winter, jazz, pop and classical concerts can be enjoyed in the cities. The first snow on the Sierra Nevada marks the start of the skiing season. Note that dates for all events, especially *fiestas*, may change from year to year; check with the tourist board (*see p237*).

Almond trees in blossom on the lush hillsides of Andalusia

SPRING

EW PARTS OF THE WORLD can match the beauty of spring in Andalusia. After winter rains, the hills and plains are green and lush, and water cascades along riverbeds and irrigation channels. Country roads are a riot of wild flowers; almond blossom covers the hillsides and strawberries are harvested. Popular festivals abound, many of them religious, though often linked with pagan ceremonies marking the end of winter.

MARCH

Cristo de la Expiración (*Friday, nine days before Palm Sunday*), Orgiva (*see p190*). One of Andalusia's most ear-splitting *fiestas*; shotguns are fired and rockets, gunpowder and firecrackers are set off.
Semana Santa (*Palm Sunday– Good Friday*). Seville

celebrates this event spectacularly (*see p36*), and there are processions in every town and village. On Holy Wednesday in Málaga (*see pp172–3*), a prisoner is freed from jail and in gratitude joins in one of the processions. This tradition began two centuries ago, when prisoners, braving a plague, carried a holy image through the city's streets. In Baena (*see p143*), the streets vibrate to the sound of thousands of drums.

APRIL

Fiesta de San Marcos (*25 April*), Ohanes, Sierra Nevada. Accompanying the image of San Marcos through the streets are young men leading eight bulls. The bulls are persuaded to kneel before the saint.
Feria de Abril (*two weeks after Easter*), Seville (*see p36*).
Romería de Nuestra Señora de la Cabeza (*last Sunday in April*), Andújar (*see p37*). Major pilgrimage.

MAY

Día de la Cruz (*first week of May*), Granada (*see pp182–8*) and Córdoba (*see p36*).
Feria del Caballo (*first week of May*), Jerez de la Frontera (*see p158*). Horse fair.
Festival Internacional de Teatro y Danza (*throughout May*), Seville. World-class companies perform in Teatro de la Maestranza (*see pp66–7*).
Festival de los Patios (*second week in May*), Córdoba (*see p36*). Patios are on display.
Romería de San Isidro (*15 May*). *Romerías* are held in many towns, including Nerja (*see p172*), for San Isidro.
Concurso Nacional de Flamenco (*second week in May; every third year: 1998, 2001*), Córdoba. National flamenco competition.
Feria de Mayo (*last week of May*), Córdoba (*see p36*).
Romería del Rocío (*late May or early June*), El Rocío (*see p36*).

Feria del Caballo, held in Jerez de la Frontera in May

AVERAGE DAILY HOURS OF SUNSHINE

Hours

Jan Feb Mar Apr May Jun Jul Aug Sep Oct Nov Dec

Sunshine Chart
Even in winter, few days in Andalusia are entirely without sunshine. From the spring, the sunshine starts to build up progressively, and by midsummer it can be dangerous to go out even for a short time without adequate skin protection.

Bullrunning during the Lunes de Toro *fiesta* in Grazalema

SUMMER

DURING THE HOT summer months, the *siesta* (afternoon nap) comes into its own. Many people finish work at lunch time and most of the entertainment takes place in the cool of evening. Foreign tourists flocking to the coasts are joined by thousands of Spaniards. Large pop concerts are held in coastal towns.

JUNE

Corpus Christi (*late May or early June*) is commemorated in Granada (*see p37*). In Seville, the *seises*, young boys dressed in doublet and hose, dance before the cathedral altar. At Zahara, near Ronda, (*see p166*) houses and streets are decked out with greenery.
Día de San Juan (*23, 24 June*). The evening of 23 June sees dancing, drinking and singing around bonfires on beaches across Andalusia in honour of

St John the Baptist. Lanjarón (*see p181*) celebrates with a water battle in its streets in the early hours of 24 June.
Romería de los Gitanos (*third Sunday in June*), Cabra (*see p143*). A procession made up of thousands of gypsies heads for a hilltop shrine.
Festival Internacional de Música y Danza (*mid-June– early July*), Granada (*see pp182–8*). Performers come to Granada from all over the world. Many events are held in the Alhambra (*see pp186–7*).

JULY

Festival de la Guitarra (*first two weeks of July*), Córdoba (*see pp136–42*). Guitar festival presenting all musical styles, from classical to flamenco.
Fiesta de la Virgen del Carmen (*around 15 July*). This Virgin is honoured in many coastal communities by regattas and other sporting events. In the evening, the Virgin's image is put aboard a fishing boat, which parades

across the sea accompanied by the crackle of fireworks.
Lunes de Toro (*Around 17 July*), Grazalema (*see p166*). Bullrunning daily for a week.

AUGUST

Fiestas Colombinas (*Around 3 August*), Huelva (*see p123*). A Latin American dance and music festival in celebration of Columbus's voyage. It is dedicated to a different Latin American country every year.
Fiestas Patronales de Santa María de la Palma (*15 August*), Algeciras (*see p162*). A saint's image is rescued from the sea. It is cleaned, before being carried in a procession of boats to a beach. Afterwards it is returned to the sea.
Fiestas de la Exaltación del Río Guadalquivir (*third week in August*), Sanlúcar de Barrameda (*see p158*). Horse races are held on the beach.
Feria de Málaga (*last two weeks in August, see p37*).
Feria de Almería (*last week in August, see p37*).

The Costa del Sol – popular with tourists and with the Spanish

AVERAGE MONTHLY RAINFALL

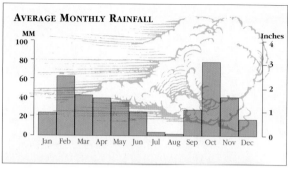

Rainfall Chart

Rain can be heavy in early spring, but summer is almost dry. Humidity and rainfall increase through September until October, when torrential rains can fall. In recent years, the rains have failed resulting in severe drought in the area.

Chirimoya harvest on the subtropical coast at Almuñécar *(see p181)*

AUTUMN

THIS IS A most pleasant time to visit Andalusia. The weather is settled, but without the searing summer heat, and the holiday crowds are easing. Grape harvests are in full swing and being celebrated in towns and villages. The theatres start to open for drama and concerts. Along the subtropical coast of the Mediterranean, sweet potatoes and *chirimoyas* (custard apples) are harvested. Inland, mushrooms, freshly picked, figure on menus.

SEPTEMBER

Feria de Pedro Romero *(first two weeks in September)*, Ronda *(see pp168–9)*. This *fiesta* celebrates the founder of modern bullfighting *(see p169)*. All participants in the Corrida Goyesca, the highlight, wear costumes designed by Goya, a great bullfighting fan.

Fiestas Patronales de la Virgen de la Piedad *(6 September)*, Baza *(see p190)*. A bizarre *fiesta* in which a figure known as Cascamorras comes from neighbouring Guadix to try to steal a statue of the Virgin. Youths covered with oil taunt him and chase him out of town. He is sent back to Guadix empty-handed, where he receives further punishment for his failure.

Moros y Cristianos *(15 September)*, Válor *(see p191)*. This *fiesta* features the re-creation of Reconquest battles.

Fiesta de la Vendimia *(second or third week of September)*, La Palma del Condado *(see p125)*. A lively *fiesta* to bless the first grape juice.

Romería de San Miguel *(last Sunday of September)*, Torremolinos *(see p174)*. One of the largest *romerías* in Andalusia.

Bienal de Arte Flamenco *(last two weeks of September, even-numbered years)*, Seville. A fabulous opportunity for enthusiasts to see world-class flamenco artists, such as Cristina Hoyos.

Sevilla en Otoño *(September–November)*, Seville. A variety of cultural events, including dance, theatre and exhibitions, and, in addition, sports.

Moros y Cristianos fiesta, Válor *(see p191)*

OCTOBER

Fiesta del Vino *(5–9 October)*, Cadiar *(see p191)*. A feature of this *fiesta* in the mountains of the Alpujarras is the construction of a fountain which gushes forth wine.

Festival Iberoamericano de Teatro *(last two weeks of October)*, Cádiz *(see pp160–61)*. Latin American theatre festival.

NOVEMBER

Festival Internacional de Jazz *(early November)*, Granada *(see pp182–8)* and Seville.

Festival de Cine Iberoamericano *(last two weeks of November)*, Huelva *(see p123)*. Latin American film festival.

Oil-covered youths chasing Cascamorras in Baza

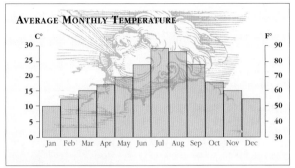

AVERAGE MONTHLY TEMPERATURE

Temperature Chart
Andalusia enjoys a warm Mediterranean climate throughout the year, although it can become cold at night. Temperatures rise from January to the summer months when, in some cities inland, they can far exceed the average for the region.

Medieval music at the Fiesta de los Verdiales in Málaga

WINTER

AT THIS TIME OF YEAR the ripe olives are harvested in abundance. The restaurants serve venison, wild boar and partridge dishes as this is the hunting season. Skiers flock to the Sierra Nevada. Though winter is the rainy season and it is cold at night, many days have sunshine. By February, almond blossom and strawberries begin to appear again.

DECEMBER

La Inmaculada Concepción *(8 December)*, Seville. The *tuna*, groups of wandering minstrels, take to the streets around the Plaza del Triunfo and Santa Cruz *(see pp70–71)*.
Fiesta de los Verdiales *(28 December)*, Málaga *(see pp172–3)*. On Spain's equivalent of April Fool's Day, *El Día de los Santos Inocentes*, thousands of town and country folk gather at the Venta del Túnel, on the outskirts of Málaga.

They come to hear *pandas* (bands) compete in performing *verdiales*, wild, primitive music from Moorish times, played on medieval instruments.

JANUARY

Día de la Toma *(2 January)*, Granada *(see pp182–8)*. This *fiesta* recalls the ousting of the Moors in 1492 *(see p46)*. Queen Isabel's crown and King Fernando's sword are paraded through the streets, and the royal standard flies from the balcony of the Ayuntamiento.
Día de Reyes *(6 January)*. On the evening before this public holiday, the Three Kings arrive, splendidly dressed, to parade through town centres across Andalusia. They ride in small carriages that are drawn either by tractors or horses and, during processions, throw sweets to the excited children.
Certamen Internacional de Guitarra Clásica Andrés Segovia *(first week of January)*, Almuñécar *(see p181)*. Classical guitar competition in homage to the master.

FEBRUARY

Los Carnavales *(second or third week in February)*. Carnival is widely celebrated with tremendous enthusiasm, particularly in the western part of Andalusia and, most spectacularly, in Cádiz *(see p37)*. The coastal town of Isla Cristina *(see p122)* is famed for its exuberant festivities.
Festival de Música Antigua *(February and March)*, Seville. Early music is performed on historic instruments.

Ski station on the snow-covered slopes of the Sierra Nevada *(see p189)*

Fiestas in Andalusia

THERE IS NOTHING quite like a Spanish *fiesta* or *feria*, and those of Andalusia are among the most colourful. *Fiestas* may commemorate an historic event or a change of season. More often they mark a religious occasion; Semana Santa (Holy Week), for example, is celebrated all over Andalusia. Feasting, dancing, singing, drinking – often right around the clock – are all integral to a *fiesta*. At a *feria* there will often be a decorated fairground, revellers dressed in traditional flamenco attire, and processions of horses and carriages. Throughout Andalusia you will also come across *romerías*, in which processions carry holy effigies through the countryside to a shrine.

Costume, Semana Santa, Córdoba

Horsemen and women in their finery at Seville's Feria de Abril

SEVILLE

SEMANA SANTA, or Holy Week (Palm Sunday–Good Friday) is celebrated in flamboyant style in Seville. More than 100 *pasos* (floats bearing religious effigies) are carried through the streets of the city. They are accompanied by *nazarenos*, members of some 50 brotherhoods dating back to the 13th century, wearing long robes and tall pointed hoods. As the processions sway through the streets, appointed singers burst into *saetas*, shafts of song in praise of the Virgin. Emotion reaches fever-pitch in the early hours of Good Friday, when the Virgen de La Macarena is paraded, accompanied by 2,500 *nazarenos* (see p87).

During their Feria de Abril, the spring fair held around two weeks after Easter, the *sevillanos* go on a spree for a week.

Daily, from about 1pm, elegant horsemen and women wearing *mantillas* (lace headdresses) show off their finery in a parade known as the *cabalgata*. At night, *casetas* (entertainment booths) throb to *sevillanas*, a popular dance that has a flamenco accent.

(Out of a thousand *casetas*, about a quarter are open to the public.) Spain's best matadors feature in bullfights in the Maestranza bullring *(see p66)*.

HUELVA AND SEVILLA

ONE OF SPAIN'S most popular *fiestas*, the Romería del Rocío, is held during Pentecost. More than 70 brotherhoods trek to the shrine of El Rocío *(see p125)* amid Las Marismas, the marshlands at the mouth of the Guadalquivir. They are joined by pilgrims travelling on horseback, on foot or by car. All pay homage to the Virgen del Rocío, also called the White Dove or the Queen of the Marshes. There is drinking and dancing for several days and nights, until the early hours of Monday morning when the Virgin is brought out of the shrine. Young men from the nearby town of Almonte carry her through the crowds for up to 12 hours, fighting off anybody who tries to get near.

CÓRDOBA AND JAÉN

MAY IS A NONSTOP FIESTA in Córdoba *(see pp136–42)*. The Día de la Cruz – the Day of the Cross – is held on the first three days of the month. Religious brotherhoods and neighbourhoods compete with each other to create the most colourful, flower-decorated crosses, which are set up in squares and at street corners. Following this is the Festival de los Patios (5–15 May), when the patios of the city's old quarter are thrown

Pilgrims taking part in the Romería del Rocío in Huelva province

open for visitors to come and admire. Crowds go from patio to patio, at each one launching into flamenco dance or song.

During the last week of May, Córdoba holds its lively *feria*. It is as colourful as the Feria de Abril in Seville, but more accessible to strangers. This festival, with roots in Roman times, welcomes the spring.

The Romería de Nuestra Señora de la Cabeza takes place on the last Sunday in April at the Santuario de la Virgen de la Cabeza *(see p147)*, a remote shrine in the Sierra Morena. Over 250,000 people attend, some making the pilgrimage on foot or on horseback. At the site, flames shoot up day and night from a torch fed by candles lit by the faithful. Then the Virgin, known as La Morenita, is borne through the crowd to cries of *¡Guapa, guapa!* (beautiful, beautiful!).

Penitents at the Romería de Nuestra Señora de la Cabeza in April

CÁDIZ AND MÁLAGA

FOR TWO WEEKS in February, Los Carnavales (Carnival) is celebrated with more flair and abandon in Cádiz *(see p160)* than anywhere else in Andalusia. Some say it rivals the carnival in Río de Janeiro. Groups of singers practise for months in advance, composing outrageous satirical ditties that poke fun at anything from the current fashions to celebrities, especially politicians. Often sumptuously costumed, they perform their songs in the Falla Theatre in a competition lasting for several days. Then they take part in a parade. The whole city puts on fancy dress

Costumed revellers at the February Carnival (Los Carnavales) in Cádiz

and crowds of revellers throng the narrow streets of the city's old quarter, shouting, singing, dancing and drinking.

The Feria de Málaga in the middle of August each year, celebrates the capture of the city from the Moors by the Catholic Monarchs *(see p46)*. Eager to outdo Seville, Málaga *(see pp172–3)* puts on a fine show. The residents, famous for their ability to organize a good party, put on traditional costume and parade, along with decorated carriages and elegant horsefolk, through the city centre and the fairground. The entertainment goes on for a week nonstop, and top bullfighters perform at the city's bullring *(see p173)* in La Malagueta.

GRANADA AND ALMERÍA

CORPUS CHRISTI, held in late May or early June, is one of the major events in Granada *(see pp182–8)*. On the day before Corpus a procession of bigheads (costumed caricatures with outsized heads) and giants parades through the city, led by the *tarasca*, a woman on a huge dragon. The next day, the *custodia*, or monstrance, is carried from the cathedral all through the streets. For a week afterwards there is bullfighting, flamenco and general revelry.

The *feria* in Almería *(see pp192–3)*, which is held at the end of August, is in honour of the Virgen del Mar. There are funfairs, processions, sporting events and bullfights. The city's Virgin dates back to 1502, when a coastguard on the lookout for Berber pirates found an image of the Virgin washed up on a beach.

Feria de Málaga, celebrating the capture of the city from the Moors

THE HISTORY OF SEVILLE AND ANDALUSIA

ANDALUSIA'S early history is an extraordinary tale of ancient cities – Cádiz *(see pp160–61),* founded in 1100 BC, is the oldest city in Europe – and waves of settlers, each one contributing new ideas and customs.

Hominids first inhabited the region about one million years ago. *Homo sapiens* had arrived by 25,000 BC, and by the Iron Age a strong Iberian culture had emerged. Later, trade and cultural links developed first with the Phoenicians, then with the Greeks and Carthaginians. These ties and the abundance of natural raw materials, such as iron, gold and copper ore, made this part of Iberia one of the wealthiest and most sophisticated areas of the Mediterranean.

The Romans were attracted by its riches and made their first forays into southern Spain in 206 BC. They ruled for almost 700 years. Their place was eventually taken by the Visigoths as the Western Roman Empire crumbled in the 5th century AD. The Moors,

Stone carving of an Iberian warrior

who followed, flourished first in Córdoba, then in Seville, and, towards the end of their almost 800 year rule, in the Nasrid kingdom of Granada.

After the fall of Granada to the Christians in 1492, Spain entered an era of expansion and prosperity. The conquest of the New World made Seville one of the most affluent cities in Europe, but much of this wealth was squandered on wars by the Habsburg kings. By the 18th century Spain had fallen into economic decline; in the 19th and early 20th centuries poverty led to political conflict and, ultimately, to the Civil War.

The years following the Civil War saw continuing poverty, though mass tourism in the 1960s and '70s did much to ease this. With Franco's death and Spain's entry into the EU, the Spanish began to enjoy increasing prosperity and democratic freedoms. Andalusia still lagged behind, however, and the Expo '92 was part of government policy to foster its economic growth.

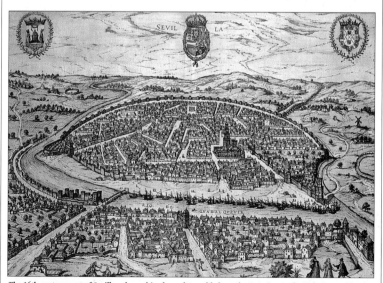

The 16th-century port of Seville, where ships brought wealth from the Americas to the Holy Roman Empire

◁ **18th-century lithograph of the Puerta de la Justicia in the Alhambra** *(see pp186–7)*

Early Andalusia

Neanderthal skull

NEANDERTHALS inhabited Gibraltar around 50,000 BC. *Homo sapiens* arrived 25,000 years later and Neolithic tribespeople from Africa settled in Spain from about 7000 BC. By the time the Phoenicians arrived to trade in precious metals, they were met by a sophisticated Iberian culture. They later established trading links with the semi-mythical Iberian kingdom of Tartessus. The Greeks, already settled in northeastern Spain, started to colonize the south from about 600 BC. Meanwhile, Celts from the north had mixed with Iberians. This culture, influenced by the Greeks, created beautiful works of art. The Carthaginians arrived in about 500 BC and, according to legend, destroyed Tartessus.

AREAS OF INFLUENCE

| | Greek |
| | Phoenician |

The short sword and shield denote an Iberian warrior.

Burial Sight at Los Millares
Los Millares (see p193) was the site of an early metal-working civilization in about 2300 BC. Up to 100 corpses were buried on a single site; the huge burial chambers were covered with earth to make a gently sloping mound.

This figure's arms are outstretched in an attitude of prayer.

Cave Paintings
From approximately 25,000 BC, people painted caves in Andalusia. They portrayed fish, land animals, people, weapons and other subjects with a skilful naturalism.

IBERIAN BRONZE FIGURES

These bronze figurines from the 5th–4th centuries BC are votive offerings to the gods. They were discovered in a burial ground near Despeñaperros in the province of Jaén. The Romans regarded the Iberians who crafted them as exceptionally noble.

TIMELINE

1,000,000–750,000 BC Stones worked by hominids at Puerto de Santa María, Cádiz *Stone tool*	**25,000–18,000 BC** *Homo sapiens* make cave paintings and rock engravings	**4000 BC** Burials at Cueva de los Murciélagos in Granada leave Neolithic remains; esparto sandals, religious offerings and other items **4500 BC** Farmers begin to grow crops and breed cattle			
1,000,000 BC	**50,000 BC**	**10,000 BC**	**8000 BC**	**6000 BC**	**4000 BC**
	50,000 BC Neanderthals inhabit Gibraltar	**7000 BC** Neolithic colonists arrive, perhaps from North Africa. Farming begins on Iberian Peninsula		*Neolithic ochre pot*	

Goddess Astarte
The Phoenicians founded Cádiz in about 1100 BC. They brought their own goddess, Astarte, who became popular across Andalusia as the region absorbed eastern influences.

WHERE TO SEE EARLY ANDALUSIA

Cave paintings can be seen in the Cueva de la Pileta near Ronda la Vieja *(p167)* and in the Cuevas de Nerja *(p172)*. At Antequera *(p171)* there are Bronze Age dolmens dating from 2500 BC; at Los Millares *(p193)* there are burial chambers. The replicas of the famous Tartessian Carambolo Treasure are in the Museo Arqueológico in Seville *(p95)* and Iberian stone carvings from Porcuna are exhibited in Jaén *(p145)*.

The Toro de Porcuna *(500–450 BC) was found at Porcuna near Jaén with other sculptures.*

Greek Urn
The ancient Greeks imported many artifacts from home; their style of decoration had a strong influence on Iberian art.

The headdress shows this is a votaress, devoted to her god.

The hand of this priestess is raised in benediction.

Dama de Baza
This female figure, dating from around 500–400 BC, may represent an Iberian goddess. It is one of several such figures found in southern Spain.

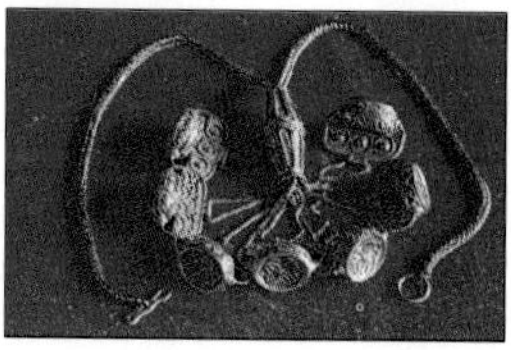

Carambolo Treasure
Phoenician in style, this treasure is from Tartessus. Although many artifacts have been uncovered, the site of this kingdom has yet to be found.

2300 BC Beginning of the Bronze Age; dolmen-style burials take place at Los Millares *(see p193)*

800–700 BC Kingdom of Tartessus at its height, influenced by the Phoenicians

Tartessian buckle

241 BC First Punic War between Carthage and Rome

2000 BC	1000 BC	800 BC	600 BC	400 BC

1100 BC Foundation of Cádiz by the Phoenicians

800 BC Celts from northern Europe move southwards

600 BC Greek colonists settle on the coasts of Andalusia

500 BC Carthage colonizes southern Spain

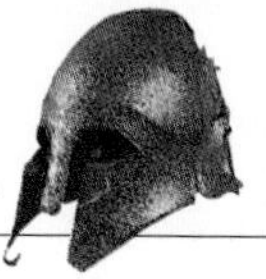

Greek helmet

219 BC Carthaginians take Sagunto, eastern Spain

Romans and Visigoths

THE ROMANS came to Spain during a war against Carthage in 206 BC. Attracted by the wealth of the peninsula, they stayed for 700 years; in 200 years they conquered Spain and split it into provinces. Baetica, with Corduba (Córdoba) as its capital, corresponded roughly to what is now Andalusia. Cities were built, while feudal lords created vast estates, exporting olive oil and wheat to Rome. Baetica became one of the wealthiest of Rome's provinces with a rich, Ibero-Roman culture. The Visigoths who followed continued to assert Roman values until the Moors arrived in AD 711.

Visigothic capital

ROMAN TERRITORY AD 100

☐ *Roman Baetica*

☐ *Other Roman provinces*

Hadrian

Emperors Hadrian and Trajan were born in Baetica. A great many politicians, writers and philosophers from the province also moved to Rome, some enjoying great fortune.

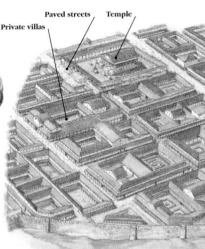

Private villas · Paved streets · Temple

Roman Mosaics in Andalusia

Private houses, temples and public buildings all had mosaic floors. Many themes, from the gods to hunting, were represented.

ITÁLICA RECONSTRUCTED

Scipio Africanus founded Itálica (see p128) in 206 BC after his defeat of the Carthaginians. The city reached its height in the 2nd and 3rd centuries AD and was the birthplace of the emperors Hadrian and Trajan. Unlike Córdoba, it was not built over in post-Roman times and today Itálica is a superbly preserved example of a Roman city.

TIMELINE

206 BC Scipio Africanus gains victory against the Carthaginians at Alcalá del Río; Itálica is founded

55 BC Birth of Seneca the Elder in Córdoba

AD 27 Andalusia is named Baetica

Suicide of Seneca

65 Suicide of Seneca the Younger after plotting against Nero

117 Hadrian is crowned Emperor

200 BC	100 BC	AD 1	100	200

200 BC Romans conquer southern Spain and reach Cádiz

61 BC Julius Caesar is governor of Hispania Ulterior (Spain)

Julius Caesar

98–117 Trajan, from Itálica, is emperor. Spanish senators enjoy influence in Rome

69–79 Emperor Vespasian grants Roman status to all towns in Hispania

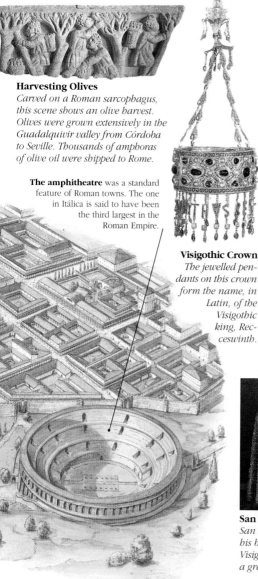

Harvesting Olives
Carved on a Roman sarcophagus, this scene shows an olive harvest. Olives were grown extensively in the Guadalquivir valley from Córdoba to Seville. Thousands of amphoras of olive oil were shipped to Rome.

The amphitheatre was a standard feature of Roman towns. The one in Itálica is said to have been the third largest in the Roman Empire.

Visigothic Crown
The jewelled pendants on this crown form the name, in Latin, of the Visigothic king, Recceswinth.

WHERE TO SEE ROMAN AND VISIGOTHIC ANDALUSIA

Extensive Roman remains can be seen at the sights of Itálica *(see p128)*, Carmona *(p128)* and Ronda la Vieja *(p167)*; In Málaga there is a partially excavated Roman amphitheatre, and Roman columns can be seen at the Alameda de Hércules in Seville *(p86)*. The Museo Arqueológico in Seville *(p95)*, Córdoba *(p139)* and Cádiz *(p160)* all have Roman artifacts on display. Visigothic pillars and capitals can be viewed in the Mezquita in Córdoba *(pp140–41)*.

The Roman ruins at Itálica (see p128) are situated 9 km (5.5 miles) north of Seville.

San Isidoro and San Leandro
San Isidoro (560–635) of Seville, like his brother, San Leandro, converted Visigoths to Christianity; he also wrote a great scholastic work, Etymologies.

300	400	500	600	

415 Visigoths arrive in Spain from northern Europe

446 Tarraconensis in north still Roman; Rome attempts to win back rest of Spain

Illuminated cover of Etymologies *by San Isidoro*

632 Death of Prophet Muhammad

409 Vandals sack Tarraconensis (Tarragona)

Theodosius

476 Visigoths control whole of Spain

589 Third Council of Toledo in central Spain. Visigothic King Reccared converted from Arianism to Catholicism

635 Death of San Isidoro of Seville

The Moorish Conquest

10th-century ivory cask

CALLED IN TO RESOLVE a quarrel among the Visigoths, the Moors first arrived in 710. They returned in 711 to conquer Spain; within 10 years, the north alone remained under Christian control. The Moors named their newly conquered territories Al Andalus and in 929 they established an independent caliphate. Córdoba, its capital, was the greatest city in Europe, a centre for art, science and literature. In the 11th century the caliphate collapsed into 30 feuding *taifas* (party states). Almoravids, tribesmen from North Africa, invaded the region in 1086, and in the 12th century Almohads from Morocco ousted the Almoravids and designated Seville their capital.

MOORISH DOMAIN AD 800

☐ *Al Andalus*

Abd al Rahman III receives the Byzantine envoy

Apocalypse
An 11th-century account of an 8th-century text, Commentaries on the Apocalypse *by Beato de Liébana, this illustration shows Christians going to war.*

Bronze Stag
This 10th-century caliphal-style bronze is from Medina Azahara.

THE COURT OF ABD AL RAHMAN III

Abd al Rahman III began his palace of Medina Azahara *(see p134)* in 936. This 19th-century painting by Dionisio Baixeres shows a Byzantine envoy presenting the caliph with the works of the Greek scientist Dioscorides. The Moors of Córdoba possessed much knowledge of the ancient world, which was later transmitted to Europe. The Medina was sacked by Berber mercenaries in 1010.

TIMELINE

Visigothic king and Moorish chief

756 Abd al Rahman I reaches Spain and asserts himself as ruler, declaring an independent emirate based around Córdoba

936 Medina Azahara begun

929 Abd al Rahman III proclaims caliphate in Córdoba

700	800	900

711 Invasion under Tariq ben Ziyad

710 First Moorish intervention in Spain

785 The Mezquita *(see pp140–41)* begun at Córdoba

822–52 Rule of Abd al Rahman II

Coin from the reign of Abd al Rahman III

912–61 Rule of Abd al Rahman III

961–76 Al Hakam II builds great library at Medina Azahara; expands Mezquita

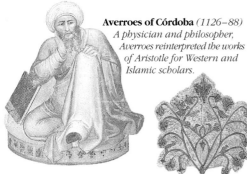

Averroes of Córdoba *(1126–88)*
*A physician and philosopher,
Averroes reinterpreted the works
of Aristotle for Western and
Islamic scholars.*

Horseshoe arches were a major
feature here, as in the Mezquita
(see pp140–41) at Córdoba.

Mozarabic Bible
*Moorish society
integrated Jews and
Mozarabs (Christians
living an Islamic
lifestyle). Illustrations
like this one, from a
10th-century Bible,
are in a Moorish
decorative style.*

Clerics prepare
the manuscript to
be given to Abd
al Rahman III.

WHERE TO SEE MOORISH ANDALUSIA

The Mezquita in Córdoba *(see
pp140–41)* and the ruins of
the palace at Medina Azahara
(p134) are the most complete
remnants of Spain's Moorish
caliphate. Artifacts found at
Medina Azahara can be seen
in the Museo Arqueológico
in Córdoba *(see p139)*. The
Alcazaba at Almería *(see p192)*
dates from the 10th century,
when this city was still part
of the caliphate, while the
Alcazaba at Málaga *(see p173)*
was built during the ensuing
Taifa period. The Torre del
Oro *(see p67)* and La Giralda
(see p76) in Seville are both
Almohad structures.

The Alcazaba in Almería
(p192), *dating from the 10th
century, overlooks the old town.*

Cufic Script
*Islamic artists,
forbidden to use
representations of
the human figure,
made ample use
of calligraphy
for decoration.*

Irrigation in Al Andalus
*The water wheel was vital to irrigation,
which the Moors used to grow newly
imported crops such as rice and oranges.*

Al Mansur	**1086** Almoravids invade	**1120** Almoravid power starts to wane	
1012 *Taifas* emerge as splinter Moorish states		**1126** Birth of Averroes, Arab philosopher	
1031 Caliphate ends		**1147** Almohads arrive in Seville; build Giralda and Torre del Oro	
1000	**1100**		**1200**
976–1002 Al Mansur, military dictator, comes to power	**1085** Fall of Toledo in north to Christians decisively loosens Moorish control over central Spain	**1135** Maimónides, Jewish philosopher, born in Córdoba	**1175–1200** Height of Almohad power. Previously lost territory won back from Christians
1010 Medina Azahara sacked by Berbers		*Maimónides*	

The Reconquest

Christian horseman

THE WAR BETWEEN Moors and Christians, which started in northern Spain, arrived in Andalusia with a landmark Christian victory at Las Navas de Tolosa in 1212; Seville and Córdoba fell soon afterwards. By the late 13th century only the Nasrid kingdom of Granada remained under Moorish control. Meanwhile, Christian monarchs such as Alfonso X and Pedro I employed Mudéjar *(see p22)* craftsmen to build churches and palaces in the reconquered territories – Mudéjar literally means "those permitted to stay". Granada eventually fell in 1492 to Fernando and Isabel of Aragón and Castilla, otherwise known as the Catholic Monarchs.

MOORISH DOMAIN IN 1350

☐ *Nasrid kingdom*

The Catholic Monarchs enter Granada; Fernando and Isabel were awarded this title for their services to Christendom.

Boabdil

Cantigas of Alfonso X
Alfonso X, who won back much of Andalusia from the Moors, was an enlightened Christian monarch. His illuminated Cantigas are a vivid account of life in Reconquest Spain.

THE FALL OF GRANADA
This relief by Felipe de Vigarney (1480–c.1542), in Granada's Capilla Real *(see p182)*, shows Boabdil, the last Moorish ruler, surrendering the city in 1492. Trying to establish a Christian realm, the Catholic Monarchs converted the Moors by force and expelled the Jews. The same year, Columbus got funds for his voyage to America *(see p123).*

Almohad Banner
This richly woven tapestry is widely believed to be the banner captured from the Moors by the Christians at the battle of Las Navas de Tolosa.

TIMELINE

1226 Fernando III takes Baeza

1236 Fernando III conquers Córdoba

1252–84 Alfonso X reconquers much of Andalusia. Toledo Translators' School in the north continues to translate important works of Moorish literature

Pedro I of Castilla

1333 Moors add tower to the 8th-century Keep *(see p164)* on Gibralta

1220	1260	1300	1340

1212 Almohad *(see p44)* power broken by Christian victory at Las Navas de Tolosa

1248 Fernando III takes Seville

1238 Nasrid dynasty established in Granada. Alhambra *(see p186)* begun

1350–69 Reign of Pedro I of Castilla, who rebuilds Seville Alcázar in Mudéjar style. His lack of Spanish patriotism provokes civil war against Henry II of Trastámara

Alfonso X

Chivalry
*The Moors lived by chivalric codes –
this jousting scene is in the Sala de
los Reyes in the Alhambra (see p186).*

Nasrid warriors

Crown
*This Mudéjar-style
crown, bearing the
coats of arms of Castilla
and León, is made of
silver, ivory and coral.*

Astrolabe
*As this 15th-century
navigation tool shows,
the Moors had great
technical expertise.*

Boabdil's Demise
*Legend has it that
Boabdil wept as he left
Granada. He moved
to Laujar de Andarax
(see p189) until 1493,
then later to Africa.*

WHERE TO SEE RECONQUEST ANDALUSIA

Many of the Reconquest
buildings in Andalusia are
Mudéjar in style *(see p22)*.
The most notable are the
Palacio Pedro I in the Reales
Alcázares *(p81)* and parts
of the Casa de Pilatos *(p75)*,
both in Seville. Christian
churches built in Andalusia
during the 13th, 14th and 15th
centuries are also either completely Mudéjar in style or
have Mudéjar features such
as a minaret-like bell tower
or portal; as, for example, the
Iglesia de San Marcos *(p88)*
in Seville. During this period
the Nasrids of Granada built
the most outstanding example of Moorish architecture
in Spain, the Alhambra and
Generalife *(pp186–8)*. Seville
Cathedral *(pp76–7)* was constructed in the 15th century
as a high Gothic assertion of
the Catholic faith.

The Palacio Pedro I (see
p81) *in Seville is considered to
be the most complete example of
Mudéjar architecture in Spain.*

1369 Henry II of Trastámara
personally kills Pedro I;
lays seeds of monolithic
Castilian regime

La Pinta, *one of
Columbus's ships*

PINTA

1492 Fall of Granada to
the Catholic Monarchs

1380	1420	1460

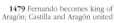

*Forced baptism
of the Moors*

1469 Marriage of Fernando
of Aragón to Isabel of Castilla

1474 Isabel proclaimed queen in Segovia

1479 Fernando becomes king of
Aragón; Castilla and Aragón united

1492
Columbus
sails to
America

Seville's Golden Age

THE 16TH CENTURY saw the rise of a monolithic Spanish state, led by the Catholic Monarchs. Heretics were persecuted and the remaining Moors treated so unjustly that they often rebelled. In 1503 Seville was granted a monopoly on trade with the New World and Spain entrusted with "converting" the Indians by the pope. In 1516 the Habsburg Carlos I came to the throne, later to be elected Holy Roman Emperor; Spain became the most powerful nation in Europe. Constant war, however, consumed the wealth that its main port, Seville, generated. By the 1680s the Guadalquivir had silted up, trade had passed to Cádiz and Seville declined.

Mexican Indian

SPANISH EMPIRE IN 1700

☐ *Spanish territories*

La Giralda *(see p76)*, once an Almohad minaret, is now the belfry of Seville's cathedral.

Carlos I *(1516–56)*
Carlos I of Spain was made Holy Roman Emperor Carlos V in 1521. His election enabled the Holy Roman Empire to gain access to the immense wealth that Spain, Seville in particular, generated at this time.

Map of Central America
Within 30 years of Columbus's first voyage, the distant lands and seas of Central America had become familiar territory to Spanish navigators.

SEVILLE IN THE 16TH CENTURY

This painting by Alonso Sánchez Coello (1531–88) shows Seville at its height. With the return of treasure fleets from the New World, astonishing wealth poured into the city and it became one of the richest ports in Europe. The population grew, religious buildings proliferated and artistic life found new vigour. Despite the prosperity of the city, poverty, crime and sickness were endemic.

TIMELINE

1502 Moors rebel in Las Alpujarras *(see pp190–91)*; they are baptized or expelled by the Inquisition	**1516** Death of Fernando	*Seville Inquisition banner*	**1588** Spanish Armada fails in attack on England
	1519 Hernán Cortés conquers Mexico	**1559** Inquisition persecutes Protestants in Seville	**1587** Cádiz raided by Drake
			1580 Seville becomes largest city in Spain

1500		**1525**		**1550**		**1575**

	1516–56 Reign of Carlos I, later Holy Roman Emperor	**1532** Pizarro conquers Peru	**1556–98** Reign of Felipe II
		1519 Magellan sails from Sanlúcar de Barrameda on first circumnavigation of the world	**1558** Second Moorish rebellion in Las Alpujarras
1506 Death of Isabel			*Ferdinand Magellan (1480–1521)*

Inquisition
Fears of heresy laid the ground for the Spanish Inquisition to be set up in the 15th century. In the 16th century autos-da-fé (trials of faith) were held in Seville in the Plaza de San Francisco (see p72).

Unloading and loading took place virtually in the heart of the city.

Velázquez
Born in Seville in 1599, Diego Velázquez paint-ed his earliest works in the city, but later became a court painter in Madrid. This cru-cifix is a detail of a painting he made at the be-hest of Felipe IV.

Ships from other parts of Europe brought goods to the city; this merchan-dise would be traded later in the New World.

The Last Moors
The last Moors were expelled in 1609; this destroyed southern Spain's agriculture, which had taken over 700 years to develop.

WHERE TO SEE THE GOLDEN AGE IN ANDALUSIA

The Isabelline style *(see p22)*, lasting testament to national-istic fervour of the early 16th century, can be seen in the Capilla Real *(p182)* in Granada and the Palacio de Jabalquinto in Baeza *(pp148–9)*. Baeza and Úbeda *(pp150–51)* both prospered during the Renais-sance in Spain and contain some of the best architecture of this period in Andalusia. The Plateresque *(p23)* façade of the Ayuntamiento *(pp72–3)* in Seville is a good example of the style, and the Palacio Carlos V *(p183)* in Granada is the best example of Classical Renaissance architecture in Spain. The Archivo de Indias *(pp78–9)* was built according to the principles of Herreran style *(p23)*. The Hospital de la Caridad *(p67)* is a fine 17th-century Baroque building.

The Capilla Real (see p182) *in Granada was built to house the bodies of the Catholic Monarchs, Fernando and Isabel.*

	1608 Cervantes, active in Madrid and Seville, publishes *Don Quixote*		*Original edition of Don Quixote*	
1598–1621 Reign of Felipe III	**1609** Expulsion of Moors by Felipe III		**1649** Plague in Seville kills one in three	
1600		**1625**	**1650**	**1675**
		1630 Madrid becomes Spain's largest city. Zurbarán moves to Seville		**1665–1700** Carlos II, last of the Spanish Habsburgs
1599 Velázquez born in Seville				*Young beggar by Murillo (1617–82)*
1596 Sack of Cádiz by the English fleet	**1617** Murillo born in Seville			

Bourbon Kings

Joseph Bonaparte

THE 13-YEAR War of the Spanish Succession saw Bourbons on the throne in place of the Habsburgs and, under the Treaty of Utrecht, the loss of Gibraltar to the British *(see pp164–5)*. Later, ties with France dragged Spain into the Napoleonic Wars: following the Battle of Trafalgar, the Spanish king Carlos IV abdicated and Napoleon Bonaparte placed his brother Joseph on the Spanish throne. The Peninsular War ensued and, with British help, the French were driven out of Spain. After the Bourbon restoration, Spain, weakened by further strife, began to lose her colonies. Andalusia became one of Spain's poorest regions.

SPAIN IN EUROPE (1812)

▨ *Napoleonic dependencies*

☐ *Napoleonic rule*

Romantic Andalusia
Andalusia's Moorish legacy helped to establish it as a land of beauty and myth, making it popular with travellers of the Romantic era.

The Constitution
is proclaimed to the people of Cádiz.

Carlos III
A Bourbon monarch of the Enlightenment and an innovator in matters of society and science, Carlos III tried to establish colonies of farm workers in the sparsely populated Sierra Morena.

THE 1812 CONSTITUTION
During the Peninsular War, Spain's Parliament met in Cádiz, and in 1812 produced an advanced liberal constitution. However, after the Bourbon restoration in 1814, Fernando VII banned all liberal activity. Ironically, during the First Carlist War, Fernando's daughter, Isabel II, contesting her right to the throne against her uncle Don Carlos, turned to the liberals for support.

TIMELINE

1700	1725	1750	1775
1701 Felipe V of Bourbon begins his reign	**1717** American trade moves to Cádiz		**1779–8** Great Siege of Gibraltar
	1726 Spain tries to retake Gibraltar		
1701–13 War of the Spanish Succession	**1724** Felipe V abdicates but is reinstated	**1759–88** Carlos III	
	1713 Treaty of Utrecht; Gibraltar ceded to Britain	**1746–59** Reign of Fernando VI	
		1771 Royal Tobacco Factory in Seville is completed	
			1788–1808 Carlos IV

Battle of Bailén
In 1808, at Bailén, a Spanish army comprising local militias beat an experienced French army, taking 22,000 prisoners.

Battle of Trafalgar
In 1805, the Spanish, allied at the time to Napoleon, lost their fleet to the British admiral, Nelson.

Support for the constitution came from a wide section of society, including women.

WHERE TO SEE BOURBON ANDALUSIA

Eighteenth-century Baroque architecture can be seen all over Andalusia. The prime examples in Seville are the former Royal Tobacco Factory, now the city's Universidad *(see pp94–5)*, and the Plaza de Toros de la Maestranza *(p66)*. Osuna *(p129)*, Écija *(p129)* and Priego de Córdoba *(p146)* all have fine examples of the style. The lower levels of Cádiz Cathedral *(p160)* are the most complete example of a Baroque church found in Spain. The Puente Isabel II *(p101)* is a fine example of 19th-century *arquitectura de hierro* (iron architecture).

The Puente Isabel II *is an example of the architecture of Andalusia's "industrial" age.*

Washington Irving
In Tales of the Alhambra *(1832) the American diplomat Washington Irving perpetuated a highly romanticized view of Andalusia.*

Seville's Tobacco Factory
Carmen *(1845), by Prosper Mérimée (see p94), was inspired by the women – over 3,000 of them – who worked in the tobacco factory.*

Isabel II

1808 Joseph Bonaparte made king of Spain. Battle of Bailén	**1812** Liberal constitution drawn up in Cádiz	**1870–73** Reign of King Amadeo	**1873–4** First Republic
	1814–33 (Bourbon restoration) Reign of Fernando VII	**1868** Isabel II loses her throne in "glorious" revolution	

1800	**1825**	**1850**	**1875**

	1814 South American colonies begin struggle for independence	**1843** Isabel II accedes to throne	**1846–9** Second Carlist War **1872–6** Third Carlist War	
1805 Battle of Trafalgar			**1874** Second Bourbon restoration: Alfonso XII made king	
	1808–14 Peninsular War	**1833** First Carlist War		*Alfonso XII*

The Seeds of Civil War

General Franco

Ａ NDALUSIA CONTINUED to decline, remaining so deeply feudal that by the early 20th century social protest was rife. The 1920s brought dictator General Primo de Rivera and relative, but short-lived, social order. In 1931, a Republican government, initially comprising liberals and moderate socialists, came to power. A rigid social order made real reforms slow to arrive, however, and 1931–36 saw growing conflict between extreme left and right wing (including the Falange) elements. Finally, in 1936, the Nationalist General Franco, leading a Moroccan garrison, invaded Spain, declaring war on the Republic.

ANDALUSIA IN 1936

▨ Nationalist territory

☐ Republican territory

Moorish Revival
By the late 19th century, re-gionalism, andalucismo, led to a revival of Moorish-style architecture. An example is Seville's Estación de Córdoba.

Women fought along-side men against the Nationalist army.

Picasso
Pablo Picasso, shown in this self-portrait, was born in Málaga in 1881. His most famous work, Guernica, de-picts the tragic effects of the Civil War.

THE REPUBLICAN ARMY
In Andalusia, Franco attacked the Republican army at the very start of the war. Cádiz and Seville fell to Nationalists, but other Andalusian towns held out longer. Franco seized Málaga in 1937, executing thousands of Republicans.

TIMELINE

1876 Composer Manuel de Falla born in Cádiz	**1882–1912** Growing militancy of farm workers	
	1885–1902 Regency of María Cristina	*Spanish soldiers, Cuban War*
		1895–8 Cuban War

1880	**1890**	**1900**

1881 Pablo Picasso born	**1893** Guitarist Andrés Segovia born near Jaén	**1898** Cuba gains indepen-dence with US aid; Cádiz and Málaga begin to decline	**1902–31** Reign of Alfonso XIII
	1885 Anarchist group *Mano Negra* active in Andalusia		

Casas Viejas

In 1933, peasants were massacred after an uprising by anarchists at Casas Viejas in the province of Cádiz. The incident further served to undermine the Republican government.

WHERE TO SEE EARLY 20TH-CENTURY ARCHITECTURE IN ANDALUSIA

This period is characterized by architectural revivals. The regionalist style can be seen at the Plaza de España *(see p96),* the Museo Arqueológico *(p97),* and the Museo de Artes y Costumbres Populares *(p97),* all in the Parque María Luisa. The Teatro Lope Vega *(p95)* is in a Neo-Baroque style.

The Pabellón Real (see p97) *in the Parque María Luisa is a pastiche of the late Gothic, Isa-belline (see p21) style.*

1929 Exposition

This trade fair was intended to boost Andalusia's economy. Unfortunately, it coincided with the Wall Street Crash.

Arms were supplied to the Republican army by the then Soviet Union.

General Queipo de Llano

Queipo de Llano broadcast radio propaganda to Seville as part of the Nationalists' strategy to take the city.

Federico García Lorca

This poster is for Lorca's play, Yerma. The outspoken poet and playwright was murdered by local Falangists in his home town, Granada, in 1936.

Republican poster

1923–30 Dictatorship of General Primo de Rivera	**1933** Massacre at Casas Viejas
	1929 Ibero-American Exposition, Seville

1936 Civil War starts

1910 — **1920** — **1930**

1917–20 Bolshevik Triennium; communists lead protests in Andalusia

José Antonio Primo de Rivera

1931–39 Second Republic

1933 Falange founded by José Antonio Primo de Rivera; later supports Franco

1936 Franco becomes head of state

1939 Civil War ends

Modern Andalusia

Andalusian flag

By 1945 Spain remained the only Nationalist state in Europe. She was denied aid until 1953, when Franco allowed US bases to be built on Spanish soil. The 1960s and '70s saw economic growth, Andalusia in particular benefiting from tourism. When Franco died in 1975 and Juan Carlos I came to the throne, Spain was more than ready for democracy; the regions clamoured for devolution from Franco's centralized government. In 1982 the Sevillian Felipe González came to power and, in the same year, Andalusia became an autonomous region.

AUTONOMOUS REGIONS

Present-day Andalusia

The Puente de Chapina is distinguished by a geometrically designed canopy running along the top of it.

Feria
Despite the repressive regime that Franco established, the spirit of the Andalusian people remained evident in events such as the feria *in Seville.*

The Hungry Years
After the Civil War, Spain was isolated from Europe and after World War II received no aid; amid widespread poverty and rationing, many Andalusians left to work abroad.

NEW BRIDGES

Despite its recent autonomy, Andalusia still lagged behind much of the rest of Spain economically. Funds were provided by central government to build the new infrastructure needed to support Expo '92. Five bridges, all of the most innovative, modern design, were built over the Guadalquivir river.

TIMELINE

1940 Franco refuses to allow Hitler to attack Gibraltar from Spanish territory	**1953** Spain is granted economic aid in return for allowing US bases on Spanish soil	**1966** Palomares incident: two US aircraft collide and four nuclear bombs fall to earth, one in the sea, but do not explode. The Duchess of Medina Sidonia, "the red duchess", leads protest march on Madrid
1940	**1950**	**1960**
1940–53 The Hungry Years		**1962** Development of Costa del Sol begins
	Franco meets American President Eisenhower (1953)	**1969** Spain closes its border with Gibraltar

Franco's Funeral (1975)
Franco's death was mourned as much as it was welcomed; most people, though, saw the need for democratic change.

Package Holidays
New building for mass tourism transformed Andalusia's coast.

WHERE TO SEE MODERN ANDALUSIA

The most striking buildings of modern Andalusia were built in the early part of the 1990s. Expo '92 left Seville with five new bridges over the Guadalquivir river, while at La Cartuja *(see p102)* Expo's core pavilions still stand, soon to be the site of new attractions. The new Teatro de la Maestranza *(pp66–7)*, in El Arenal, was also built during this period.

The Omnimax cinema *(see p102) on the former Expo '92 site was originally built as part of the Pavilion of Discoveries.*

The Puente del Alamillo
(Harp) has a single upward arm supporting its weight.

The Puente de la Barqueta, a unique
suspension bridge supported by a single overhead beam, spans 168 m (551 ft).

Felipe González
In 1982, the year after an attempted coup by the Civil Guard colonel Antonio Tejero, Felipe González, leader of the socialist PSOE, claimed a huge electoral victory.

Expo '92
Hosted by Seville, Expo '92 placed Andalusia at the centre of a world stage. In 1996, however, Spain was still recovering the cost.

1976 Adolfo Suárez appointed prime minister and forms centre-right government	**1982** Felipe González elected prime minister; Andalusia becomes an autonomous region	*Royal wedding of Elena de Borbón*	
		1985 Spain-Gibraltar border opens	**1995** Elena de Borbón, eldest daughter of Juan Carlos I, marries in Seville Cathedral
1980		**1990**	**2000**
1975 Franco dies. Third Bourbon restoration; Juan Carlos I accedes to the throne	**1981** Colonel Tejero attempts coup and holds Spanish Parliament hostage; Juan Carlos intervenes	**1992** Expo '92, Seville *Colonel Tejero*	**1998-9** The Basque separatist terrorist group, ETA, declares a ceasefire - it only lasts a year
			1996 In the general election González loses to a coalition led by Aznar

SEVILLE AREA
BY AREA

Seville at a Glance

Baroque doorway, Parlamento de Andalucía *(see p87)*

THE CAPITAL OF ANDALUSIA is a compact and relaxing city with a rich cultural heritage. Conveniently, many of its principal sights can be found within or very near the city centre which is set on the east bank of the Río Guadalquivir. Most visitors head straight for the cathedral and La Giralda, Reales Alcázares and Museo de Bellas Artes. Among other highly popular monuments are the exquisite Renaissance palace of Casa de Pilatos and Seville's bullring, the Plaza de Toros de la Maestranza. There are, however, many other churches, monuments and neighbourhoods to discover in the four central areas described in this section, and more, further afield, across the river.

The splendid ceiling of Museo de Bellas Artes *(see pp64–5)*

EL ARENAL
Pages 60–67

Plaza de Toros de la Maestranza seen from the river *(see p66)*

Patio of Real Fábrica de Tabacos, today the Universidad *(see p94)*

The Moorish Torre del Oro, built to defend Seville *(see p67)*

| 0 metres | 400 |
| 0 yards | 400 |

◁ La Giralda by night over the rooftops of El Arenal

One of many elaborate floats in the Basílica de la Macarena, Seville's shrine for cult worship *(see p87)*

LA MACARENA
Pages 82–9

SANTA CRUZ
Pages 68–81

Roman relief of Leda and the Swan, Casa de Pilatos *(see p75)*

La Giralda rising above the massive Gothic cathedral *(see pp76–7)*

Sumptuous Mudéjar arches and decor in Salón de Embajadores, Reales Alcázares *(see pp80–81)*

PARQUE MARIA LUISA
Pages 90–97

Plaza de España in the green oasis of Parque María Luisa *(see pp96–7)*

EL ARENAL

BOUNDED BY the Río Guadalquivir and guarded by the mighty, 13th-century Torre del Oro, El Arenal used to be a district of munitions stores and shipyards. Today this quarter is dominated by the dazzling white bullring, Plaza de Toros de la Maestranza, where the Sevillians have been staging *corridas* for more than two centuries. The many classic bars and wine cellars in neighbouring streets get extra busy during the summer bullfighting season.

Torre del Oro shown on 20th-century tiles

Once central to the city's life, the influence of the Guadalquivir declined as it silted up during the 17th century. By then El Arenal had become a notorious underworld haunt clinging to the city walls. After being converted into a canal in the early 20th century, the river was restored to its former navigable glory just in time for Expo '92. The east riverfront was transformed into a tree-lined, shady promenade with excellent views of Triana and La Cartuja across the river *(see pp102–3).* Boat trips and sightseeing tours depart from the Torre del Oro. Close by is the smart, new Teatro de la Maestranza, where opera, classical music and dance take place before well-informed audiences.

The Hospital de la Caridad testifies to the city's continuing love affair with the Baroque. Its church is filled with famous paintings by Murillo, and the story of the Seville School is told with pride in the immaculately restored Museo de Bellas Artes further north. The city's stunning collection of great works by Zurbarán, Murillo and Valdés Leal is reason enough to visit Seville.

SIGHTS AT A GLANCE

Historic Buildings
Hospital de la Caridad **5**
Plaza de Toros de la Maestranza **3**
Torre del Oro **6**

Museums
Museo de Bellas Artes
pp64–5 **1**

Churches
Iglesia de la Magdalena **2**

Theatres
Teatro de la Maestranza **4**

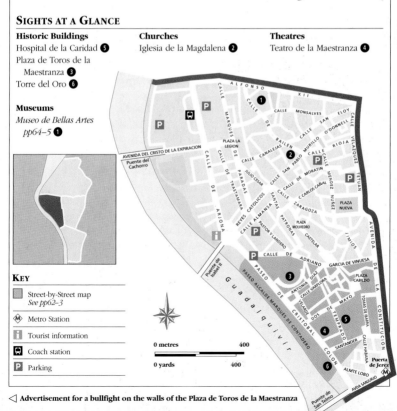

KEY

▢	Street-by-Street map *See pp62–3*
Ⓜ	Metro Station
ℹ	Tourist information
🚌	Coach station
P	Parking

0 metres   400
0 yards   400

Street-by-Street: El Arenal

Statue of Carmen

ONCE HOME TO THE PORT of Seville, El Arenal also housed the artillery headquarters and ammunition works. Now its atmosphere is set by Seville's bullring, the majestic Plaza de Toros de la Maestranza, which is located here. During the bullfighting season (*see pp24–5*) bars and restaurants are packed, but for the rest of the year the backstreets remain quiet. The riverfront is dominated by one of Seville's best-known monuments, the Moorish Torre del Oro, while the long, tree-lined promenade beside Paseo de Cristóbal Colón is the perfect setting for a romantic walk along the Guadalquivir.

★ Plaza de Toros de la Maestranza
Seville's 18th-century bullring, one of Spain's oldest, has a Baroque façade in white and ochre ❸

Carmen (*see p94*), sculpted in bronze, stands opposite the bullring.

CALLE DE ADRIANO

CALLE ANTONIA DIAZ

PASEO DE CRISTOBAL COLON

Teatro de la Maestranza
This showpiece theatre and opera house opened in 1991. Home of the Orquesta Sinfónica de Sevilla, it also features international opera and dance companies ❹

Paseo Alcalde Marqués de Contadero

STAR SIGHTS

- ★ Plaza de Toros de la Maestranza
- ★ Torre del Oro
- ★ Hospital de la Caridad

The Guadalquivir used to cause catastrophic inundations. Following floods in 1947 a barrage was constructed. Today, tourists enjoy peaceful boat trips, starting from Torre del Oro.

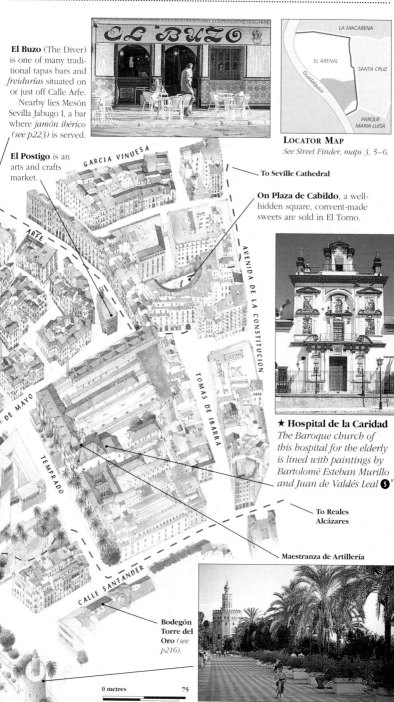

El Buzo (The Diver) is one of many traditional tapas bars and *freidurías* situated on or just off Calle Arfe. Nearby lies Mesón Sevilla Jabugo I, a bar where *jamón ibérico* (see p223) is served.

El Postigo is an arts and crafts market.

To Seville Cathedral

On Plaza de Cabildo, a well-hidden square, convent-made sweets are sold in El Torno.

GARCIA VINUESA

ARFE

US DE MAYO

TEMPRADO

AVENIDA DE LA CONSTITUCION

TOMAS DE IBARRA

CALLE SANTANDER

LOCATOR MAP
See Street Finder, maps 3, 5–6.

LA MACARENA

EL ARENAL

SANTA CRUZ

Guadalquivir

PARQUE MARIA LUISA

★ **Hospital de la Caridad**
The Baroque church of this hospital for the elderly is lined with paintings by Bartolomé Esteban Murillo and Juan de Valdés Leal ❺

To Reales Alcázares

Maestranza de Artillería

Bodegón Torre del Oro *(see p216).*

★ **Torre del Oro**
Built in the 13th century in order to protect the port, this crenellated Moorish tower now houses a small maritime museum ❻

0 metres 75

0 yards 75

KEY

– – – Suggested route

Museo de Bellas Artes ●

Baroque cherubs in Sala 5

THE FORMER Convento de la Merced Calzada has been restored to create one of the finest art museums in Spain. The convent, which was completed in 1612 by Juan de Oviedo, is built around three patios, which today are adorned with flowers, trees and *azulejos* (see p74). The museum's impressive collection of Spanish art and sculpture extends from the medieval to the modern, focusing on the work of Seville School artists such as Bartolomé Esteban Murillo, Juan de Valdés Leal and Francisco de Zurbarán.

🛗 👥 **for disabled**

La Inmaculada
This boisterous In-maculada (1672), by Valdés Leal (1622–90) is in Sala 8, a gallery devoted to the artist's forceful religious paintings.

★ San Hugo en el Refectorio (1655)
One of several works by Zurbarán for the monastery at La Cartuja (see p103), this scene depicts the Carthusian Order of monks first renouncing the eating of meat.

First floor

The Claustro de los Bojes is enclosed by Tuscan-style arches.

STAR EXHIBITS
★ La Virgen de la Servilleta
★ Domed Ceiling
★ Claustro Mayor
★ San Jerónimo Penitente by Pietro Torrigiano
★ San Hugo en el Refectorio by Zurbarán

★ San Jerónimo Penitente (1528)
Sculpted by the Florentine Torrigiano, this master-piece in terracotta brought the vitality of the Italian Renaissance to Seville.

★ La Virgen de la Servilleta
This Virgin and Child (1665–8), painted on a napkin (servilleta), is one of Murillo's most popular works.

VISITORS' CHECKLIST

Pl del Museo 9. **Map** 5 B2. (95) 422 07 90. 43, C1, C2, C3, C4. 3–8pm Tue, 9am– 8pm Wed– Sat, 9am–2pm Sun.   www. juntadeandalucia.es/cultura

★ Domed Ceiling
The magnificent ceiling of the convent church, now restored to its Baroque glory, was painted by Domingo Martínez in the 18th century.

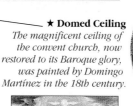

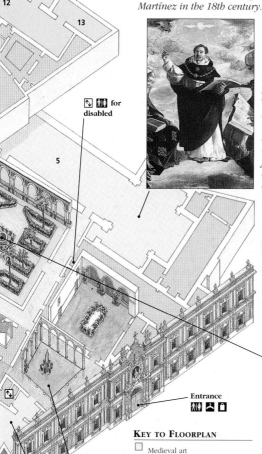

14

12

13

↑ for disabled

5

Apoteosis de Santo Tomás de Aquino
Zurbarán accomplished this work in 1631, at the age of 33. His sharp characterization of the figures and vivid use of colour bring it to life, as can be seen on this detail.

↑

★ Claustro Mayor
The main cloister of the monastery was remodelled by architect Leonardo de Figueroa in 1724.

Entrance

GALLERY GUIDE
Signs provide a self-guided chronological tour through the museum's 14 galleries, starting by the Claustro del Aljibe. Works downstairs progress from the 14th century through to Baroque; those upstairs from the Baroque to the early 20th century.

↑

1

Claustro del Aljibe

Ground floor

KEY TO FLOORPLAN

☐ Medieval art

☐ Renaissance art

☐ Baroque art

☐ 19th- and 20th-century art

☐ Non-exhibition space

Museo de Bellas Artes ❶

See pp64–5.

Madonna and Child in the Baroque Iglesia de la Magdalena

Iglesia de la Magdalena ❷

Calle San Pablo 10. **Map** 3 B1 (5 B2).
📞 95 422 96 03. 🕐 7:30–11am, 6:30–9pm Mon–Sat; 7:30am–1:30pm, 6:30–9pm Sun.

Tʜɪs ɪᴍᴍᴇɴsᴇ ʙᴀʀᴏQᴜᴇ church by Leonardo de Figueroa, completed in 1709, is gradually being restored to its former glory. In its southwest corner is the Capilla de la Quinta Angustia, a Mudéjar chapel with three cupolas. This chapel survived from an earlier church where the great Spanish painter Bartolomé Murillo *(see pp64–5)* was baptized in 1618. The font which was used for his baptism today stands in the baptistry of the present building. The sheer west front is surmounted by a belfry painted in vivid colours.

Among the religious works in the church are a painting by Francisco de Zurbarán, *St Dominic in Soria*, housed in the Capilla Sacramental (to the right of the south door), and frescoes by Lucas Valdés above the sanctuary depicting *The Allegory of the Triumph of Faith*. On the wall of the north transept is a cautionary fresco which depicts a medieval auto-da-fé (trial of faith).

Plaza de Toros de la Maestranza ❸

Paseo de Colón 12. **Map** 3 B2 (5 B4).
📞 95 422 45 77. 🕐 9am–7pm daily; 9:30am–3pm on bullfight days. 🖼 ✔

Sᴇᴠɪʟʟᴇ's ꜰᴀᴍᴏᴜs bullring is arguably the finest in the whole of Spain and is a perfect venue for a first experience of the *corrida*, or bullfight *(see pp24–5)*. Although the art of the matador (bullfighter) is now declining in popularity, the sunlit stage, with its white-washed walls, blood red fences and merciless circle of sand, remains crucial to the city's psyche. Even if you dislike the idea of bullfighting, this arcaded arena, dating from 1761 to 1881, is an aesthetic marvel and well worth a visit.

The bullring accommodates as many as 12,500 spectators. Guided tours start from the main entrance on Paseo de Cristóbal Colón. On the west side stands the Puerta del Príncipe (Prince's Gate), through which the very best of the matadors are carried triumphant on the shoulders of admirers from the crowd.

Passing the *enfermería* (emergency hospital), visitors reach a museum which details the history of the bullfight in Seville. Among its collection of costumes, portraits and posters are scenes showing early contests held in the Plaza de San Francisco and a purple cape painted by Pablo Picasso. The tour continues to the chapel where matadors pray for success, and then on to the

stables where the horses of the *picadores* (lance-carrying horsemen) are kept.

The bullfighting season starts on Easter Sunday and continues intermittently until October. Most *corridas* are held on Sunday evenings. Tickets can be bought from the *taquilla* (booking office) at the bullring itself.

Entrance with 19th-century iron-work, Teatro de la Maestranza

Teatro de la Maestranza ❹

Paseo de Colón 22. **Map** 3 B2 (5 C5).
📞 95 422 65 73 (information).
🕐 for performances. 🚫 ♿
🌐 www.teatromaestranza.com

Nᴏᴛ ꜰᴀʀ ꜰʀᴏᴍ the Plaza de Toros, and with echoes of its circular bulk, is Seville's 1,800-seat opera house and theatre. It opened in 1991 and many international opera companies perform here *(see*

Arcaded arena of the Plaza de Toros de la Maestranza, begun in 1761

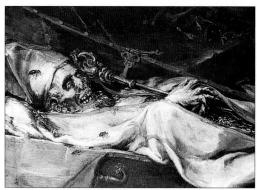

Finis Gloriae Mundi by Juan de Valdés Leal in the Hospital de la Caridad

p231). Like many of the city's buildings built during the run-up to Expo '92 *(see pp54–5),* it was designed in a rather austere style by architects Luis Marín de Terán and Aurelio del Pozo. Ironwork remnants of the 19th-century ammunition works that first occupied the site decorate the river façade. Tickets are sold from the box office situated in the adjacent Jardín de la Caridad.

Hospital de la Caridad ❺

Calle Temprado 3. **Map** 3 B2 (5 C5).
[95 422 32 32.] 9am–1:30pm, 3:30–7:30pm Mon–Sat, 9am–1pm Sun & public hols. ▣

THIS CHARITY HOSPITAL was founded in 1674 and it is still used today as a sanctuary for elderly and infirm people. In the gardens opposite the entrance stands a statue of its benefactor, Miguel de Mañara. The complex was designed by Pedro Sánchez Falconete. The façade of the hospital church, with its whitewashed walls, terracotta stonework and framed *azulejos (see p74)* provides a glorious example of Sevillian Baroque.

Inside are two square patios adorned with plants, 18th-century Dutch *azulejos* and fountains with Italian statues depicting Charity and Mercy. At their northern end a passage to the right leads to another patio, where a 13th-century arch from the city's shipyards survives. A bust of Mañara stands amid rose bushes.

Inside the church there are many original canvases by some of the leading artists of the 17th century, despite the fact that some of its greatest artworks were looted by Marshal Soult at the time of the Napoleonic occupation of 1810 *(see p51).* Immediately above the entrance is the ghoulish *Finis Gloriae Mundi* (The End of the World's Glories) by Juan de Valdés Leal, while opposite hangs his morbid *In Ictu Oculi* (In the Blink of an Eye). Many of the other works are by Murillo, including *St John of God Carrying a Sick Man,* portraits of the Child Jesus, *St John the Baptist as a Boy* and *St Isabel of Hungary Curing the Lepers.* Looking south from the hospital's

entrance you can see the octagonal Torre de Plata (Tower of Silver) rising above Calle Santander. Like the Torre del Oro nearby, it dates from Moorish times and was built as part of the city defences.

Torre del Oro ❻

Paseo de Colón s/n. **Map** 3 B2 (5 C5).
[95 422 24 19.] 10am–2pm Tue–Fri, 11am–2pm Sat & Sun. ● Aug. ▣ (free Tue).

IN MOORISH SEVILLE the Tower of Gold formed part of the walled defences, linking up with the Reales Alcázares *(see pp80–81)* and the rest of the city. It was constructed as a defensive lookout in 1220, when Seville was under the control of the Almohads *(see pp44–5),* and had a companion tower on the opposite river bank. A mighty chain would be stretched between the two to prevent ships from sailing upriver. In 1760 the turret was added.

The gold in the tower's name may refer to gilded *azulejos* which once clad its walls, or to New World treasures unloaded here. The tower has been used as a chapel, a prison, a gun powder store and port offices. Now it is the Museo Marítimo, exhibiting maritime maps and antiques.

The Torre del Oro, built by the Almohads

DON JUAN OF SEVILLE

Miguel de Mañara (1626–79), founder and subsequent benefactor of the Hospital de la Caridad, is frequently linked with Don Juan Tenorio. The amorous conquests of the legendary Sevillian seducer were first documented in 1630 in a play by Tirso de Molina. They have since inspired works by Mozart, Molière, Byron and Shaw. Mañara is thought to have led an equally dissolute life prior to his conversion to philanthropy – apparently this was prompted by a premonition of his own funeral which he experienced one drunken night.

The legendary Don Juan with two of his conquests

SANTA CRUZ

THE BARRIO DE SANTA CRUZ, Seville's old Jewish quarter, is a warren of white alleys and patios that has long been the most picturesque corner of the city. Many of the best-known sights are grouped here: the cavernous Gothic cathedral with its landmark Giralda; the splendid Real Alcázar with the royal palaces and lush gardens of Pedro I and Carlos V; and the Archivo de Indias, whose documents tell of Spain's exploration and conquest of the New World.

Spreading northeast from these great monuments is an enchanting maze of whitewashed streets. The

Ornate streetlamp, Plaza del Triunfo

artist Bartolomé Esteban Murillo lived here in the 17th century while his contemporary, Juan de Valdés Leal, decorated the Hospital de los Venerables with fine Baroque frescoes.

Further north, busy Calle de las Sierpes is one of Seville's favourite shopping streets. Its adjacent market squares, such as the charming Plaza del Salvador, provided backdrops for Cervantes' stories. Nearby, the ornate façades and interiors of the Ayuntamiento and the Casa de Pilatos, a gem of Andalusian architecture, testify to the great wealth and artistry that flowed into the city in the 16th century.

SIGHTS AT A GLANCE

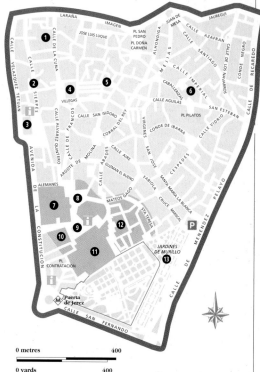

KEY

Street-by-Street map
See pp70–71

Ⓜ Metro Station

ℹ Tourist information

Ⓟ Parking

0 metres 400
0 yards 400

◁ **La Giralda seen from the gardens of the Reales Alcázares**

Street-by-Street: Santa Cruz

THE MAZE of narrow streets to the east of Seville cathedral and the Real Alcázar represents Seville at its most romantic and compact. As well as the expected souvenir shops, tapas bars and strolling guitarists, there are plenty of picturesque alleys, hidden plazas and flower-decked patios to reward the casual wanderer. Once a Jewish ghetto, its re-

Window grille, Santa Cruz

stored buildings, with characteristic window grilles, are now a harmonious mix of up-market residences and tourist accommodation. Good bars and restaurants make the area well worth an evening visit.

Plaza Virgen de los Reyes
Horse carriages line this plaza which has an early 20th-century fountain by José Lafita **8**

Palacio Arzobispal,
the 18th-century Archbishop's Palace, is still used by Seville's clergy.

★ Seville Cathedral and La Giralda
This huge Gothic cathedral and its Moorish bell tower are Seville's most popular sights **7**

Convento de la Encarnación
(See p78)

Archivo de Indias
Built in the 16th century as a merchants' exchange, the Archive of the Indies now houses documents relating to the Spanish colonization of the Americas **10**

Plaza del Triunfo
A Baroque column celebrates the city's survival of the great earthquake of 175... Opposite is a mode... statue of the Imma... late Conception

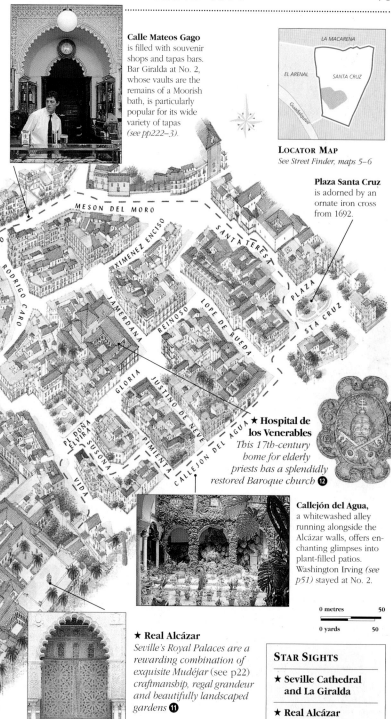

Calle Mateos Gago
is filled with souvenir
shops and tapas bars.
Bar Giralda at No. 2,
whose vaults are the
remains of a Moorish
bath, is particularly
popular for its wide
variety of tapas
(see pp222–3).

LOCATOR MAP
See Street Finder, maps 5–6

Plaza Santa Cruz
is adorned by an
ornate iron cross
from 1692.

★ **Hospital de
los Venerables**
*This 17th-century
home for elderly
priests has a splendidly
restored Baroque church* ⑫

Callejón del Agua,
a whitewashed alley
running alongside the
Alcázar walls, offers en-
chanting glimpses into
plant-filled patios.
Washington Irving *(see
p51)* stayed at No. 2.

| 0 metres | 50 |
| 0 yards | 50 |

★ **Real Alcázar**
*Seville's Royal Palaces are a
rewarding combination of
exquisite Mudéjar (see p22)
craftmanship, regal grandeur
and beautifully landscaped
gardens* ⑪

KEY

– – – Suggested route

STAR SIGHTS

★ **Seville Cathedral
and La Giralda**

★ **Real Alcázar**

★ **Hospital de los
Venerables**

Mosaic, from Itálica *(see p128)*, **in the Casa de la Condesa Lebrija**

Casa de la Condesa Lebrija ❶

Calle Cuna 8. **Map** 1 C5; 3 C1 (5 C2).
📞 95 422 78 02. ⏱ *mid-Jun–Sep:*
10am–1:30pm, 5–8pm Mon–Fri,
10am–2pm Sat; Oct–mid-Jun: 10am–
1:30pm, 4:30–7:30pm Mon–Fri, 10am–
2pm Sat. 🎫 🖪

THE HOME OF the family of
the Countess Lebrija, this
mansion illustrates palatial life
in Seville. The ground floor
houses Roman and medieval
exhibits. A guided tour of the
first floor features a library
and art, such as the Moorish
inspired *azulejos (see p74)*.

The house itself dates from
the 15th century and has some
Mudéjar *(see p22)* features.
Many of its Roman treasures
were taken from the ruins at
Itálica *(see p128)*, including the
mosaic floor in the main patio.
The *artesonado* ceiling above
the staircase came from the
palace of the Dukes of Arcos

in Marchena, near Seville.
Ancient roman glass ware,
coins and later examples of
marble from Medina Azahara
(see p134) are displayed in
rooms off the main patio.

Calle de las Sierpes ❷

Map 3 C1 (5 C3).

THE STREET of the snakes,
running north from Plaza
de San Francisco, is Seville's
main pedestrianized shopping
promenade. Long-established
stores selling the Sevillian
essentials – hats, fans and the
traditional *mantillas* (lace headdresses) stand alongside clothes
boutiques, souvenir shops,
bargain basements and lottery
kiosks. The best time to stroll
along it is when the *sevillanos*
themselves do – during the
early evening *paseo*.

The parallel streets of Cuna
and Tetuán on either side also
offer some enjoyable window-
shopping. Look out for the
splendid 1924 tiled advert for
Studebaker automobiles *(see
p74)* at Calle Tetuán 9.

At the southern end of Calle
de las Sierpes, on the wall of
the Banco Central Hispano, a
plaque marks the site of the
Cárcel Real (Royal Prison),
where the famous Spanish
writer Miguel de Cervantes
(1547–1616) *(see p49)* was
incarcerated. Walking north
from here, Calle Jovellanos to
the left leads to the Capillita
de San José. This small, rather
atmospheric chapel, built in
the 17th century, contrasts

sharply with its commercial
surroundings. Further on, at
the junction with Calle Pedro
Caravaca, you can take a look
back into the anachronistic,
upholstered world of the Real
Círculo de Labradores, a private
men's club founded in 1856.
Right at the end of the street,
take the opportunity to peruse
Seville's best-known *pastelería*
(cake shop), La Campana.

Ayuntamiento ❸

Plaza Nueva 1. **Map** 3 C1 (5 C3).
📞 95 459 01 01. ⏱ 5:30 & 6:30pm
Tue–Thu. 🖪

Plateresque doorway, part of the façade of Seville's Ayuntamiento

SEVILLE'S CITY HALL stands
between the historic Plaza
de San Francisco and the modern expanse of Plaza Nueva.

In the 15th–18th centuries,
Plaza de San Francisco was the
venue for autos-da-fé, public
trials of heretics held by the
Inquisition *(see p49)*. Those
found guilty would be taken
to the Quemadero and burnt
alive. (This site is now the
Prado de San Sebastián, north
of Parque María Luisa, *see
pp96–7*.) These days, Plaza de
San Francisco is the focus of
activities in Semana Santa and
Corpus Christi *(see pp32–3)*.

Plaza Nueva was once the
site of the Convento de San
Francisco. In its centre is an
equestrian statue of Fernando
III, who liberated Seville from
the Moors and was eventually
canonized in 1671 *(see p46)*.

The Ayuntamiento, begun in
1527, was finisished in 1534.
The east side, looking on to

Tables outside La Campana, Seville's most famous *pastelería*

Plaza de San Francisco, is a fine example of the ornate Plateresque style *(see p23)* favoured by the architect Diego de Riaño. The west front is part of a Neo-Classical extension built in 1891. It virtually envelops the original building, but richly sculpted ceilings survive in the vestibule and in the lower Casa Consistorial (Council Meeting Room). This room contains Velázquez's *Imposition of the Chasuble on St Ildefonso*, one of many artworks in the building. The upper Casa Consistorial has a dazzling gold coffered ceiling and paintings by Zurbarán and Valdés Leal *(see pp64–5)*.

Iglesia del Salvador ❹

Pl del Salvador. **Map** 3 C1 (6 D3). ☎ *95 421 16 79.* ⬤ *for refurbishment until 2007.*

Baroque façade of the Iglesia del Salvador on the Plaza del Salvador

THIS CHURCH'S cathedral-like proportions result in part from the desire of Seville's Christian conquerors to outdo the architectural splendours of the Moors. The mosque of Ibn Addabas first occupied the site; part of the Moorish patio survives beside Calle Córdoba. It is boxed in by arcades incorporating columns with Roman and Visigothic capitals.

By the 1670s the mosque, long since consecrated for Christian worship, had fallen into disrepair. Work started on a new Baroque structure, designed by Esteban García. The church was completed in 1712 by Leonardo de Figueroa.

Inside, the nave is by José Granados, architect of Granada cathedral *(see p182)*. In the Capilla Sacramental there is a fine statue, *Jesus of the Passion*, made in 1619 by Juan Martínez Montañés (1568–1649). In the northwest corner, a door leads to the ornate Capilla de los Desamparados and a Moorish patio. Over the exit on Calle Córdoba, the bell tower rests on part of the original minaret.

Adjacent to the church is the Plaza del Salvador, which has become a meeting place for Seville's young crowd, with several great tapas bars. The bronze statue commemorates the sculptor Montañés. On the east side of the church, the Plaza Jesús de la Pasión is given over to shops catering to weddings – the Iglesia del Salvador is a favourite among *sevillanos* for getting married.

Plaza del Alfalfa ❺

Map 3 C1 (6 D3). 🏠 *(pets) Sun am.*

NAMED AFTER ALFALFA, a clover-like plant widely cultivated for fodder, this small, tree-shaded square was once used as a hay market. Now, a pet market is held there on Sunday mornings. There are cages of birds and puppies, tanks of exotic fish, and stalls selling tortoises, lizards, mice and even silkworms.

A short walk east of the plaza, down Calle Jesús de las Tres Caídas, stands the colourfully restored Iglesia de San Isidoro. Dating from the 14th century, it has a neat Gothic portal capped by a Mudéjar star, facing Calle San Isidoro. Inside there stands a dramatic statue of Simón Cirineo which was sculpted by Antonio Francisco Gijón around 1687.

THE SIGN OF SEVILLE

The curious abbreviation "no8do" is emblazoned everywhere from the venerable walls of the Ayuntamiento to the sides of the municipal buses. It is traditionally said to stand for "No me ha dejado" ("She has not deserted me"). These words were reputedly uttered by Alfonso the Wise, after the city remained loyal to him in the course of a dispute with his son Sancho during the Reconquest *(see pp46–7)*. The double-loop symbol in the middle represents a skein of wool, the Spanish word for which is madeja, thus no (madeja)do.

The traditional emblem of Seville, here in stone on the Ayuntamiento

The Art of Azulejos

COOL IN SUMMER, durable and colourful, glazed ceramic tiles have been a striking feature of Andalusian façades and interiors for centuries. The techniques for making them were first introduced by the Moors – the word *azulejo* derives from the Arabic *az-zulayj* or "little stone". Moorish *azulejos* are elaborate mosaics made of unicoloured stones.

16th-century *azulejos*, Salones de Carlos V *(p80)*

In Seville the craft flourished and evolved in the potteries of Triana *(see pp100–101)*. A later process, developed in 16th-century Italy, allowed tiles to be painted in new designs and colours. The onset of the Industrial Revolution enabled *azulejos* to be mass-produced in ceramics factories including, until 1980, the famous "Pickman y Cia" at the monastery of La Cartuja *(see p103)*.

MUDÉJAR-STYLE AZULEJOS

The Moors created fantastic mosaics of tiles in sophisticated geometric patterns as decoration for their palace walls. The colours used were blue, green, black, white and ochre.

16th-century Mudéjar tiles, Casa de Pilatos

Interlacing motifs, Patio de las Doncellas

Mudéjar tiles in the Patio de las Doncellas, Reales Alcázares

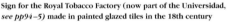

AZULEJOS FOR COMMERCIAL USE

As techniques for making and colouring *azulejos* improved, their use was extended from interior decor to decorative signs and shop façades. Even billboards were produced in multicoloured tiles. The eye-catching results can still be seen all over Andalusia.

Sign for the Royal Tobacco Factory (now part of the Universidad, *see pp94–5)* made in painted glazed tiles in the 18th century

Contemporary glazed ceramic beer tap

Azulejo billboard advertising the latest model of Studebaker Motor Cars (1924), situated on Calle Tetuán, off Calle de las Sierpes *(see p72)*

Genoan fountain and Gothic balustrades in the Mudéjar Patio Principal of the Casa de Pilatos

Casa de Pilatos ⑥

Plaza de Pilatos 1. **Map** 4 D1 (6 E3).
📞 95 422 52 98. 🕐 9am–7pm
(6pm in winter) daily. 🎫 🖼 1st floor.
♿ ground floor.

In 1518 the first Marquess of Tarifa departed on a Grand Tour of Europe and the Holy Land. He returned two years later, enraptured by the architectural and decorative wonders of High Renaissance Italy. He spent the rest of his life creating a new aesthetic, which was very influential. His palace in Seville, called the House of Pilate because it was thought to resemble Pontius Pilate's home in Jerusalem, became a luxurious showcase for the new style.

Lantern in the entrance portal

Over the centuries, subsequent owners added their own embellishments. The Casa de Pilatos is now the residence of the Dukes of Medinaceli and is still one of the finest palaces in Seville.

Visitors enter it through a marble portal, commissioned by the Marquess in 1529 from Genoan craftsmen. Across the arcaded Apeadero (carriage yard) is the Patio Principal. This courtyard is essentially Mudéjar (see p22) in style with azulejos and intricate plasterwork. It is surrounded by irregularly spaced arches capped with delicate Gothic balustrades. In its corners stand three Roman statues, Minerva, a dancing muse and Ceres, and a Greek fourth statue, a 5th century BC original of the goddess Athena. In its centre is a fountain imported from Genoa. To the right, through the Salón del Pretorio with its coffered ceiling and marquetry, is the Corredor de Zaquizamí. Among the antiquities in adjacent rooms are a bas-relief of *Leda and the Swan* and two Roman reliefs commemorating the Battle of Actium of BC 31. Further along, in the Jardín Chico there is a pool with a bronze of Bacchus.

Coming back to the Patio Principal, you turn right into the Salón de Descanso de los Jueces. Beyond this is a rib-vaulted chapel, which has a sculpture dating from the 1st century AD, *Christ and the Good Shepherd*. Left through the Gabinete de Pilatos, with its small central fountain, is the Jardín Grande. The Italian architect, Benvenuto Tortello, created the loggias in the 1560s.

Returning once more to the main patio, behind the statue of Ceres, a tiled staircase leads to the apartments on the upper floor. It is roofed with a wonderful *media naranja* (half orange) cupola built in 1537. There are Mudéjar ceilings in some rooms, which are filled with family portraits, antiques and furniture. Plasterwork by Juan de Oviedo and frescoes by Francisco de Pacheco still survive in rooms which bear these artists' names.

West of the Casa de Pilatos, the Plaza de San Ildefonso is bounded by the Convento de San Leandro, famous for the *yemas* (sweets made from egg yolks) sold from a *torno* (drum). Opposite the convent is the Neo-Classical Iglesia de San Ildefonso, which has statues of San Hermenegildo and San Fernando by Pedro Roldán.

Escutcheons in the coffered ceiling of the Salón del Pretorio

Seville Cathedral and La Giralda ❼

16th-century stained glass

Sᴇᴠɪʟʟᴇ's ᴄᴀᴛʜᴇᴅʀᴀʟ occupies the site of a great mosque built by the Almohads *(see pp44–5)* in the late 12th century. La Giralda, its bell tower, and the Patio de los Naranjos are a legacy of this Moorish structure. Work on the Christian cathedral, the largest in Europe, began in 1401 and took just over a century to complete. As well as enjoying its Gothic immensity and the works of art in its chapels and Treasury, visitors can climb La Giralda for superb views over the city.

★ La Giralda
The bell tower is crowned by a bronze weathervane (giraldillo) *depicting Faith, from which it takes its name. A replica has replaced the original vane.*

Entrance

★ Patio de los Naranjos
In Moorish times worshippers would wash hands and feet in the fountain under the orange trees before praying.

The Rise of La Giralda

The minaret was finished in 1198. In the 14th century the original Muslim bronze spheres at its top were replaced by Christian symbols. In 1568 Hernán Ruiz added the Renaissance belfry, which blends perfectly with the Moorish base.

| 1198 | 1400 | 1557 (plan) | 1568 |

Puerta del Perdón

Roman pillars brought from Itálica *(see p128)* surround the cathedral steps.

Retablo Mayor
*Santa María de la Sede,
the cathedral's patron
saint, sits at the high
altar below a waterfall
of gold. The 44 gilded
relief panels of the
retablo were carved
by Spanish and
Flemish sculptors
between 1482
and 1564.*

VISITORS' CHECKLIST

Avenida de la Constitucion s/n.
Map 3 C2 (5 C4). 95 456 33
21. *many routes.* **Cathedral & La Giralda** 11am–5pm
Mon–Sat; 2:30–6pm Sun (9:30am–
3:30pm Jul–Aug).
8:30am, 10am, noon, 5pm
Mon–Sun (also 8pm Sat, 11am,
1pm & 6pm Sun).

**The Sacristía
Mayor** houses
many works of
art, including
paintings by
Murillo.

★ **Capilla Mayor**
*The overwhelming, golden
Retablo Mayor in the
main chapel is
enclosed by
monumental iron
grilles forged in
1518–32.*

**The Tomb of
Columbus** dates from
the 1890s. His coffin
is carried by bearers
representing the king-
doms of Castile, León,
Aragón and Navarra *(see p46).*

**Puerta
del Bautismo**

STAR FEATURES

★ **La Giralda**

★ **Patio de los
Naranjos**

★ **Capilla Mayor**

Iglesia del Sagrario,
a large 17th-century
chapel, is now used
as a parish church.

Puerta de la Asunción
*Though Gothic in style, this portal
was not completed until 1833. A
stone relief of the Assumption of the
Virgin decorates the tympanum.*

Upper part of the Baroque doorway of the Palacio Arzobispal

Plaza Virgen de los Reyes **8**

Map 3 C2 (6 D4). **Palacio Arzobispal** ● *to the public.* **Convento de la Encarnación** ● *to the public.*

THE PERFECT PLACE to pause for a while and admire the Giralda *(see pp76–7)*, this plaza presents an archetypal Sevillian tableau: horse-drawn carriages, orange trees, gypsy flower-sellers and religious buildings. At its centre is an early 20th-century monumental lamppost and fountain by José Lafita, with grotesque heads copied from Roman originals in the Casa de Pilatos *(see p75)*.

At the north of the square is the Palacio Arzobispal (Arch-bishop's Palace), begun in the 16th century, finished in the 18th, and commandeered by Marshal Soult during the Napoleonic occupation of 1810 *(see pp50–51)*. A fine Baroque palace, it has a jasper staircase and paintings by Zurbarán and Murillo. On the opposite side of

the square is the whitewashed Convento de la Encarnación, which was founded in 1591. The convent stands on grounds that have also been the site of a mosque and of a hospital.

The Plaza Virgen de los Reyes was once home to the Corral de los Olmos, a rogues' inn which features in the writings of Miguel de Cervantes *(see p49)* – on one of the convent walls a plaque bears an inscription testifying to this.

Plaza del Triunfo **9**

Map 3 C2 (6 D4).

LYING BETWEEN the cathedral *(see pp76–7)* and the Real Alcázar *(see pp80–81)*, the Plaza del Triunfo was built to celebrate the triumph of the city over an earthquake in 1755. The quake devastated the city of Lisbon, over the border in Portugal, but caused comparatively little damage in Seville – a salvation attributed to the city's great devotion to the

Decorative Giralda relief on the Archivo de Indias

Virgin Mary. She is honoured by a Baroque column beside the Archivo de Indias, while in the centre of the Plaza del Triunfo a monument comm-emorates Seville's belief in the Immaculate Conception.

In Calle Santo Tomás, which leads off from the southeastern corner of the Plaza del Triunfo, lies a building now used by the Archivo de Indias. Formerly the Museo de Arts Contem-poráneo – now in the Monasterio de Santa Mariá de las Cuevas *(see p103)* – the building is no longer open to the public. Dating from 1770 it was once a barn where tithes collected by the Church were stored. Parts of the Moorish city walls were uncovered during the renovation of the building.

Archivo de Indias **10**

Avda de la Constitución s/n. **Map** 3 C2 (6 D5). ☎ *95 421 12 34.* ◻ *phone for details.* ⊘

Façade of the Archivo de Indias by Juan de Herrera

THE ARCHIVE of the Indies punches home Seville's pre-eminent role in the colonization and exploitation of the New World. Built between 1584–98 to designs by Juan de Herrera, co-architect of El Escorial near Madrid, it was originally a *lonja* (exchange), where merchants traded. In 1785, Carlos III had all Spanish documents relating to the "Indies" collected under one roof, creating a fascinating archive. It contains letters from Columbus, Cortés, Cervantes, and George Washington, the first American president, and the extensive correspondence of Felipe II. The vast collection amounts to some 86 million handwritten pages and 8,000 maps and drawings. Some of the documents are now being stored digitally on CD-ROM.

Visitors to the Archivo de Indias climb marble stairs to library rooms where drawings, maps and facsimile documents are exhibited in a reverential atmosphere. Displays change on a regular basis; one might include a watercolour map from the days when the city of Acapulco was little more than a castle, drawings recording a royal *corrida* (bullfight) which was held in Panama City in 1748 or designs and plans for a town hall in Guatemala.

Real Alcázar ⓫

See pp80–81.

Hospital de los Venerables ⓬

Plaza de los Venerables 8. **Map** 3 C2 (6 D4). 95 456 26 96. 10am–2pm, 4–8pm daily. except Sun evening.

LOCATED IN THE HEART of the Barrio de Santa Cruz, the Hospital of the Venerables was founded as a home for elderly priests. It was begun in 1675 and completed around 20 years later by Leonardo de Figueroa. The hospital has recently been restored as a cultural centre by FOCUS (Fundación Fondo de Cultura de Sevilla).

It is built around a central, sunken patio. The upper floors, along with the infirmary and the cellar, are used as galleries for exhibitions. A separate guided tour visits the hospital church, a showcase of Baroque splendours, with frescoes by Juan de Valdés Leal and his son Lucas Valdés.

Other highlights include the sculptures of St Peter and St Ferdinand by Pedro Roldán, flanking the east door; and *The Apotheosis of St Ferdinand* by Lucas Valdés, top centre in the *retablo* of the main altar. Its frieze (inscribed in Greek) advises visitors to "Fear God and Honour the Priest".

In the sacristy, the ceiling has an effective *trompe l'oeil* depicting *The Triumph of the Cross* by Juan de Valdés Leal.

Jardines de Murillo ⓭

Map 4 D2 (6 E5).

THESE FORMAL GARDENS at the southern end of the Barrio de Santa Cruz once used to be orchards and vegetable plots in the grounds of the Real Alcázar. They were donated to the city in 1911. Their name commemorates Seville's best-known painter, Bartolomé Murillo (1617–82), who lived in nearby Calle Santa Teresa. A long promenade, Paseo de Catalina de Ribera, pays tribute to the founder of the Hospital de las Cinco Llagas, which is now the seat of the Parlamento de Andalucía *(see p87)*. Rising

Monument to Columbus in the Jardines de Murillo

above the garden's palm trees is a monument to Columbus, incorporating a bronze of the *Santa María*, the caravel that bore him to the New World in the year of 1492 *(see p123)*.

Fresco by Juan de Valdés Leal in the Hospital de los Venerables

Real Alcázar ⓫

Mudéjar stucco

IN 1364 PEDRO I *(see p46)* ordered the construction of a royal residence within the palaces built by the city's Almohad *(see pp44–5)* rulers. Within two years, craftsmen from Granada and Toledo had created a jewel box of Mudéjar patios and halls, the Palacio Pedro I, which now forms the heart of Seville's Real Alcázar. Later monarchs added their own distinguishing marks – Isabel I *(see p47)* despatched navigators to explore the New World from her Casa de la Contratación, while Carlos V *(see p48)* had grandiose, richly decorated apartments built.

Jardín de Troya

Gardens of the Alcázar
Laid out with terraces, fountains and pavilions, these gardens provide a delightful refuge from the heat and bustle of Seville.

★ **Salones de Carlos V**
Vast tapestries and lively 16th-century azulejos decorate the vaulted halls of the apartments and chapel of Carlos V.

Patio del Crucero lies above the old baths.

PLAN OF THE REAL ALCÁZAR

The complex includes the Palacio Pedro I and Spanish National Trust offices. The palace's upper floor is used by the Spanish royal family.

KEY

◻ Area illustrated above

◻ Gardens

★ **Patio de las Doncellas**
The Patio of the Maidens boasts plasterwork by the top craftsmen of Granada.

★ Salón de Embajadores
Built in 1427, the dazzling dome of the Ambassadors' Hall is made up of carved and gilded, interlaced wood.

VISITORS' CHECKLIST

Patio de Banderas. **Map** 3 C2 (6 D4). ☎ 95 450 23 23. 🚌 C3, C4, 21, 22. ⏰ 9:30am–7pm Tue–Sat, 9:30am–5pm Sun (Oct–Mar: until 5pm Tue–Sat, 1:30pm Sun). 🎫

Horseshoe Arches
Azulejos and complex plasterwork decorate the Ambassadors' Hall, which has three symmetrically arranged, ornate archways, each with three horseshoe arches.

Casa de la Contratación

The Patio de la Montería was where the court met before hunting expeditions.

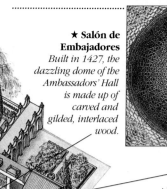

The façade of the Palacio Pedro I is a unique example of Mudéjar style.

Puerta del León (entrance)

Patio de las Muñecas
With its adjacent bedrooms and corridors, the Patio of the Dolls was the domestic heart of the palace. It derives its name from two tiny faces that decorate one of its arches.

STAR FEATURES

★ **Patio de las Doncellas**

★ **Salón de Embajadores**

★ **Salones de Carlos V**

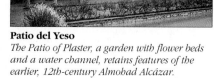

Patio del Yeso
The Patio of Plaster, a garden with flower beds and a water channel, retains features of the earlier, 12th-century Almohad Alcázar.

LA MACARENA

THE NORTH of Seville, often overlooked by visitors, presents a characterful mix of decaying Baroque and Mudéjar churches, old-style neighbourhood tapas bars and washing-filled back streets. Its name is thought to derive from the Roman goddess, Macaria, the daughter of the hero Hercules. La Macarena is a traditional district and the power of church and family is still strong there.

The best way to enter this quarter is to walk north up Calle Feria to the Basílica de la Macarena, a cult-worship shrine to Seville's much-venerated Virgen de la Esperanza Macarena. Beside this

**Roman column,
Alameda de Hércules**

modern church stands a restored entrance gate and remnants of defensive walls, which enclosed the city during the Moorish era.

Among many churches and convents in this quarter, the Monasterio de San Clemente and Iglesia de San Pedro retain the spirit of historic Seville, while the Convento de Santa Paula offers a rare opportunity to peep behind the walls of a closed religious community. The 13th-century Torre de Don Fadrique in Convento de Santa Clara is a notable sight to the west of the area. Further north is the former Hospital de las Cinco Llagas, now restored as the seat of Andalusia's Parliament.

SIGHTS AT A GLANCE

Churches and Convents
Basílica de la Macarena ❹
Convento de Santa Paula ❽
Iglesia de San Marcos ❼
Iglesia de San Pedro ❾
Iglesia de Santa Catalina ❿
Monasterio de San Clemente ❶

Historic Buildings
Parlamento de Andalucía ❺
Torre de Don Fadrique ❷

Monuments
Murallas ❻

Markets
Alameda de Hércules ❸

KEY

▨ Street-by-Street map
　See pp84–5

🅿 Parking

| 0 metres | 500 |
| 0 yards | 500 |

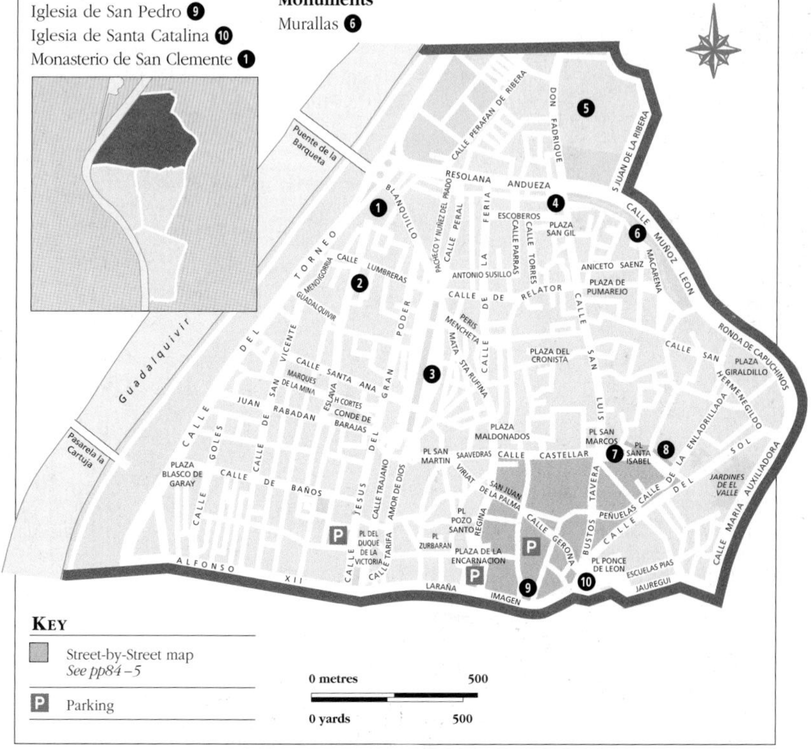

◁ **Float of Virgen de la Esperanza Macarena during the Semana Santa processions**

Street-by-Street: La Macarena

A STROLL IN THIS AREA provides a glimpse of everyday life in a part of Seville that has so far escaped developing the rather tourist-oriented atmosphere of Santa Cruz. Calle de la Feria, the main street for shopping and browsing, is best visited in the morning when there is plenty of activity and its market stalls are filled with fresh fish and

Tiled image of Santa Paula vegetables. Early evening, meanwhile, is a good time to discover the area's large number of fine churches, which are open for Mass at that time. It is also the time when local people visit the bars of the district for a drink and tapas.

Palacio de las Dueñas, boxed in by the surrounding streets and houses, is a 15th-century Mudéjar palace with an elegant main patio. It is the private residence of the Dukes of Alba, whose tiled coat of arms can be seen above the palace entrance.

Iglesia San Juan de la Palma is a small Mudéjar church. Its brickwork belfry was added in 1788.

Calle de la Feria is a lively street full of small shops. Thursday morning is the busiest time, when *El Jueves,* Seville's oldest market, takes place.

★ **Iglesia de San Pedro**
The church where Velázquez was baptized is a mix of styles, from Mudéjar to these modern tiles on its front 9

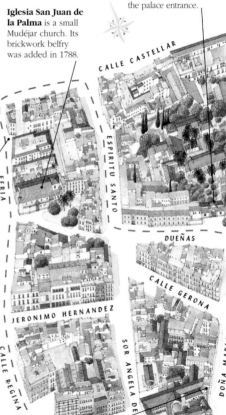

In Convento de Santa Inés the nuns make and sell cakes.

CALLE CASTELLAR

FERIA

ESPIRITU SANTO

DUEÑAS

CALLE GERONA

DOÑA MARIA CORONEL

JERONIMO HERNANDEZ

CALLE REGINA

SOR ANGELA DE LA CRUZ

KEY

— — — Suggested route

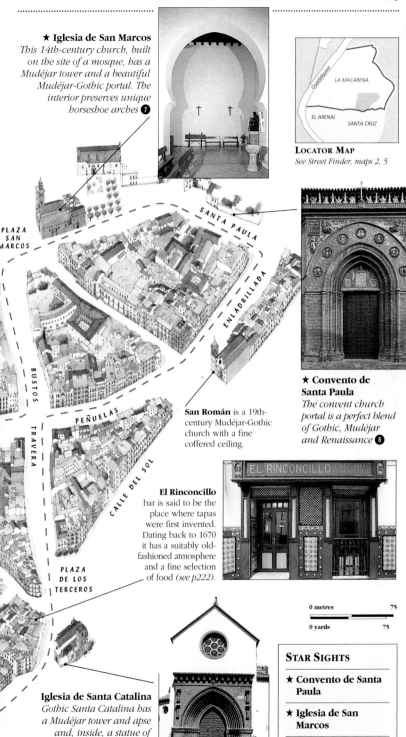

★ **Iglesia de San Marcos**
This 14th-century church, built on the site of a mosque, has a Mudéjar tower and a beautiful Mudéjar-Gothic portal. The interior preserves unique horseshoe arches **7**

LOCATOR MAP
See Street Finder, maps 2, 5

★ **Convento de Santa Paula**
The convent church portal is a perfect blend of Gothic, Mudéjar and Renaissance **8**

San Román is a 19th-century Mudéjar-Gothic church with a fine coffered ceiling.

El Rinconcillo bar is said to be the place where tapas were first invented. Dating back to 1670 it has a suitably old-fashioned atmosphere and a fine selection of food *(see p222)*.

Iglesia de Santa Catalina
Gothic Santa Catalina has a Mudéjar tower and apse and, inside, a statue of Santa Lucía, patron saint of the blind, by Roldán **10**

0 metres 75
0 yards 75

STAR SIGHTS

★ **Convento de Santa Paula**

★ **Iglesia de San Marcos**

★ **Iglesia de San Pedro**

Monasterio de San Clemente ❶

Calle Reposo 9. **Map** 1 C3.
🕿 95 437 80 40. **Church** ☐ *for Mass only: 8:30am Mon–Sat, 9:30am Sun & public hols.*

BEHIND THE ancient walls of the Monasterio de San Clemente is a tranquil cloister with palms and fruit trees, and an arcade with a side entrance to the monastery's church.

This atmospheric church can also be entered through an arch in Calle Reposo. Its features range from the 13th to 18th centuries, and include a fine Mudéjar *artesonado* ceiling, *azulejos (see p74)* dating from 1588, a Baroque main *retablo* by Felipe de Rivas and early 18th-century frescoes by Lucas Valdés.

Torre de Don Fadrique ❷

Convento de Santa Clara, Calle Santa Clara 40. **Map** 1 C4.
🕿 95 437 99 05. ● *currently for refurbishment.*

ONE OF THE best-preserved historical surprises in Seville, this 13th-century tower stands like a chess-piece castle

Torre de Don Fadrique in the patio of Convento de Santa Clara

in the Convento de Santa Clara. This is entered from Calle Santa Clara, passing through an arch to a sleepy patio with orange trees and a fountain. To the left is a second courtyard, where the tower is hidden away. The Gothic entrance to the court-yard was built during the 16th century as part of Seville's first university and transplanted here in the 19th century.

Constructed in 1252, the tower formed part of the defences for the palace of the Infante Don Fadrique. On the façade Romanesque windows sit below Gothic ones. More than 80 steps lead to the upper floor, from which there are impressive views across the city towards La Giralda and Puente de la Barqueta.

The convent of Santa Clara was founded in 1260, though the present buildings date from the 15th century. The Mannerist entrance portico is by Juan de Oviedo. Inside, the nave has a Mudéjar coffered ceiling and an outstanding main *retablo* sculpted by Juan Martínez Montañés in 1623.

Gargoyle on the Torre de Don Fadrique

Marble columns at the southern end of Alameda de Hércules

Alameda de Hércules ❸

Map 2 D4.

THIS TREE-LINED boulevard was originally laid out in 1574. The former marshy area was thus turned into a fashionable promenade for use by *sevillanos* of the Golden Age *(see pp48–9)*.

Since the relocation of the Sunday morning flea market to Charco de la Pava *(see p102)*, efforts have been made to improve the Alameda, long seen as one of Seville's seedier areas.

At the southern end of the boulevard stand two marble columns. They were brought here from a Roman temple dedicated to Hercules in what is now Calle Mármoles (Marbles Street), where three other columns remain. Time-worn statues of Hercules and Julius Caesar cap the Alameda's columns.

The area boasts an eclectic mix of bars, restaurants, cafes and Moroccan-style tea houses.

Basílica de la Macarena ❹

Calle Bécquer 1. **Map** 2 F3.
📞 95 437 01 95. 🕐 9:30am–1pm,
5–9pm daily. **Treasury** 🕐 9:30am–
1pm, 5–8pm daily. 🌑 Easter hols. 📷

THE BASILICA de la Macarena was built in 1949 in the Neo-Baroque style by Gómez Millán as a new home for the much-loved Virgen de la Esperanza Macarena. It butts on to the 13th-century Iglesia de San Gil, where the Virgin was housed until a fire in 1936.

The adored image of the Virgin stands above the principal altar amid waterfalls of gold and silver. It has been attributed to Luisa Roldán (1656–1703), the most talented woman artist of the Seville School. A chapel on the east wall includes a sculpture made by Morales Nieto in 1654, *Christ under Sentence*.

The wall-paintings, by Rafael Rodríguez Hernández, were not executed until 1982. The themes focus on the Virgin Mary, such as a scene of the Immaculate Conception.

In a room to the right of the main entrance you can buy mementos associated with the

Float of the Virgen de la Macarena in Semana Santa processions

Virgin, and tickets for the museum entirely devoted to her cult which is housed in the Treasury. Among a wealth of magnificent processional garments and props are gowns made from *trajes de luces* (suits of lights) donated by famous and no doubt grateful bullfighters. There is also a display of the Virgin's jewels. The floats used in Semana Santa (*see p36*), among them La Macarena's elaborate silver platform, can also be admired.

VIRGEN DE LA MACARENA

Devotions to the Virgen de la Macarena reach their peak during Semana Santa (*see p36*), when her statue is borne through the streets on a canopied float decorated with swathes of white flowers, candles and ornate silverwork. Accompanied by hooded penitents and cries of *¡guapa!* (beautiful!) from her followers, the virgin travels along a route from the Basílica de la Macarena to the cathedral (*see pp76–7*) in the early hours of Good Friday.

Renaissance façade and Baroque portal of Parlamento de Andalucía

Parlamento de Andalucía ❺

C/ Parlamento de Andalucia s/n.
Map 2 E3. 🕐 By written application or call the protocol office. 📞 954 59 21 00. ♿ 📷
🌐 www.parlamento-and.es

THE PARLIAMENT of Andalusia has its seat in an impressive Renaissance building, the Hospital de las Cinco Llagas (five wounds). The hospital, founded in 1500 by Catalina de Ribera, was originally sited near Casa de Pilatos. In 1540 work began on what was to become Europe's largest hospital. Designed by a succession of architects, its south front has a Baroque central portal by Asensio de Maeda.

The hospital was completed in 1613, and admitted patients until the 1960s. In 1992 it was restored for the Parliament.

At the heart of the complex, the Mannerist church, built by Hernán Ruiz the Younger in 1560, has today been turned into a debating chamber.

Virgen de la Macarena – the main reredos in Basílica de la Macarena

Murallas

Map 2 E3.

A SECTION of the defensive walls that once enclosed Seville survives along calles Andueza and Muñoz León. It runs from the rebuilt Puerta de la Macarena at the Basílica de la Macarena (*see p87*) to the Puerta de Córdoba some 400 m (1,300 ft) further east.

Dating from the 12th century, it was constructed as a curtain wall with a patrol path in the middle. The original walls had over 100 towers; the Torre Blanca is one of seven that can be seen here. At the eastern end stands the 17th-century Iglesia de San Hermenegildo, named after the Visigothic king who was allegedly martyred on the site. On the southern corner of this church remains of Moorish arches can be seen.

Iglesia de San Marcos **7**

Plaza de San Marcos. **Map** 2 E5 (6E1).
[C] *95 450 26 16.* [ ] *7:30–8:30pm Mon–Sat.*

T HIS 14TH-CENTURY church retains several Mudéjar features, notably its Giralda-like tower (based on the minaret of an earlier mosque) and the decoration on the Gothic portal on Plaza de San Marcos. The restoration of the interior, gutted by fire in 1936, has highlighted unique horseshoe arches in the nave. A statue of St Mark with book and quill pen, attributed to Juan de Mesa, is in the far left corner. In the plaza at the back of the

The Gothic-Mudéjar portal of the 14th-century Iglesia de San Marcos

church is the Convento de Santa Isabel, founded in 1490. It became a women's prison in the 19th century. The church dates from 1609. Its Baroque portal, facing onto Plaza de Santa Isabel, has a bas-relief of *The Visitation* sculpted by Andrés de Ocampo.

Convento de Santa Paula **8**

C/ Santa Paula 11. **Map** 2 E5 (6 F1).
[C] *95 453 63 30.* [ ] *10am–1pm, 4:30–6:30pm Tue–Sun.*

S EVILLE HAS MANY ENCLOSED religious complexes, but few are accessible. This is one of them, a convent set up in 1475 and still home to 40 nuns. The public is welcome to enter through two different doors in the Calle Santa Paula. Bang on the brown one, marked No. 11, to have a look at the convent museum. Steps lead to two galleries crammed with

religious paintings and artifacts. The windows of the second look onto the nuns' cloister, which echoes with laughter in the afternoon recreation hour. The nuns make a phenomenal range of marmalades and jams, which visitors may purchase in a room near the exit.

Ring the bell by a brick doorway nearby to visit the convent church, reached by crossing a meditative garden. Its portal vividly combines Gothic arches, Mudéjar brickwork, Renaissance medallions, and ceramics by the Italian artist, Nicola Pisano. Inside, the nave has an elaborate wooden roof carved in 1623. Among its statues are St John the Evangelist and St John the Baptist, carved by Juan Martínez Montañés.

St John the Baptist by Montañés in the Convento de Santa Paula

---

SEVILLIAN BELL TOWERS

Bell towers rise above the rooftops of Seville like bookmarks flagging the passing centuries. The influence of La Giralda (*see p76*) is seen in the Moorish arches and tracery adorning the 14th-century tower of San Marcos, and the Mudéjar brickwork which forms the base for San Pedro's belfry. The churches of Santa Paula and La Magdalena reflect the ornate confidence of the Baroque period, while the towers of San Ildefonso illustrate the Neo-Classical tastes of the 19th century.

San Marcos

San Pedro

Santa Paula

Intricate pattern on a chapel door in the Iglesia de San Pedro

Iglesia de San Pedro ❾

Plaza San Pedro. **Map** 2 D5 (6 E2).
📞 95 422 91 24. ⭘ 8:30–11:30am,
7–8:30pm Mon–Sat; 9:30am–1:30pm,
7–8:30pm Sun. ♿

THE CHURCH where the painter Diego Velázquez was baptized in 1599 presents a typically Sevillian mix of architectural styles. Mudéjar elements survive in the lobed brickwork of its tower, which is surmounted by a Baroque belfry. The principal portal, facing Plaza de San Pedro, is another Baroque adornments added by Diego de Quesada in 1613. A statue of St Peter looks disdainfully down at the heathen traffic below.

The poorly lit interior has a Mudéjar wooden ceiling and west door. The vault of one of its chapels is decorated with exquisite geometric patterns formed of interlacing bricks. Behind the church, in Calle Doña María Coronel, cakes and biscuits are sold from a revolving drum in the wall of the Convento de Santa Inés. An arcaded patio fronts its restored church, with frescoes by Francisco de Herrera and a nun's choir separated from the public by a screen. The preserved

body of Doña María Coronel, the convent's 14th-century founder, is honoured in the choir every 2 December.

Iglesia de Santa Catalina ❿

Plaza Ponce de León. **Map** 2 D5
(6 E2). 📞 95 421 74 41. ⬤ for
restoration until 2010.

BUILT ON THE FORMER site of a mosque, this 14th-century church has a Mudéjar tower modelled on La Giralda *(see p76)* (best viewed from Plaza Ponce de Léon) which has been spared the customary Baroque hat. On the west side, by Calle Alhóndiga, the Gothic portal is originally from the Iglesia de Santa Lucía, which was knocked down in 1930. Within its entrance is a horseshoe arch. At the far left end of the nave, the Capilla Sacramental is by Leonardo de Figueroa. On the right, the Capilla de la Exaltación has a decorative ceiling, circa 1400, and a figure of Christ by Pedro Roldán.

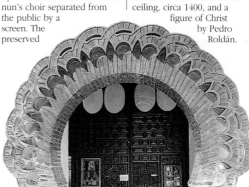

Detail of horseshoe arch in the Iglesia de Santa Catalina

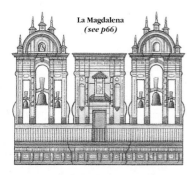

La Magdalena
(see p66)

San Ildefonso
(see p75)

PARQUE MARÍA LUISA

THE AREA SOUTH of the city centre is dominated by the extensive, leafy Parque María Luisa, Seville's principal green area. A great part of it originally formed the grounds of the Baroque Palacio de San Telmo, dating from 1682. Today the park is devoted to recreation; with its fountains, flower gardens and mature trees it provides a welcome place to relax during the long, hot summer months. Just north of the park lies Prado de San Sebastián, the former site of the *quemadero*, the platform where many victims of the Inquisition *(see p49)* were burnt do death. The last execution took place here in 1781.

Many of the historic buildings situated within the park were erected for the Ibero-American Exposition of 1929. This international jamboree sought to reinstate Spain and Andalusia on the world map. Exhibitions from Spain, Portugal and Latin America were displayed in attractive, purpose-built pavilions that are today used as museums, embassies, military headquarters and also cultural and educational institutions. The grand five-star Hotel Alfonso XIII and the crescent-shaped Plaza de España are the most striking legacies from this surge of Andalusian pride. Nearby is the Royal Tobacco Factory, forever associated with the fictional gypsy heroine, Carmen, who toiled in its sultry halls. Today it is part of the Universidad, Seville's university.

Ceramic urn in the Parque María Luisa

SIGHTS AT A GLANCE

Museums
Museo Arqueológico **7**
Museo de Artes y Costumbres Populares **6**

Theatres
Teatro Lope de Vega **4**

Gardens
Parque María Luisa pp96–7 **5**

Historic Buildings
Hotel Alfonso XIII **1**
Palacio de San Telmo **2**
Universidad **3**

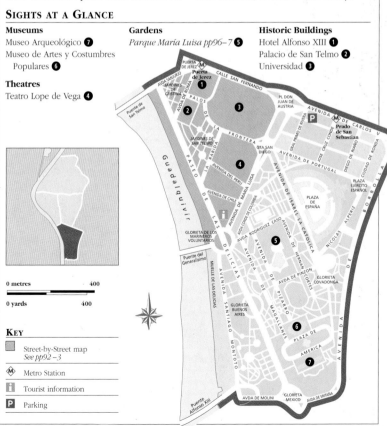

0 metres   400
0 yards   400

KEY

▨ Street-by-Street map
See pp92–3

Ⓜ Metro Station

ℹ Tourist information

Ⓟ Parking

◁ **Horse-drawn carriage on Calle San Fernando**

Street-by-Street: Around the Universidad

Statue of El Cid by Anna Huntington

SOUTH OF the Puerta de Jerez, a cluster of stately buildings stands between the river and Parque María Luisa. The oldest ones owe their existence to the Guadalquivir itself – the 17th-century Palacio de San Telmo was built as a training school for mariners, while the arrival of tobacco from the New World prompted the construction of the monumental Royal Tobacco Factory, today the Universidad de Sevilla. The 1929 Ibero-American Exposition added pavilions in various national and historic styles and also the opulent Hotel Alfonso XIII, creating an area of proud and pleasing architecture that will entertain visitors as they walk towards the Parque María Luisa.

To Triana

Paseo de las Delicias, a riverside walk flanking the Jardines de San Telmo, is a busy road despite its name, the "walk of delights".

Pabellón de Chile is now the Escuela de Artes Aplicadas (School of Applied Arts).

Pabellón de Perú, which is modelled on the Archbishop's Palace in Lima, has a vividly carved façade. It is typical of the nationalistic designs used for the Exposition buildings.

Pabellón de Uruguay

Costurero de la Reina, the "Queen's sewing box", used to be a garden lodge which Princess María Luisa enjoyed visiting. Today it houses the municipal tourist office.

Monument to El Cano, who completed the first world circumnavigation in 1522 after Magellan was killed on route.

0 metres	75
0 yards	75

KEY

– – – Suggested route

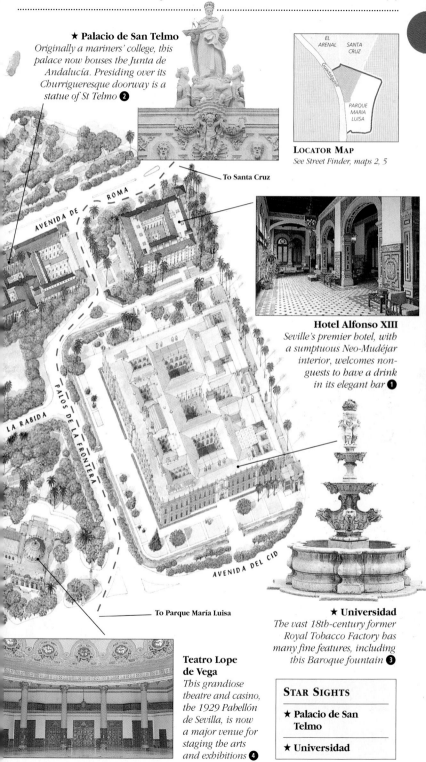

★ **Palacio de San Telmo**
Originally a mariners' college, this palace now houses the Junta de Andalucía. Presiding over its Churrigueresque doorway is a statue of St Telmo ❷

LOCATOR MAP
See Street Finder, maps 2, 5

To Santa Cruz

AVENIDA DE ROMA

PALOS DE LA FRONTERA

LA RÁBIDA

Hotel Alfonso XIII
Seville's premier hotel, with a sumptuous Neo-Mudéjar interior, welcomes non-guests to have a drink in its elegant bar ❶

AVENIDA DEL CID

To Parque María Luisa

★ **Universidad**
The vast 18th-century former Royal Tobacco Factory has many fine features, including this Baroque fountain ❸

Teatro Lope de Vega
This grandiose theatre and casino, the 1929 Pabellón de Sevilla, is now a major venue for staging the arts and exhibitions ❹

STAR SIGHTS

★ **Palacio de San Telmo**

★ **Universidad**

Hotel Alfonso XIII ❶

Calle San Fernando 2. **Map** 3 C3 (6 D5). ☎ *95 491 70 00.* ♿ *except toilets.* ☑ *www.westin.com*

AT THE SOUTHEAST corner of Puerta de Jerez is Seville's best-known luxury hotel. This is named in honour of King Alfonso XIII *(see p52)*, who reigned from 1902 until 1931, when Spain became a republic. It was built between 1916–28 for visitors to the 1929 Ibero-American Exposition *(see p53)*. The building is in Regionalista style, decorated with *azulejos (see p74)*, wrought iron and ornate brickwork. Its centre-piece is a grand patio with a fountain and orange trees. Non-residents are welcome to visit the bar or to dine in the hotel's Itálica restaurant.

Central patio with fountain in the elegant Hotel Alfonso XIII

Churrigueresque adornments of the portal of Palacio de San Telmo

Palacio de San Telmo ❷

Avenida de Roma s/n. **Map** 3 C3. ☎ *95 503 55 05.* ☐ *Mon & Wed.* ☒ ♿ ☐ ☑ *www.juntadeandalucia.es*

THIS IMPOSING PALACE was built in 1682 to serve as a marine university, training navigators and high-ranking officers. It is named after St Telmo, the patron saint of navigators. In 1849 the palace became the residence of the Dukes of Montpensier – until 1893 its vast grounds included what is now the Parque María Luisa *(pp96–7)*. The palace became a seminary in 1901, and today it is the presidential head-quarters of the Junta de Anda-lucía (regional government).

The palace's star feature is the exuberant Churrigueresque portal overlooking Avenida de Roma by Antonio Matías de Figueroa, completed in 1734. Surrounding the Ionic columns are allegorical figures of the Arts and Sciences. St Telmo can be seen holding a ship and charts, flanked by the sword-bearing St Ferdinand and St Hermenegildo with a cross. The north façade, which is on Avenida de Palos de la Frontera, is crowned by a row of Sevillian celebrities. These sculptures were added in 1895 by Susillo. Among them are representations of several notable artists such as Murillo, Velázquez and Montañés.

Façade detail of the Universidad

Universidad ❸

Calle San Fernando 4. **Map** 3 C3. ☎ *95 455 10 00.* ☐ *8am–8:30pm Mon–Fri.* ● *public hols.*

THE FORMER Real Fábrica de Tabacos (Royal Tobacco Factory) is now part of Seville University. It was a popular attraction for 19th-century travellers in search of Romantic Spain. Three-quarters of Europe's cigars were then manufactured here. They were rolled on the thighs of over 3,000 *cigar-reras* (female cigar-makers), who were "reputed to be more impertinent than chaste", as the writer Richard Ford observed in his 1845 *Handbook for Spain*. The factory complex is the largest building in Spain after El Escorial in Madrid and was built between 1728–71. The

CARMEN

The hot-blooded *cigarreras* working in Seville's Royal Tobacco Factory inspired the French author, Prosper Mérimée, to create his famous gypsy heroine, *Carmen*. The short story he wrote in 1845 tells the tragic tale of a sensual and wild woman who turns her affections from a soldier to a bullfighter and is then murdered by her spurned lover. Bizet based his famous opera of 1875 on this impassioned drama, which established Carmen as an incarnation of Spanish romance.

Carmen and Don José

moat and watchtowers are evidence of the importance given to protecting the king's lucrative tobacco monopoly. To the right of the main entrance, on Calle San Fernando, is the former prison where workers caught smuggling tobacco were kept. To the left is the chapel, which is now used by university students.

The discovery of tobacco in the New World is celebrated in the principal portal, which has busts of Columbus *(see p123)* and Cortés. This part of the factory was once used as residential quarters – to either side of the vestibule lie small patios with plants and green ironwork. Ahead, the Clock Patio and Fountain Patio lead to the former working areas. The tobacco leaves were first dried on the roof, then shredded by donkey-powered mills below. Production now takes place in a modern factory situated on the other side of the river, by the Puente del Generalísimo.

Baroque fountain in one of the patios in the Universidad

Teatro Lope de Vega **❹**

Avenida María Luisa s/n. **Map** 3 C3.
📞 95 459 08 67 (ticket office).
🖥 www.sevilla.org/cultura. 🕐 for performances. ♿

L OPE DE VEGA (1562–1635), often called "the Spanish Shakespeare", was a brilliant playwright of more than 1,500 plays. This Neo-Baroque theatre which honours him was opened in 1929 as a casino and theatre for the Ibero-American Exposition *(see p53)*. Its colon-

Dome of the Neo-Baroque Teatro Lope de Vega, opened in 1929

naded and domed buildings are still used to stage performances and exhibitions *(see pp230–31)*. Visitors to the Café del Casino have an opportunity to relax and to enjoy a coffee amid its faded opulence.

Parque María Luisa **❺**

See pp96–7.

Museo de Artes y Costumbres Populares **❻**

Pabellón Mudéjar, Parque María Luisa.
Map 4 D5. 📞 95 423 25 76.
🕐 3–8pm Tue, 9am–8pm Wed–Sat, 9am–2pm Sun & public hols. 🚫 ♿

H OUSED IN the Mudéjar Pavilion of the 1929 Ibero-American Exposition *(see p53)*, this museum is devoted to the popular arts and traditions of Andalusia. Exhibits in the basement include a series of

workshop scenes detailing crafts such as leatherwork, ceramics and cooperage. There is also an informative account of the history of the *azulejo*. Upstairs is a display of 19th-century costumes, furniture, musical instruments and rural machinery. Romantic images of flamenco, bullfighting, and the Semana Santa and Feria de Abril *(see p36)* are a compendium of the Sevillian cliché.

Museo Arqueológico **❼**

Plaza de América, Parque María Luisa.
Map 4 D5. 📞 95 423 24 01.
🕐 3–8pm Tue, 9am–8pm Wed–Sat, 9am–2pm Sun & public hols. 🚫 ♿

T HE RENAISSANCE PAVILION of the 1929 Ibero-American Exposition is now Andalusia's museum of archaeology. The basement houses Paleolithic to early-Roman exhibits, such as copies of the remarkable Tartessian Carambolo treasures *(see p41)*. This hoard of 6th-century BC gold jewellery was discovered near Seville in 1958.

Upstairs, the main galleries are devoted to the Roman era, with statues and fragments rescued from Itálica *(see p128)*. Highlights include a 3rd-century BC mosaic from Écija *(see p129)* and sculptures of local-born emperors Trajan and Hadrian. The rooms continue to Moorish Spain via Palaeo-Christian sarcophagi, Visigothic relics and artifacts discovered at Medina Azahara *(see p134)*.

Museo de Artes y Costumbres Populares, the former Mudéjar Pavilion

Parque María Luisa ❺

Statue of María Luisa (1929)

THIS VAST PARK takes its name from Princess María Luisa de Orleans, who donated part of the grounds from the Palacio de San Telmo *(see p94)* to the city in 1893. The area was landscaped by Jean-Claude Forestier, director of the Bois de Boulogne in Paris, who created a leafy setting for the pastiche pavilions of the 1929 Ibero-American Exposition *(see p53)*. The most dazzling souvenirs from this extravaganza are the Plaza de España and Plaza de América, both the work of Aníbal González, which set the park's theatrical mood. Sprinkling fountains, flowers and cool, tree-shaded avenues all go to make this park a refreshing retreat from the heat and dust of the city.

★ **Plaza de España**
Tiled benches line this semicircular plaza, centrepiece of the 1929 Exposition.

Glorieta de la Infanta
has a bronze statue honouring the park's benefactress, the Princess María Luisa de Orleans.

Starting point for horse and carriage rides

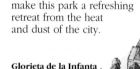

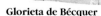

Glorieta de Bécquer
Allegorical figures, depicting the phases of love, add charm to this tribute to Gustavo Adolfo Bécquer (1836–70), the Romantic Sevillian poet. It was sculpted by Lorenzo Coullaut Valera in 1911.

Isleta de los Patos
In the centre of the park is a lake graced by ducks and swans. A gazebo situated on an island provides a peaceful resting place.

Fuente de los Leones
Ceramic lions guard this octagonal fountain, which is surrounded by myrtle hedges. Its design was inspired by the fountain in the Patio de los Leones at the Alhambra (see p187).

VISITORS' CHECKLIST

Map 4 D4. 🚌 *C1, C2, 31, 30, 33, 34, 70, 72.* **Museo de Artes y Costumbres Populares** *(see p95).* **Museo Arqueológico** *(see p95).* ♿ 🍴

★ Museo de Artes y Costumbres Populares
The pavilions of Plaza de América evoke the triumph of the Mudéjar, Gothic and Renaissance styles. The Pabellón Mudéjar houses a museum of Andalusian folk arts ❻

Pabellón Real

The Monte Gurugú is a minimountain with a tumbling waterfall.

★ Museo Arqueológico
The Neo-Renaissance Pabellón de las Bellas Artes today houses a regional archaeological museum. Many finds from nearby Roman Itálica (see p128) are among the exhibits ❼

Ceramics
Brightly painted Sevillian ceramics from Triana decorate the park in the form of floral urns, tiled benches and playful frogs and ducks placed around the fountains.

STAR FEATURES

★ Plaza de España

★ Museo Arqueológico

★ Museo de Artes y Costumbres Populares

Across the River

On THE WEST BANK of the Guadalquivir, old Seville meets the new. Since Roman times, pottery has been made in Triana, which was named after the emperor Trajan. It has traditionally been a working-class district, famous for the bullfighters and flamenco artists that came from its predominantly gypsy community. With cobbled streets and shops selling ceramics, it still has an authentic, lived-in feel. Iglesia de Santa Ana is a fine Mudéjar-Gothic church. From the riverside restaurants and bars along Calle Betis there are views of Seville's towers and belfries.

Tile from Triana, a manufacturing centre for *azulejos* and ceramics

In the 15th century, a Carthusian monastery was built in what was then a quiet, isolated area north of Triana – hence the name that the district acquired: Isla de la Cartuja. Later Columbus resided here, planning his future exploits. Mainly due to this connection, La Cartuja was the site for Expo '92 *(see pp102–03)*. The monastery buildings were restored and several pavilions of strikingly modern design built at considerable cost. The majority of the pavilions are now closed and the Expo site has been redeveloped to include the Isla Mágica theme park *(see p102)*.

Sights at a Glance

Theme Parks
Cartuja '93 ❷
Charco de la Pava
   Flea Market ❸
Isla Mágica ❶

Traditional Areas
Triana pp100–101 ❺

Churches and Monasteries
Iglesia de Nuestra Señora
   de la O ❻
Iglesia de Santa Ana ❼
Monasterio de Santa María de
   las Cuevas ❹

0 kilometres 1

0 miles 1

Key

- Seville city centre
- Built-up area
- Greater Seville
- 🚉 Railway station
- Coach terminus
- Motorway
- Major road
- Minor road

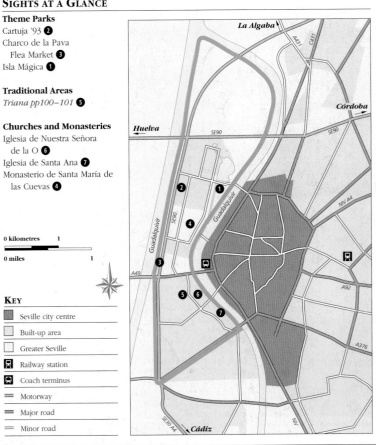

◁ **Pabellón de Andalucía, built for the Expo '92 on Isla de la Cartuja**

Triana ❺

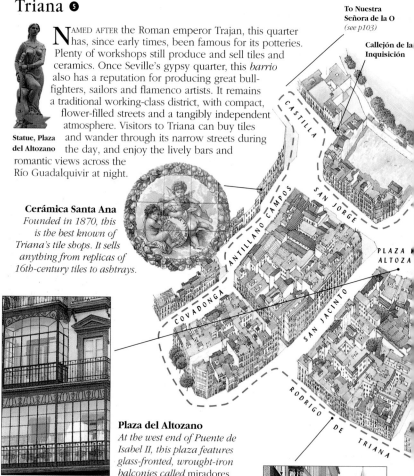

NAMED AFTER the Roman emperor Trajan, this quarter has, since early times, been famous for its potteries. Plenty of workshops still produce and sell tiles and ceramics. Once Seville's gypsy quarter, this *barrio* also has a reputation for producing great bull-fighters, sailors and flamenco artists. It remains a traditional working-class district, with compact, flower-filled streets and a tangibly independent atmosphere. Visitors to Triana can buy tiles and wander through its narrow streets during the day, and enjoy the lively bars and romantic views across the Río Guadalquivir at night.

Statue, Plaza del Altozano

To Nuestra Señora de la O *(see p103)*

Callejón de la Inquisición

Cerámica Santa Ana
Founded in 1870, this is the best known of Triana's tile shops. It sells anything from replicas of 16th-century tiles to ashtrays.

Plaza del Altozano
At the west end of Puente de Isabel II, this plaza features glass-fronted, wrought-iron balconies called miradores.

SANTA JUSTA AND SANTA RUFINA

Two Christians working in the Triana potteries in the 3rd century have become Seville's patron saints. The city's Roman rulers are said to have thrown the young women to the lions after they refused to join a pro-cession venerating Venus. This martyrdom has inspired many works by Sevillian artists, including Murillo and Zurbarán *(see pp64–5)*. The saints are often shown with the Giralda, which, appar-ently, they protected from an earthquake in 1755.

Santa Justa and Santa Rufina as represented by Murillo (c.1665)

Calle Rodrigo de Triana
This street in white and ochre is named after the Andalusian sailor who first caught sight of the New World on Columbus's epic voyage of 1492 (see p49).

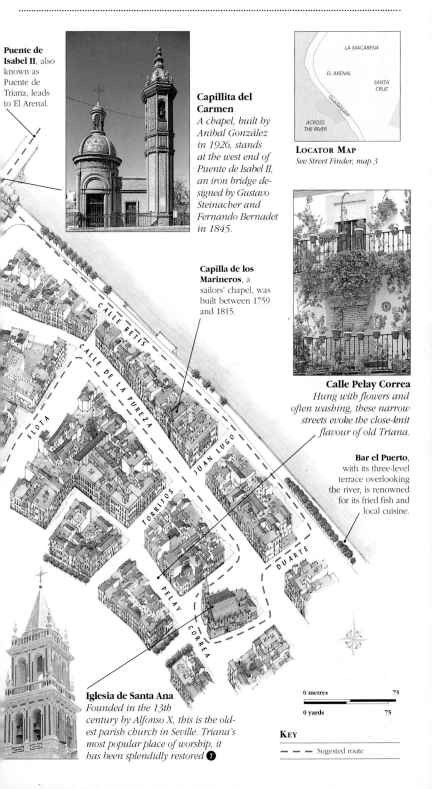

Puente de Isabel II, also known as Puente de Triana, leads to El Arenal.

Capillita del Carmen
A chapel, built by Aníbal González in 1926, stands at the west end of Puente de Isabel II, an iron bridge designed by Gustavo Steinacher and Fernando Bernadet in 1845.

LOCATOR MAP
See Street Finder, map 3

LA MACARENA

EL ARENAL

SANTA CRUZ

ACROSS THE RIVER

Guadalquivir

Capilla de los Marineros, a sailors' chapel, was built between 1759 and 1815.

Calle Pelay Correa
Hung with flowers and often washing, these narrow streets evoke the close-knit flavour of old Triana.

Bar el Puerto, with its three-level terrace overlooking the river, is renowned for its fried fish and local cuisine.

Iglesia de Santa Ana
Founded in the 13th century by Alfonso X, this is the oldest parish church in Seville. Triana's most popular place of worship, it has been splendidly restored ❼

CALLE BETIS

CALLE DE LA PUREZA

FLOTA

JUAN LUGO

TORRIJOS

PELAY

CORREA

DUARTE

0 metres   75

0 yards   75

KEY

– – – Sugested route

A thrill ride at the Isla Mágica theme park

Isla Mágica ❶

Pabellón de España, Isla de la Cartuja.
Map 1 B2. ☎ *902 16 17 16 (info).*
⚟ ◨ *Apr– mid-Jun & mid-Sep–Oct: 11am–7pm daily; mid-Jun–mid-Sep: 11am–10pm or midnight daily.*
◗ *Nov–Mar.* ⊞ *www.islamagica.es*

Opened in 1997, the Isla Mágica theme park occupies part of the Isla de la Cartuja site redeveloped for Expo '92 *(see pp54–5)*, including the Pabellón de España and the the dramatically leaning Pabellón de Andalucía.

The park recreates the exploits of the explorers who set out from Seville in the 16th century on voyages of discovery to the New World. The first of the eight zones which visitors experience is Seville, Port of the Indies, followed by among others Quetzal, the Fury of the Gods, the Gateway to the Americas, Amazonia, the Pirate's Lair and El Dorado.

The Jaguar is the most thrilling ride, a rollercoaster

hurtling at 85 km/h (53 mph) along its looping course, but head also for The Anaconda, a flume ride, and The Orinoco Rapids on which small boats are buffeted in swirling water. The Fountain of Youth is designed for children, with carousels and fighting pirates.

Shows in the park include street performances and dance shows as well as screenings on the IMAX cinema. The shows provide the historical background and incorporate special effects and audience participation. New shows are added every season with some shows running throughout the season and others featuring for just a few weeks. Check the Isla Magica website for up-to-date information on all performances.

Cartuja '93 ❷

Paseo del Oeste (renamed Calle Leonardo da Vinci). **Map** 1 A3.

This new science and technology park occupies the western side of the Expo '92 site. Visitors can walk along Calle Leonardo da Vinci and the service roads for close-up views of some of Expo '92's most spectacular pavilions. These buildings, however, now part of the Andalusian World Trade Centre, belong to public and private companies and are closed to visitors, although there are plans to develop the area. Groups of buildings south and east of the Parque Alamillo

The Pabellón de Andalucía, built on Isla de la Cartuja for Expo '92

are part of Seville University, which has links with Cartuja '93. To its south lie the gardens surrounding the ancient Monasterio de Santa María de las Cuevas *(see p103).*

Charco de la Pava Flea Market ❸

◨ *Sun am.*

Situated beyond the Olympic Stadium, along the River Guadalquivir, is the Charco de La Pava flea market. The market occupies a large open space on the far side of the Cartuja and is held on Sunday mornings. It is a popular spot among locals and tourists who come here for a leisurely browse through the bric-a-brac. Stretched out along the ground are all manner of goods for sale, from rusty farming tools to brass ornaments, paintings and old photographs. The market was, for many years, held at Alameda de Hércules *(see p86)* in the La Macarena area to the north of the city.

Despite its proximity to the city centre, Charco de la Pava, and the area immediately surrounding it, has little in the way of cafés and restaurants, so stock up with a hearty breakfast before heading out in search of a bargain.

Passenger boat at the Isla Mágica theme park

Main entrance of the Carthusian Monasterio de Santa María de las Cuevas, founded in 1400

Monasterio de Santa María de las Cuevas ❹

Calle Americo Vespucio 2, Isla de la Cartuja. **Map** 1 A4. 🕿 95 503 70 70. **Monastery & Centro Andaluz de Arte Contemporaneo** ◯ Oct–Mar: 10am–8pm (last adm 7:30pm) Tue–Fri, 11am–8pm Sat, 10am–3pm Sun; Apr–Sep: 10am–9pm (last adm 8:30pm) Tue–Fri, 11am–9pm Sat, 10am–3pm Sun. 🎟 (free Tue). ♿ 📷

T HIS HUGE complex, built by the Carthusian monks in the 15th century, is closely tied to Seville's history. Columbus stayed and worked here, and even lay buried in the crypt of the church, Capilla Santa Ana, from 1507 to 1542. The Carthusians lived here until 1836 and commissioned some of the finest works of the Seville School, including masterpieces by Zurbarán and Montañés, now housed in the Museo de Bellas Artes (see pp64–5).

In 1841 Charles Pickman, a British industrialist, built a ceramics factory on the site. After decades of successful business, production ceased in 1980 and the monastery was restored as a central exhibit for Expo '92. Also of interest are the Capilla de Afuera by the main gate, and the Casa Prioral, which has an exhibition of the restoration. There is a Mudéjar cloister of marble and brick. The chapter house has tombstones of rich patrons of the monastery.

The Centro Andaluz de Arte Contemporáneo features contemporary art exhibitions, as part of the Museo de Arte Contemporaneo. The centre's permanent collection is mostly by 20th century Andalusian artists while its temporary exhibitions include paintings, photographs, installations and performance art by international artists. Past exhibitions have featured everything from sculpture to internet art.

Triana ❺

See pp100–101.

The colourful belfry of Nuestra Señora de la O in Triana

Iglesia de Nuestra Señora de la O ❻

C/ Castilla. **Map** 3 A1. 🕿 95 433 75 39. ◯ 10am–1pm, 6–9pm daily.

T HE CHURCH OF Our Lady of O, built in the late 17th century, has a brightly painted belfry decorated with azulejos made locally. Inside, Baroque sculptures include a Virgin and Child with silver haloes, attributed to Duque Cornejo, in the far chapel to the left as you enter. On the other side of the high altar is a fine group by Pedro Roldán depicting St Anne, St Joachim and Mary, the Virgin; a Jesus of Nazareth bearing his cross in the main chapel on the far wall is also by the same sculptor.

The church is in Calle de Castilla, whose name comes from the notorious castle in Triana where the Inquisition had its headquarters from the 16th century. The Callejón de la Inquisición, a nearby alley, leads down to the river.

Iglesia de Santa Ana ❼

C/ de la Pureza 84. **Map** 3 B2. 🕿 95 427 08 85. ◯ 9am–3pm, 7–9pm daily.

O NE OF THE FIRST churches built in Seville after the Reconquest (see pp46–7), Santa Ana was founded in 1276 but has been much remodelled over the centuries. Today it is a focal point for the residents and cofradias (the religious brotherhoods) of Triana.

The vaulting of the nave is similar to Burgos cathedral's vaulting, suggesting that the same architect worked on the two churches. The west end of the nave has a 16th-century retablo, richly carved by Alejo Fernández. The sacramental chapel in the north wall has a Plateresque entrance.

In the baptistery is the Pila de los Gitanos, or Gypsy Font, which is believed to pass on the gift of flamenco song to the children of the faithful.

Street Finder Index

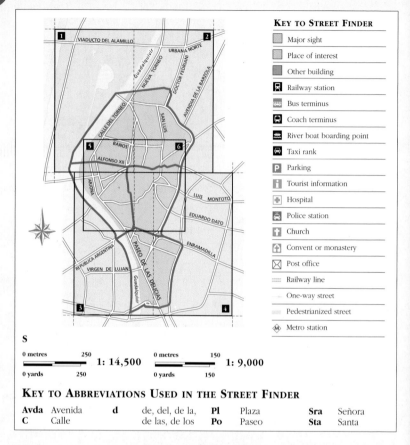

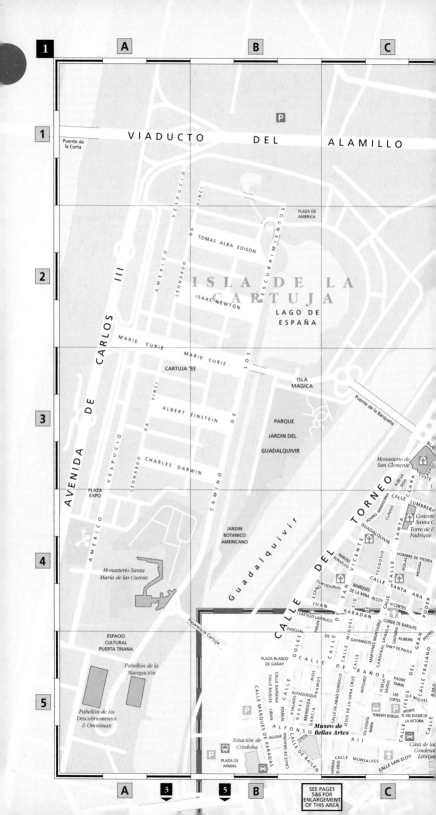

SEE PAGES
5&6 FOR
ENLARGEMENT
OF THIS AREA

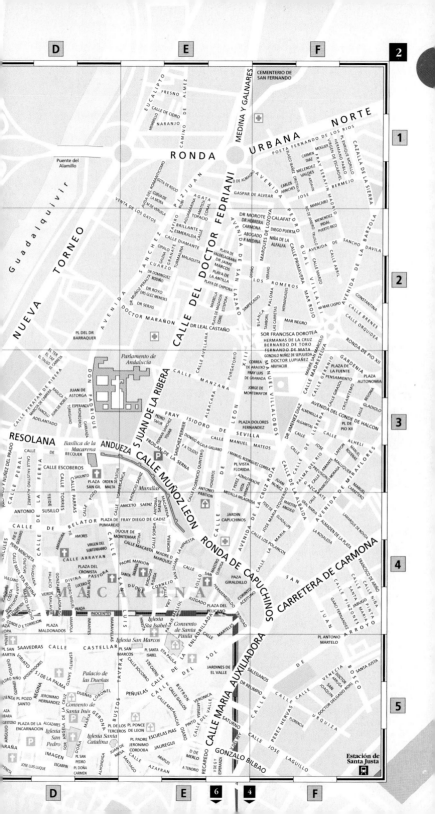

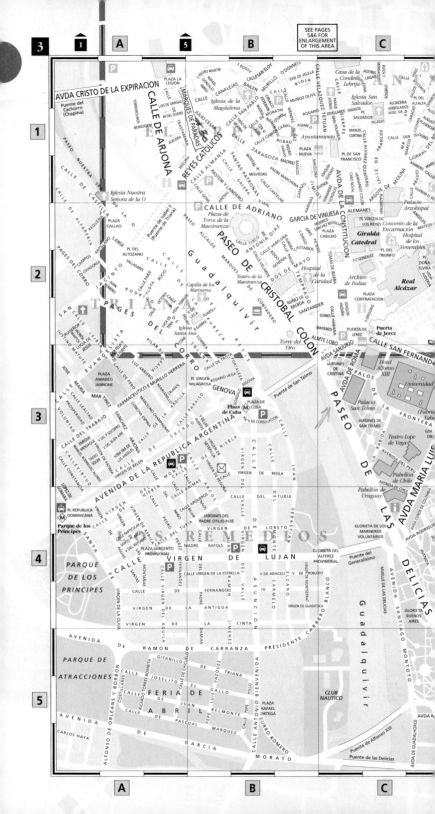

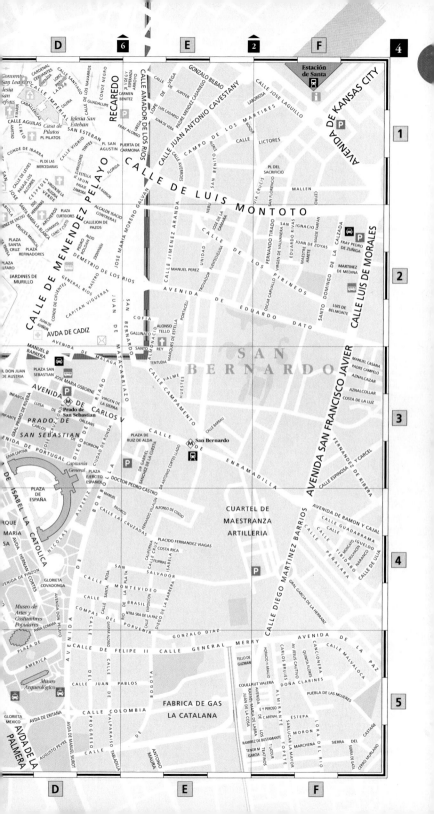

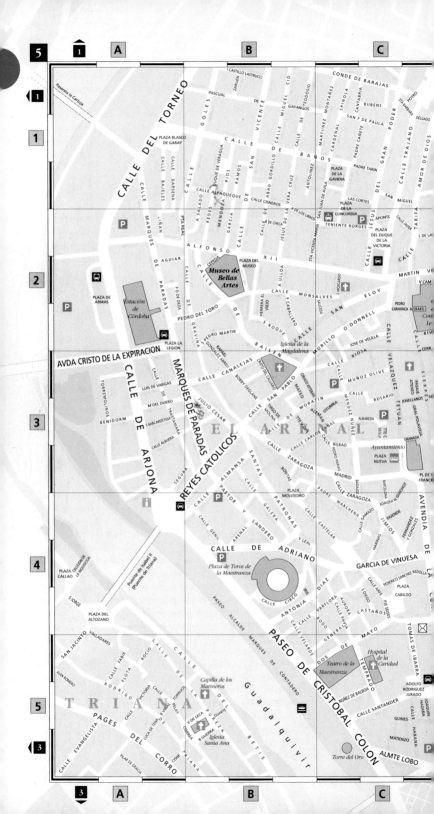

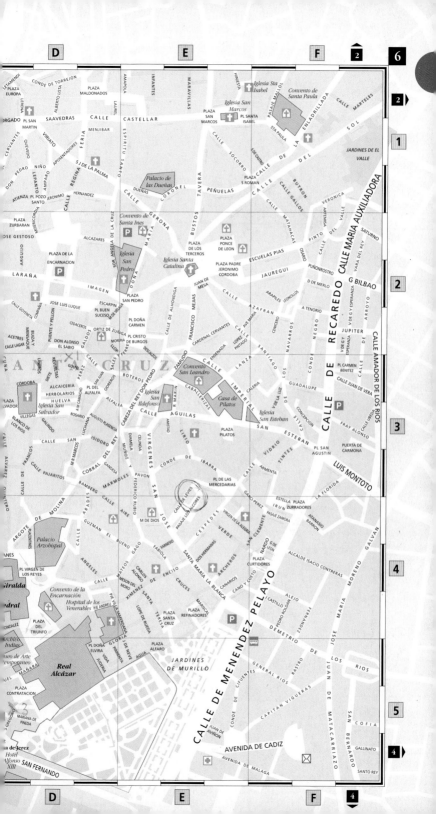

ANDALUSIA
AREA BY AREA

Andalusia at a Glance

A NDALUSIA IS A REGION OF CONTRASTS where
snowcapped mountains rise above deserts
and Mediterranean beaches, and Moorish palaces can be found standing next to Christian
cathedrals. Its eight provinces, which in this
guide are divided into four areas, offer busy
towns such as Granada and Córdoba with their
astonishing architectural treasures, in addition
to sleepy villages, endless olive groves and
nature reserves of great beauty.

**Roof of the Mihrab in the Mezquita,
Córdoba's top sight** *(see pp140–41)*

The amphitheatre in the Roman city of Itálica
(see p42 and 128), **just outside Seville**

**HUELVA AND
SEVILLA**
Pages 118–29

**CADIZ AND
MALAGA**
Pages 154–75

**Golden chalice from the
rich treasury of Cádiz
cathedral** *(see p160)*

Arcos de la Frontera, one of the pretty *pueblos blancos*
(white towns, *see pp166–7)* **so typical of Andalusia**

**The Puente Nuevo, leading to
Ronda's old town** *(see pp168–9)*

Baroque west front of the elegant
cathedral in Jaén *(see p144)*

The imposing Moorish castle of Baños de la Encina
(see p147) in the province of Jaén

CORDOBA
AND JAEN
Pages 130–53

GRANADA AND
ALMERIA
Pages 176–95

Magical Alhambra overlooking the Albaicín, Granada *(see pp182–8)*

0 kilometres   50

0 miles   25

Cabo de Gata, a nature reserve
with excellent beaches *(see p194)*

HUELVA AND SEVILLA

A NDALUSIA'S WESTERN EXTREMITIES *and the plains surrounding Seville are rarely explored by travellers in southern Spain. There are isolated beaches along Huelva province's Atlantic coast and good walking country in the northern sierras. The Parque Nacional de Doñana on the Guadalquivir delta is Europe's largest nature reserve; inland, orange groves straddle the river's valley.*

As Roman legions under Scipio Africanus crossed southern Spain on their westward trek in the 3rd century BC, they founded a formidable metropolis, Itálica. Its ruins remain north of Seville. Later, the Moors held the region as part of the Emirate of al Andalus. They peppered it with their whitewashed, fortified towns, of which Carmona, in Sevilla province, is a fine example.

After the Christian Reconquest *(see pp46–7)*, Moorish traditions persisted through Mudéjar architecture *(see pp22–3)*, blending with Baroque and Renaissance in cities such as Osuna, which flourished in the 16th century.

Huelva province is inextricably bound up with another chapter in the history of world conquest – in 1492 Columbus set out on his epic voyage from Palos de la Frontera, which at the time was an important port. He stayed nearby, at the Franciscan Monasterio de la Rábida, built earlier that century. Running along Huelva's northern border is a ridge of mountains, of which the forested Sierra de Aracena forms part. This ridge continues into Sevilla province as the Sierra Norte de Sevilla. Here, goats forage, birds of prey fly overhead and streams gush through chasms. The landscape erupts in a riot of wild flowers in spring, turning brown as the searing summer sets in.

The Parque Nacional de Doñana preserves the dunes and marshlands near the mouth of the Guadalquivir to the south. Here, teeming birdlife and wetland fauna thrive on the mudflats and shallow, saline waters.

Iglesia de Nuestra Señora del Rocío, El Rocío, where many pilgrims converge each Pentecost Sunday

◁ The famed *jamón ibérico* (cured ham) hanging in a bar in Jabugo, Sierra de Aracena

Exploring Huelva and Sevilla

COSMOPOLITAN SEVILLE *(see pp56–113)* is the natural base from which to explore the far-flung corners of Huelva and Sevilla provinces, such as the little-visited and awesomely beautiful Sierra de Aracena and the rugged Sierra Norte. The Atlantic coast offers a virtually unbroken stretch of beaches and the Parque Nacional de Doñana features a fascinating marsh landscape abundant in wildlife. Between the coast and the mountains are rolling agricultural plains, interrupted by vine-yards in fertile El Condado. Among the region's historic towns are Écija and Osuna, with fine Baroque features, while the history of Columbus can be traced in the towns around Huelva.

The mines of Riotinto, Sierra de Aracena

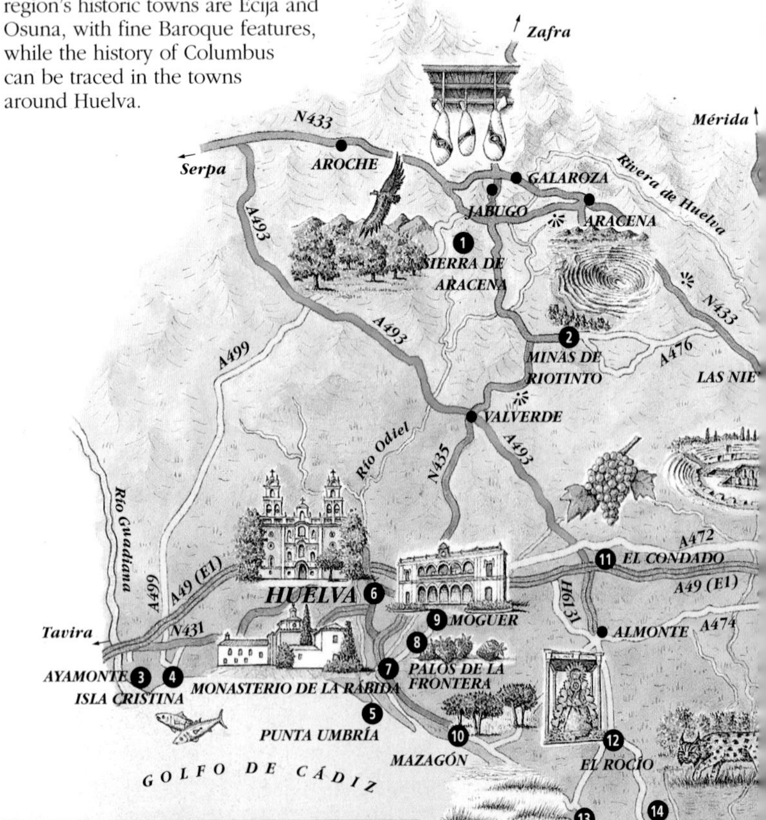

Zafra

Mérida

Serpa

N433

AROCHE

GALAROZA

JABUGO

ARACENA

SIERRA DE
ARACENA ❶

Rivera de Huelva

A493

A493

A499

N433

A476

MINAS DE
RIOTINTO ❷

LAS NIE

VALVERDE

Río Odiel

N435

A493

Río Guadiana

A472

❶❶ EL CONDADO

A49 (E1)

A49 (E1)

HUELVA ❻

MOGUER ❾

ALMONTE   A474

Tavira

N431

❽

A49/N

Río Tinto

AYAMONTE ❸ ❹
ISLA CRISTINA

MONASTERIO DE LA RÁBIDA

❼ PALOS DE LA
FRONTERA

PUNTA UMBRÍA

❺

MAZAGÓN

❿

EL ROCÍO ❿❷

GOLFO DE CÁDIZ

MATALASCAÑAS ❶❸

❶❹ PARQUE
NACIONA
DE DOÑA

Fishing boats at anchor in the harbour of Punta Umbría

0 kilometres   20

0 miles   10

GETTING AROUND

The busy NIV (E5) linking Córdoba with Seville slices through the eastern half of the region, bypassing Écija and Carmona, then streaks on down to Jerez de la Frontera and Cádiz. Another motorway, the A92, brings traffic from Málaga and Granada. All join a ring-road at Seville, with the A49 (E1) continuing to Huelva and Portugal. All these cities are also connected by rail. A complex and inexpensive bus network run by many different companies links most towns. To explore the more remote parts of the region, particularly the beautiful mountain roads, it is essential to have private transport.

A well-known *bodega* advertisement in the rolling hills of the Sierra de Aracena

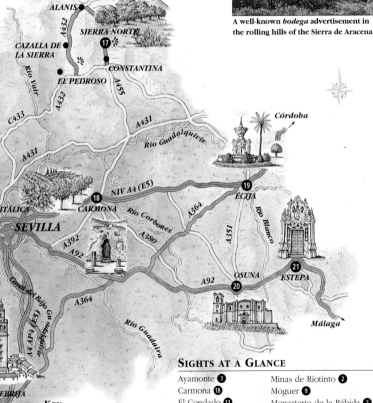

SIGHTS AT A GLANCE

KEY

▬▬	Motorway
▬▬	Major road
▭▭	Minor road
▬▬	Scenic route
▬▬	River
☀	Viewpoint

A ham shop in Jabugo, Sierra de Aracena

Sierra de Aracena ❶

Huelva. **Road map** A3. 🚍 *El Repilado.*
🚌 *Aracena.* 🛈 *Plaza San Pedro s/n,
Aracena (959 12 82 06).* 🖐 *Sat.*
🌐 *www.sierradearacena.net*

T HIS WILD MOUNTAIN RANGE in
northern Huelva province
is one of the most remote
and least visited corners of
Andalusia. Its slopes, covered
with cork, oak, chestnut and
wild olive, are cut by rushing
streams and many extremely
tortuous mountain roads.

The main town of the region,
Aracena, squats at the foot of
a ruined Moorish fortress on
a hillside pitted with caverns.
One of these, the **Gruta de las
Maravillas**, can be entered to
see its underground lake in a
chamber hung with stalactites.
Near the fortress, the **Iglesia
del Castillo**, which was built
in the 13th century by the
Knights Templar, has a Mudéjar
tower and foundations.

The village of **Jabugo** also
nestles amid these mountains.
It is famed across Spain for its
tasty cured ham, *jamón ibérico*,
or *pata negra (see p223).*

🌋 Gruta de las Maravillas
Pozo de la Nieve. 📞 *959 12 83 55.*
⏰ *10am–1:30pm, 3–6pm.* 📷 ✔

Minas de
Riotinto ❷

Huelva. **Road map** B3. 🚍 *Riotinto.*
📞 *959 59 00 25.* ⏰ *10:30am–
3pm, 4–7pm daily.* ⬤ *25 Dec, 1 & 6
Jan* 📷 ♿ ✔
🌐 *parquemineroderiotinto.sigadel.com*

A FASCINATING DETOUR off the
N435 between Huelva city
and the Sierra de Aracena leads
to the opencast mines at Riotinto. These have been excavated since Phoenician times; the
Greeks, Romans and Visigoths
exploited their reserves of iron,
copper, silver and mineral ores.

The lip of the crater overlooks walls of rock streaked
with green and red fissures.
Below, the trucks at work in
the mines appear toy-sized.
The **Museo Minero** in the
village explains the history of
the mines and of the Riotinto
Company. At weekends and on
public holidays there is a train
tour in restored 1900 carriages.

🏛 Museo Minero
Plaza del Museo s/n. 📞 *959 59 00
25.* ⏰ *daily.* 📷 ♿ ✔ ▢

Ayamonte ❸

Huelva. **Road map** A4. 🚹 *18,000.*
🚍 🛈 *Avda Ramon y Cajal, s/n
(959 47 09 88).* 🖐 *Sat morning.*

B EFORE THE ROAD BRIDGE over
the lower Guadiana river
was completed in 1992, anyone crossing between southern
Andalusia and the Algarve coast
of Portugal had to pass through
Ayamonte. The small, flat-
bottomed car ferry across the
jellyfish-infested mouth of the
Guadiana river still operates
and is an alternative for those
making the journey between
the two countries. Visitors
can watch the ferry from the
tower of Ayamonte's **Iglesia
San Francisco**, which has a
fine Mudéjar ceiling.

Isla Cristina ❹

Huelva. **Road map** A4. 🚹 *18,000.*
🚍 🛈 *Av. de Madrid s/n (959 33
26 94).* 🖐 *Thu.*
🌐 *www.islacristina.org*

O NCE A DISTINCT ISLAND, Isla
Cristina is now surrounded
by marshes. Situated near the
mouth of the Guadiana river,
it is an important fishing port,
home to a fleet of tuna and
sardine trawlers. With a fine
sandy beach, it has, in recent
years, also become a popular
summer resort. There is an
excellent choice of restaurants
situated on the main seafront,
which serve delicious, freshly
landed fish and seafood.

Tuna and sardine trawlers moored for the night in the port of Isla Cristina

Frescoes depicting the life of Columbus at Monasterio de la Rábida

Punta Umbría ❺

Huelva. **Road map** A4. 14,000.
🚌 ℹ️ *Ciudad de Huelva s/n (959 31 46 19).* 🚢 *Mon.*

Punta Umbria is one of the main beach resorts in Huelva province. It sits at the end of a long promontory, with the Marismas del Odiel wetlands to one side and an outstanding sandy beach bordering the Gulf of Cádiz to the other. The Riotinto Company first developed the resort in the late 19th century for its British employees. These days, however, it is mainly Spanish holiday-makers who stay in the beachside villas.

A long bridge crosses the marshes, giving road access from Huelva. It is more fun to follow a trail blazed by Riotinto expatriates seeking the sun and take the ferry across the bird-rich wetlands.

Huelva ❻

Huelva. **Road map** A3. 130,000.
🚌 🚌 ℹ️ *Avenida Alemania 12 (959 25 74 03).* 🚢 *Fri.*

Founded as onuba by the Phoenicians, the town had its grandest days as a Roman port. It prospered again in the early days of trade with the Americas, but Seville soon took over. Its decline culminated in 1755, when Huelva was almost wiped out by the great Lisbon earthquake. Today, industrial suburbs sprawl around the

Odiel quayside, from which the Riotinto Company once exported its products all over the commercial world.

That Columbus set sail from Palos de la Frontera, across the estuary, is Huelva's main claim to international renown. This fact is celebrated in the excellent **Museo Provincial**, which also has several exhibitions charting the history of the mines at Riotinto. Some archaeological finds from the very early days of mining are cleverly presented. To the east of the centre the Barrio Reina Victoria is a bizarre example of English suburbia in the very heart of Andalusia. It is a district of bungalows in mock-Tudor style, built by the Riotinto Company for its staff in the early 20th century.

South of the town, at Punta del Sebo, the Monumento a

Bronze jug, Museo Provincial, Huelva

Colón, a rather bleak statue of Columbus created by Gertrude Vanderbuilt Whitney in 1929, dominates the Odiel estuary.

🏛 **Museo Provincial**
Alameda Sundheim 13. 📞 *959 25 93 00.* 🕐 *9am–8pm Tue–Sat, 9am–3pm Sun & public hols.* ♿

Monasterio de la Rábida ❼

Huelva. **Road map** A4. 🚌 *from Huelva.* 📞 *959 35 04 11.* 🕐 *10am–1pm, 4–6:15pm Tue–Sun.* 💺 *www.monasteriodelarabida.com*

In 1491, a dejected Genoese explorer found refuge in the Franciscan friary at La Rábida, across the Odiel estuary from Huelva. King Fernando and Queen Isabel had refused to back his plan to sail west to the East Indies. The prior, Juan Pérez, who as the confessor of the queen had great influence, eventually succeeded in getting this decision reversed. The following year, this sailor, by name Columbus, became the first European to reach the Americas since the Vikings.

La Rábida friary, which was built on Moorish ruins in the 15th century, is now a shrine to Columbus. Frescoes painted by Daniel Vásquez Díaz in 1930 glorify Columbus's life. The Sala de las Banderas contains a small casket of soil from every Latin American country. Worth seeing are the Mudéjar cloisters, the lush gardens and the beamed chapterhouse.

COLUMBUS IN ANDALUSIA

Cristóbal Colón – Christopher Columbus to the English-speaking world – was born in Genoa in Italy, trained as a navigator in Portugal and conceived the idea of reaching the Indies by sailing westwards. In 1492 he sailed from Palos de la Frontera and later the same year landed on Watling Island in the Bahamas, believing that he had fulfilled his ambition.

Columbus made three further voyages from bases in Andalusia, reaching mainland South America and other islands in what are still termed the West Indies in deference to his mistake. He died at Valladolid in 1506.

Columbus takes his leave before setting sail

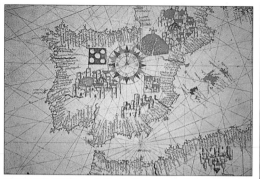

Historic map, Casa Museo de Martín Alonso Pinzón, Palos de la Frontera

Palos de la Frontera **8**

Huelva. **Road map** A4. 🏛 *12,000.* ⊟ 🛈 *Parque Botánico José Celestino Mutis, Paraje de la Rábida (959 53 05 97).* 🚌 *Sat.*

Palos is an unprepossessing agricultural town on the eastern side of the Río Odiel's marshy delta. Yet it is a major attraction on the Columbus heritage trail.

On 3 August 1492, Columbus put out to sea from Palos in his caravel, the *Santa María,* with the *Pinta* and the *Niña,* whose captains were Martín and Vicente Pinzón, brothers from Palos. A statue of Martín Pinzón stands in the town's main square, and his former home has been turned into a small museum of exploration, named the **Casa Museo de Martín Alonso Pinzón**.

The Gothic-Mudéjar **Iglesia San Jorge,** dates from the 15th century. It has a fine portal, through which Columbus left after hearing Mass before his famous voyage. Afterwards, he boarded the *Santa María* at a pier which is now forlornly silted up.

These days, Palos's prosperity comes from the thousands of hectares of strawberry beds in the surrounding fields, which soak up the sun.

🏛 Casa Museo de Martín Alonso Pinzón

Calle Colón 24. 📞 *959 35 01 99.* ⭘ *Mon–Sat.*

Moguer **9**

Huelva. **Road map** A3. 🏛 *15,000.* ⊟ 🛈 *Calle Castillo s/n (959 37 18 98).* 🚌 *Thu.* 🖳 *www.aytomoguer.es*

A beautiful, whitewashed town, Moguer is a network of shaded courtyards and narrow streets lined with flower boxes. It is a delight to stroll around, exploring treasures such as the 16th-century hermitage of **Nuestra Señora de Montemayor** and the Neo-Classical **Ayuntamiento.** Moguer is also the birthplace of the poet and 1956 Nobel laureate, Juan Ramón Jiménez. The **Museo de Zenobia y Juan Ramón**

The 16th-century Nuestra Señora de Montemayor in Moguer

Jiménez, charts his life and work in a relocated setting – in 2004 the museum will return to the poet's restored former home.

The walls of the 14th-century **Convento de Santa Clara** enclose some splendid, stone-carved Mudéjar cloisters. The nuns' dormitory, kitchen and refectory capture some of the atmosphere of their life inside the enclosure.

The **Monasterio de San Francisco** is worth seeing for its church, with a superb white tower and Baroque portals.

🏛 Museo de Zenobia y Juan Ramón Jiménez

Calle Rivera 2. 📞 *959 37 21 48.* ⭘ *Tue–Sun.* ⬤ *Sun pm & public hols.* 📷 🟢

⛪ Convento de Santa Clara

Plaza de las Monjas. 📞 *959 37 01 07.* ⭘ *Tue –Sat.* ⬤ *public hols.* 📷

Mazagón's sandy beach on the Costa de la Luz

Mazagón **10**

Huelva. **Road map** A4. 🏛 *3,500.* ⊟ 🛈 *Edificio Mancomunidad, Avda Descubridores s/n (959 37 60 44).* 🚌 *Fri evening.*

One of the more remote beach resorts of the Costa de la Luz, Mazagón shelters among pine woods 23 km (14 miles) southeast of Huelva. Virtually deserted in winter, it comes to life in summer when mainly Spanish holiday-makers arrive to fish, sail and enjoy the huge, and often windswept, beach. Visitors to the resort may still take pleasure in the solitude, however, while walking for miles along the endless Atlantic shoreline and among the sand dunes.

Moorish walls surrounding Niebla in El Condado

El Condado ⓫

Huelva. **Road map** B3. 🚉 🚌 *Palma del Condado*. 🛈 *Calle Campo Castillo s/n, Huelva (959 36 22 70).* 🌐 *www.castillodeniebla.com*

THE ROLLING, fecund hills to the east of Huelva produce several of Andalusia's finest wines. El Condado, defined roughly by Niebla, Palma del Condado, Bollullos del Condado and Rociana del Condado, is the heart of this wine-growing district.

Niebla is of ancient origin. Its bridge is Roman, but its solid walls are Moorish, as is the now ruined, 12th-century **Castillo de los Guzmanes**.

Around Niebla, vineyards spread out over the landscape, which is dotted with villages close to the main *bodegas*. These include Bollullos del Condado, which has the largest cooperative winery in Andalusia and also the **Museo del Vino**. Here you can learn about wine-growing techniques and also taste their wines before making your purchase.

Bollullos and Palma del Condado are good examples of the popular young white wines produced in the region.

Palma del Condado is best visited in September when the inhabitants celebrate the year's *vendimia* (grape harvest).

⚜ **Castillo de los Guzmanes**
C/ Campo Castillo s/n. 📞 *959 36 22 70.* ⬜ *Mon–Sun.*
🍷 **Museo del Vino**
Plaza Idelfonso Pinto s/n, Bollullos del Condado. 📞 *959 41 05 13.*
⬜ *Jun–Sep: 9am–2:30pm; Oct–May: 10am–2pm, 4–7pm. Phone to visit on weekends & public hols.*

El Rocío ⓬

Huelva. **Road map** B4. 🚶 *2,500.* 🚌 🛈 *Centro Doñana, Avda de la Canaliega s/n. 959 44 38 08.* 🎪 *Tue.*

BORDERING the wetlands of the Doñana region *(see pp126–7)*, the village of El Rocío is for most of the year a tranquil, rural backwater which attracts few visitors.

At the Romería del Rocío *(see pp36–7)* in May, however, nearly a million people converge on the village. Many are pilgrims who travel from all over Spain by bus, car, horse, or even on gaudily decorated ox-carts or on foot. They come to **Ermita de Nuestra Señora del Rocío**, which has a statue reputed to have been behind miraculous apparitions since 1280. Pilgrims are joined by revellers, who are enticed by the promise of plentiful wine, music and a great party.

Matalascañas ⓭

Huelva. **Road map** B4. 🚶 *1,200.* 🚌 🛈 *Avenida de las Adelfas s/n. 959 43 00 86.* 🎪 *Thu.* 🌐 *www.aytoalmonte.es*

MATALASCAÑAS is the largest Andalusian beach resort west of the Guadalquivir river. Thousands holiday here, lying in the sun, riding, sailing or water-skiing by day and dancing to the latest disco beat at night. At the Romería del Rocío, the resort overflows with pilgrims and revellers.

Matalascañas is totally self-contained. To one side there are dunes and forests stretching as far as Mazagón, to the other the wild peace of the Doñana *(see pp126–7)*.

Iglesia de Nuestra Señora del Rocío in the village of El Rocío

Parque Nacional de Doñana 🔾

THE NATIONAL PARK of Doñana is ranked among Europe's greatest wetlands. Together with its adjoining protected areas (Parque Natural de Doñana), the park covers over 50,000 hectares (185,000 acres) of marshes and sand dunes. The area used to be hunting grounds *(coto)* belonging to the Dukes of Medina Sidonia and was never suitable for human settlers. The wildlife flourished and, in 1969, the area became officially protected. In addition to a wealth of endemic species, thousands of migratory birds stay in winter when the marshes flood again, after months of drought.

Bird-spotting from boat on the Guadalquivir

Shrub Vegetation
Backing the sand dunes is a thick carpet of lavender, rock rose and other low shrubs.

Prickly Juniper
This species of juniper (Juniperus oxycedrus) *thrives in the wide dune belt, putting roots deep into the sand. The trees may get buried beneath the dunes.*

Palacio del Acebrón

El Rocío

La Rocina

H612

El Acebuche

Matalascañas

Palacio de Doñana

Laguna de Santa Olaya

Coastal Dunes
Softly rounded, white dunes, up to 30 m (99 ft) high, fringe the park's coastal edge. The dunes, ribbed by prevailing winds off the Atlantic, shift constantly.

Monte de Doñana, the wooded area behind the sand dunes, provide shelter for lynx, deer and boar.

Official Tour
Numbers of visitors are controlled very strictly. On official day tours along rough tracks, the knowledgeable guides point out elusive animals while ensuring minimal environmental impact.

KEY

☐	Marshes
☐	Dunes
•••	Parque Nacional de Doñana
•••	Parque Natural de Doñana
▬	Road
❋	Viewpoint
ℹ	Visitors' centre
P	Parking
🚌	Coach station

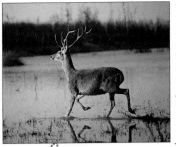

Deer
Fallow deer (Dama dama) *and larger Red deer* (Cervus elaphus) *roam the park. Stags engage in fierce contests in late summer as they prepare for breeding.*

Visitors' Checklist

Huelva & Sevilla. **Road map** B4. **Marginal areas** *daily.* *25 Dec, 1 Jan, 6 Jan & Pentecost.* ***La Rocina:*** *959 44 23 40;* ***Palacio del Acebrón:*** *exhibition "Man and the Doñana".* *10am–9pm.* ***El Acebuche:*** *reception, audiovisual exhibition, café and shop.* *8am–9pm.* *959 44 87 11.* ***Self-guided footpaths:*** *La Rocina and Charco de la Boca; El Acebrón from Palacio del Acebrón; Laguna del Acebuche from Acebuche.* **Inner park areas** *summer: Mon– Sat; winter: Tue–Sun. Guided tour only. Jeeps leave El Acebuche 8:30am & 3pm. Bookings* *959 43 04 32.* *Opening hours change; phone first.*

Río Guadiamar
José Antonio Valverde
Marisma de Iznalcázar
Marisma Gallega
Río Guadalquivir
Sanlúcar de Barrameda
Fábrica de Hielo
0 kilometres 5
0 miles 5

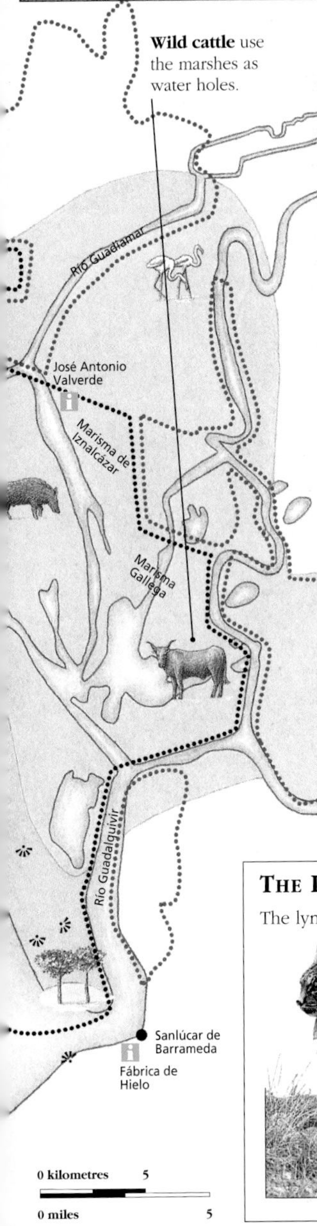

Wild cattle use the marshes as water holes.

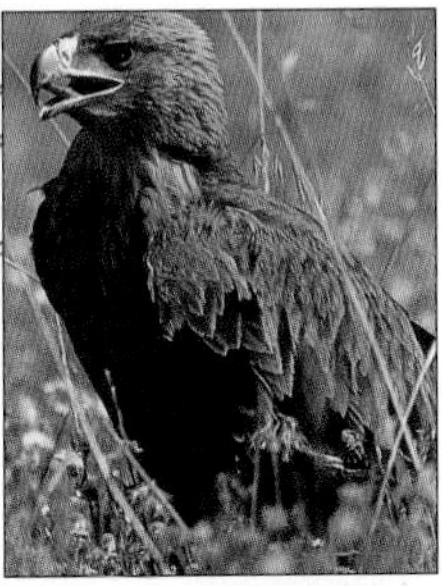

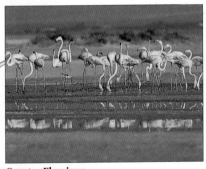

Imperial Eagle
The very rare Imperial eagle (Aquila adalberti) *preys on small mammals.*

Greater Flamingo
During the winter months, the salty lakes and marshes provide the beautiful, pink Greater flamingo (Phoenicopterus ruber) *with crustaceans, its main diet.*

The Lynx's Last Refuge

The lynx is one of Europe's rarest mammals. In Doñana about 30 individuals of Spanish lynx (Lynx pardinus) have found a refuge. They have yellow-brown fur with dark brown spots and pointed ears with black tufts. A research programme is under way to study this shy animal, which tends to stay hidden in scrub. It feeds mainly on rabbits and ducks, but sometimes also deer fawn.

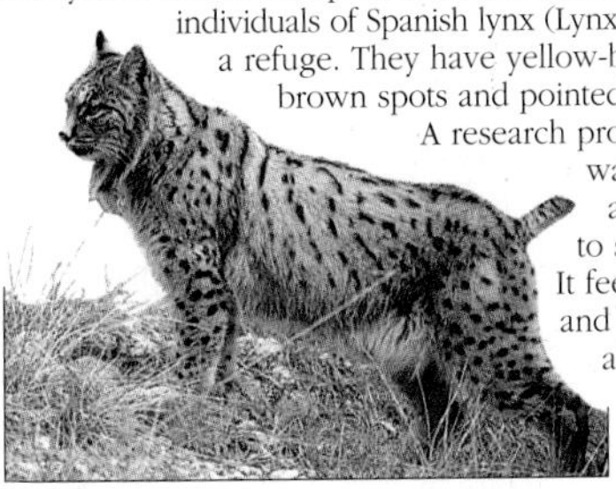

The elusive lynx, only spotted with patience

Scenic view over the rooftops of Lebrija with their distinctive red tiles

Lebrija

Sevilla. **Road map** B4. 🏠 *24,000.*
🚉 🚌 ℹ *Casa de Cultura, Calle
Tetuán 15 (95 597 40 68).* 🛒 *Tue.*

THE PRETTY, WALLED town of
Lebrija enjoys panoramic
views over the neighbouring
sherry-growing vineyards of
the Jerez region *(see p214)*.
Narrow cobbled streets lead
to **Iglesia de Santa María de
la Oliva**. This is a 12th-century
Almohad mosque with many
original Islamic features, which
was consecrated as a church
by Alfonso X *(see p46)*.

Itálica

Sevilla. **Road map** B3. 🚌 *from
Plaza de Armas, Seville.* ☎ *95
599 73 76.* ◯ *Apr–Sep: 8:30am–
8:30pm Tue–Sat, 9am–3pm Sun &
public hols; Oct–Mar: 9am–5:30pm
Tue–Sat, 10am–4pm Sun.*

SCIPIO AFRICANUS established
Itálica in 206 BC, as one of
the first cities founded by the
Romans in Hispania. Later, it
burgeoned, both as a military
headquarters and as a cultural
centre, supporting a population of several thousand.
Emperors
Trajan and
Hadrian
were both
born in Itálica.
The latter bestowed
imperial largesse on
the city during his reign in
the 2nd century AD,
adding marble temples
and other fine buildings.
Archaeologists have
speculated that the changing

**Roman mosaic
from Itálica**

course of the Guadalquivir
may have led to the demise
of Itálica. Certainly, the city
declined steadily after the fall
of the Roman Empire, unlike
Seville, which flourished.
At the heart of the site you
may explore the crumbling
remains of a vast amphitheatre,
which once seated 25,000.
Next to it is a display of finds
from the site, although many
of the treasures are displayed
in the Museo Arqueológico in
Seville *(see p195)*. Visitors can
wander among the traces of
streets and villas. Little remains
of the city's temples or baths,
as most stone and marble was
plundered by builders over
the subsequent centuries.
The village of **Santiponce**
lies just outside the site. Here,
some better-preserved Roman
remains, including baths and a
theatre, have been unearthed.

Sierra Norte

Sevilla. **Road map** B3. 🚌 *Estación de
Cazalla y Constantina.* 🚌 *Constantina;
Cazalla.* ℹ *El Robledo (95 588 15 97).*

AN AUSTERE mountain range
flanks the northern border
of Sevilla province. Known as
the Sierra Norte de Sevilla, it
is a part of the greater Sierra
Morena, which forms a
natural frontier be-
tween Andalusia
and the plains
of La Mancha
and Extrema-
dura. The region,
gashed by rushing
streams, is sparsely
populated and, as it is relatively
cool in summer, it can offer

a much needed escape from
the relentless heat of Seville.
In winter, you may meet the
occasional huntsman carrying
a partridge or hare.
    Cazalla de la Sierra, the
main town of the area, seems
surprisingly cosmopolitan and
is highly popular with young
sevillanos at weekends. It has
made a unique contribution
to the world of drink, namely
Liquor de Guindas. This is a
concoction of cherry liqueur
and aniseed, whose taste is
acquired slowly, if at all.
    Constantina, to the east, is
more peaceful and has superb
views across the countryside.
A romantic aura surrounds the
ruined castle, which is situated
high above the town.

**Grazing cow in the empty expanses
of the Sierra Norte de Sevilla**

Carmona

Sevilla. **Road map** B3. 🏠 *25,000.* 🚌
ℹ *Alcázar de la Puerta de Sevilla s/n
(95 419 09 55).* 🛒 *Mon & Thu.*
🌐 *www.turismo.carmona.org*

TRAVELLING EAST from Seville
on the NIV E5, Carmona is
the first major town you come
to. It rises above expansive
agricultural plains. Sprawling
suburbs spill out beyond the
Moorish city walls, which can
be entered through the old
Puerta de Sevilla. Inside,
there is a dense concentration
of mansions, Mudéjar churches,
squares and cobbled streets.
    The grandeur of Plaza de San
Fernando is characterized by
the strict Renaissance façade
of the old **Ayuntamiento**. The
present town hall, located just
off the square, dates from the

Tomb of Servilia, Necrópolis Romana, Carmona

18th century; in its courtyard are some fine Roman mosaics. Close by lies **Iglesia de Santa María la Mayor**. Built in the 15th century over a mosque, whose patio still survives, this is the finest of the churches. Dominating the town, however, are the imposing ruins of the **Alcázar del Rey Pedro**, once a palace of Pedro I, also known as Pedro el Cruel (the Cruel) *(see p46)*. Parts of it now form a parador *(see p202)*.

Just outside Carmona is the **Necrópolis Romana**, the extensive remains of a Roman burial ground. A site museum displays some of the worldly goods buried with the bodies. These include statues, glass and jewellery, as well as urns.

🏛 **Ayuntamiento**
Calle Salvador 2. 📞 95 414 00 11.
🕐 8am–3pm Mon–Fri. ⬤ public hols.
🏛 **Necrópolis Romana**
Avenida Jorge Bonsor 9. 📞 95 414 08 11. 🕐 Tue–Sat. ⬤ public hols.

Écija ⑲

Sevilla. **Road map** C3. 🏠 40,000.
🚉 ℹ Plaza de España 1,
Ayuntamiento (95 590 29 33).
🚌 Thu. 🌐 www.ecija.org

ECIJA IS NICKNAMED "the frying pan of Andalusia" owing to its famously torrid climate. In the searing heat, the palm trees which stand on the Plaza de España provide some blissful shade. This is an ideal place to sit and observe daily life. It is also the focus of evening strolls and coffee-drinking.

Écija has 11 Baroque church steeples. Most are adorned with gleaming *azulejos (see p74)* and together they make an impressive sight. The most florid of these is the **Iglesia**

de Santa María overlooking Plaza de España. **Iglesia de San Juan**, adorned with an exquisite bell tower, is a very close rival.

The **Palacio de Peñaflor** is also in Baroque style. Its pink marble doorway is topped by twisted columns, while a pretty wrought-iron balcony runs along the front façade.

🏛 **Palacio de Peñaflor**
C/ Caballeros 32. 📞 95 483 02 73.
🕐 Mon–Sun (courtyard only).

Osuna ⑳

Sevilla. **Road map** C4.
🏠 17,500. 🚉 🚌 ℹ Plaza Major s/n (95 481 57 32).
🚌 Mon.

Iglesia del Carmen statuary

OSUNA was once a key Roman garrison town before being eclipsed during the Moorish era. The Dukes of Osuna, who wielded immense power, restored the town to prominence in the 16th century. During the 1530s they founded the grand collegiate church, **Colegiata de Santa**

María. Inside is a Baroque *retablo,* and paintings by José de Ribera. The dukes were also the founders of the town's **Universidad**, a rather severe building with a beautiful patio.

Some fine mansions, among them the Baroque **Palacio del Marqués de la Gomera**, are also a testament to the former glory of this town.

Estepa ㉑

Sevilla. **Road map** C4. 🏠 12,000. 🚉
ℹ Calle Saladillo, 12, Casa de Cultura (95 591 27 71). 🚌 Mon, Wed & Fri.
🌐 www.estepa.com

LEGEND HAS IT that when the invading Roman army closed on Estepa in 207 BC, the townsfolk committed mass suicide rather than surrender.

These days, life in this small town in the far southeast of Sevilla province is far less dramatic. Its fame today derives from the production of its renowned biscuits – *mantecados* and *polvorones (see p213)*. Wander among the narrow streets of iron-grilled mansions, and sit on the main square to admire the beautiful black and white façade of the Baroque church, **Iglesia del Carmen**.

Wall painting on the ornate Baroque façade of Palacio de Peñaflor, Écija

CÓRDOBA AND JAÉN

ÓRDOBA, WITH ITS MAGNIFICENT MOSQUE *and pretty Moorish patios, is northern Andalusia's star attraction. Córdoba province encompasses the Montilla and Moriles wine towns and also Baroque treasures such as Priego de Córdoba. Jaén's mountain passes are gateways to the province's beautiful Renaissance towns of Úbeda and Baeza, and to the great wildlife reserves of the mountain ranges.*

Córdoba, on Andalusia's great river Guadalquivir, was a Roman provincial capital 2,000 years ago, but its golden age came with the Moors. In the 10th century it was the western capital of the Islamic empire, rivalling Baghdad in wealth, power and sophistication. Today it is an atmospheric city, its ancient quarters and great buildings reflecting a long and glorious history.

Córdoba's surrounding countryside is dotted with monuments to its Moorish past – like the Caliph's palace of Medina Azahara. To the south lies the Campiña, an undulating landscape covered in regiments of olives and vines, and green and gold expanses of sunflowers and corn. Here and there are whitewashed villages and hilltop castles with crumbling walls.

Running across the north of Córdoba and Jaén provinces is the Sierra Morena. Deer and boar shelter in the forest and scrub of this broad mountain range. The sierras dominate Jaén province. The great Río Guadalquivir springs to life as a sparkling trout stream in the Sierra de Cazorla, the craggy wilderness along its eastern border. Through the ages, mule trains, traders, highwaymen and armies have used the cleft in Sierra Morena, known as Desfiladero de Despeñaperros, to cross from La Mancha and Castilla to Andalusia.

Ancient castles perched on heights, once strategic outposts on the Muslim/Christian frontier, now overlook the peaceful olive groves punctuated by historic towns preserving gems of post-Reconquest architecture.

The city of Jaén with its cathedral in the foreground, as viewed from Castillo de Santa Catalina

◁ **Elaborate stonework and Islamic inscriptions on the mihrab of Córdoba's Mezquita**

Exploring Córdoba and Jaén

THIS REGION OF ROLLING FIELDS and craggy heights is divided by the fertile Guadalquivir valley. On the northern banks of the river is Córdoba with its famous Mezquita. The wild, uninhabited Sierra Morena lies to the north, while southward is a prosperous farming area dotted with historic towns, such as Priego de Córdoba. Further east, amid the olive groves of Jaén, are the Renaissance jewels, Baeza and Úbeda. From these towns it is an easy excursion to the nature reserve of Cazorla, which offers dramatic scenery and a glimpse of deer and wild boar.

Main street of Cabra during siesta

BELALCÁZAR

HINOJOSA
DEL DUQUE

1 SIERRA MORENA

A420

AÑORA

A430

PEDROCHE

POZOBLANCO

Puertollano

PEÑARROYA-
PUEBLONUEVO

N502

CO421

VILLANUEVA
DE CÓRDOBA

A420

A432

FUENTE
OBEJUNA

BELMEZ

SANTUAR
VIRGEN
LA CABE

Embalse de
Puente Nuevo

N432

Embalse de
Guadalmellato

MONTORO **6**

N420

Embalse
de Yeguas **1**

ANDÚJAR

CO142

MEDINA AZAHARA **4**

5

Río Guadalquivir

CÓRDOBA

NIV A4 (E5)

A306

A321

A431

3 CASTILLO DE
ALMODÓVAR
DEL RÍO

A309

2

PALMA
DEL RÍO

A453

NIV A4 (E5)

Sevilla

MONTILLA

N432

7

11 BAENA

A3

ALCAUDETE

CV241

8

AGUILAR

10 CABRA

PRIEGO DE
CÓRDOBA

A340

12

9

LUCENA

N331

A331

N321

Málaga

Embalse de
Iznájar

Olive groves stretching across the countryside

SIGHTS AT A GLANCE

**The town of Cazorla on the border of
the nature reserve**

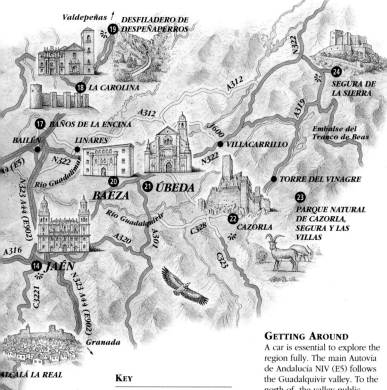

KEY

▨	Motorway
▨	Major road
▨	Minor road
▨	Scenic route
⌒	River
☀	Viewpoint

0 kilometres   20

0 miles   10

GETTING AROUND

A car is essential to explore the region fully. The main Autovía de Andalucía NIV (E5) follows the Guadalquivir valley. To the north of the valley public transport is sparse, but there are frequent bus services to the south. Córdoba is well served by trains, including the AVE high-speed train with fast connections to Seville, Madrid and as far as Lleida. Jaén, however, is not so well served, with only one direct train per day to Córdoba.

Palma del Río ❷

Córdoba. **Road map** C3. 🏠 *19,000.* 🚌 🚏 🛈 *Cardenal Portocarrero (957 64 43 70).* 🕎 *Tue.*

REMAINS OF THE WALLS built by the Almohads in the 12th century are a reminder of the frontier days of this farming town. The Romans established a settlement here, on the main route from Córdoba to Itálica *(see p128)*, almost 2,000 years ago. The Baroque **Iglesia de la Asunción** dates from the 18th century. The monastery of San Francisco is now a delightful hotel *(see p207)*, and guests dine in the 15th-century refectory of the Franciscan monks. Palma is the home town of El Cordobés, one of

Bell tower, La Asunción

Spain's most famous matadors. As a youth he would creep out into the fields around the town to practise with the bulls. His biography, *Or I'll Dress You in Mourning*, gives a vivid view of Palma and of the days of desperate hardship which followed the end of the Civil War.

Castillo de Almodóvar del Río ❸

Córdoba. **Road map** C3. 📞 *957 63 40 55.* ⏰ *May–mid-Sep: 11am–2:30pm, 4–8pm (7pm mid-Sep –Apr).* 📷 W *www.castillodealmodovar.com*

ONE OF ANDALUSIA'S most dramatic silhouettes breaks the skyline as the traveller approaches Almodóvar del Río. The Moorish castle, with parts dating back to the 8th century, looks down on the white-washed town and surrounding fields of cotton and cereals.

Detail of wood carving in the main hall of Medina Azahara

Medina Azahara ❹

Córdoba. **Road map** C3. 📞 *957 32 91 30.* ⏰ *10am–6:30pm Tue–Sat (8:30pm May–Sep), 10am–2pm Sun & public hols.* 📷 *(free for EU citizens).*

JUST A FEW KILOMETRES to the northwest of the city lies the remains of a Moorish palace. Built in the 10th century for Caliph Abd al Rahman III,

Sierra Morena Tour ❶

THE AUSTERE SIERRA MORENA runs across northern Andalusia. This route through Córdoba province takes in a region of oak- and pine-clad hills, where hunters stalk deer and boar. It also includes the open plain of Valle de los Pedroches, where storks make their nests on church towers. The area, little visited by tourists, is sparsely populated. Its individual character is more sober than the usual image of Andalusia and it makes a delightful excursion on a day out from Córdoba.

Hinojosa del Duque ④
"Catedral de la Sierra", the vast, 15th-century pile of the Gothic-Renaissance Iglesia San Juan Bautista, dominates the town. It has a Churrigueresque *retablo*.

RISING AT FUENTE OBEJUNA

On 23 April 1476, townsfolk stormed the palace of the hated lord, Don Fernando Gómez de Guzmán. He was hurled from a palace window, then hacked to pieces in the main plaza. When questioned by a judge who committed the crime, the men and women replied as one, "Fuente Obejuna, señor!" Nobody was punished, at least according to Lope de Vega's best-known play, named after the village.

Lope de Vega (1562–1635)

Peñarroya-Pueblonuevo ②
This was once an important copper- and iron-mining centre.

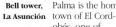

Fuente Obejuna ③
The Plaza Lope de Vega is often the venue for Lope de Vega's famous play. The parish church, Nuestra Señora del Castillo, was built in the 15th century.

Bélmez ①
Remains of a 13th-century castle crown a hill, from which there are fine views.

who named it after his wife. More than 4,000 camels, 15,000 mules and 10,000 workers ferried building materials from as far as North Africa.

The palace is built on three levels and includes a mosque, the caliph's residence and fine gardens. Alabaster, ebony, jasper and marble decoration adorned its many halls and, it is said, shimmering pools of quicksilver added lustre.

Unfortunately, the glory was short-lived. The palace was sacked by Berber invaders in 1010. Then, over centuries, it was ransacked for its building materials. Now, the ruins give only glimpses of its former splendour – a Moorish main hall, for instance, with marble carvings and a fine wooden ceiling. The palace is being restored, but progress is slow.

Córdoba ❺

See pp136–42.

Montoro ❻

Córdoba. **Road map** D3. 🏠 *9,600.*
🚌 🛈 *Plaza de España 8 (957 16 00 89).* 🛒 *Tue.*
🌐 *www.pagina.de/montoro*

Spread over five hills which span a bend in the River Guadalquivir, Montoro dates from the times of the Greeks and Phoenicians. Today the economy of this rather lethargic town depends on its olive groves. The solid bridge was designed by Enrique de Egas, was started in the time of the Catholic Monarchs

(see pp46–7) and took more than 50 years to finish. The townswomen sold their jewellery to raise funds for the bridge, hence its name: **Puente de las Donadas** (Bridge of the Donors).

Steep streets give the town charm. In Plaza de España are the **Ayuntamiento**, former seat of the ducal rulers, with a Plateresque façade, and the Gothic-Mudéjar **Iglesia de San Bartolomé**.

Leather bags and embossed saddlery are among several enduring crafts which are still produced in Montoro.

The 16th-century bridge spanning the Guadalquivir at Montoro

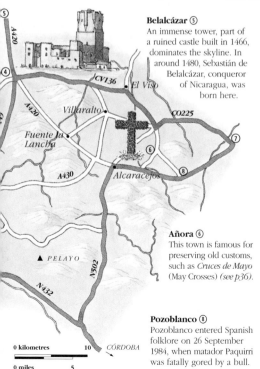

Belalcázar ⑤
An immense tower, part of a ruined castle built in 1466, dominates the skyline. In around 1480, Sebastián de Belalcázar, conqueror of Nicaragua, was born here.

Añora ⑥
This town is famous for preserving old customs, such as *Cruces de Mayo* (May Crosses) *(see p36)*.

Pozoblanco ⑧
Pozoblanco entered Spanish folklore on 26 September 1984, when matador Paquirri was fatally gored by a bull.

Tips for Drivers

Length: *190 km (118 miles).*
Stopping-off points: *There are many shady places to stop along the way to have a picnic. Some of the villages along this route, such as Fuente Obejuna, have restaurants and bars.*

Pedroche ⑦
A 56-m (184-ft) high granite church tower, with an alarming crack in it, rises above this village.

Key

▨▨▨	Tour route
⹀	Other roads
▲	Mountain peak

0 kilometres 10

0 miles 5

Street-by-Street: Córdoba ❺

Statue of Maimónides

THE HEART OF CORDOBA is the old Jewish quarter near the Mezquita, known as the Judería. A walk around this area gives the visitor the sensation that little has changed since this was one of the greatest cities in the Western world. Narrow, cobbled streets where cars cannot penetrate, secluded niches, wrought iron gates, tiny workshops where silversmiths create fine jewellery – all appears very much as it was 1,000 years ago. Traffic roars along the riverfront, past the replica of a Moorish water wheel and the towering walls of the Great Mosque. Most of the sights are in this area, while modern city life takes place some blocks north, around the Plaza de las Tendillas.

Sinagoga
Hebrew script covers the interior walls of this medieval synagogue, the only one remaining in Andalusia.

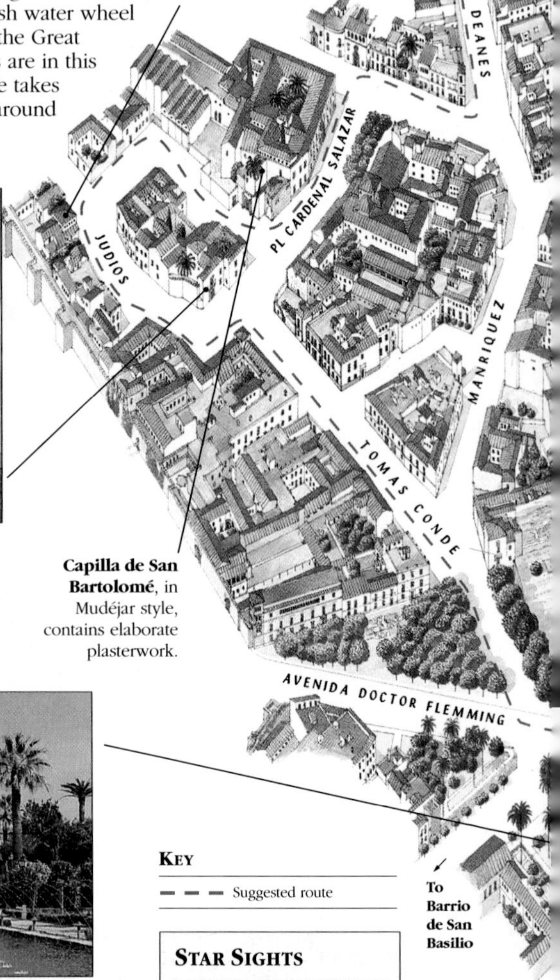

Museo Taurino
A replica of the tomb of the famous torero, *Manolete, and the hide of the bull that killed him (see p25) are in this museum of bullfighting.*

Capilla de San Bartolomé, in Mudéjar style, contains elaborate plasterwork.

★ **Alcázar de los Reyes Cristianos**
Water terraces and fountains add to the tranquil atmosphere of the gardens belonging to the palace-fortress of the Catholic Monarchs, constructed in the 14th century.

KEY

– – – Suggested route

To
Barrio de San Basilio

STAR SIGHTS

★ **Mezquita**

★ **Alcázar de los Reyes Cristianos**

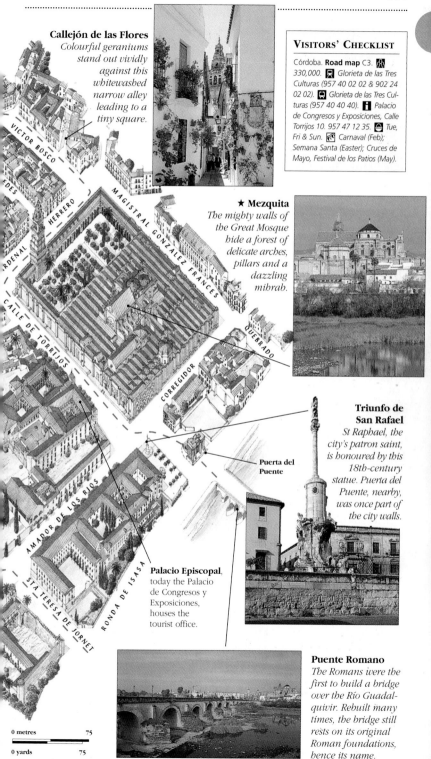

Callejón de las Flores
*Colourful geraniums
stand out vividly
against this
whitewashed
narrow alley
leading to a
tiny square.*

VISITORS' CHECKLIST

Córdoba. **Road map** C3.
330,000. Glorieta de las Tres
Culturas (957 40 02 02 & 902 24
02 02). Glorieta de las Tres Cul-
turas (957 40 40 40). Palacio
de Congresos y Exposiciones, Calle
Torrijos 10. 957 47 12 35. Tue,
Fri & Sun. Carnaval (Feb);
Semana Santa (Easter); Cruces de
Mayo, Festival de los Patios (May).

★ Mezquita
*The mighty walls of
the Great Mosque
hide a forest of
delicate arches,
pillars and a
dazzling
mihrab.*

**Triunfo de
San Rafael**
*St Raphael, the
city's patron saint,
is honoured by this
18th-century
statue. Puerta del
Puente, nearby,
was once part of
the city walls.*

**Puerta del
Puente**

Palacio Episcopal,
today the Palacio
de Congresos y
Exposiciones,
houses the
tourist office.

Puente Romano
*The Romans were the
first to build a bridge
over the Río Guadal-
quivir. Rebuilt many
times, the bridge still
rests on its original
Roman foundations,
hence its name.*

0 metres   75
0 yards   75

Exploring Córdoba

CORDOBA'S CORE is the old city around the Mezquita on the banks of the Guadalquivir. Its origins are probably Carthaginian; the name may be derived from Kartuba, Phoenician for "rich and precious city". Under the Romans it was a provincial capital and birthplace of philosopher Seneca. However, Córdoba's golden age was in the 10th century when Abd al Rahman III created an independent caliphate with Córdoba as its capital. Its influence spread to North Africa and the Balearic Islands. Córdoba was a centre of trade, industry and learning, where Jews and Christians lived alongside Muslims. Civil war *(see pp44–5)* ended the caliphate and the city was pillaged. It declined after falling to Fernando III in 1236, although a number of fine buildings have since been erected.

Sculpture by Mateo Inurria

Naranjas y Limones in Museo Julio Romero de Torres

🕌 Mezquita
See pp140–41.

♠ Alcázar de los Reyes Cristianos
C/ Caballerizas Reales s/n. 📞 957 42 01 51. ⏰ Oct–May: 10am–2pm, 4:30–6:30pm Tue–Sat, 9:30am–3pm Sun; Jun & Sep: 8:30am–2pm, 5:30–7:30pm Tue–Sun. 📷

This palace-fortress was built in 1328 on the orders of Alfonso XI. Fernando II and Isabel stayed here during their campaign to conquer Granada from the Moors *(see p46)*. Later it was used by the Inquisition *(see p49)*, and then as a prison.

The gardens with ponds and fountains make for a pleasant stroll and are open in the evenings in July and August. Behind the palace's walls are Roman mosaics and a Roman sarcophagus dating from the 3rd century AD.

✡ Sinagoga
Calle Judíos 20. 📞 957 20 29 28. ⏰ 10am–2pm, 3:30–5:30pm Tue–Sat; 10am–1:30pm Sun.

Constructed around 1315, the small Mudéjar-style synagogue is one of three in Spain preserved from that era. The other two are both in Toledo, just south of Madrid. The women's gallery and decorative plasterwork, with Hebrew script, are of particular interest.

The synagogue lies in the Judería, the Jewish quarter, which has hardly changed since Moorish times. It is a labyrinth of narrow streets, with whitewashed houses and patios. In a plaza nearby is a statue of Maimónides, a 12th-century Jewish sage.

🏛 Museo Taurino
Plaza Maimónides 1. 📞 957 20 10 56. ⏰ 10am–2pm, 4:30–6:30pm Tue–Sat (8am–3pm Jun–Sep); 9:30am–2:30pm Sun & public hols. 📷

This museum displays stuffed heads of famous bulls, posters and other relics of the *corrida (see pp24–5)*. Rooms are dedicated to local idols, matadors Manolete, Lagartijo and Machaquito. The legendary Manolete was gored to death by the bull Islero in Linares in 1947.

🏛 Museo Julio Romero de Torres
Plaza del Potro 1. 📞 957 49 19 09. ⏰ 10am–2pm, 5:30–7:30pm Tue–Sat (4:30–6:30pm Oct–May), 9am–2:30pm Sun. 📷 (free Fri).

Julio Romero de Torres (1874–1930), who was born in this house, captured the soul of Córdoba in his paintings. Many depict nudes in stilted poses; others are painfully mawkish, including the deathbed scene *Look How Lovely She Was* (1895). His unpredictable style varied from the macabre *Cante Hondo* (1930) to the humorous *Naranjas y Limones* (Oranges and Lemons) (1928).

🏛 Museo de Bellas Artes
Plaza del Potro 1. 📞 957 47 33 45. ⏰ 2:30–8:30pm Tue, 9am–8:30pm Wed–Sat, 9am–2:30pm Sun.

Located in a former charity hospital, this museum exhibits sculptures by local artist Mateo Inurria (1867–1924) as well as paintings by Murillo, Valdés Leal and Zurbarán of the Seville School *(see p64)*.

⛲ Plaza de la Corredera
Built in the 17th century in Castilian style, this handsome, arcaded square has been the scene of bullfights and other

Daily market in the arcaded Plaza de la Corredera

public events. The buildings are gradually being restored, but the cafés under the arches still retain an air of the past. A market is held here.

🏛 Palacio de Viana

Plaza Don Gome 2. ☎ 957 49 67 41. ◯ Oct–May: 10am–1pm, 4–6pm Mon–Fri, 10am–1pm Sat; Jun–Sep: 9am–2pm Mon–Sat. ● 1–15 Jun, public hols. 🎟 Tapestries, furniture, porcelain and paintings are displayed in this 17th-century mansion.

Central fountain in the garden of the 17th-century Palacio de Viana

Purchased by a savings bank in 1981, the former home of the Viana family is kept much as they left it. There are 14 beautiful patios and a delightful garden of citrus trees, date palms and rose bushes around a fountain.

🏛 Museo Arqueológico

Plaza Jerónimo Páez 7. ☎ 957 47 40 11. ◯ 2:30–8:30pm Tue, 9am–8:30pm Wed–Sat, 9am–2:30pm Sun & public hols. 🎟 Roman remains, including mosaics and pottery are on display in this Renaissance mansion. Other exhibits include Moorish items such as a 10th century bronze stag found at Medina Azahara *(see p134)*.

🏛 Puente Romano

This arched bridge has Roman foundations, but was rebuilt by the Moors. Nearby, south of the Mezquita, stands the Puerta del Puente, designed by Hernán Ruiz in 1571.

Moorish bronze stag in the Museo Arqueológico

🏛 Torre de la Calahorra

An impressive end to the Puente Romano, this tower was built for defence during the 14th century. It houses an intriguing little museum which explains the life, culture and philosophy of 10th-century Córdoba through models and audiovisual shows.

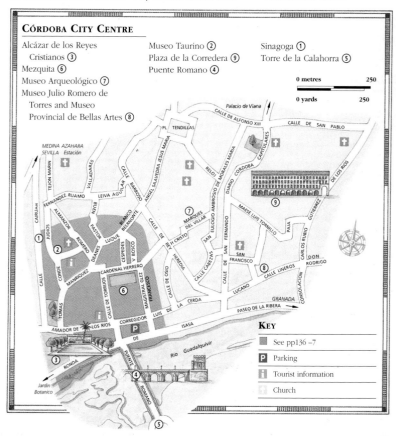

CÓRDOBA CITY CENTRE

Alcázar de los Reyes Cristianos ③
Mezquita ⑥
Museo Arqueológico ⑦
Museo Julio Romero de Torres and Museo Provincial de Bellas Artes ⑧

Museo Taurino ②
Plaza de la Corredera ⑨
Puente Romano ④

Sinagoga ①
Torre de la Calahorra ⑤

0 metres 250
0 yards 250

KEY

See pp136–7

P Parking

i Tourist information

Church

Córdoba: the Mezquita

CORDOBA'S GREAT MOSQUE, dating back
12 centuries, embodied the power of
Islam on the Iberian peninsula. Abd al
Rahman I *(see p44)* built the original
mosque between 785 and 787. The
building evolved over the centuries,
blending many architectural forms.
In the 10th century al Hakam II
(see p44) made some of the most
lavish additions, including the
elaborate *mihrab* (prayer niche)
and the *maqsura* (caliph's
enclosure). In the 16th century a
cathedral was built in the heart
of the reconsecrated mosque,
part of which was destroyed.

Patio de los Naranjos
*Orange trees grow in the courtyard
where the faithful washed
before prayer.*

Torre del Alminar
*This bell tower, 93 m (305
ft) high, is built on the site
of the original minaret.
Steep steps lead to the top
for a fine view of the city.*

**The Puerta del
Perdón** is a Mudéjar-
style entrance gate, built
during Christian rule in
1377. Penitents were
pardoned here.

**Puerta de San
Esteban** is set in
a section of wall
from an earlier
Visigothic church.

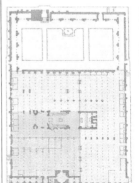

EXPANSION OF THE MEZQUITA

Abd al Rahman I built the
original mosque. Extensions
were added by Abd al Rahman
II, al Hakam II and al Mansur.

KEY TO ADDITIONS

☐ Mosque of Abd al Rahman I
☐ Extension by Abd al Rahman II
☐ Extension by al Hakam II
☐ Extension by al Mansur
☐ Patio de los Naranjos

STAR FEATURES

★ **Mihrab**

★ **Capilla de Villaviciosa**

★ **Arches and Pillars**

Cathedral

Part of the mosque was destroyed to accommodate the cathedral, started in 1523. Featuring an Italianate dome, it was chiefly designed by members of the Hernán Ruiz family.

VISITORS' CHECKLIST

Calle Torrijos. ☎ 957 47 05 12.
🕐 Apr–Jun: 10am–7:30pm
Mon–Sat; Jul–Oct: 10am–7pm
Mon–Sat, 9–10:45am, 2–7:30pm
Sun (Nov–Mar: 10am–5:30pm).
📷 ✝ 9:30am Mon–Sat; 11am,
noon & 1pm Sun & public hols.

The cathedral choir has Churrigueresque stalls, carved by Pedro Duque Cornejo in 1758.

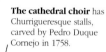

Capilla Mayor

Capilla Real

★ **Arches and Pillars**
More than 850 columns of granite, jasper and marble support the roof, creating a dazzling visual effect. Many were taken from Roman and Visigothic buildings.

★ **Mihrab**
This prayer niche, richly ornamented, held a gilt copy of the Koran. The worn flagstones indicate where pilgrims circled it seven times on their knees.

★ **Capilla de Villaviciosa**
The first Christian chapel to be built in the mosque, in 1371, the Capilla de Villaviciosa has stunning multi-lobed arches.

The Patios of Córdoba

SINCE EARLY TIMES, family and social life in Andalusia have revolved around the courtyard or patio, which is at the heart of the classic Mediterranean house. The sleeping accommodation and living rooms were built round this space, which introduces air and light into the house. Brick arches, colourful tiles, ironwork, orange and lemon trees,

Regional pottery as patio decoration

and pots full of flowers add to the charm of these cool and tranquil retreats. Córdoba takes pride in all its patio gardens, be they palatial spaces in the grandest residences or tiny courtyards in humble homes, shared by many. There are traditional patios in the San Lorenzo and Judería quarters and in Barrio San Basilio, west of the Mezquita.

Whitewashed walls   **Tiled portrait of saint**   **Orange trees**

Festival de los Patios, when scores of patios are thrown open to the public, takes place in early May (see pp36–7). The most beautifully decorated patio wins a prestigious prize.

ANDALUSIAN PATIO

This scene, painted by García Rodríguez (1863–1925), evokes a style of patio that is still common in Andalusia. The patio walls are usually immaculately whitewashed, contrasting with the colourful display of geraniums and carnations in terracotta pots. Fragrant blooms of jasmine add to the atmosphere.

Moorish-style lamps, *which now have electric bulbs, light the patio in the late evening.*

Azulejos, *a reminder of the region's Moorish past, decorate many patios, adding to their colourful display.*

Cancelas *are attractively designed iron gates which screen the private patio from the street outside.*

A central fountain *or well traditionally provided water and remains a feature of many patios today.*

Montilla ➐

Córdoba. **Road map** C3. 🏠 *23,000.*
🚌 🚍 🛈 *Calle Capitan Alonso de Vargas 3 (957 65 24 62).* 🛒 *Fri.*

MONTILLA IS THE CENTRE of an important wine-making region, but one that finds it difficult to emerge from the shadow of a more famous rival. The excellent white wine is made in the same way as sherry *(see pp28–9)* and tastes rather like it but, unlike sherry, does not need fortifying with alcohol. Some *bodegas*, including **Alvear** and **Pérez Barquero**, are happy to welcome visitors.

The Mudéjar **Convento de Santa Clara** dates from 1512 and the **castle** from the 18th century. The town library is in the **Casa del Inca**, so named because Garcilaso de la Vega, who wrote about the Incas, lived there in the 16th century.

The historic crest of the Bodega Pérez Barquero

🍷 **Bodega Alvear**
Avenida María Auxiliadora 1. 📞 *957 66 40 14.* 🕐 *daily (call first to arrange visit).* ⬤ *Sun & public hols.*
🍷 **Bodega Pérez Barquero**
Avenida Andalucía 27. 📞 *957 65 05 00.* 🕐 *8:30am–2pm, 3:30–6:30pm Mon–Thu, 8:30–2:30pm Fri.*

Aguilar ➑

Córdoba. **Road map** C3. 🏠 *13,500.*
🚌 🚍 🛈 *Cuesta de Jesús 2, Edificio Antiguo Posito (957 66 15 67).* 🛒 *Tue, Thu & Fri.*

CERAMICS, WINE and olive oil are important products in Aguilar, which was settled in Roman times. There are several seigneurial houses, and the eight-sided **Plaza de San José**. Built in 1810, it houses the town hall. Nearby is a Baroque clock tower.

Lucena ➒

Córdoba. **Road map** D3. 🏠 *40,000.*
🚌 🛈 *Castillo del Moral s/n (957 51 32 82).* 🛒 *Wed.*
🌐 *www.turlucena.com*

LUCENA PROSPERS from furniture making and from its brass and copper manufactures, and produces interesting ceramics. Under the caliphs of Córdoba *(see p44)* it was an important trading and intellectual centre, with a dynamic, independent, Jewish community.

Iglesia de Santiago, with a Baroque turret, was built on the site of a synagogue in 1503. The **Torre del Moral** is the only remaining part of a Moorish castle. Granada's last sultan, Boabdil, was captured in 1483, and imprisoned here. Nearby, the 15th-century **Iglesia de San Mateo** has a flamboyant Baroque sacristy and three naves with delicate arches.

On the first Sunday in May Lucena stages an elaborate ceremony which honours the Virgen de Araceli.

Cabra ➓

Córdoba. **Road map** D3. 🏠 *21,000.*
🚌 🛈 *Calle Santa Rosalia 2 (957 52 01 10).* 🛒 *Mon.* 🌐 *www.cabra.net*

SET AMID FERTILE fields and vast olive groves, Cabra was an episcopal seat in the 3rd century. On a rise stands the former castle, which is

Statue of Santo Domingo, Iglesia Santo Domingo in Cabra

now a school. There are also some noble mansions and the **Iglesia Santo Domingo** with a Baroque façade.

Just outside the town, the **Fuente del Río**, source of the Río Cabra, is a pleasantly leafy spot in which to picnic.

Baena ⓫

Córdoba. **Road map** D3. 🏠 *20,000.*
🚌 🛈 *Virrey del Pino 5 (957 67 17 57).* 🛒 *Thu.* 🌐 *www.ayto-baena.es*

BAENA'S OLIVE OIL has been famed since Roman times. At the top of the whitewashed town is **Iglesia Santa María la Mayor**. On the Plaza de la Constitución stands the handsome, modern town hall. The **Casa del Monte**, an arcaded mansion dating from the 18th century, flanks it on one side.

Easter week is spectacular, when thousands of drummers take to the streets *(see p32)*.

Decoration on façade of the 18th-century Casa del Monte, Baena

Jaén ⓮

THE MOORS KNEW JAEN as *geen*, meaning "way station of caravans". Their lofty fortress, later rebuilt as the Castillo de Santa Catalina, symbolizes Jaén's strategic importance on the route to Andalusia from the more austere Castile. For centuries this area was a battleground between Moors and Christians *(see pp46–7)*. The older, upper part of the city holds most interest. Around the cathedral and towards the Barrio San Juan are numerous seigneurial buildings, long winding streets and steep alleys. The city centre is filled with smart shops, and in the evenings the narrow streets near Plaza de la Constitución are filled with people enjoying the *tapeo* in the many bars.

Bamboo crucifix at Santa Clara

Mighty ramparts of Castillo de Santa Catalina

⛪ Castillo de Santa Catalina
Carretera al Castillo. 📞 953 12 07 33 *(tourist centre)*, 953 23 00 00 *(parador)*. ⬤ Tue–Sun. ⬤ public hols.
Hannibal is believed to have erected a tower on this rocky pinnacle, high above the city. Later the Moors established a fortress, only to lose it to the crusading King Fernando III in 1246. A larger castle was then built with huge ramparts. This has been restored and a medieval-style *parador* (inn) built next door *(see pp202–3)*.
It is worthwhile taking the sinuous road up to the Torre del Homenaje and the castle chapel. Even more rewarding are the great views of the city, the mountains and the landscape, thick with olive trees.

⛪ Catedral
Andrés de Vandelvira, responsible for many of Ubeda's fine buildings *(see pp150–51)*, designed the cathedral in the 16th century. Later additions include the two handsome 17th-century towers which flank the west front. Inside are beautifully carved choir stalls. There is also a museum which contains valuable works of art.
Every Friday, between 11:30am and 12:45pm, worshippers can view the Lienzo del Santo Rostro. St Veronica is said to have used this piece of cloth to wipe Christ's face, which left a permanent impression on it.

Statuary on the cathedral façade

♨ Baños Arabes
Palacio Villardompardo, Plaza Santa Luisa de Marillac. 📞 953 24 80 68. ⬤ 9am–8pm Tue–Fri, 9:30am–2:30pm Sat & Sun. ⬤ public hols.
These 11th-century baths are known as the baths of Ali, a Moorish chieftain. They were restored during the 1980s. The interior features horseshoe arches, ceilings decorated with tiny star-shaped windows, a hemispherical dome and two earthenware vats in which bathers once immersed themselves. The baths are entered through the Palacio Villardompardo, which also houses a museum of local arts and crafts.

OLIVE OIL

Olive oil is the life-blood of Jaén and its province. Since the Phoenicians, or possibly the Greeks, brought the olive tree to Spain it has flourished in Andalusia, particularly in Jaén, which today has an annual production of more than 200,000 tonnes of oil. Harvesting, mostly by hand, takes place from December onwards. Quality is controlled by a system known as *Denominación de Origen Controlada*. The best product, virgin olive oil, is made from the first cold-pressing, so that the full flavour, vitamins and nutrients of the oil are preserved.

Harvest time in one of the many olive groves in Andalusia

Horseshoe arches supporting the dome at the Baños Arabes

Shrine of Virgen de la Capilla in Iglesia San Ildefonso

🔒 Capilla de San Andrés

Tucked away in a narrow alley next to a college lies this Mudéjar chapel. It was founded in the 16th century, possibly on the site of a synagogue, by Gutiérrez González, who was treasurer to Pope Leo X and endowed with extensive privileges. A magnificent gilded iron screen by Maestro Bartolomé de Jaén is the highlight of the chapel.

🔒 Iglesia San Ildefonso

This mainly Gothic church has façades in three different styles. One is Gothic, with a mosaic of the Virgin descending on Jaén during a Moorish siege in 1430. A second is partly Plateresque *(see p23)* and the third, by Ventura Rodríguez in the late 18th century, is Neo-Classical. Inside, the high altar is by Pedro and José Roldán. There is also a chapel which enshrines the Virgen de la Capilla, Jaén's patron saint. The museum next door is devoted to the Virgin.

🔒 Real Monasterio de Santa Clara

Founded in the 13th century, just after the Reconquest of the city by Christian forces, this is one of the most ancient monasteries in Jaén. It has a lovely cloister, which dates from about 1581. The church has an *artesonado* ceiling and shelters a curious 16th-century bamboo image of Christ made in Ecuador. Sweet cakes are offered for sale by the nuns from the convent.

VISITORS' CHECKLIST

Jaén. **Road map** D3. 🚗
115,000. 🚉 Paseo de la Estación
s/n (902 24 02 02). 🚌 Plaza Coca
de la Piñera s/n. 953 25 01 06. 🛈
Calle Maestra 13 (953 24 26 24).
🛒 Thu. 🎉 Semana Santa
(Easter); Festividad de Nuestra
Señora de la Capilla (11 Jun); Feria
de San Lucas (18 Oct); Romería de
Santa Catalina (25 Nov).

🏛 Museo Provincial

Paseo de la Estación 29. 📞 953 25 06
00. 🕐 3–8:30pm Tue, 9am–8:30pm
Wed–Sat, 9am–2:30pm Sun.
⬤ public hols.

This building incorporates remains of the Iglesia de San Miguel and the façade of a 16th-century granary. A Palaeo-Christian sarcophagus, Roman mosaics and sculptures, and Greek and Roman ceramics are among the articles on display.

A short walk along Paseo de la Estación is the Plaza de las Batallas and a memorial to the defeats of Napoleon at Bailén *(see p51)* and of the Moors at Las Navas de Tolosa *(see p46)*.

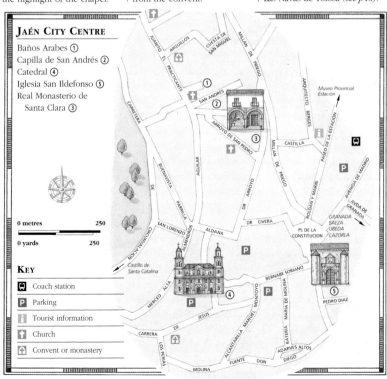

JAÉN CITY CENTRE

Baños Arabes ①
Capilla de San Andrés ②
Catedral ④
Iglesia San Ildefonso ⑤
Real Monasterio de
    Santa Clara ③

0 metres   250
0 yards   250

KEY

🚌 Coach station
🅿 Parking
🛈 Tourist information
⛪ Church
🏛 Convent or monastery

The Moorish Castillo de la Mota and the ruined church crowning the hill above Alcalá la Real

Priego de Córdoba ⑫

Córdoba. **Road map** D3. 🏠 23,000. 🚌 🛈 Calle del Río 33 (957 70 06 25). 🏛 Sat. W www.aytopriego decordoba.es

PRIEGO DE CORDOBA lies on a fertile plain at the foot of La Tiñosa, the highest mountain in Córdoba province. It is a pleasant small town with an unassuming air, well away from the main routes, and yet it claims to be the capital of Córdoba Baroque. The title is easy to accept in view of the dazzling work of local carvers, gilders and ironworkers.

The town's labyrinthine old quarter was the site of the original Arab settlement. But the 18th century, when silk manufacture prospered, was Priego's golden age. During this time elegant houses were built and money was lavished on fine Baroque architecture, particularly churches.

A recently restored Moorish fortress, standing on Roman foundations, introduces visitors to the fine medieval quarter which is called **Barrio de la Villa**. Whitewashed buildings line its narrow streets and flower-decked squares. Paseo Colombia leads to the Adarve, a long promenade with views of the surrounding countryside.

The nearby **Iglesia de la Asunción** is an outstanding structure. Originally Gothic in style, it was converted to a Baroque church by Jerónimo Sánchez de Rueda in the 18th century. Its *pièce de résistance* is the sacristy chapel, created in 1784 by local artist Francisco Javier Pedrajas. Its sumptuous ornamentation in the form of sculpted figures and plaster scrolls and cornices can be overwhelming. The main altar is in Plateresque style *(see p23)*.

The **Iglesia de la Aurora** is another fine Baroque building. At midnight every Saturday the cloaked brotherhood, Nuestra Señora de la Aurora, parades the streets singing songs to the Virgin and collecting alms.

Silk merchants built many of the imposing mansions that follow the curve around the Calle del Río. Niceto Alcalá Zamora was born at No. 33 in 1877. A brilliant orator, he became Spain's president in 1931, but was forced into exile during the Civil War. Today this building is the tourist office.

At the end of the street is the **Fuente del Rey**, or King's Fountain. This is a Baroque extravaganza, with three pools, 139 spouts gushing water, and includes Neptune among its exuberant statuary.

May is one of the liveliest months to visit Priego. Every Sunday a procession celebrates the town's deliverance from a plague which devastated the population centuries ago.

Fine statuary ornaments the 16th-century Fuente del Rey at Priego de Córdoba

Alcalá la Real ⑬

Jaén. **Road map** D3. 🏠 22,000. 🚌 🛈 Fortaleza de la Mota (639 64 77 96). 🏛 Tue. W www.alcalareal.com

ALCALÁ WAS A STRATEGIC point held by the military Order of Calatrava during Spain's Reconquest *(see pp46–7)*. On the hilltop of La Mota are the ruins of the Moorish **Fortaleza de la Mota**, built by the rulers of Granada in the 14th century, with later additions. Nearby are ruins of the town's main church. There are splendid views over the countryside and the historic town, with its air of past glories. The Renaissance **Palacio Abacial** and **Fuente de Carlos V** are the chief attractions to be found around the plaza in the centre of the town.

Jaén ⓮

See pp144–5.

Andújar ⓯

Jaén. **Road map** D3. 🏘 *39,000.* 🚊
🚌 ℹ️ *Torre del Reloj Plaza de Santa
Maria s/n. 953 50 49 59.* 🕑 *Tue.*

THIS STRATEGICALLY situated
town was once the site of
Iliturgi, an Iberian town which
was destroyed by Scipio's army
in the Punic Wars *(see p42)*. A
15-arched bridge built by the
Roman conquerors still spans
the Guadalquivir river.

In the central plaza is the
Gothic **Iglesia San Miguel**,
with paintings by Alonso Cano.
The **Iglesia Santa María la
Mayor** features a Renaissance
façade and a splendid Mudéjar
tower. Inside is the painting
Christ in the Garden of Olives
(c.1605) by El Greco.

The town is also renowned
for its potters, who still turn
out ceramics in traditional style.
Olive oil *(see p144)*, which is
produced in Andújar, figures
strongly in the local cuisine.

Santuario Virgen de la Cabeza ⓰

Padres Trinitarios. **Road map** D2. 📞
953 54 90 15. 🕙 *10am–8pm daily.*
🚡 🌐 *www.santuariovirgencabeza.org*

NORTH OF Andújar, amid the
oak trees and bull ranches
of the Sierra Morena, is the
Santuario Virgen de la Cabeza.
Within this grim stone temple

Roman bridge spanning the Guadalquivir at Andújar

from the 13th century, is a
much-venerated Virgin. According to tradition her image
was sent to Spain by St Peter.

Much of the building and
the original statue of the Virgin
were destroyed in 1937 in the
Civil War *(see pp52–3)*. For
nine months 230 civil guards
held out against Republican
forces. 20,000 men
attacked the sanc-
tuary before it
burned down.
Captain Santiago
Cortés, the
commander of
the civil guard,
died from his
battle wounds.

On the last
Sunday in April
every year, many
thousands make
a pilgrimage to the
sanctuary to pay
homage to the Virgin *(see p37)*.

**Façade of the palace of
Pablo de Olavide**

Baños de la Encina ⓱

Jaén. **Road map** D2. 🚌 *from
Linares & Jaén.* 📞 *Callejon del
Castillo 1. 953 61 30 04
(Ayuntamiento).* 🕙 *Wed–Sun.*

CALIPH AL-HAKAM II *(see p44)*
ordered the construction
of this fortress in the foothills
of the Sierra Morena in AD 967.
Rising above the village, it is
a daunting sight with its 15
towers and soaring ramparts.
Its heights give views across
pastures and olive groves.

During the spring fair there
is a *romería (see p36)* to the
town's shrine of the Virgen de
la Encina. According to local
tradition, the Virgin made a
miraculous appearance on an
encina (holm oak tree).

La Carolina ⓲

Jaén. **Road map** E2. 🏘 *15,500.*
🚌 ℹ️ *Carretera Madrid–Cádiz
km 269. 953 68 08 82.* 🕑 *Tue & Fri.*

FOUNDED in 1767, La Carolina
was populated by settlers
from Germany and Flanders.
This was an ill-fated plan to
develop the area
and to make it safer
for travellers.
The person in
charge, Carlos III's
minister, Pablo
de Olavide,
had a palace
built on the main
square. Just out-
side town is a
monument to a
battle at Las Navas
de Tolosa in 1212.
Alfonso VIII, king
of Castile, was led
by a shepherd over the hills
to Las Navas, where he
crushed the Moors. His
victory began the reconquest
of Andalusia *(see pp46–7)*.

Desfiladero de Despeñaperros ⓳

Jaén. **Road map** E2. ℹ️ *Auto via de
Andalucia (A4) km 257 Santa Elena,
Jaén. 953 66 43 07.*

THIS SPECTACULAR PASS in the
Sierra Morena is the main
gateway to Andalusia. Armies,
stage-coaches, mule-trains
and brigands all used the pass,
so hold-ups were common.

The four-lane Autovía de
Andalucía and a railway line
thread their way through the
chasm, which offers views of
rock formations – *Los Organos*
(the organ pipes) and the *Salto
del Fraile* (monk's leap).

**Replica of the statue of the Virgin
Mary, Santuario de la Cabeza**

Street-by-Street: Baeza ⑳

NESTLING AMID THE OLIVE groves that characterize much of Jaén province, beautiful Baeza is a small town, unusually rich in Renaissance architecture. Called Beatia by the Romans and later the capital of a Moorish fiefdom, Baeza is portrayed as a "royal nest of hawks" on its

Coat of arms, Casa del Pópulo

coat of arms. It was conquered by Fernando III in 1226 – the first town in Andalusia to be definitively won back from the Moors – and was then settled by Castilian knights. An era of medieval splendour followed, reaching a climax in the 16th century, when Andrés de Vandelvira's splendid buildings were erected. In the early 20th century, Antonio Machado, one of his generation's greatest poets, lived here for some years.

★ Palacio de Jabalquinto
An Isabelline (see p22) style façade, flanked by elaborate, rounded buttresses, fronts this splendid Gothic palace.

Antigua Universidad
From 1542 until 1825, this Renaissance and Baroque building was the site of one of Spain's first universities.

Torre de los Aliatares is a 1,000-year-old tower built by the Moors.

To Úbeda

PLAZA DE ESPAÑA

Ayuntamiento
Formerly a jail and a courthouse, the town hall is a dignified Plateresque structure (see p23). The coats of arms of Felipe II, Juan de Borja and of the town of Baeza adorn its upper façade.

SAN FELIPE

PLAZA SANTA CRUZ

BEATO AVILA

COMPAÑIA

ROMAN

BARBACANA

MERCADERIAS

PASEO DE LA CONSTITUCION

PASEO DE TUNDIDORES

O. NARVAEZ

GASPAR BECERRA

Casas Consistoriales Bajas

La Alhóndiga, the old corn exchange, has impressive triple-tier arches running along its front.

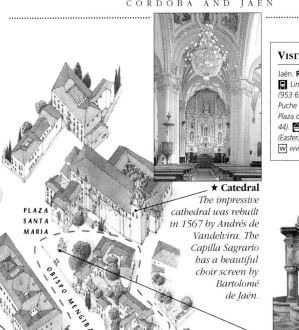

VISITORS' CHECKLIST

Jaén. **Road map** E3. 👥 18,000.
🚉 Linares-Baeza 15 km (9 miles)
(953 65 02 02). 🚌 Avda Alcalde
Puche Pardo (953 74 04 68). 🛈
Plaza del Pópulo s/n (953 74 04
44). 🛒 Tue. ⚑ Semana Santa
(Easter); Feria (mid-Aug).
Ⓦ www.andalucia.org

★ Catedral
*The impressive
cathedral was rebuilt
in 1567 by Andrés de
Vandelvira. The
Capilla Sagrario
has a beautiful
choir screen by
Bartolomé
de Jaén.*

Fuente de Santa María
*Architect-sculptor Ginés
Martínez of Baeza designed
this fountain in the form of
a triumphal arch. It was
completed in 1564.*

**Antigua
Carnicería** now
houses the offices of the
Justice Department.

**Puerta de Jaén y
Arco de Villalar**
*This gateway in the city
ramparts is adjoined by
an arch erected in 1521
to appease Carlos I (see
p48) after a rebellion.*

| 0 metres | 75 |
| 0 yards | 75 |

KEY

🛈 Tourist information

- - - Suggested route

To
Jaén

★ Plaza del Pópulo
*The Casa del Pópulo, a fine Plateresque palace,
now the tourist office, overlooks this square. In
its centre is the Fuente de los Leones, a fountain
with an Ibero-Roman statue flanked by lions.*

STAR SIGHTS

**★ Palacio de
Jabalquinto**

★ Catedral

★ Plaza del Pópulo

PLAZA
SANTA
MARIA

OBISPO MENGIBAR

SAN GIL

Úbeda ㉑

Hospital de Santiago, detail

ᴘᴇʀᴄʜᴇᴅ ᴏɴ ᴛʜᴇ crest of a ridge, Úbeda is a showcase of Renaissance magnificence. Thanks to the patronage of some of Spain's most influential men of the 16th century, such as Francisco de los Cobos, secretary of state, and his great nephew, Juan Vázquez de Molina, a number of noble buildings are dotted about the town. The Plaza de Vázquez de Molina is surrounded by elegant palaces and churches and is undoubtedly the jewel in the crown. The narrow streets of the old quarter contrast sharply with modern Úbeda, which expands north of the Plaza de Andalucía. In 2003 Úbeda became a UNESCO World Heritage Site.

Maestro Bartolomé's choir screen at Capilla del Salvador

🏛 Capilla del Salvador

Three architects, Andrés de Vandelvira (credited with refining the Renaissance style), Diego de Siloé and Esteban Jamete helped design this 16th-century landmark. It was built as the personal chapel of Francisco de los Cobos, whose tomb lies in the crypt.

Although the church was pillaged during the Civil War (see pp52–3), it retains a number of treasures. These include a carving of Christ, which is all that remains of an altarpiece by Alonso de Berruguete, Maestro Bartolomé de Jaén's choir screen, and a sacristy by Vandelvira.

Behind the church are two other buildings dating from the 16th century – Cobos's palace, which is graced by a Renaissance façade, and the Hospital de los Honrados Viejos (Honoured Elders). At the end of Baja del Salvador is the Plaza de Santa Lucía. A promenade leads from this point along the Redonda de Miradores, following the line of the old walls and offering views of the countryside.

🏛 Palacio de las Cadenas

Pl de Vázquez de Molina. ☎ 953 75 04 40. ☐ 10am–2pm, 5–9pm Mon–Fri; 10am–2pm Sat–Sun & public hols. W www.ubedainteresa.com

Two stone lions guard Úbeda's town hall, which occupies this palace built for Vázquez de Molina by Vandelvira during the mid-16th century. The building gets its name from the iron chains (cadenas) once attached to the columns supporting the main doorway.

Crowning the corners of the Classical façade are carved stone lanterns. A museum of local pottery is in the basement. The building also houses the tourist information office.

🏛 Parador de Úbeda

Plaza de Vázquez de Molina s/n. ☎ 953 75 03 45. **Patio** ☐ to non-guests daily. See also p203.

Built in the 16th century but considerably altered in the 17th century, this was the residence of Fernando Ortega Salido, Dean of Málaga and chaplain of El Salvador. The austere palace has been turned into a hotel, which is also known as the Parador del Condestable Dávalos in honour of a warrior famed during the Reconquest (see pp46–7). Its patio is an ideal place to have a drink.

🏛 Santa María de los Reales Alcázares

Built on the site of an original mosque, this church, mainly dating from the 13th century, is now undergoing restoration. Inside there is fine ironwork by Maestro Bartolomé. The Gothic cloister, with pointed arches and ribbed vaults, and a Romanesque doorway, are particularly noteworthy.

Near the church is the Cárcel del Obispo (Bishop's Jail), so called because nuns punished by the bishop were confined there. Today the building contains the town's courthouse.

Stone lions guarding the Palacio de las Cadenas

🏛 Museo Arqueológico

Casa Mudéjar, C/ Cervantes 6. [📞] *953 75 37 02.* [🕐] *2:30–8:30pm Tue, 9am–8pm Wed–Sat, 9am–2:30pm Sun.* [⚫] *public hols.*

This archaeological museum exhibits artifacts from Neolithic times to the Moorish era. The display includes tombstones from the 1st century AD and Moorish and Mudéjar works in wood and plaster. It is located in the 15th-century Casa Mudéjar, among the many palaces and churches gracing the streets of the old quarter.

⚕ Hospital de Santiago

Calle Obispo Cobos s/n. [📞] *953 75 08 42.* [🕐] *8am–3pm, 4–10pm Mon–Fri, 11am–2pm, 4–9:30pm Sat & Sun.*

Created on the orders of the Bishop of Jaén around 1562, this colossal former hospital was designed by Vandelvira. The façade is flanked by square towers, one topped with a distinctive blue-and-white tiled steeple. Marble columns grace the patio with its central fountain. A broad staircase leads up to the gallery roofed by a frescoed ceiling.

Today the building houses the Palacio de Congresos y Exposiciones. At the entrance is an information office, and in a corner of the patio there is a stone-vaulted café.

Nearby, on Avenida de la Constitución, is Úbeda's bullring, open during the *fiesta*.

Distinctive steeple above the Hospital de Santiago

VISITORS' CHECKLIST

Jaén. **Road map** D3. [🏠] *34,000.* [🚌] *to Linares-Baeza (953 62 00 62 & 902 24 02 02).* [🚌] *Calle San José 6 (953 75 21 57).* [ℹ] *Palacio Marques de Contadero, Calle Baja del Marques 4 (953 75 08 97).* [📅] *Fri.* [🎉] *Semana Santa (Easter).* [W] *www.ubedainteresa.com*

Statuary on the main entrance of Iglesia de San Pablo

⛪ Iglesia de San Pablo

The three doors of this church all date from different periods. The main entrance is in late Gothic style while the others are in transitional Romanesque and Isabelline. Inside is an apse which dates from the 13th century and a beautiful 16th-century chapel by Vandelvira. The church is surmounted by a Plateresque tower (1537).

Nearby on Plaza de Vázquez de Molina is a monument to the poet and mystic San Juan de la Cruz (1549–91).

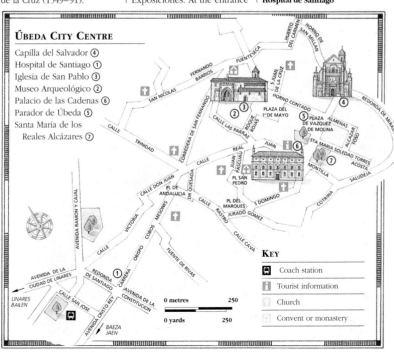

ÚBEDA CITY CENTRE

Capilla del Salvador ④
Hospital de Santiago ①
Iglesia de San Pablo ③
Museo Arqueológico ②
Palacio de las Cadenas ⑥
Parador de Úbeda ⑤
Santa María de los Reales Alcázares ⑦

KEY

🚌 Coach station
ℹ Tourist information
⛪ Church
✠ Convent or monastery

0 metres 250
0 yards 250

Ruins of La Iruela, spectacularly situated above the road outside Cazorla

Cazorla ㉒

Jaén. **Road map** E3. 🏃 *8,500.* 🚌
ℹ️ *Paseo del Santo Cristo 17 (953 71 01 02).* 🚌 *Mon & Sat.*

CAZORLA WAS WEALTHY in ancient times when the Romans mined the surrounding mountains for silver. Today it is better known as the jumping-off point for those who wish to visit the Parque Natural de Cazorla, Segura y Las Villas.

Modern buildings have proliferated, but it is pleasant to stroll along the crooked streets between the Plaza de la Corredera and the charming Plaza Santa María. The ruined Iglesia de Santa María forms a picturesque backdrop to this popular meeting place. Above stands the imposing Moorish **Castillo de la Yedra** which houses a folklore museum.

On the road leading to the park are the remains of **La Iruela**, a much-photographed fortress atop a rocky spur.

On 14 May the locals pay homage to a former resident of Cazorla, San Isicio, one of seven apostles who preached Christianity in Spain before the arrival of the Moors.

🏛 **Castillo de la Yedra**
📞 *953 71 00 39.* 🕐 *9am–8pm Wed–Sat, 3–8pm Tue, 9am–3pm Sun & hols.*

Parque Natural de Cazorla, Segura y Las Villas ㉓

Jaén. **Road map** E3. 🚌 *Cazorla.*
ℹ️ *Quercus Sociedad Cooperativa Andaluza, Calle Martinez Falero, 41 Bajo, Cazorla (953 72 01 15).*
🌐 *www.excursionesquercus.com*

FIRST-TIME VISITORS are amazed by the spectacular scenery of this 214,336-ha (529,409-acre) nature reserve with its thick woodland, tumbling streams and abundant wildlife. Bristling mountains rise over 2,000 m (6,500 ft) above

the source of the Guadalquivir. The river flows north through a delightful valley before reaching the Tranco de Beas dam, where it turns to run down towards the Atlantic.

Cars are allowed only on the main road. Many visitors explore on foot, but horses and bikes can be hired from the **Centro de Recepción e Interpretación de la Naturaleza**, in the reserve. It provides a lot of useful information. There are also opportunities for hunting and angling.

🏛 **Centro de Recepción e Interpretación de la Naturaleza**
Carretera del Tranco km 49, Torre del Vinagre. 📞 *953 72 01 15.* 🕐 *daily.*

Segura de la Sierra ㉔

Jaén. **Road map** E2. 🏃 *2,200.* 🚌
ℹ️ *Ayuntamiento, Calle Regidor Juan de Isla 1 (953 48 02 80).*

THIS TINY VILLAGE at 1,200 m (4,000 ft) above sea level is dominated by its restored Moorish **castillo** (ask for keys in the village). From the ramparts there are splendid views of the harsh mountain ranges. Below is an unusual bullring, partly chipped out of rock. It sees most action at the *fiesta* in the first week of October.

Olive oil in the Segura de la Sierra area is one of four which bear Spain's prestigious *Denominación de Origen Controlada* label *(see p144).*

Moorish castillo at Segura de la Sierra, surrounded by olive groves

Wildlife in Cazorla, Segura and Las Villas

T HE NATURE RESERVE of Sierra de Cazorla, Segura and Las Villas protects a profusion of wildlife. Most is native to the region, but some species have recently been introduced or reintroduced for hunting. More than 100 species of birds live in

Mouflon
(Ovis musimon)

Cazorla, some very rare. It is the only habitat in Spain, apart from the Pyrenees, where the lammergeier can be seen. The extensive forests are home to a range of plant life, such as the indigenous *Viola cazorlensis (see p19)*, which grows among rocks.

The golden eagle (Aquila chrysaetus), *king of the air, preys on small mammals living in the reserve.*

Griffon vultures (Gyps fulvus) *circle high above the reserve, descending rapidly when they catch sight of their prey.*

The lammergeier (Gypaetus barbatus) *drops bones from a height on to rocks to smash them and eat the marrow.*

LANDSCAPE

The area's craggy limestone heights and riverside meadows are part of its attraction. Water trickles down the mountains, filling the lakes and brooks of the valley. This lush landscape provides ideal habitats for a diversity of wildlife.

Red deer (Cervus elaphus), *reintroduced to the area in 1952, are most commonly seen in the autumn months.*

The Spanish ibex (Capra pyrenaica) *is amazingly sure-footed on the rocky terrain. Today, the few that remain only emerge at dusk in order to feed.*

Otters (Lutra lutra) *live around lakes and streams and are active at dawn and dusk.*

Wild boar (Sus scrofa) *hide in woodland by day and forage at night for anything from acorns to roots, eggs of ground-nesting birds and small mammals.*

CÁDIZ AND MÁLAGA

A NDALUSIA'S SOUTHERN PROVINCES *offer striking contrasts. Behind Málaga's suburbs are forested mountains with awesome natural wonders, such as the Garganta del Chorro. Behind the tourist resorts of the Costa del Sol is the Serranía de Ronda, habitat of elusive wildlife. Here, white Moorish towns command strategic hilltop locations. East of Gibraltar are the sherry towns of Cádiz province and the raw coastal strands of the Costa de la Luz.*

In Málaga province the mountains fall steeply to the Mediterranean. The ancient port of Málaga town was a wintering place for English travellers in the 19th century; then in the 1960s, the narrow strip of coast to its east and west was claimed by the nascent tourist industry as the "Costa del Sol".

A rash of high-rise development around the beaches of grey sand at its eastern end soon made the name "Torremolinos" synonymous with the excesses of cheap package holidays for the mass market. Meanwhile, at Marbella, further east, an exclusive playground for international film stars and Arab royalty was taking shape.

Gibraltar, a geographical and a historical oddity, is a decisive full stop at the end of the Costa del Sol. The mountains of North Africa loom across the Strait of Gibraltar, and the spirit of the Moors can be felt very clearly in Tarifa and Cádiz – author Laurie Lee's city "sparkling with African light".

Between these two towns is the Cádiz section of the Costa de la Luz ("Coast of Light") *(see p30)* which continues up north along the shores of Huelva province. Little developed, it is characterized by long stretches of windswept sand, popular with locals.

North of Cádiz is sherry country, with its hills and large vineyards. To taste sherry visit Jerez de la Frontera – a link in a chain of towns on the frontier of the Christian war to reconquer Andalusia from its Muslim rulers.

Ronda with its 18th-century bridge spanning the Guadalevín river

◁ **Beach life at Nerja, east of Málaga, one of the Costa del Sol's busy resorts**

Exploring Cádiz and Málaga

WITH A NEW NETWORK of excellent roads across the region, the mountains of Málaga province's interior are easily accessible to holiday-makers who are staying on the Costa del Sol. Day trips can be made from either Marbella or Torremolinos to the glorious Montes de Málaga and Grazalema nature reserves or to the Serranía de Ronda, with lunch stops at classic *pueblos blancos*. In the heart of this characteristic Andalusian landscape lies the captivating town of Ronda, ensouled by clear, stark light and the lingering aura of Moorish times.

Further west, on the Atlantic coast beyond Tarifa where mass-market developers fear to tread, the same spirit lingers. The once great city of Cádiz and the small ports of El Puerto de Santa María, Chipiona and Sanlúcar de Barrameda all make excellent bases for exploring sherry country.

Outside dining at a restaurant close to the cathedral in Málaga

KEY

▬	Motorway
▬	Major road
▬	Minor road
▬	Scenic route
▬	River
❀	Viewpoint

SIGHTS AT A GLANCE

The beach of Nerja, situated at the foot of Sierra de Almijara on the Costa del Sol

GETTING AROUND

Málaga's international airport *(see p246)* is the busiest airport in Andalusia. From here, the fast, new N340 (E5) dual carriageway traces the coastline as far as Algeciras, but bypasses Torremolinos, Fuengirola and Marbella. After Algeciras, the road narrows and continues to Cádiz. The new highway A376 from San Pedro de Alcántara northwards to Ronda is a sensationally beautiful route. The A382 cuts across the north of both provinces from Jerez to Antequera. At this point it continues as a dual carriageway, also known as the A92, to Granada. A railway running along the Costa del Sol links Málaga, Torremolinos and Fuengirola. Another heads north from Málaga, stopping at Álora, El Chorro and Fuente de Piedra. Although you will find it possible to explore remote corners of Cádiz and Málaga provinces using the complex bus network, it requires some patience.

Entrance to the Barbadillo *bodega* in Sanlúcar de Barrameda

Sanlúcar de Barrameda ❶

Cádiz. **Road map** B4. 🏠 *62,000.*
🚌 ℹ️ *Calzada del Ejército s/n
(956 36 61 10).* 🚌 *Wed.*

A FISHING PORT at the mouth of the Guadalquivir river, Sanlúcar is overlooked by the Moorish **Castillo de Santiago**. The Parque Nacional de Doñana *(see pp126–7)*, over the river, can be reached by boat from the riverside quay. From here Columbus set off on his third trip to the Americas, in 1498, and in 1519 Ferdinand Magellan left the port intending to circumnavigate the globe.

However, Sanlúcar is now best known for its *manzanilla (see p28)*, a light, dry sherry from, among other producers, **Bodegas Barbadillo**.

Tourists and wine enthusiasts alike can watch the sun set over the river, sip a *copita* (little glass) of *manzanilla* and enjoy the local shellfish, *langostinos*.

Sights in the town include the **Iglesia de Nuestra Señora de la O** *(see p22)*, which has superb Mudéjar portals.

🍷 Bodegas Barbadillo
C/ Luis de Eguilaz 11. 📞 *956 38 55 00.*
📷 *noon & 1pm Mon–Sat.* 🎥 ♿

Chipiona ❷

Cádiz. **Road map** B4. 🏠 *17,000.*
ℹ️ *Calle Larga 74, Edificio San Luis
(956 37 71 50).* 🚌 *Mon.*
🌐 *www.chipiona.org*

A LIVELY LITTLE resort town, Chipiona is approached through sherry vineyards. It has a great beach and a holiday

atmosphere in the summer. Days on the beach are followed by a *paseo* along the quay or the main street of the Moorish old town, where many cafés and ice-cream parlours *(heladerías)* stay open well past midnight. There are also street entertainers and horse-drawn carriages. The **Iglesia de Nuestra Señora de Regla**, the main church, has a natural spring feeding a fountain, and an adjoining cloister decorated with 17th-century *azulejos*.

Jerez de la Frontera ❸

Cádiz. **Road map** B4. 🏠 *186,000.* ✈️
🚌 ℹ️ *Alameda Cristina, 7 (956 33 11 50).* 🚌 *Mon.*

J EREZ, THE CAPITAL of sherry production, is surrounded by chalky countryside blanketed with long rows of vines. British merchants have been involved for centuries in producing and shipping sherry, and have created Anglo-Andaluz dynasties like Sandeman and John Harvey – names which can be seen emblazoned over the *bodega* entrances. A tour of a *bodega*, through cellars piled high with *soleras (see p29)*, will enable visitors to learn how to distinguish a *fino* from an *amontillado* and an *oloroso* sherry *(see p28)*.

Jerez has a second claim to world fame, the **Real Escuela Andaluza de Arte Ecuestre** – the school of equestrian art. On selected days, in a display of exquisite dressage, the horses dance to music amid colourful pageantry. Visitors can arrange to watch horses being trained.

Nearby is **La Atalaya Theme Centre**, which includes two museums: the magical **Palacio del Tiempo**, home to the most impressive clocks in Europe, and **El Misterio de Jerez**, which pays tribute to the history of sherry in the area.

The old city walls flank the Barrio de Santiago. On Plaza de San Juan is the 18th-century **Palacio de Pemartín**, the home of the Centro Andaluz de Flamenco, which, through exhibitions and audiovisual shows, offers an insight to this music and dance tradition *(see pp26–7)*. The 16th-century Gothic **Iglesia de San Mateo** is just one of several interesting churches nearby.

The partially restored, 11th-century **Alcázar** includes a well-preserved mosque, now a church. Just to the north of the Alcázar is the **Catedral del Salvador**, whose most interesting sight, *The Sleeping Girl* by Zurbarán, is in the sacristy.

🏛️ Real Escuela Andaluza de Arte Ecuestre
Avenida Duque de Abrantes s/n.
📞 *956 31 96 35 (information, press 2 for English). Call to arrange visit.* 🎥 ♿
🌐 *www.realescuela.org*
♠ Alcázar
Alameda Vieja s/n. 📞 *956 31 97 98.*
🕐 *daily.* ● *25 Dec, 1 & 6 Jan* 🎥 📷
🏛️ La Atalaya Theme Centre
Calle Cervantes 3. 📞 *956 18 21 00.*
🕐 *Tue–Sun.* 🎥 📷 ♿
🏛️ Palacio de Pemartín
Centro Andaluz de Flamenco, Plaza de San Juan 1. 📞 *956 34 92 65.*
🕐 *Mon–Fri.* ● *public hols.*

Antique clock in the Museo de Relojes, Jerez de la Frontera

El Puerto de Santa María ❹

Cádiz. **Road map** B4. 🏠 *76,000.* ✈
🚉 🚌 ℹ *Calle Luna 22 (956 54 24 13).* 🎡 *Tue.* 🅦 *www.elpuertosm.es*

SHELTERED from the Atlantic wind and waves of the Bay of Cádiz, El Puerto de Santa María is a tranquil town which has burgeoned as one of the main ports for the exportation of sherry in Andalusia. A number of sherry companies, such as **Terry** and **Osborne**, have *bodegas* here, which can be visited for tours and tasting.

Among the town's sites are the 13th-century **Castillo San Marcos** and a **Plaza de Toros** – one of the largest and most famous bullrings in Spain. The town's main square, the Plaza Mayor, is presided over by the 13th-century, Gothic **Iglesia Mayor Prioral**, which is worth a look for its unusual choir.

Scattered around the town are several fine old *palacios*, or stately houses, adorned with the coats of arms of wealthy families who prospered in the port during colonial times.

The waterfront is lined with quite a few first-rate seafood restaurants, among them La Resaca (the Hangover), where, when it is dark, gypsies perform fiery flamenco.

♟ Castillo San Marcos
Plaza Alfonso X, El Sabio. ⬛ *956 85 17 51.* ◯ *Oct– May: Tue, Thu, Sat; Jun–Sep: Tue–Sun.* 🈺

🎪 Plaza de Toros
Plaza Elias Ahuja s/n. ⬛ *956 54 15 78.* ◯ *Tue–Sun.* ♿

🍷 Bodegas Osborne
Calle de los Moros. ⬛ *956 86 91 00.* ◯ *Mon–Fri (phone to arrange).* ⬤ *public hols.* ♿ 🈺

🍷 Bodegas Terry
Calle Toneleros s/n. ⬛ *956 85 77 00.* ◯ *Mon–Fri (phone to arrange).* ⬤ *public hols.* ♿ 🈺

El Puerto de Santa María's 13th-century Castillo San Marcos

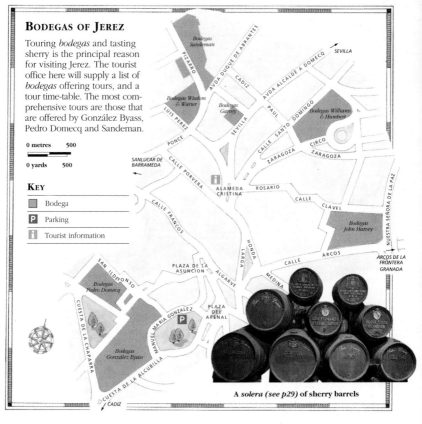

BODEGAS OF JEREZ

Touring *bodegas* and tasting sherry is the principal reason for visiting Jerez. The tourist office here will supply a list of *bodegas* offering tours, and a tour time-table. The most comprehensive tours are those that are offered by González Byass, Pedro Domecq and Sandeman.

0 metres   500
0 yards   500

KEY

🟦 Bodega

🅿 Parking

ℹ Tourist information

A *solera* (see p29) of sherry barrels

Cádiz

Egyptian mask, the Museo de Cádiz

JUTTING OUT OF the Bay of Cádiz, and almost entirely surrounded by water, Cádiz can lay claim to being Europe's oldest city. Legend names Hercules as its founder, although history credits the Phoenicians with establishing the town of Gadir in 1100 BC. Occupied by the Carthaginians, Romans and Moors in turn, the city also prospered after the Reconquest *(see pp46–7)* on wealth taken from the New World. In 1587 Sir Francis Drake raided the port in the first of many British attacks in the war for world trade. In 1812 Cádiz briefly became Spain's capital when the nation's first constitution was declared here *(see p50)*.

Saint Bruno in Ecstasy by Zurbarán in the Museo de Cádiz

Exploring Cádiz

Writers have waxed lyrical over Cádiz for centuries: " . . . the most beautiful town I ever beheld . . . and full of the finest women in Spain," gushed Lord Byron in 1809. Modern Cádiz is a busy port, with a few ugly suburbs to get through before arriving at the historic centre. This is situated on a peninsula that juts sharply into the sea, and consists of haphazardly heaped, Moorish-style houses.

The joy of visiting Cádiz is to wander the harbour quayside, with its well-tended gardens and open squares, then plunging into the centre.

The old town is full of narrow, dilapidated alleys, where flowers sprout from rusting cans mounted on walls beside religious tile paintings. Markets pack into tiny squares, alive with the bartering of fish and vegetables, and street vendors selling pink boiled shrimps in newspaper.

The pride of Cádiz is Los Carnavales *(see p37)*, an explosion of festivities. Under the dictator Franco *(see pp54–5)*, Cádiz was the only city where the authorities failed to suppress the anarchy of carnival.

⛪ Catedral

🕐 *Wed, Fri & Sun.*

Known as the Catedral Nueva (New Cathedral) because it was built over the site of an older one, this huge Baroque and Neo-Classical church is one of Spain's largest. Its dome of yellow tiles looks like gilt glinting in the sun. The carved stalls inside came from a Carthusian

monastery. In the crypt are the tombs of the composer Manuel de Falla (1876–1946) and writer José María Pemán (1897–1981), both natives of Cádiz.

The cathedral's treasures are stored in a museum in Plaza Fray Félix. The collection includes jewel-studded monstrances of silver and gold, painted wood panels and notable paintings.

CÁDIZ CATHEDRAL

🏛 Museo de Cádiz

Plaza de Mina s/n. 📞 *956 21 22 81.* 🕐 *9:30am–8pm Tue–Sat, 9:30am–2:30pm Sun.* 🚫 *public hols.* ♿

On the ground floor there are archaeological exhibits charting the history of Cádiz, including statues of Roman leaders, such as emperor Trajan, and Phoenician stone sarcophagi. Upstairs is one of Andalusia's largest art galleries, displaying

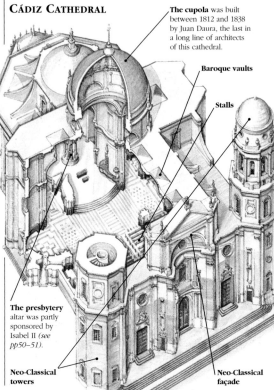

The cupola was built between 1812 and 1838 by Juan Daura, the last in a long line of architects of this cathedral.

Baroque vaults

Stalls

The presbytery altar was partly sponsored by Isabel II *(see pp50–51)*.

Neo-Classical towers

Neo-Classical façade

VISITORS' CHECKLIST

Cádiz. **Road map** B4.
🏃 150,000. 🚉 Plaza de Sevilla
s/n (902 24 02 02). 🚌 Plaza de
la Hispanidad s/n (902 19 92 08).
🚹 Calle Nueva 6 (956 25 86
46). 🚠 Mon. 🎭 Los Carnavales
(Feb), Semana Santa (Easter).
🌐 www.cadizturismo.com

works by Rubens, Murillo and
Zurbarán, as well as paintings
by recognized contemporary
Spanish artists. On the third
floor is a collection of puppets
made for village *fiestas* around
Andalusia. There are also some
more recent ones satirizing
current political figures.

**Commemorative plaques on the
Oratorio de San Felipe Neri**

♛ Oratorio de San Felipe Neri
Calle Santa Inés s/n. 🕿 956 21 16
12. ◻ 10am–1pm Mon–Sat.
People visit this 18th-century
church to pay homage to an
event of 1812. As Napoleon
tightened his grip on Spain, a
provisional government, which
had been set up in Cádiz, proclaimed a liberal constitution
(*see p50*). The site has been a
shrine to liberalism ever since.

🏛 Museo de las Cortes
Calle Santa Inés s/n. 🕿 956 22 17 88.
◻ Tue–Sun. ● public hols.
This museum is devoted to the
declaration of the constitution
in 1812. The exhibits include
a mural of the declaration and
the original documents.

🏛 Torre Tavira
Calle Marqués del Real Tesoro 10.
🕿 956 21 29 10. ◻ daily. 📷 ✔
The city's official watchtower
in the 18th century has now
been converted into a camera
obscura, and offers great views.

Medina Sidonia ❻

Cádiz. **Road map** B5. 🏃 11,500.
🚉 🚌 Plaza Iglesia Mayor s/n (956
41 24 04). 🚠 Mon.

As you drive along the N440,
between Algeciras and
Jerez, Medina Sidonia appears
startlingly white atop a conical
hill. The town was taken from
the Moors in 1264 by Alfonso
X, and during the 15th century
the Guzmán family were established as the Dukes of Medina
Sidonia to defend the territory
between here and the Bay of
Cádiz. After the Reconquest
(*see pp46–7*), the family grew
rich from investments in the
Americas and Medina Sidonia
became one of the most important ducal seats in Spain.
    Much of the town's medieval
walls still stand and cobbled
alleys nestle beneath them.
    The **Iglesia Santa María la
Coronada** is the town's most
important building. Begun on
the foundations of a castle in
the 15th century, after the Reconquest, it is a fine example
of Andalusian Gothic. Inside,
there is a collection of religious
works of art dating from the
Renaissance, including paintings and a charming *retablo*
with beautifully carved panels.

Costa de la Luz ❼

Cádiz. **Road map** B5. 🚉 Cádiz.
🚌 Cádiz, Tarifa. 🚹 2nd floor Plaza de
San Antonio 3, Cádiz (956 80 70 61).

The costa de la luz between
Cádiz and Tarifa is a raw,
wind-harassed stretch of coast.
Strong, pure light characterizes

**Carved *retablo*, Iglesia de Santa
María la Coronada, Medina Sidonia**

this unspoilt region and is the
source of its name. From the
Sierra del Cabrito, just to the
west of Algeciras (*see p162*),
are views across the Strait of
Gibraltar. On clear days you
can just make out the outline
of Tangier (*see pp162–3*) and
the parched Moroccan landscape – not unlike the Costa
de la Luz – visible below the
purple-tinged Rif mountains.
    Off the N340, at the end of
a long, narrow road, which
strikes out across a wilderness
of cacti, sunflowers and lone-
some cork trees, is **Zahara de
los Atunes**, a modest holiday
resort with a few hotels.
    Conil de la Frontera to the
west, divided from Zahara by
a large area reserved for the
military, is busier. It specializes
in the cheaper end of the market for domestic tourism.
    Other fine beaches on this
coast include Caños de Meca
and Bolonia (*see pp30–31*).

Fishing boats at the resort of Zahara de los Atunes on the Costa de la Luz

Tarifa ⓼

Cádiz. **Road map** B5. 🏛 16,000. 🌐
ℹ *Paseo de la Alameda s/n (956 68 09
93).* 🚌 *Tue.* 🔲 *www.tarifaweb.com*

Tarifa, europe's windsurfing
capital *(see p30)* takes its
name from Tarif ben Maluk,
an 8th-century Moorish
commander.

The 10th-century **Castillo de
Guzmán el Bueno** is the site
of a legend. In 1292, Guzmán,
who was defending Tarifa from
the Moors, was told his host-
age son would die if he did
not surrender; rather than give
in, Guzmán threw down his
dagger for the captors to use.

♟ Castillo de Guzmán el
Bueno
Calle Guzmán el Bueno. 🅲 *956 68
46 89.* ⏱ *Tue–Sun.* 🈶

Castillo de Guzmán el Bueno

Algeciras ⓽

Cádiz. **Road map** C5. 🏛 200,000.
🚉 🚌 ℹ *Calle Juan de Cierva s/n
(956 57 26 36).* 🚌 *Tue.*

The town of algeciras was
central to General Franco's
attempts to regain Spanish control over Gibraltar by economic
rather than military means. In
1969, the frontier was closed
and massive investment made
to develop Algeciras as an industrial base to absorb surplus
labour and end the depend-
ence of the area on Gibraltar.
The resulting urban sprawl of
factories and refineries is given
a wide berth by most travellers except those on their way
to or from North Africa.

Tangier ⓾

**Water seller,
Grand Socco**

Tangier is only a couple of hours by ferry
from Algeciras, making it a perfect day
trip. Despite its proximity, this ancient port,
founded by the Berbers before 1000 BC,
will be a sharp culture shock for those used
to life in Europe. Tangier is vibrant with
eastern colour, and the vast, labyrinthine
Medina, the market quarter, pulsates with noise.
From their workshops in back alleys, craftsmen make traditional goods for busy shops
and stalls in the crowded streets. Yet behind
wrought-iron railings the traveller will see tranquil courts
decorated with mosaics, cool fountains and mosques.

🏛 Dar El Makhzen
Place de la Kasbah. 🅲 *212 39
93 20 97.* ⏱ *Wed–Mon.* 🈶
Sultan Moulay Ismail,
who unified Morocco
in the 17th century,
had the Dar El Makh-
zen built within the
Kasbah. The sultans
lived here with their
wives, harems and
entourages until 1912.
It is now a museum ex-
hibiting traditional crafts
such as carpets, ceramics,
embroidery and wrought
ironwork. The exhibits are
arranged round a central
courtyard, decorated with
beautifully carved stone-work,
and in cool rooms with carved
ceilings that are decorated with
painted tiles. There are illuminated Korans in the Fez room
and a courtyard in the style of
Andalusian Moorish gardens.

🕌 Kasbah
The Kasbah or citadel, built in
Roman times and where the
Sultans once held court, is at
the Medina's highest point. It
is separated from its alleys by
sturdy fortress walls and four
massive stone gateways. From
the battlements there are views
over the Medina, the port and
the Strait of Gibraltar.

The Kasbah encloses the Dar
El Makhzen and other palaces,
the treasury house, the old prison and the law courts around
the Mechour square. Villas that
were once owned by American
and European celebrities, such
as Paul Bowles, the author of
The Sheltering Sky, who came
here during the early part of
the 20th century, are also situated within the Kasbah walls.

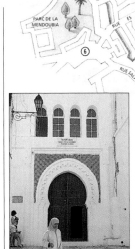

**Façade of the Dar El Makhzen, the
museum of Moroccan arts**

View into the labyrinthine Medina from the Grand Socco

⌂ American Legation

Rue du Portugal. **☎** *212 39 93 53 17.* ○ *Mon, Wed & Thu or by appt.*
This former palace, a gift from Sultan Moulay Slimane in 1821, was the United States' first diplomatic mission and remained the American Embassy until 1961. It is now an art museum and holds regular exhibitions.

⌂ Hôtel Continental

Rue Dar El Baroud. **☎** *212 39 93 10 24.* ○ *daily.*
Numerous intrigues have been played out in this hotel overlooking the port. Today it is a fine place to sit and drink tea.

⌂ Rue es Siaghin

The Medina's main artery, offering a staggering array of merchandise; shop owners along the street will offer you mint tea in a bid to get you to buy.

The carved façade of Tangier's Grand Mosque

0 metres   100
0 yards   100

KEY

▦	Old city walls
🏠	Church
☪	Mosque

SIGHTS AT A GLANCE

American Legation ⑦
Dar El Makhzen ①
Grand Mosque ④
Grand Socco ⑥
Hôtel Continental ③
Kasbah ②
Rue es Siaghin ⑤

☪ Grand Mosque

Green and white minarets rise above this massive edifice built in the 17th century by Sultan Moulay Ismail. An exquisitely carved gateway suggests more treasures within – non-Muslims, however, are forbidden from entering any mosque.

⌂ Grand Socco

Traders from the Rif mountains come to barter their goods at this busy main square at the heart of Tangier. The square's official name, Place du 9 Avril 1947, commemorates a visit by Sultan Muhammad V.

THE INTERNATIONAL ERA

From 1932 until its incorporation into Morocco in 1956, Tangier was an international zone, tax free and under the control of a committee of 30 nations. This was an era that was characterized by financial fraud, espionage, large-scale smuggling, outrageous sexual licence and profligacy by wealthy tax exiles, such as heiress Barbara Hutton. Celebrities such as Henri Matisse, Jack Kerouac and Orson Welles added colour to the scene.

Orson Welles, once a familiar sight on the streets of Tangier

Gibraltar ⑪

NATIVE GIBRALTARIANS are descendents of British, Genoese Jews, Portuguese and Spanish who remained after the Great Siege *(see p50)*. Britain seized Gibraltar during the War of the Spanish Succession in 1704, and was granted it "in perpetuity" by the Treaty of Utrecht *(see p50)* nine years later. As the gateway to the Mediterranean, the Rock was essential to Britain in colonial times, and the treaty is still invoked in response to Spanish claims to Gibraltar. Each year, around 4 million people stream across the frontier at La Línea to visit this speck of England bolted on to Andalusia. Pubs, pints of ale, fish and chips, pounds sterling and bobbies on the beat all contrast with Spain. Most visitors are Spaniards, seduced by the island's shopping.

Gibraltarian barbary ape

The Keep
The lower part of this Moorish castle, built in the 8th century, is still used to house Gibraltar's prison population.

Siege Tunnels
Soldiers' barracks and storerooms fill 50 km (31 miles) of tunnels.

Spanish border and customs

Cable Car
A cable car runs from the centre of the town to the Top of the Rock, Gibraltar's summit, which, at 450 m (1,475 ft) high, is often shrouded in mist.

The airport runway crosses over the main road from La Línea to Gibraltar.

St Michael's Cave
During World War II these caves served as a bomb-proof military hospital. These days classical concerts are performed here.

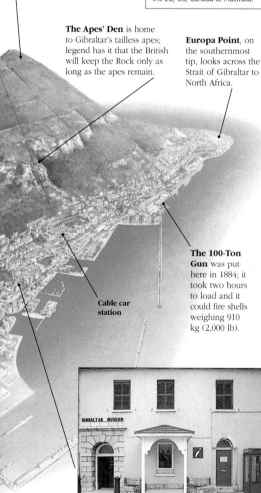

The Apes' Den is home to Gibraltar's tailless apes; legend has it that the British will keep the Rock only as long as the apes remain.

Europa Point, on the southernmost tip, looks across the Strait of Gibraltar to North Africa.

Cable car station

The 100-Ton Gun was put here in 1884; it took two hours to load and it could fire shells weighing 910 kg (2,000 lb).

La Línea de la Concepción, with Gibraltar in the distance

La Línea de la Concepción ⑫

Cádiz. **Road map** C5. 👥 60,000.
🚌 🛈 *Avenida de 20 Abril s/n (956 76 99 50).* 🛒 *Wed.*

LA LÍNEA is a town on the Spanish side of the border with Gibraltar. Its name, "The Line", refers to the old walls that once formed the frontier, but which were demolished during the Napoleonic wars to prevent the French using them for defence. Now it is a lively trading town, with several hotels patronized by people who want to avoid the higher prices of Gibraltar hotels.

The elegant marina at Sotogrande

Sotogrande ⑬

Cádiz. **Road map** C5. 👥 2,000. 🚌
San Roque. 🛈 *Plaza de la Iglesia s/n, Palacio de los Gobernadores (956 69 40 05).* 🛒 *Sun.*

JUST ABOVE Gibraltar, on the Costa del Sol, Sotogrande is an exclusive residential seaside town where wealthy Gibraltarians, who commute daily to the Rock, reside in exclusive villas. The marina is filled with expensive yachts and lined with excellent sea-food restaurants. Nearby there are several immaculately mani-cured golf courses *(see p30).*

Gibraltar Museum
This museum, built on the foundations of Moorish baths, houses an exhibition of Gibraltar's history under British rule.

A Tour Around the Pueblos Blancos ⑭

INSTEAD OF SETTLING on Andalusia's plains, where they would have fallen prey to bandits, some Andalusians chose to live in fortified hilltop towns and villages. The way of life in these *pueblos blancos* – so called because they are whitewashed in the Moorish tradition – has barely changed for centuries. Touring the *pueblos blancos,* which crown the mountains rising sharply from the coast, will show visitors a world full of references to the past. Yet today they are working agricultural towns, not just tourist sights.

Zahara de la Sierra ③ This fine *pueblo blanco*, a tightly huddled hillside village below a castle ruin, has been declared a national monument.

Ubrique ②
This town, nestling at the foot of the Sierra de Ubrique, has become a flourishing producer of leather goods.

Grazalema ④ At the heart of the Parque Natural de la Sierra de Grazalema, this village has the highest rainfall in Spain. Lush vegetation fills the park.

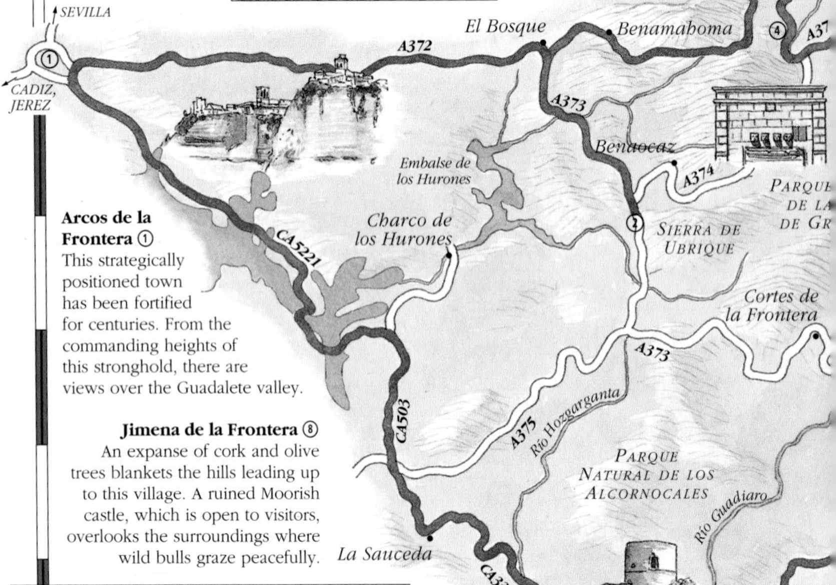

Arcos de la Frontera ①
This strategically positioned town has been fortified for centuries. From the commanding heights of this stronghold, there are views over the Guadalete valley.

Jimena de la Frontera ⑧
An expanse of cork and olive trees blankets the hills leading up to this village. A ruined Moorish castle, which is open to visitors, overlooks the surroundings where wild bulls graze peacefully.

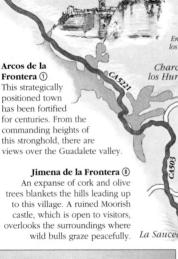

Gaucín ⑦
From here there are unsurpassed vistas over the Mediterranean, the Atlantic, the great hump of Gibraltar and across the strait to the Rif mountains of North Africa.

SEVILLA

CADIZ, JEREZ

El Bosque   Benamahoma

A372

A373

Embalse de los Hurones

Charco de los Hurones

CA5221

Benaocaz

A374

PARQUE DE LA DE GR

SIERRA DE UBRIQUE

Cortes de la Frontera

A373

A375

Río Hozgarganta

CA503

PARQUE NATURAL DE LOS ALCORNOCALES

Río Guadiaro

La Sauceda

CA3331

A369

Embalse de Zahí

CA5013

A37

0 kilometres   1

0 miles   5

Setenil ⑤
The streets of this white town are formed from the ledge of a gorge, carved from tufa rock by the river Trejo.

Ronda ⑥
With the Tajo gorge as an efficient moat, Ronda was one of the last towns recaptured from the Moors. It later became the cradle of modern bullfighting (see pp168–9).

KEY

▰▰▰ Tour route

= Other roads

TIPS FOR DRIVERS

Tour length: 205 km (135 miles).
Stopping-off points: Ronda has a wide range of hotels (see p208) and restaurants (see p220). Arcos de la Frontera has a parador (see p207), other hotels and some restaurants. Gaucín, Jimena de la Frontera and Zahara de la Sierra also have a few places to stay and eat. Both Grazalema and Setenil have a couple of bars and a hotel. Ubrique has just one hotel.

Arcos de la Frontera ⑮

Cádiz. **Road map** B4. 🏘 30,000.
🚌 ℹ️ *Plaza del Cabíldo s/n (956 70 22 64)*. 🚩 *Fri.*
ⓦ *www.ayuntamientoarcos.org*

Aᴿᴄᴏs ʜᴀs ʙᴇᴇɴ inhabited since prehistoric times. Its strategic position encouraged settlement, first as the Roman town of Arcobriga, and later as the stronghold of Medina Arkshon under the Caliphate of Córdoba (see p44). It was captured by Alfonso X's (see p46) Christian forces in 1264.

An archetypal white town, it has a labyrinthine Moorish quarter that twists up to its ruined castle. At its centre is the Plaza de España, one side of which gives views across sunbaked plains. Fronting the square are the superb **Parador de Arcos de la Frontera** (see p207) and the **Iglesia de Santa María de la Asunción**, a late Gothic-Mudéjar building worth seeing for its extravagant choir stalls and altarpiece. A small museum displays the church treasures. More striking is the massive, Gothic **Parroquia de San Pedro**. Its thick-set tower provides a view over the sheer drop down to the Guadalete river. Nearby is the **Palacio del Mayorazgo** with an ornate, Renaissance façade. The **Ayuntamiento** is also worth seeing, particularly to view its beautiful Mudéjar ceiling.

🏛 **Palacio del Mayorazgo**
Calle San Pedro 2. 📞 *956 70 30 13 (Casa de Cultura)*.
🔓 *daily.* ♿
🏛 **Ayuntamiento**
Plaza del Cabildo 1. 📞 *956 70 00 02.* 🔓 *Mon–Fri.*
● *public hols.*

Roman theatre set amid the ruins of Acinipo (Ronda la Vieja)

Ronda la Vieja ⑯

Málaga. **Road map** C4. 🚌 🚌 *Ronda.*
📞 *952 21 36 40 & 630 42 99 49.*
ℹ️ *Plaza España 9 (952 87 12 72).*
🔓 *9am–3:30pm Wed–Sat, 10am–3pm Sun.* **Cuevas de la Pileta** by guided tour (twice daily).
ⓦ *www.turismoderonda.es*

Rᴏɴᴅᴀ ʟᴀ ᴠɪᴇᴊᴀ is the modern name for the remains of the Roman city of Acinipo, 12 km (7 miles) northwest of Ronda (see pp168–9). An important town in the 1st century AD, it later declined, unlike the growing town of Ronda, which was called Arunda by the Romans.

The ruins are beautifully sited on a hillside where only a fraction of the town has been excavated. The town's most important sight is the theatre, but lines of stones also mark foundations of houses, and of the forum and other public buildings.

Along the C339, 22 km (12 miles) from Ronda la Vieja, are the Cuevas de la Pileta, the site of prehistoric cave paintings dating from about 25,000 BC (see p41).

The Gothic-Mudéjar Iglesia de Santa María de la Asunción

Street-by-Street: Ronda ⓱

Plate handpainted in Ronda

O NE OF THE MOST spectacularly located cities in Spain, Ronda sits on a massive rocky outcrop, straddling a precipitous limestone cleft. Because of its impregnable position this town was one of the last Moorish bastions, finally falling to the Christians in 1485. On the south side perches a classic Moorish *pueblo blanco* (*see p166*) of cobbled alleys, window grilles and dazzling whitewash – most historic sights are in this old town. Across the gorge in El Mercadillo, the newer town, is one of Spain's oldest bullrings.

★ Puente Nuevo
Building the "New Bridge" over the nearly 100 m (330 ft) deep Tajo gorge was a feat of civil engineering in the late 18th century.

Convento de Santo Domingo was the local headquarters of the Inquisition.

To El Mercadillo, Plaza de Toros and Parador de Ronda (*see p208*)

Casa del Rey Moro
From this 18th-century mansion, built on the foundations of a Moorish palace, 365 steps lead down to the river.

Mirador El Campillo

★ Palacio Mondragón
Much of this palace was rebuilt after the Reconquest (see pp46–7), but its arcaded patio is adorned with original Moorish mosaics and plasterwork.

0 metres 75
0 yards 75

STAR SIGHTS
★ Palacio Mondragón
★ Puente Nuevo

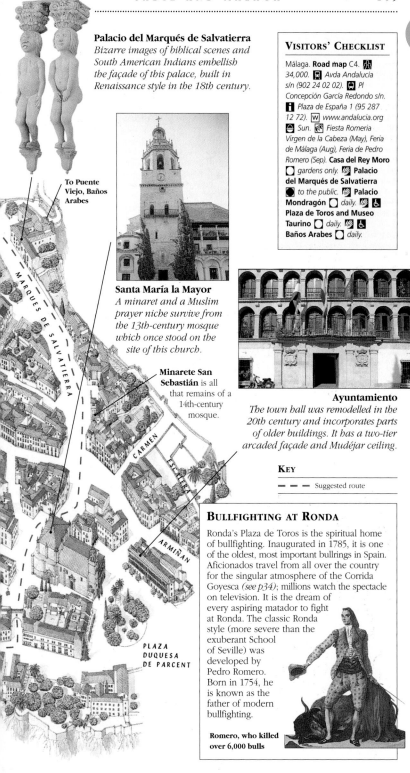

Palacio del Marqués de Salvatierra
Bizarre images of biblical scenes and South American Indians embellish the façade of this palace, built in Renaissance style in the 18th century.

VISITORS' CHECKLIST

Málaga. **Road map** C4. 🏠 34,000. 🚉 *Avda Andalucía s/n (902 24 02 02).* 🚌 *Pl Concepción García Redondo s/n.* 🅸 *Plaza de España 1 (95 287 12 72).* 🅆 *www.andalucia.org* 🗓 *Sun.* 🎉 *Fiesta Romería Virgen de la Cabeza (May), Feria de Málaga (Aug), Feria de Pedro Romero (Sep).* **Casa del Rey Moro** ⬤ *gardens only.* 🖼 **Palacio del Marqués de Salvatierra** ⬤ *to the public.* 🖼 **Palacio Mondragón** ⬤ *daily.* 🖼 ♿ **Plaza de Toros and Museo Taurino** ⬤ *daily.* 🖼 ♿ **Baños Arabes** ⬤ *daily.*

To Puente Viejo, Baños Arabes

MARQUES DE SALVATIERRA

Santa María la Mayor
A minaret and a Muslim prayer niche survive from the 13th-century mosque which once stood on the site of this church.

Minarete San Sebastián is all that remains of a 14th-century mosque.

CARMEN

ESCALERA

Ayuntamiento
The town hall was remodelled in the 20th century and incorporates parts of older buildings. It has a two-tier arcaded façade and Mudéjar ceiling.

KEY

– – – Suggested route

ARMIÑAN

PLAZA DUQUESA DE PARCENT

BULLFIGHTING AT RONDA

Ronda's Plaza de Toros is the spiritual home of bullfighting. Inaugurated in 1785, it is one of the oldest, most important bullrings in Spain. Aficionados travel from all over the country for the singular atmosphere of the Corrida Goyesca *(see p34)*; millions watch the spectacle on television. It is the dream of every aspiring matador to fight at Ronda. The classic Ronda style (more severe than the exuberant School of Seville) was developed by Pedro Romero. Born in 1754, he is known as the father of modern bullfighting.

Romero, who killed over 6,000 bulls

Carratraca ⓘ

Málaga. **Road map** C4. 🏃 *900.*
📮 🛈 *Ayuntamiento Glorieta 2 (95
245 80 16).* 🚌 *Sat.*

A STEEP, TWISTING mountain
road leads up to this small
village, which in the 19th and
early 20th centuries attracted
Europe's highest society and
members of royalty. They came
here for the healing powers of
the village's natural sulphurous
spring. Lord Byron, Alexandre
Dumas and Empress Eugénie
of France are on the town's list
of illustrious past visitors.

These days, Carratraca retains
a faded glory, and there is a
forlorn atmosphere amid the
long-closed casinos and in the
Hostal el Príncipe, where the
famous and the sick used to
stay. Water still gushes out of
the mountainside – at a rate of
700 litres (155 gal) per minute
– and the outdoor baths remain
open, although they are little
used these days. A pungent
smell of sulphur in the air
ensures that the existence of
the springs is not forgotten.

Outdoor hot baths in the
village of Carratraca

Álora ⓘ

Málaga. **Road map** C4. 🏃 *13,000.*
📮 📮 🛈 *Avenida Constitución s/n (95
249 83 80).* 🚌 *Mon.*

SITUATED in the Guadalhorce
river valley, Álora is an important agricultural centre. It
is a classic white town (*pueblo
blanco, see pp166–7*), perched

on a hillside overlooking an
expanse of wheat fields, citrus
orchards and olive groves.

The town's cobbled streets
radiate from the 18th-century
Iglesia de la Encarnación.
At the weekly market, stalls of
farm produce and clothing fill
nearby streets. On the higher
of Álora's twin hills stands the
Castillo with a cemetery of
niche tombs set in neat blocks.

♣ Castillo Árabe

Calle Ancha. 📞 *95 249 83 80
(tourist office).* ○ *daily.*

Garganta del Chorro ⓘ

Málaga. **Road map** C4. 📮 *El Chorro.*
📮 *Parque Ardales.* 🛈 *Avenida
Constitución s/n (95 249 83 80).*

UP THE FERTILE Guadalhorce
valley, 12 km (7 miles) on
from Álora, is one of the geographical wonders of Spain.
The Garganta del Chorro is an
immense gaping chasm 180 m
(590 ft) high, slashing through
a limestone mountain. In some
places, where the Guadalhorce
river hurtles through, waters
foaming white, it is only 10 m
(30 ft) wide. Below the gorge
is a hydroelectric plant, which
detracts slightly from the wild-
ness of the place.

The **Camino del Rey** was
opened in 1921 to give visitors a sense of the gorge's
dizzying dimensions. This precipitous catwalk clings to the
rock face and crosses from one
side of the gorge to the other
via a precarious bridge. It is
now unsafe in places and is
currently closed to visitors.
The nearby village of **El
Chorro** offers a wide range
of outdoor activities.

Fuente de Piedra ⓘ

Málaga. **Road map** C4. 📮 📮
🛈 *Cerro del Palo Centro de
Visitantes de Laguna de Fuente de
Piedra (95 211 10 50).*

THE LARGEST of several lakes
in an expanse of wetlands
north of Antequera, the Laguna
de la Fuente de Piedra teems
with bird life, including huge
flocks of flamingos. In March,

The Garganta del Chorro, rising high above the Guadalhorce river

every year, up to 25,000 of them arrive to breed before migrating back to West Africa. Visitors should note that if there is drought in the region, the birds breeding. Apart from flamingos, there are also cranes, herons, bee-eaters, snow-white egrets, as well as many species of ducks and geese. Their numbers have increased since conservation and anti-hunting laws were introduced and the area declared a sanctuary. A road off the N334 leads to the lake side, from where visitors can watch the birds. Restraint is required: it is forbidden to join the waders in the lake. Information is available from a visitors' centre near the village of Fuente de Piedra.

The triumphal, 16th-century Arco de los Gigantes, Antequera

Antequera ⓜ

Málaga. **Road map** D4. 🏔 *42,000.*
🚌 🚐 🛈 *Plaza San Sebastián 7 (95 270 25 05).* 🚍 *Tue.*
🌐 *www.aytoantequera.com*

A BUSY MARKET TOWN and commercial centre in the Guadalhorce river valley, the town of Antequera has long been strategically important; first as Roman Anticaria and later as a Moorish border fortress defending Granada.

Of all Antequera's churches the **Iglesia de Nuestra Señora del Carmen**, with its vast, Baroque altarpiece, is not to be missed. To the west of here, at the opposite end of the town, is the 19th-century **Plaza de Toros**, where there is a museum of bullfighting.

Limestone formations in the Parque Natural del Torcal

High on a hill overlooking the town is the **Castillo Arabe**, a Moorish castle built in the 13th century on the site of a Roman fort. Visitors cannot go inside, but can walk round the castle walls – the approach is through the 16th-century **Arco de los Gigantes**. There are fine views from the **Torre del Papabell-otas**, which is located on the best-preserved part of the wall. In the town below, the 18th-century **Palacio de Nájera** is the setting for the Municipal Museum; the star exhibit here is a 2,000-year-old statue, in bronze, of a Roman boy.

Just outside of town, to the northeast, there are massive prehistoric dolmens. They are thought to be between 4,000 and 4,500 years old, the burial chambers of some of the region's early tribal leaders.

🐂 **Plaza de Toros**
Crta de Sevilla s/n. 🛈 *95 270 81 42.*
◯ *Tue–Sun.* **Museo Taurino**
◯ *Sat, Sun, public hols.*
🏛 **Palacio de Nájera**
Coso Viejo s/n. 🛈 *95 270 40 21.*
◯ *Tue–Sun.* 📷

El Torcal ⓝ

Málaga. **Road map** D4. 🚌 🚐 *Ante-qùera.* 🛈 *Antequera (95 270 25 05).*

A HUGE EXPOSED HUMP of limestone upland, which has been battered into bizarre formations by wind and rain, the **Parque Natural del Torcal** is very popular with hikers. Most follow a network of footpaths leading from a visitors' centre in the middle, on which short walks of up to two hours are

marked by yellow arrows; the longer walks are marked in red. There are canyons, caves, mushroom-shaped rocks and other geological curiosities to see. The park is also a joy for natural historians, with fox and weasel populations, and colonies of eagles, hawks and vultures. It also protects rare plants and flowers, among them species of wild orchid.

Archidona ⓞ

Málaga. **Road map** D4. 🏔 *8,200.*
🚌 🚐 🛈 *Plaza Ochavada 2 (95 271 64 79).* 🚍 *Mon.*

T HIS SMALL TOWN is worth a stop to see its extraordinary **Plaza Ochavada**. This is an octagonal square built in the 18th century in a French style, but which also incorporates traditional Andalusian features.

From the **Ermita Virgen de Gracia** on a hillside above the town, there are commanding views over rolling countryside.

The 18th-century, octagonal Plaza Ochavada in Archidona

Nerja ㉕

Málaga. **Road map** D4. 🏠 *18,000.*
🚌 🛈 *Calle Puerta del Mar 2
(95 252 15 31).* 🚍 *Tue.*
🖥 *www.nerja.org*

THIS FASHIONABLE resort at the eastern extremity of the Costa del Sol lies at the foot of the beautiful mountains of the Sierra de Almijara, and is perched on a cliff above a succession of sandy coves. The main area for tourist activity in the resort centres around the promenade, running along a rocky promontory known as **El Balcón de Europa** (the Balcony of Europe). Ranged along its length are cafés and restaurants with outdoor tables, and there are sweeping views up and down the coast. On the edges of town, holiday villas and apartments proliferate.

Due east of the town are the **Cuevas de Nerja**, a series

The town of Nerja overlooking the sea from El Balcón de Europa

of vast caverns of considerable archaeological interest, which were discovered in 1959. Wall paintings *(see p40)* found in them are believed to be about 20,000 years old but they are closed to public view. Only a few of the many cathedral-sized chambers are open to public view. One of

these has been turned into an impressive underground auditorium large enough to hold audiences of several hundred. Concerts are held there in the summer.

♠ **Cuevas de Nerja**
Carretera de las Cuevas de Nerja.
📞 *95 252 95 20.* ⊙ *daily.* 🈚

Málaga ㉘

Málaga. **Road map** D4. 🏠 *650,000.*
✈ 🚉 🚌 🛈 *Pasaje de Chinitas 4
(95 221 34 45).* 🚍 *Sun.*
🖥 *www.andalucia.org*

A THRIVING PORT, Málaga is Andalusia's second largest city. Initial impressions tend to be of ugly suburbs, high-rise blocks and lines of rusting cranes, but this belies a city that is rich with history, and is filled with monuments and the vibrancy of Andalusia.

Malaca, the Phoenician *(see pp40–41)* city, was an important trading port on the Iberian peninsula. After Rome's victory against Carthage in 206 BC *(see p42)*, it became a major port for Roman trade with Byzantium. Málaga's heyday came in the years after 711, when it fell to the Moors and became their main port serving Granada. It was recaptured by the Christians in 1487 after a bloody siege. The Moors who stayed behind were expelled *(see pp48–9)* after a rebellion.

Following a long decline, the city flourished once again

**Façade detail,
Málaga Cathedral**

during the 19th century, when Málaga wine became one of Europe's most popular drinks. Unfortunately, phylloxera, the vine disease that ravaged the vineyards of Europe, reached Málaga, putting paid to the prosperity of its vineyards. This, however, was when tourists – the British especially – began to winter here.

The old town at the heart of Málaga radiates from the **catedral**. It was begun in 1528 by Diego de Siloé, but it is a bizarre mix of styles. Its construction was interrupted by an earth-

quake in 1680. The half-built second tower, abandoned in 1765 when funds ran out, is the reason for the cathedral's nickname: La Manquita (the one-armed one).

Málaga's former Museo de Bellas Artes is being adapted to house a new **Museo de Picasso**, displaying works by the native artist *(see p52)*. The **Casa Natal de Picasso**, where

Amphitheatre

**Puerta
Principal**

Entrance

**Puerta de
las Columnas**

Plaza de Armas

Vélez Málaga 26

Málaga. **Road map** D4. 🎿 *55,000.*
🚆 🛈 *Avda Andalucia 52, Torre del Mar (95 254 11 04).* ⛴ *Thu.*
🌐 *www.ayto-velezmalaga.es*

O N THE COSTA DEL SOL, just 5 kilometres (3 miles) inland from Torre del Mar is the market town of Vélez-Málaga, in the fertile Vélez river valley. The modern district is sprawling and industrial, while the old Moorish town is dominated by the **Fortaleza de Vélez**, a fortress with a restored tower that juts out dramatically from a rocky outcrop against the sky.

Immediately below the fortress is the medieval **Barrio de San Sebastián** with its dark cobbled alleys, whitewashed walls and iron window-grilles. Here, two churches stand out: the **Iglesia de Santa María la Mayor**, which still retains an original Moorish minaret; and

the **Iglesia de Nuestra Señora de la Encarnación**, which was once a Visigothic church and then, later, a mosque.

⛪ **Fortaleza de Vélez**
Vélez Málaga Alta. ◯ *daily.*

Narrow street in the Barrio de San Sebastián, Vélez Málaga

Montes de Málaga 27

Málaga. **Road map** D4. 🚌 *to Colmenar.* 🛈 *Lagar de Torrijos, on C345 at km 544,3 (95 104 51 00).*

T O THE NORTH and east of Málaga are the beautiful hills of Montes de Málaga. A wide area is undergoing reforestation and forms the **Parque Natural de Montes de Málaga**. Wildlife thrives in the strongly scented undergrowth of lavender and wild herbs. Occasionally, there are glimpses of wild cats, stone martens, wild boars, eagles and other birds of prey.

Walkers can follow marked trails. A farmhouse has been restored and converted into an ethnological museum. Along the C345 road between Málaga and the park, there are sensational views down to the sea.

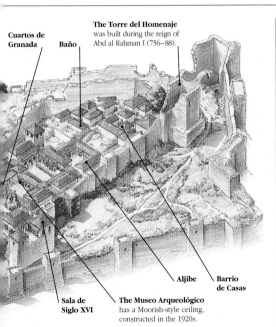

Cuartos de Granada

Baño

The Torre del Homenaje was built during the reign of Abd al Rahman I (756–88).

Aljibe

Barrio de Casas

Sala de Siglo XVI

The Museo Arqueológico has a Moorish-style ceiling, constructed in the 1920s.

Malaga's Alcazaba
Málaga's vast Alcazaba was built between the 8th and 11th centuries on the site of a Roman town. The two are curiously juxtaposed, with the Roman amphitheatre, discovered in 1951 and only partially excavated, just outside the entrance. The remains of Moorish walls can be seen, but the real attraction is the Museo Arqueológico, housing collections of Phoenician, Roman and Moorish artifacts, including fine ceramics.

the painter spent his early years, is now the headquarters of the Picasso Foundation.

On the hill directly behind the Alcazaba are the ruins of the **Castillo de Gibralfaro**, a 14th-century Moorish castle. Connected to the fortress by a pair of parallel ramparts, it can be reached through some beautiful gardens. There are views over the old town, the port and the Málaga bullring, immediately below. The road to the Parador de Málaga also leads to the top of this hill; there are commanding views over the city from both.

East of Málaga on the road to Vélez Málaga is the unspoilt family beach of Rincón de la Victoria (*see p31*).

🏛 **Museo de Picasso**
Calle San Agustín 8. 🛈 *95 260 27 31.*
◯ *10am–8pm Tue–Sun.* 🅿

🏛 **Casa Natal de Picasso**
Plaza de la Merced 15. 🛈 *95 206 02 15.* ◯ *10am–2pm, 5–8pm Mon–Sat, 10am–2pm Sun & public hols.*

⛪ **Castillo de Gibralfaro**
◯ *9am–6pm Tue–Sun.*

⛪ **Alcazaba**
Calle Alcazaba s/n. 🛈 *95 221 60 05.* ◯ *8:30am–7pm Tue–Sun.*

🏛 **Museo Arqueológico**
Calle Alcazabilla. 🛈 *95 221 60 05.* ◯ *9:30am–8pm Tue–Sun.*

Torremolinos, the brash capital of the Costa del Sol's tourist industry

Torremolinos ㉙

Málaga. **Road map** D4. 🏛 *50,000.*
🚌 🚉 ℹ *Plaza Blas Infante 1
(952 37 95 12).* 🛒 *Thu.*
🌐 *www.ayto.torremolinos.org*

Torremolinos was a pioneer in the development of mass tourism in Spain and, until the mid-1970s, an archetype of the successful sun-and-beach resort. Later, a victim of its own success, Torremolinos became a byword for all that is wrong with unchecked development.

"Torrie" or "T-Town" to its friends, is a high-rise holiday metropolis rounding a headland dividing two beaches. It grew from a village in the 1950s to one of the busiest resorts on the Costa del Sol, where British, and to a lesser extent, German holiday-makers enjoyed their cheap package holidays. It also developed its red-light district and a raffish nightlife to provide "relaxation" and "recreation" for sailors of the US navy in port at Málaga.

Recently, the town has been cleaned up as part of a scheme that has seen huge sums spent on new squares, a promenade, green spaces and enlarging the beach with millions of tonnes of fine golden sand.

Although Torremolinos still has scores of English bars run by expatriates, the atmosphere is now decidedly less brash, especially at Carihuela beach towards the adjoining resort of Benalmádena. Bajondillo beach is nearer the busy town centre. As elsewhere on the Costa del Sol, Torremolinos has a thriving scene in winter, as well as in the summer.

Fuengirola ㉚

Málaga. **Road map** C4. 🏛 *53,000.*
🚌 🚉 ℹ *Avda Jesús Santos Rein 6
(95 246 74 57).* 🛒 *Tue, Sat & Sun.*
🌐 *www.fuengirola.org*

Sprawling along the foot of southern Andalusia's grey and ochre Serranía de Ronda, which drops steeply down to the edge of the Mediterranean, Fuengirola is another cheap, package holiday resort. In recent years, some of the wilder elements of its, mostly British, clientele have moved on to newer pastures elsewhere. Nowadays it is mainly families who take their sun-and-sea summer holidays here. During the mild winter months, retired people arrive from the UK; they stroll along the seaside promenade, go to English bars and waltz the afternoons away at hotel dances.

Boxes of fresh fish, Fuengirola

Marbella ㉛

Málaga. **Road map** C4. 🏛 *120,000.*
🚉 ℹ *Glorieta de la Fontanilla s/n,
Paseo Marítimo (95 277 14 42).*
🛒 *Mon & Sat (Puerto Banús).*
🌐 *www.marbella.es*

In glittering contrast with Torremolinos and Fuengirola, Marbella is one of Europe's most exclusive holiday resorts. Royalty, film stars and other members of the jet set spend their summers here in smart villas, or else stay at one of

Yachts and motorboats in the exclusive marina of Marbella – the summer home of the international jet set

19th-century lithograph of the harbour at Málaga

LIFE IN THE SUN

The idealized image of the Costa del Sol before tourism is of idyllic fishing villages where life was always at an easy pace. It is true to say that local economies have turned away from fishing and agriculture, and that the natural beauty of this coast has been marred by development. Any measured view, however, should consider the situation described by Laurie Lee, the writer who in 1936 wrote of ". . . salt-fish villages, thin-ribbed, sea-hating, cursing their place in the sun". Today, few Andalusians curse their new-found prosperity.

Marbella's luxury hotels. In winter, the major attraction is the golf *(see pp30–31)*. A short walk from many of the smartest hotels is an old town of spotlessly clean alleys, squares, courtyards and smart restaurants. One of the delights of Marbella is eating outside in **Plaza de los Naranjos**, the main square, shaded by orange trees. The **Ayuntamiento**, overlooking the square, has a panelled Mudéjar ceiling. The **Iglesia de Nuestra Señora de la Encarnación**, just off the square, is a cool, peaceful refuge. Devotees of Picasso can visit the **Museo del Grabado Español Contemporáneo**, where some of his least-known work is exhibited.

Anybody who is interested in the nightlife should come with a full wallet; luckily the beaches – Victor's, Cabopino, Don Carlos, Babaloo and Las Dunas *(see pp30–31)* – are free.

🏛 **Museo del Grabado Español Contemporáneo**
C/ Hospital Bazan s/n. 📞 952 76 57 41. ⬜ Tue–Sat. ⬤ public hols. 🎟
🏛 **Ayuntamiento**
Plaza de los Naranjos 1. 📞 95 276 11 00. ⬜ Mon–Fri.

San Pedro de Alcántara ㉜

Málaga. **Road map** D4. 🏃 26,000.
🚉 🛈 Avda Marques del Duero, 69 (95 278 52 52). ⬤ Thu.

SAN PEDRO IS A SMALL, rather exclusive resort which lies within Marbella's sphere of influence. It is quiet, with a sleepy atmosphere, especially in the Plaza de la Iglesia, the town square, set back from the modern marina. Most of the smart holiday developments are on the town's fringes, set amid a number of golf courses *(see pp30–31)*, on the lower slopes of the Sierra Blanca.

Estepona ㉝

Málaga. **Road map** C5. 🏃 46,000.
🚉 🛈 Avda San Lorenzo 1 (95 280 09 13). ⬤ Wed & Sun.
🌐 www.infoestepona.com

THIS FISHING VILLAGE, situated midway between Marbella and Gibraltar, has been altered, but not totally overwhelmed, by tourist developments. It is not particularly attractive at first sight, with big hotels and

The leafy Plaza de las Flores hidden in Estepona's backstreets

apartment blocks fronting the town's busy main tourist area. Behind, however, there are endearing pockets of all that is quintessentially Spanish – orange trees lining the streets, and the lovely **Plaza Arce** and **Plaza de las Flores**, peaceful squares where old men sit reading newspapers while around them children kick footballs about. There are also a few good, relatively inexpensive fish restaurants and tapas bars. The beach is pleasant enough and evenings in the town tend to be quiet, which makes the resort popular for families with young children.

Not far away from Estepona, however, is a popular nudist beach called the Costa Natura *(see pp30–31)*.

Relaxing in sleepy San Pedro de Alcántara

GRANADA AND ALMERÍA

EASTERN ANDALUSIA *is dominated by the Sierra Nevada, Iberia's highest range and one of Spain's premier winter sports venues. At its foot is Granada, once a Moorish kingdom, with a royal palace, the Alhambra, straight out of* One Thousand and One Nights. *Ruined fortresses, relics of a warring past, dominate the towns of Granada province. In Almería's arid interior, film directors have put to use atmospheric landscapes reminiscent of Arabia or the Wild West.*

At the point where the mountains of the Sierra Nevada meet the plain, 670 m (2,200 ft) above sea level, nestles the ancient city of Granada, founded by the Iberians. For 250 years it was the capital of a Moorish kingdom whose borders enclosed both Almería and Málaga provinces. On a ridge overlooking the city rises the royal citadel of the Alhambra, a complex of spacious palaces and water gardens.

The mountainous terrain of Granada province is starkly impressive. Amid the ravines, crags and terraced fields of Las Alpujarras on the southern flank of the Sierra Nevada, the villages seem to cling to the sheer slopes.

Along the coastal strip of Granada province, avocados and custard apples flourish in the subtropical climate.

Hotels, villas and holiday apartment blocks are also much in evidence here.

East of Granada, the landscape becomes more arid. Around the town of Guadix, founded in Phoenician and Roman times, thousands of people live in cave-houses. A statue of an Iberian goddess from pre-Roman times was found at Baza, and at Los Millares, near Almería, there are traces of a 4,000-year-old settlement.

Almería, a flourishing port in the Moorish era, has been revitalized by a new form of agriculture. Plastic greenhouses now cover hectares of its surrounding province, producing fruit and vegetables all year round.

Along the sparsely populated coast of Cabo de Gata, little-visited villages and bays doze in year-round sunshine.

The Renaissance castle of Lacalahorra at the foot of the Sierra Nevada

◁ Patio de los Leones, Alhambra, Granada; a fountain resting on the backs of 12 lions

Exploring Granada and Almería

G RANADA AND THE ALHAMBRA are the obvious
highlights of this region, but are only a
part of its appeal. Improved roads make it
easy to reach most places within a few hours,
and from Granada it is possible to explore the
Sierra Nevada, plunge into the clear waters of
the Costa Tropical, or wander through beautiful, spectacularly situated old towns, such as
Montefrío and Alhama de Granada. From
Almería it is a short hop to the Arizona-like
country around Tabernas, where spaghetti
westerns were made, or to the secluded
beaches of the Parque Natural de Cabo de
Gata. Each town and whitewashed village
that lies in between has its own charm.

**The Alhambra, with the snow-covered Sierra
Nevada mountain range in the background**

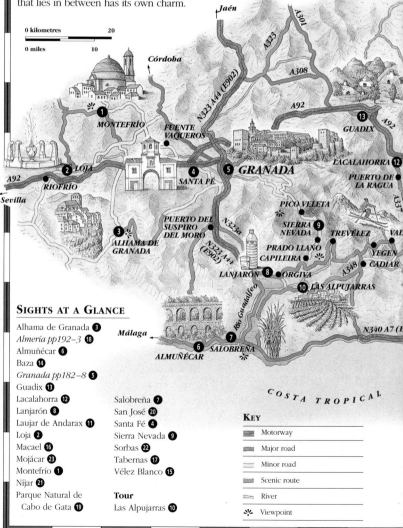

SIGHTS AT A GLANCE

KEY

▬▬	Motorway
▬▬	Major road
‒‒	Minor road
▭▭	Scenic route
∿∿	River
❊	Viewpoint

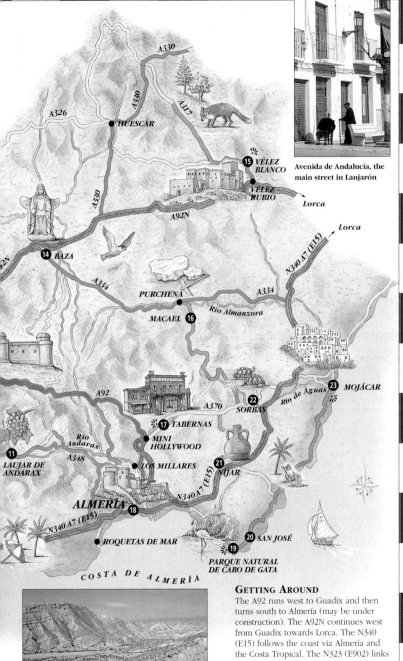

Avenida de Andalucía, the
main street in Lanjarón

A330

A326

HUESCAR

A317

A330

15 VÉLEZ
BLANCO

VÉLEZ
RUBIO

Lorca

A92N

Lorca

N340 A7 (E15)

14 BAZA

2N

A334

PURCHENA

A334

Río Almanzora

MACAEL **16**

23 MOJÁCAR

A92

A370

22
SORBAS

Río de Águas

17 TABERNAS

MINI
HOLLYWOOD

Río
Andarax

A348

LOS MILLARES

21
NÍJAR

N340 A7 (E15)

11
LAUJAR DE
ANDARAX

ALMERÍA **18**

N340 A7 (E15)

ROQUETAS DE MAR

20 SAN JOSÉ

19

PARQUE NATURAL
DE CABO DE GATA

COSTA DE ALMERÍA

Spaghetti-western-style landscape near Tabernas

GETTING AROUND

The A92 runs west to Guadix and then
turns south to Almería (may be under
construction). The A92N continues west
from Guadix towards Lorca. The N340
(E15) follows the coast via Almería and
the Costa Tropical. The N323 (E902) links
the coast with Granada and the A348
connects the villages of the Alpujarras.

There are three trains a day between
Granada and Almería, but no coastal rail
service. Frequent buses run from both
cities to towns on main routes.

Whitewashed houses on the edge of the gorge at Alhama de Granada, surrounded by olive groves

Montefrío ❶

Granada. **Road map** D3. 🏃 7,000.
🚌 🛈 *Plaza de España 1 (958 33
60 04).* 🚌 *Mon.*

MONTEFRÍO IS the archetypal
Andalusian town, which,
approached by road from the
south, offers wonderful views
of tiled rooftops and whitewashed houses running up to
a steep crag. The village is
surmounted by remains of
Moorish fortifications and
the 16th-century Gothic
Iglesia de la Villa, which
is attributed to Diego
de Siloé. Located in
the centre of town
stands the **Iglesia de
la Encarnación**, in
Neo-Classical design;
the architect Ventura
Rodríguez (1717–85)
is credited with its
design. Montefrío
is also famed for
the high quality of
its pork products.

Loja ❷

Granada. **Road map** D4. 🏃 21,000.
🚌 🚌 🛈 *Calle las Tiendas, 1 (958 32
39 49).* 🚌 *Mon.* 🌐 *www.aytoloja.org*

ARUINED MOORISH fort rises
above the crooked streets
of the old town of Loja, which
was built at a strategic point on
the Río Genil. The Renaissance
Templo de San Gabriel
(1566) has a striking façade,
designed by Diego de Siloé.
Known as "the city of water",
Loja also has some beautiful
fountains. East of the town,

the fast-flowing Río Genil cuts
through **Los Infiernos** gorge.
To the west is **Riofrío,** where
the local trout is served in a
number of restaurants.

Alhama de Granada ❸

Granada. **Road map** D4. 🏃 6,000.
🚌 🛈 *Paseo Montes Jovellar s/n
(958 36 06 86).* 🚌 *Fri.*

ALHAMA IS a charming
little town balanced
above a gorge. It was
known as Al hamma
(hot springs) to the
Arabs. Their baths
can still be seen in
Hotel Balneario
on the edge of the
town. Alhama's fall
to the Christians in
1482 was a major
Moorish defeat. It
led to the final
humiliation of the
Nasrid kingdom at
Granada in 1492
(*see p46*).

**Belfry of Templo de San
Gabriel at Loja**

The 16th-century **Iglesia
de Carmen** has a number
of very fine paintings on
its dome, which had
to be restored after
damage incurred
during the Spanish
Civil War (*see pp52–3*).
Narrow, immaculately whitewashed streets lead to the
Iglesia de la Encarnación,
which was founded by the
Catholic Monarchs (*see
pp46–7*) in the 16th
century. Some of the
vestments worn by the
present-day priests are

said to have been embroidered
by Queen Isabel herself. The
church also has a Renaissance
bell tower designed by Diego
de Siloé. Nearby is the 16th-
century **Hospital de la Reina**,
now a library housing a fine
artesonado ceiling.

🏨 **Hotel Balneario**
Calle Balneario. 📞 958 35 00 11.
🔵 Apr–Nov.

🏨 **Hospital de la Reina**
Calle Vendederas s/n. 📞 958 36 06
43. 🔵 11am–1:30pm, 4–8pm
Tue–Fri, 10am–1pm Sat.

Santa Fé ❹

Granada. **Road map** D4. 🏃 12,500.
🚌 🛈 *Arco de Sevilla, Calle Isabel la
Católica, 7 (958 44 12 58).* 🚌 *Thu.*

THE ARMY of the Catholic
Monarchs camped here
as it lay siege to Granada (*see
p46*). The camp burned down,
it is said, after a maid placed
a candle too close to a curtain
in Isabel's tent. Fernando
ordered a model town to
be built. Its name, "holy
faith", was chosen by the
devout Isabel. In 1492
the Moors made a
formal surrender at
Santa Fé and here,
in the same year,
the two monarchs
backed Columbus's
voyage of exploration
(*see p123*). An earthquake
destroyed some of the
town in 1806. A Moor's
severed head, carved
in stone, decorates
the spire of the
parish church.

**Spire-tip of the
church, Santa Fé**

Granada ❺

See pp182–8.

Almuñécar ❻

Granada. **Road map** D4. 🚶 *21,000.*
🚌 ℹ️ *Avenida Europa s/n (958 63 11
25).* 🚌 *Fri.* 🔲 *www.almunecar.info*

AᴸᴹᴜÑÉᴄᴀʀ ʟɪᴇs on southern Spain's most spectacular coast, the **Costa Tropical** *(see p30)*, where mountains rise to over 2,000 m (6,560 ft) from the shores of the Mediterranean Sea. The Phoenicians founded the first settlement, called Sexi, at Almuñécar, and the Romans built an aqueduct here. When the English writer Laurie Lee made his long trek across Spain in 1936, he described Almuñécar as "a tumbling little village fronted by a strip of grey sand which some hoped would be an attraction for tourists". On returning in the 1950s, he found a village still coming to terms with the Spanish Civil War *(see pp52–3)*, which he recounts in his novel *A Rose for Winter*.

Almuñécar is now a holiday resort. Above the old town is the **Castillo de San Miguel**. In its shadow are botanic gardens, the **Parque Ornitológico** and a Roman fish-salting factory. Phoenician

Castillo de San Miguel, overlooking the village of Almuñécar

artifacts are on display in the **Museo Arqueológico Cueva de Siete Palacios**.

⛰️ **Castillo de San Miguel**
🔲 *Tue–Sun.* 📷

🦜 **Parque Ornitológico**
Plaza de Abderraman s/n. 📞 *958 63 11 25.* 🔲 *daily.* 📷

🏛️ **Museo Arqueológico Cueva de Siete Palacios**
Casco Antiguo. 🔲 *Tue–Sun.* 📷

Salobreña ❼

Granada. **Road map** E4. 🚶 *10,500.*
🚌 ℹ️ *Plaza de Goya s/n (958 61 03 14).* 🚌 *Tue & Fri.*

Fʀᴏᴍ ᴀᴄʀᴏss the coastal plain Salobreña looks like a white liner sailing above a sea of waving sugar cane.

Narrow streets wend their way up a hill first fortified by the Phoenicians. The hill later became the site of the restored **Castillo Arabe**, which gives fine views of the peaks of the Sierra Nevada *(see p189)*. Modern developments, bars and restaurants line part of this resort's lengthy beach.

⛰️ **Castillo Arabe**
Falda del Castillo, Calle Andrés Segovia.
📞 *958 61 03 14.* 🔲 *Tue–Sun.* 📷 ✉️

Lanjarón ❽

Granada. **Road map** E4. 🚶 *24,000.*
🚌 ℹ️ *Ayuntamiento, Plaza de la Constitución 29 (958 77 00 02).*
🚌 *Tue & Fri.*

Sᴄᴏʀᴇs ᴏꜰ sɴᴏᴡ-ꜰᴇᴅ springs bubble from the slopes below the Sierra Nevada, and Lanjarón, on the threshold of Las Alpujarras *(see pp190–91)*, has a long history as a spa. From June to October visitors flock to the town to take the waters and, under medical supervision, enjoy various water treatments for arthritis, obesity, nervous tension and other ailments. Lanjarón bottled water is sold all over Spain.

The town occupies a lovely site, but it can seem melancholic. The exception to this is during the early hours of the festival of San Juan *(see p33)* when a water battle takes place. Anybody who dares venture into the streets gets liberally doused.

🛁 **Balneario**
Balneario de Lanjarón. 📞 *958 77 01 37.* 🔲 *daily.* ⚫ *mid-Dec–mid Feb.* 📷 ♿

The village of Salobreña viewed across fields of sugar cane

Granada ❺

Relief at the Museo Arqueológico

THE GUITARIST ANDRES SEGOVIA (1893–1987) described Granada as a "place of dreams, where the Lord put the seed of music in my soul". It was ruled by the Nasrid dynasty *(see pp46–7)* from 1238 until 1492 when it fell to the Catholic Monarchs. Before the Moors were expelled, artisans, merchants, scholars and scientists all contributed to the city's reputation as a centre for culture. Under Christian rule the city became a focus for the Renaissance. After a period of decline in the 19th century, Granada has recently been the subject of renewed interest and efforts are being made to restore parts of it to their past glory.

🏛 Alhambra and Generalife
See pp186–188.

Façade of Granada cathedral

🔓 Catedral
On the orders of the Catholic Monarchs, work on the cathedral began in 1523 to plans in a Gothic style by Enrique de Egas. It continued under the Renaissance maestro Diego de Siloé, who also designed the façade. Corinthian pillars support his magnificent, circular Capilla Mayor. Under its dome, windows of 16th-century glass depict Juan del Campo's *The Passion*. The west front was designed by the Baroque artist Alonso Cano, who was born in Granada. His work and many of his works are housed in the cathedral. By the entrance arch are wooden statues of the Catholic Monarchs carved by Pedro de Mena in 1677.

🔓 Capilla Real
The Royal Chapel was built for the Catholic Monarchs between 1505 and 1507 by Enrique de Egas. A magnificent *reja* (grille) by Maestro Bartolomé de Jaén encloses the mausoleums and high altar. The *retablo* by the sculptor Felipe de Vigarney has reliefs depicting the fall of Granada *(see pp46–7)*. Carrara marble figures of Fernando and Isabel, designed by Domenico Fancelli in 1517, repose next to those of their daughter Juana la Loca (the Mad) and her husband Felipe el Hermoso (the Handsome), both by the sculptor Bartolomé Ordóñez.

Steps lead down to the crypt where the corpses are stored in lead coffins. In the sacristy there are yet more statues of the two monarchs and many art treasures, including paintings by Van der Weyden and Botticelli from Isabel's collection. Glass cases house Isabel's crown, Fernando's sword and their army's banners.

🏛 Palacio de la Madraza
Calle Oficios 14. 📞 958 24 34 84. ⏰ Mon–Fri. ♿
Originally an Arab university, this building later became the city hall. The façade dates from the 18th-century. Inside there is a Moorish hall with a finely decorated mihrab.

Entrance to the Moorish mihrab in the Palacio de la Madraza

🏛 Corral del Carbón
Calle Mariana Pineda s/n. 📞 958 22 59 90. ⏰ 9am–7pm daily. ♿
This galleried courtyard is a unique relic of the Moorish era. Originally it was a storehouse and inn for merchants. In Christian times it was a venue for theatrical performances; it later became a coal exchange. These days it houses local craft vendors and the main tourist office.

🏛 Casa de los Tiros
Calle Pavaneras 19. 📞 958 22 10 72. ⏰ 2:30–8pm Mon–Fri. ● public hols.
This fortress-like palace was built in Renaissance style in the 16th century. It was once the property of a family who were awarded the Generalife after the fall of Granada *(see pp46–7)*; among their possessions was a sword belonging to Boabdil *(see p47)*. The sword is represented on the façade together with five statues of Hercules, Mercury, Theseus, Hector and Jason. The building owes its name to the muskets in its battlements, *tiros* being the Spanish word for shot.

Reja by Maestro Bartolomé de Jaén enclosing the altar of the Capilla Real

🏛 Mirador de San Nicolás

From this square visitors can enjoy splendid sunset views. Tiled rooftops drop away to the Darro river, on the far side of which stands the Alhambra; the Sierra Nevada provides a suitably dramatic backdrop.

🏛 El Bañuelo

Carrera del Darro 31. ⚟ *958 22 23 39.* ⬤ *10am–2pm Tue–Sat.* ⬤ *public hols.*
These brick-vaulted Arab baths, located near the Darro river, were built in the 11th century. Roman, Visigothic and Arab capitals were all incorporated into the baths' columns.

🏛 Museo Arqueológico

Carrera del Darro 43. ⚟ *958 22 56 40.* ⬤ *2:30–8pm Tue, 9am–8:30pm Wed–Sat, 9am–2:30pm Sun.* ⬤ *public hols.*
The Renaissance Casa de Castril, with a Plateresque portal, houses this museum of Iberian, Phoenician and Roman antiquities, found in the province of Granada.

Cupola in the sanctuary of the Monasterio de la Cartuja

🏛 Palacio Carlos V

Alhambra. ⚟ *958 02 79 00.* ⬤ *9am–2:30pm Tue–Sat.* ⬤ *public hols.*
This palace in the Alhambra houses the Museo Hispano-Musulmán and the Museo de Bellas Artes. The highlight of the quite thrilling Muslim art collection is a most exquisite 15th-century vase from the Alhambra, which has amazing blue and gold designs.

🏛 Monasterio de la Cartuja

⚟ *958 16 19 32.* ⬤ *daily* 🖼
A Christian warrior, El Gran Capitán, donated the land on which this monastery was built in 1516, in thanks for surviving a skirmish with the Moors. A cupola by Antonio Palomino tops the sanctuary. The Churrigueresque sacristy *(see p23)* is by mason Luis de Arévalo and sculptor Luis Cabello.

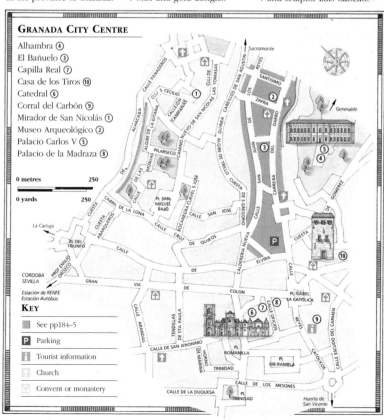

GRANADA CITY CENTRE

Alhambra ④
El Bañuelo ③
Capilla Real ⑦
Casa de los Tiros ⑩
Catedral ⑥
Corral del Carbón ⑨
Mirador de San Nicolás ①
Museo Arqueológico ②
Palacio Carlos V ⑤
Palacio de la Madraza ⑧

0 metres   250

0 yards   250

KEY

▨ See pp184–5

🅿 Parking

ℹ Tourist information

⛪ Church

⛪ Convent or monastery

Street-by-Street: the Albaicín

Ornate plaque for house in the Albaicín

THIS CORNER OF THE CITY, clinging to the hillside opposite the Alhambra, is where one feels closest to the city's Moorish ancestry. A fortress was first built here in the 13th century and there were once over 30 mosques, some of which can still be traced. Along narrow, cobbled alleys stand *cármenes*, villas with Moorish decoration and gardens, secluded from the world by their high walls. In the evening, when the scent of jasmine lingers in the air, take a walk up to the Mirador de San Nicolás. From here the view over a maze of rooftops and the Alhambra glowing in the sunset is magic.

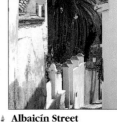

Albaicín Street
Steep and sinuous, the Albaicín streets form a virtual labyrinth. Many street names start with Cuesta, *meaning slope.*

Real Chancillería
Commissioned by the Catholic Monarchs, the Royal Chancery dates from 1530. Its patio is attributed to de Siloé.

0 metres 50
0 yards 50

Casa de los Pisa displays works of art belonging to the Knights Hospitallers, founded by Juan de Dios in the 16th century.

STAR SIGHTS

★ El Bañuelo

★ Museo Arqueológico

★ Iglesia de Santa Ana

★ Iglesia de Santa Ana
At the end of the Plaza Nueva stands this 16th-century brick church in Mudéjar style. It has an elegant Plateresque portal and, inside, a coffered ceiling.

Carrera del Darro

The road along the Río Darro leads past fine façades and crumbling bridges. At the top end, a café-terrace offers views of the Alhambra.

★ Museo Arqueológico

The ornate façade of this museum has Plateresque carvings, including reliefs of mythological figures.

VISITORS' CHECKLIST

Granada. **Road map** D4.
250,000. ✈ 12 km (7 miles) SE of city. 🚌 Avenida de Andalucia s/n (902 24 02 02).
🚆 Carretera de Jaen s/n (958 18 54 80). 🛈 Plaza de Mariana Pineda 12 (958 24 71 28).
W www.turismodegranada.org
Sat & Sun. 🎭 Día de la Cruz (3 May), Corpus Christi (May/Jun).

KEY

– – – Suggested route

To Mirador de San Nicolás

DE LOS REYES

PLAZA CONCEPCION

CARNERO

CONCEPCION BANUELO

CALLE ZAFRA

CALLE GLORIA

CARRETERA DEL SANTISIMO

CARRERA DEL DARRO

RIO DARRO

Convento de Santa Catalina de Zafra was founded in 1521.

To Sacromonte

★ El Bañuelo

Star-shaped openings in the vaults let light into these well-preserved Moorish baths, which were built in the 11th century.

SACROMONTE

Granada's gypsies formerly lived in the caves honeycombing this hillside. Travellers such as Washington Irving *(see p51)* would go there to enjoy spontaneous outbursts of flamenco. Today, virtually all the gypsies have moved away, but touristy flamenco shows of variable quality are still performed here in the evenings *(see p230)*. A Benedictine monastery, the Abadía del Sacromonte, sits at the very top of the hill. Inside, the ashes of San Cecilio, Granada's patron saint, are stored.

Gypsies dancing flamenco, 19th century

Granada: Alhambra

A MAGICAL USE of space, light, water and decoration characterizes this most sensual piece of architecture. It was built under Ismail I, Yusuf I and Muhammad V, caliphs when the Nasrid dynasty (see p46) ruled Granada. Seeking to belie an image of waning power, they constructed their idea of paradise on Earth. Modest materials were used (tiles, plaster and timber), but they were superbly worked. Although the Alhambra suffered from decay and pillage, including an attempt by Napoleon's troops to blow it up, in recent times it has undergone extensive restoration and its delicate craftsmanship still dazzles the eye.

Sala de la Barca

★ Salón de Embajadores
The ceiling of this sumptuous throne room, built between 1334 and 1354, represents the seven heavens of the Muslim cosmos.

★ Patio de Arrayanes
This pool, set amid myrtle hedges and graceful arcades, reflects light into the surrounding halls.

Patio de Machuca

Entrance

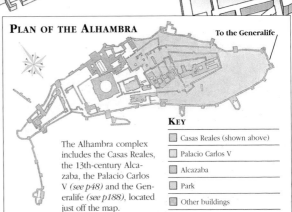

Patio del Mexuar
This council chamber, completed in 1365, was where the reigning sultan listened to the petitions of his subjects and held meetings with his ministers.

PLAN OF THE ALHAMBRA

To the Generalife

The Alhambra complex includes the Casas Reales, the 13th-century Alcazaba, the Palacio Carlos V (see p48) and the Generalife (see p188), located just off the map.

KEY

- [ ] Casas Reales (shown above)
- [ ] Palacio Carlos V
- [ ] Alcazaba
- [ ] Park
- [ ] Other buildings

Palacio del Partal

A tower and its pavilion, with a five-arched portico, are all that remain of the Palacio del Partal, the Alhambra's oldest palace.

Washington Irving's apartments

Baños Reales

Jardín de Lindaraja

The Sala de las Dos Hermanas, with its honeycomb dome, is regarded as the ultimate example of Spanish Islamic architecture.

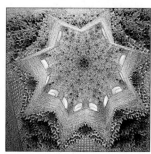

Sala de los Reyes

This great banqueting hall was used to hold extravagant parties and feasts. Beautiful ceiling paintings on leather, from the 14th century, depict tales of hunting and chivalry.

Puerta de la Rawda

★ Sala de los Abencerrajes

This hall takes its name from a noble family, who were rivals of Boabdil (see pp46–7). According to legend, he had them massacred while they attended a banquet here. The pattern of the stalactited ceiling was inspired by Pythagoras' theorem.

The Palacio Carlos V *(see p48), a fine Renaissance building, was added to the Alhambra in 1526.*

★ Patio de los Leones

Built by Muhammad V, this patio is lined with arcades supported by 124 slender marble columns. At its centre a fountain rests on 12 marble lions.

STAR FEATURES

★ **Salón de Embajadores**

★ **Patio de Arrayanes**

★ **Patio de los Leones**

★ **Sala de los Abencerrajes**

Granada: Generalife

LOCATED NORTH OF THE ALHAMBRA, the Generalife was the country estate of the Nasrid kings. Here, they could escape the intrigues of the palace and enjoy tranquillity high above the city, a little closer to heaven. The name Generalife, or Yannat al Arif, has various interpretations, perhaps the most pleasing being "the garden of lofty paradise". The gardens, begun in the 13th century, have been modified over the years. They originally contained orchards and pastures for animals. The Generalife provides a magical setting for Granada's yearly International Music and Dance Festival (see p33).

Patio de la Acequia
This enclosed oriental garden is built round a long central pool. Rows of water jets make graceful arches above it.

Sala Regia

Jardines Altos (Upper Gardens)

The Escalera de Agua is a staircase with water flowing gently down i

The Patio de los Cipreses, otherwise known as the Patio de la Sultana, was the secret meeting place for Soraya, wife of the Sultan Abu l Hasan, and her lover, the chief of the Abencerrajes.

Entrance

The Patio de Polo was the courtyard where palace visitors, arriving on horseback, would leave their horses.

Patio del Generalife
Leading up from the Alhambra to the Generalife are the Jardines Bajos (lower gardens). Above them, just before the main compound, is the Patio del Generalife.

The majestic peaks of the Sierra Nevada towering, in places, over 3,000 m (9,800 ft) above sea level

Sierra Nevada ⑨

Granada. **Road map** E4. 🚌 *from Granada.* 🏛 *Plaza Andalucía s/n, Cetursa Sierra Nevada (958 24 91 19).* 🌐 *www.sierranevadaski.com*

Fourteen peaks, more than 3,000 m (9,800 ft) high, crown the heights of the Sierra Nevada. The snow lingers until July and begins falling again in late autumn. Europe's highest road runs past the ski resort of Solynieve, at 2,100 m (6,890 ft), and skirts the two highest peaks, **Pico Veleta** at 3,398 m (11,145 ft) and **Mulhacén** at 3,482 m (11,420 ft). Its altitude and closeness to the Mediterranean account for the range of fauna and flora native to this mountain range. It is a habitat for golden eagles, rare butterflies and many wild flowers.

Visitors should take precautions for their safety. There are several mountain refuges, but hikers and climbers should let someone know their route and take tents, food and the right equipment in case they get lost or meet bad weather and cannot find a refuge.

Las Alpujarras ⑩

See pp190–91.

Laujar de Andarax ⑪

Almería. **Road map** E4. 🚶 *2,000.* 🏛 *Carretera Laujar–Berja km 1 (950 51 35 48).* 🎉 *3 & 17 of each month.*

Laujar, in the arid foothills of the Sierra Nevada, looks across the Andarax valley towards the Sierra de Gador. In this area the grapes are grown to eat but in the town a hearty red wine is produced. A legend says that the village was founded by Noah's grandson. In the 16th century, Aben Humeya, leader of a rebellion by the Moors *(see p48)*, made his base at Laujar. Christian troops crushed the rebellion cruelly and Abén Humeya was then murdered by his treacherous followers. The Moors were eventually expelled.

The 17th-century **Iglesia de la Encarnación** has a statue of the Virgin by the Granada

Painting, la Encarnación

sculptor Alonso Cano. Next to the 18th-century Baroque **Ayuntamiento** is a fountain bearing a plaque with lines by the poet and dramatist Francisco Villespesa, born in the village in 1877:

"Six fountains has my pueblo And he who drinks their waters Will never forget them, So heavenly is their taste."

A pleasant park and picnic spot has been created east of the town, at El Nacimiento.

Lacalahorra ⑫

Granada. **Road map** E4. 🚌 *Guadix.* 📞 *958 67 70 98.* 🕐 *10am–1pm, 4–6pm Wed.*

Grim, immensely thick walls with cylindrical towers encircle Lacalahorra, a castle perched on a hillock above the village. Rodrigo de Mendoza, son of Cardinal Mendoza, ordered the castle to be built for his bride between 1509 and 1512, using architects and craftsmen from Italy. Inside is a two-storey, Renaissance courtyard with a staircase and Carrara marble pillars.

The castle of Lacalahorra above the village of the same name

Whitewashed cave dwellings in the troglodyte quarter of Guadix

Guadix ❸

Granada. **Road map** E4. 👤 *20,000.*
🚌 🚉 ℹ️ *Avenida Mariana Pineda s/n*
(958 66 26 65). 📅 *Sat.*

THE TROGLODYTE QUARTER, with 2,000 caves that have been inhabited for centuries, is the town's most remarkable sight. The cave dwellers say they prefer living in caves because the temperature remains constant all year. The **Museo Al Fareria** and **Municipal Etnologica** museums show how they live underground.

Around 2,000 years ago Guadix had iron, copper and silver mines. The town thrived under the Moors and after the Reconquest (*see pp46–7*), but declined in the 18th century.

Relics of San Torcuato, who established the first Christian bishopric in Spain, are kept in the Cathedral museum. The **Catedral**, begun in 1594 by Diego de Siloé, was later finished between 1701 and 1796 by Gaspar Cayón and Vicente de Acero. Near the 9th-century **Alcazaba**, the town's Mudéjar **Iglesia de Santiago** has a fine coffered ceiling. **Palacio de Peñaflor**, dating from the 16th century, is now fully restored.

🏛 **Cueva-Museo Al Fareria**
C/San Miguel. ⬜ *daily.* 📷
🏛 **Municipal Etnologica**
Ermita Nueva s/n. ⬜ *daily.* 📷

Baza ❹

Granada. **Road map** E3. 👤 *20,000.*
🚌 ℹ️ *Plaza Mayor s/n (958 86 13 25).*
📅 *Wed.* 🌐 *www.altipla.com/baza/*

IMPRESSIVE EVIDENCE of ancient cultures based around Baza came to light in 1971, when a large, seated, female figure was

---

A Tour of Las Alpujarras ❿

LAS ALPUJARRAS lie on the southern slopes of the Sierra Nevada. The villages in this area cling to valley sides clothed with oak and walnut trees. Their flat-roofed houses are distinctive and seen nowhere else in Andalusia. Local food is rustic. A speciality is *plato alpujarreño:* pork fillet, ham, sausage and blood sausage, accompanied by a pinkish wine from the Contraviesa mountains. Local crafts include handwoven rugs (*see p228*) and curtains with Moorish-influenced designs.

Trevélez ④
Trevélez, in the shadow of Mulhacén, is built in typical Alpujarran style and is famous for its cured hams.

Orgiva ①
This is the largest town of the region, with a Baroque church in the main street and a lively Thursday market.

Poqueira Valley ②
Three villages typical of Las Alpujarras in this picturesque river valley are Capileira, Bubión and Pampaneira.

Fuente Agria ③
People come here from far and wide to drink the iron-rich, naturally carbonated waters.

▲ MULHACÉN
3,482 m
11,420 ft

S I E R R A

Trevélez

GR421

Juviles

Pórtugos

Pitres

GR413

Guadalfeo

A348

A348

LANJARÓN
GRANADA

SIERRA DE LA

found in a necropolis. She is the Dama de Baza (see p41), believed to represent an Iberian goddess, and estimated to be 2,400 years old. Subsequently, she was removed to the Museo Arqueológico in Madrid but a replica can be still seen in the **Museo Arqueológico** in Baza.

The Renaissance **Colegiata de Santa María**, nearby, has a Plateresque entrance and a fine 18th-century tower.

During the first few days of September a riotous fiesta takes place (see p34). An emissary, El Cascamorras, is despatched from the neighbouring town of Guadix to try to bring back a coveted image of the Virgin from Baza's **Convento de la Merced**. He is covered in oil and chased back to Guadix by youths, also covered in oil. There, he is taunted again for returning empty-handed.

🏛 **Museo Arqueológico**
Plaza Mayor s/n. ☎ 958 86 19 47.
◯ 10am–2pm, 5–7pm daily.

Vélez Blanco ⑮

Almería. **Road map** F3. 🏚 2,200. 🚌
Vélez Rubio. ℹ Centro de Visitantes Almacén del Trigo, Avenida Marqués de los Vélez s/n (950 41 53 54). 🛒 Wed.

DOMINATING THIS pleasant little village is the mighty **Castillo de Vélez Blanco**. It was built from 1506 to 1513 by the first Marquis de Los Vélez, and its interior richly

The village of Vélez Blanco, overlooked by a 16th-century castle

adorned by Italian craftsmen. Unfortunately for the visitor its Renaissance splendour has since been ripped out and shipped to the Metropolitan Museum of New York. There is, however, a reconstruction of one of the original patios.

A blend of Gothic, Renaissance and Mudéjar styles (see pp22–3) can be seen in the **Iglesia de Santiago**, located in the village's main street.

Just outside Vélez Blanco is the **Cueva de los Letreros**, which contains paintings from around 4000 BC. One image depicts a horned man holding sickles; another the Indalo, a figure believed to be a deity with magical powers, still used as a symbol of Almería.

♣ **Castillo de Vélez Blanco**
☎ 607 41 50 55.
◯ Thu–Tue. 🖼
⋔ **Cueva de los Letreros**
Camino de la Cueva de los Letreros.
☎ 617 88 28 08.
◯ noon–4pm daily. 🖼

Yegen ⑥
A plaque marks the house where Gerald Brenan, the author of South from Granada, lived in the 1920s.

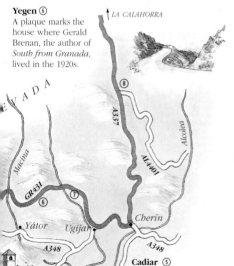

↑ LA CALAHORRA

Puerto de la Ragua ⑧
This pass, which leads across the mountains to Guadix, is nearly 2,000 m (6,560 ft) high and often snowbound in winter.

Válor ⑦
Aben Humeya, leader of a rebellion by Moriscos (see p48), was born in this village. A commemorative battle between Moors and Christians is staged each year in mid-September (see p34).

Cadiar ⑤
A fountain in the centre of this town runs with wine during the October fiesta (see p34).

KEY

▦▦	Tour route
==	Other roads
▲	Mountain peak

0 kilometres 10

0 miles 5

TIPS FOR DRIVERS

Tour length: 85 km (56 miles).
Stopping-off points: Orgiva and Trevélez have bars, restaurants and hotels (see p209). Bubión has hotels and one good restaurant (see p221). Capileira has bars and restaurants. Orgiva is the last petrol stop before Cadiar.

Almería ⑱

Taking a break in the Plaza Vieja

A COLOSSAL FORTRESS bears witness to Almería's golden age, when it was an important port for the Caliphate of Córdoba. Known as al Mariyat (the Mirror of the Sea), the city was a centre for trade and textile industries, with silk, cotton and brocade among its chief exports. After the city fell to the Catholic Monarchs *(see pp46–7)* in 1489, it went into decline for the next 300 years. During the 19th and early 20th centuries, mining and a new port revived the city's fortunes, but this period ended abruptly with the start of the Civil War *(see pp52–3)*. Today a North African air still pervades the city, with its flat-roofed houses, desert-like environs and palm trees. North African faces are common as ferries link the city with Morocco.

Detail of the Renaissance portal of Almería cathedral

The 10th-century Alcazaba overlooking the old town of Almería

♜ Alcazaba

C/ Almanzor s/n. ▮ *950 27 16 17.*
◯ *Tue–Sun.* ◼ *25 Dec, 1 Jan.*
Fine views over the city are offered by this 1,000-year old Moorish fortress. It has recently been undergoing restoration and within its walls are pleasant gardens and a Mudéjar chapel. It was the largest fortress built by the Moors and covered an area of more than 25,000 sq m (269,000 sq ft). The walls extend for 430 m (1,410 ft). Abd al Rahman III started construction in AD 955, but there were considerable additions later. The fort withstood two major sieges but fell to the Catholic Monarchs *(see pp46–7)* in 1489. Their coat of arms can be seen on the Torre del Homenaje, which was built during the monarchs' reign.

In the past, a bell in the Alcazaba was rung to advise the farmers in the surrounding countryside when irrigation was allowed. Bells were also rung to warn the citizens of Almería when pirates had been sighted off the coast.

It is inadvisable for visitors to wander around the Alcazaba district alone or after dark.

⛪ Catedral

From North Africa, Berber pirates would often raid Almería. Consequently, the cathedral looks more like a fortress than a place of worship, with four towers, thick walls and small windows. A mosque once stood on the site. It was later converted to a Christian temple, but destroyed by an earthquake in 1522. Work began on the present building in 1524 under the direction of Diego de Siloé. Juan de Orea designed the Renaissance façade. He also created the beautifully carved walnut choir stalls. The naves and high altar are Gothic.

⛪ Templo San Juan

Traces of Almería's most important mosque can still be seen here – one wall of the present church is Moorish. Inside is a 12th-century mihrab, a prayer niche with cupola. The church, built over the mosque, was damaged in the Spanish Civil War and abandoned until 1979. It has since been restored.

⛲ Plaza Vieja

Also known as the Plaza de la Constitución, this is a 17th-century arcaded square. On one side of the square is the Ayuntamiento, a flamboyant building with a cream and pink façade dating from 1899.

The pedestrianized 17th-century Plaza Vieja, surrounded by elegant arcades

Puerta de Purchena

Located at the heart of the city, the Puerta de Purchena was once one of the main gateways in the city walls. From it run a number of shopping streets, including the wide Paseo de Almería. A tree-lined thoroughfare, this is the focus of city life, with its cafés, Teatro Cervantes and nearby food market.

Centro Rescate de la Fauna Sahariana

C/ General Segura 1. **[** 950 28 10 45. **[** 8am–3pm Mon–Fri.

At the rear of the Alcazaba, this rescue centre shelters endangered species from the Sahara, in particular different kinds of gazelle. Having flourished in Almería's arid climate, some animals have been shipped to restock African nature reserves.

La Chanca

This gypsy and fishermen's quarter is near the Alcazaba. A number of families live in caves decorated with

Brightly coloured entrance to a gypsy cave in La Chanca district

flowers and brightly painted façades (though the interiors are modern). On Mondays a lively street market is held.

Though this area is picturesque, it is also desperately poor; it is unwise to walk around with valuables or at night.

ENVIRONS: One of the most important examples of a Copper Age settlement in Europe, **Los Millares**, lies

Saharan gazelle

VISITORS' CHECKLIST

Almería. **Road map** 4F.
170,000. Plaza de la Estación (902 24 02 02). Plaza de la Estación (950 26 20 98). **[i]** Parque Nicolás Salmerón s/n (950 27 43 55). Tue, Fri & Sat. Semana Santa (Easter), Feria de Almería (last week Aug). **W** www.andalucia.org

17 km (10.5 miles) north of Almería. As many as 2,000 people occupied the site from around 2700 to 1800 BC (see pp40–41). Discovered in 1891, remains of houses, defensive ramparts and a necropolis that contains more than 100 tombs have since been uncovered.

The community here lived from agriculture but also had the capability to forge tools, arms and adornments from copper, which was mined in the nearby of Sierra de Gador.

Los Millares

Santa Fé de Mondújar. **[** 677 90 34 04. **[** 10am–2pm Wed–Sun.

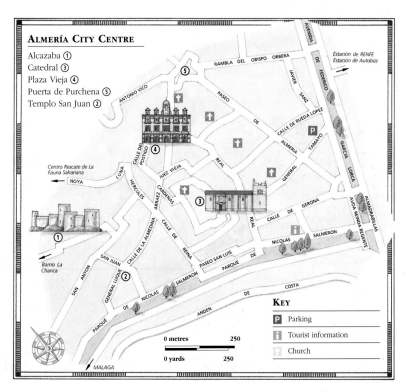

ALMERÍA CITY CENTRE

Alcazaba ①
Catedral ③
Plaza Vieja ④
Puerta de Purchena ⑤
Templo San Juan ②

Centro Rescate de La Fauna Sahariana

Estación de RENFE
Estación de Autobús

Barrio La Chanca

KEY

P Parking

[i] Tourist information

Church

0 metres   250

0 yards   250

SPAGHETTI WESTERNS

Two Wild West towns lie off the N340 highway west of Tabernas. Here, visitors can re-enact classic film scenes or watch stunt men performing bank hold-ups and saloon brawls. The Poblados del Oeste were built during the 1960s and early 1970s when low costs and eternal sunshine made Almería the ideal location for spaghetti westerns. Sergio Leone, director of *The Good, the Bad and the Ugly*, built a ranch here and film-sets sprang up in the desert. Local gypsies played Indians and Mexicans. The deserts and Arizona-style badlands are still used occasionally for television commercials and series, and by film directors such as Steven Spielberg.

Still from *For a Few Dollars More* by Sergio Leone

Macael 🔟

Almería. **Road map** F3. 👥 *6,000.*
🚌 ℹ️ *Ayuntamiento, Plaza de la Constitución 1 (950 12 81 13).* 🚆 *Fri.*

Macael is the centre of an important marble industry. Scores of local companies carve and polish the marble, which comes in white, veined grey and green. The finished product has been employed in many fine buildings, including the Alhambra in Granada *(see pp186–7)*. To the east is Purchena, where there are the remains of a strategic Moorish castle. One notable local dish is the *fritada de Purchena*, a mixture of fried tomatoes and peppers, which makes a great partner for meat dishes.

Tabernas 🔟

Almería. **Road map** F4. 👥 *3,000.*
🚌 ℹ️ *on main road (950 52 50 30).* 🚆 *Wed.*

A Moorish hilltop fortress presides over the town of Tabernas and the surrounding dusty, cactus-dotted scenery of eroded hills and dried-out riverbeds. The harsh, rugged scenery has figured in many so-called spaghetti westerns.
Not far from Tabernas is a solar energy research centre, where hundreds of heliostats follow the course of southern Andalusia's powerful sun.

Almería 🔟

See pp192–3.

Parque Natural de Cabo de Gata 🔟

Almería. **Road map** F4. 🚌 *to San José.* ℹ️ *Centro de Visitantes de las Amoladeras, Carretera Cabo de Gata km 6 (950 16 04 35).*
Park 🕙 *10am–3pm daily.*

Towering cliffs of volcanic rock, sand dunes, salt flats, secluded coves and a few fishing settlements can be found in the 29,000-ha (71,700-acre) Parque Natural de Cabo de Gata. The end of the cape, near the Arrecife de las Sirenas (Sirens' Reef), is marked by a lighthouse. The park includes a stretch of sea-bed about 2 km (1.2 miles) wide, which allows protection of the marine flora and fauna; the clear waters attract divers and snorkellers.
The area of dunes and salt-pans between the cape and the Playa de San Miguel is a habitat for thorny jujube trees. Thousands of migrating birds stop here en route to and

from Africa. Among the 170 or so bird species recorded in the park there are flamingoes, avocets, Dupont's larks and griffon vultures. Attempts are also being made to reintroduce the monk seal, which died out in the 1970s. At the northern end of the park, where there is a cormorants' fishing area, is Punta de los Muertos, ("dead man's point"); this takes its name from the bodies of shipwrecked sailors that are said to have washed ashore there.

San José 🔟

Almería. **Road map** F4. 👥 *1,000.* 🚌
ℹ️ *Calle Correos s/n (950 38 02 99).*
🚆 *Sun (Easter & summer).*

Located on a fine, sandy bay, San José is a small but fast-growing sea resort within the Parque Natural de Cabo de Gata. Rising behind it is the arid **Sierra de Cabo de Gata**, a range of bleak grandeur.

Lighthouse overlooking the cliffs of the Parque Natural de Cabo de Gata

The harbour at the traditional fishing village of La Isleta

Nearby are fine beaches, including Playa de los Genoveses *(see p31)*. Along the coast are **Rodalquilar**, a town once important for gold-mining, and **La Isleta**, a fishing hamlet.

Níjar ㉑

Almería. **Road map** F4. *3,000.* *Plaza García Blanes, Bajo (950 36 01 23).* *Wed.*

SET AMID a lush oasis of citrus trees on the edge of the Sierra Alhamilla, Níjar's fame stems from the colourful pottery and the *jarapas*, hand-woven rugs and blankets, that are made here. The town's historic quarter is typical of Andalusia, with narrow, streets and wrought-iron balconies.

The **Iglesia de Nuestra Señora de la Anunciación**, dating from the 16th century, has a coffered Mudéjar ceiling, delicately inlaid. The barren plain between Níjar and the sea has begun to blossom recently, thanks to irrigation.

In Spanish minds, the name of Níjar is closely associated with a poignant and violent incident that occurred here in the 1920s, and which later became the subject of a play by Federico García Lorca.

Sorbas ㉒

Almería. **Road map** F4. *3,000.* *Centro de Visitantes los Yesares, Calle Terraplen, 9 (950 36 44 76).* *Thu.*

BALANCED ON THE edge of a deep chasm, Sorbas overlooks the Río de Aguas, which flows far below. There are two buildings in this village worth a look: the 16th-century **Iglesia de Santa María** and a 17th-century mansion said to have once been a summer retreat for the Duke of Alba.

Another point of interest for visitors is the traditional, rustic earthenware turned out and sold by Sorbas' local potters.

Located near to Sorbas is the peculiar **Yesos de Sorbas** nature reserve. This is an unusual region of karst, where water action has carved out hundreds of subterranean galleries and chambers in the limestone and gypsum strata. Speleologists are allowed to explore the caves, but only if they are granted permission by Andalusia's environmental department. On the surface, the green, fertile valley of the Río de Aguas cuts through dry, eroded hills. Local wildlife in this area includes tortoises and peregrine falcons.

Mojácar ㉓

Almería. **Road map** F4. *7,000.* *Calle Glorieta, 1 (950 61 50 25).* *Wed & Sun.*

FROM A DISTANCE, the village of Mojácar shimmers like the mirage of a Moorish citadel, its white houses cascading over a lofty ridge near to the sea. The village was taken by the Christians in 1488 and the Moors were later expelled. In the years after the Spanish Civil War *(see pp52–3)* the village fell into ruin, as much of its population emigrated. In the 1960s Mojácar was discovered by tourists, giving rise to a new era of prosperity. The old gateway in the walls is still here, but otherwise the village has been completely rebuilt.

***Pensión* façade in the picturesque, recently rebuilt village of Mojácar**

BLOOD WEDDING AT NÍJAR

Bodas de Sangre (Blood Wedding), a play by Federico García Lorca *(see p53)*, is based on a tragic event that occurred in 1928 near the town of Níjar. A woman called Paquita la Coja agreed, under pressure from her sister, to marry a suitor, Casimiro. A few hours before the ceremony, however, she fled with her cousin. Casimiro felt humiliated and Paquita's sister, who had hoped to benefit from the dowry, was furious. The cousin was found shot dead and Paquita half-strangled. Paquita's sister and her husband, Casimiro's brother, were found guilty of the crime. Shamed by this horrific scenario, Paquita hid from the world until her death in 1987. Lorca never visited Níjar, but based his play on newspaper reports.

The dramatist Federico García Lorca (1899 – 1936)

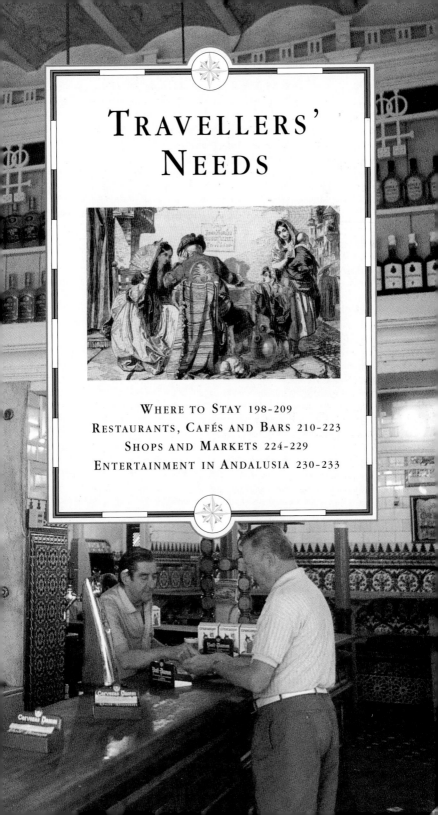

TRAVELLERS' NEEDS

WHERE TO STAY

SOME OF THE MOST charming places to stay in Spain are in Andalusia. They range from restored castles to family guesthouses, and from one of the most luxurious hotels in Europe to an organic farm deep in the countryside. For budget travel there are pensions and youth hostels, and for hikers there are mountain refuges. A night or two in a bed and breakfast is becoming

Doorman, Hotel Alfonso XIII

an increasingly popular option in rural areas. Apartments and village houses throughout the region are let by the week for self-catering holidays. Andalusia's climate is also ideal for camping, which can be a cheaper alternative.

The listings on pages 205–209 describe some of the region's best hotels in every style and all price ranges, from basic to luxurious.

The Hospedería de San Francisco in Palma del Río *(see p207)*

WHERE TO LOOK

IN SEVILLE, THE MOST appealing places to stay are mainly in the centre of town, especially around the Santa Cruz district *(see pp68–81)*, where there is a broad range of hotels. As in most cities, the cheapest hotels tend to be found around the railway station. Parking can be a problem in the town centre, so if you want a hotel with a garage or a private car park,

you may have to look around the city's outer suburbs. A reasonable alternative is to stay in a town close to Seville, such as Carmona *(see pp128–9)*.

Granada has two main hotel districts: around the Alhambra *(see pp186–7)*, which is quiet, and around the centre, which is livelier, noisier and usually cheaper. Central hotels make the best base for going out on the town at night.

In Córdoba the Judería *(see pp136–7)* is the most convenient place to stay if you plan to get around on foot. If you have a car, you may prefer a hotel on the outskirts of the city.

Hotels in Andalusia's coastal resorts are mainly the modern chains that cater for package holiday-makers or jet-setters. If you want somewhere more relaxing, there are good small hotels a short way inland; the countryside here is dotted with them. Look out for them in the white towns between Arcos de la Frontera *(see p167)* and Ronda *(see pp168–9)*, and around Cazorla *(see p152)*.

HOTEL GRADING AND FACILITIES

HOTELS IN ANDALUSIA are awarded categories and stars by the regional tourist authorities. Hotels (H is the abbreviation) are awarded between one and five stars and pensions (P) between one and two stars. The star-rating system assesses the quantity of facilities a hotel has (such as whether there is a lift or air-conditioning) rather than the quality of service to expect. Most hotels have restaurants which can be used by non-residents. Hotel-Residencias (HR), however, do not have dining rooms, although they may serve breakfast.

PARADORS

PARADORS are government-run hotels which fall into the three- to five-star classifications. The best ones occupy historic monuments, such as castles, monasteries, palaces and old hunting lodges, but a

The hillside terrace of the Alhambra Palace hotel *(see p209)*, with views across Granada

◁ **Bar on Calle Gerona, Seville**

number of them have been purpose-built in attractive settings. Though a parador will not always be the best hotel in town, they can be counted on to deliver a predictable level of comfort: regional dishes will always be on the menu and rooms are generally comfortable and often spacious. The bedroom furniture varies little from parador to parador.

If you are travelling around the paradors during high season, or intending to stay in smaller paradors, it is wise to book ahead through agents for the paradors *(see p201)*.

PRICES

HOTELS ARE OBLIGED by law to display their range of prices behind reception and in every room. As a rule the more stars a hotel has the more you pay. Rates for a double room start from 10 euros per night in a cheap one-star pension and can go as high as 180 euros in a five-star hotel.

Prices vary according to the room, and the region and season. The rural hotels are generally cheaper than the city ones. All the prices quoted on pages 205–9 are based on the rates for mid-season or high-season. High season is usually July and August, but it can also run from April to October. City hotels charge inflated rates during major *fiestas*, such as Semana Santa *(see p36)* in Seville.

Swimming pool in a courtyard of the Hotel Alfaros, Córdoba *(see p206)*

Five-star hotel restaurant logo

Note that the majority of hotels will quote prices per room and meal prices per person without *IVA* (VAT).

BOOKING AND CHECKING IN

YOU DO NOT NEED to book ahead if you are travelling off-season in rural Andalusia, unless you want to stay in a particular hotel. On the other hand, it is essential to reserve rooms by phone or through a travel agent if you travel in high season. You will also need to reserve if you want a specific room or one on the ground floor, with a good view, with a double bed (twin beds are the norm), or away from a noisy road. Hotels in many coastal resorts close between autumn and spring, so check before you travel that any hotels you want to stay in are sure to be open.

Some hotels will request a deposit of 20–25 per cent for booking during peak times, or for a long stay. Send it by a giro in Spain and by banker's draft from abroad. Try to make cancellations at least a week in advance, or you may lose all or some of your deposit. A reserved room will be held only until 8pm unless you can inform the hotel that you are going to arrive late.

When you book in you will be asked for your passport or identity card, to comply with police regulations. It will be returned to you when your details have been copied.

You are expected to check out of your room by noon or to pay for another night.

PAYING

HOTELS WHICH TAKE credit cards are indicated in the listings *(see pp205–9)*. In some large and busy hotels you may be asked at reception to sign a blank credit card pay slip on arrival. Under Spanish law it is fraudulent to ask you to do this and you are advised to refuse to sign.

Although some hotels will accept a Eurocheque, no hotel in Andalusia will take an ordinary cheque, even when it is backed by a guarantee card or drawn on a Spanish bank.

In Spain it is customary to tip the porter and the chambermaid in a hotel by 1–2 euros. The usual tip to leave in hotel restaurants is 5–10 per cent of the bill although some restaurants will have already included a service charge.

Seville's beautiful Hotel San Gil *(see p205)*, in a former mansion

Interior of Hostal de San José, Aguilar

SELF-CATERING

Villas and holiday flats let by the week are plentiful along the Costa del Sol and the coasts of Granada and Almería. Inland, an increasing number of village and farm houses are now also being let all over the region. In the UK, a number of private companies, among them **The Individual Traveller's Spain**, act as agents for owners of apartments and houses. Many agents belong to an organization called the **RAAR** (Red Andaluza de Alojamientos Rurales or Andalusian Rural Accommodation Network), through which it is possible to make direct bookings.

Prices charged for self-catering accommodation sometimes vary considerably: prices are determined by location, the season and type of property. A four-person villa with a pool costs as little as 240 euros for a week if it is inland and up to and over 950 euros per week if it is in a prime coastal location.

Another possibility is the *villa turística* (holiday village) which is half hotel, half holiday apartments. The guests can hire rooms with kitchens and use a restaurant.

BED AND BREAKFAST

Andalusia's 20 or more *casas rurales* offering bed and breakfast range from a stately *cortijo* (manor house) to a small organic farm. Do not expect usual hotel service or a long list of facilities. However, you may be met with a friendly welcome and be spoiled with good home cooking.

A stay at a bed and breakfast can be booked through **RAAR**, the owners' association, or directly. If you are booking from abroad you may be asked to send a 10 per cent deposit and to stay for at least two nights.

YOUTH HOSTELS AND MOUNTAIN REFUGES

To use Andalusia's extensive network of *albergues juveniles* (youth hostels) you have to buy an international YHA card from a hostel or show a card from your country. Bed and breakfast costs between 5 and 10 euros per person. You can book a bed or room in a hostel directly or through the central booking office of Inturjoven – **Central de Reservas de Inturjoven**.

If you backpack in remote mountain areas, you can stay in *refugios*, which are shelters with basic kitchens and dormitories. The *refugios* are marked on all good large-scale maps of the mountains and national parks. They are administered by the **Federación Andaluza de Montañismo**.

DIRECTORY

HOTELS

Asociación de Hoteles de Sevilla
Calle San Pablo 1, Casa A Bajo, 41001 Seville.
☎ 95 422 15 38.

Asociación de Hoteles Rurales de Andalucía (AHRA)
Calle Ramal Hoyo, Edificio el Congreso,1 Local 82–83, 29620 Torremolinos.
☎ 952 37 87 75.
FAX 952 37 87 84.

PARADORS

Central de Reservas
Calle Requena 3, 28013 Madrid. ☎ 91 516 66 66.
FAX 915 16 66 57/58.
W www.parador.es

Keytel
402 Edgware Road, London W2 1ED.
☎ (020) 7616 0300.
W www.keytel.co.uk

SELF-CATERING & BED & BREAKFAST

RAAR
Apto 2035, 04080 Almería.
☎ 950 26 50 18.
FAX 950 27 04 31.

The Individual Traveller's Spain
Bignor, Pulborough, West Sussex RH20 1QD.
☎ (08700) 780 194.

YOUTH HOSTELS

Central de Reservas de Inturjoven
Calle Miño 24, 41011 Seville. **Map** 3 A4.
☎ 90 251 00 00.
FAX 95 503 58 40.

MOUNTAIN REFUGES

Federación Andaluza de Montañismo,
Camino de Ronda 101, edificio Atalaya 1ª planta, oficina 7G, 18003 Granada.
☎ 958 29 13 40.
(Mon–Thu 10am–2pm, 5–9pm; Fri 9am–1pm).
W www.fedamon.com

CAMPING

Club de Camping y Caravanning de Andalucía
Calle Francisco Carrión Mejías 13, 41003 Seville.
☎ 954 22 77 66.

Camping and Caravanning Club
Coventry, UK.
☎ 024 7669 4995.

DISABLED

Viajes 2000
Paseo de la Castellana 228–30, 28046 Madrid.
☎ 91 323 10 29.
FAX 91 314 73 07.
W www.viajes2000.com

IHD
EURL, Boîte Postale 62, 83480 Puget-sur-Argens, France.
☎ (0494) 81 61 51.
FAX (0494) 81 61 43.

GENERAL INFO

Dirección General de Fomento y Promocion Turistica de la Junta de Andalucía
Torneo, 26, 41071 Seville.
☎ 95 503 07 00.
FAX 95 446 47 44. W www.juntadeandalucia.es

The rustic-style youth hostel, Cazorla, on the edge of the nature reserve

CAMP SITES

THERE ARE MORE THAN 110 camp sites scattered across the region of Andalusia, many of them along the coasts but there are also some outside the major cities and in the popular countryside areas. Most have electricity and running water; some also have launderettes, restaurants, shops, play areas for children and pools.

It is a wise to take with you a camping *carnet* (card). It can be used to check in at sites, and it also gives you third-party insurance. *Carnets* are issued by the AA, the RAC, and by camping and caravanning clubs.

A map of all the region's camp sites, entitled *Campings en Andalucía*, is published by the regional tourist authority, the **Dirección General de Turismo, Junta de Andalucía**.

DISABLED TRAVELLERS

HOTEL MANAGERS will advise on wheelchair access and staff will always assist, but few hotels are equipped for the disabled. However, some of the youth hostels are.

RADAR *(see p239)*, the Royal Association for Disability and Rehabilitation, publishes a useful booklet called *Holidays and Travel Abroad*, and **Holiday Care Service** *(see p239)* publishes a fact sheet on Spain.

In Spain, the Confederación Coordinadora Estatal de Minusválidos Fisicos de España, also known as **Servi-COCEMFE** *(see p239)*, and **Viajes 2000**

have details of hotels with special facilities in Andalusia.

IHD (International Help for the Disabled) arrange accessible accommodation, nurses, transport and other help for visitors to the Costa del Sol who have special needs.

FURTHER INFORMATION

EVERY YEAR the **Dirección General de Turismo** in Andalusia publishes its *Guía de Hoteles, Pensiones, Apartamentos, Campings y Agencias de Viajes*. This gives the star-ratings and a resumé of facilities of all hotels, pensions, camp sites and youth hostels in the area.

Having chosen the type of accommodation you want and where you want to stay, it is wise to fax or phone directly to obtain the most up-to-date information on prices and facilities. In the

Logo for a five-star hotel

hotel listings *(pp204–209)*, the hotels have been listed under higher rather than lower price bands. This means that prices for specific rooms on certain nights, or for an apartment or pension out of season, may turn out to be cheaper.

El Nacimiento bed and breakfast hotel, Almería *(see p209)*

Andalusia's Best: Paradors

PARADOR IS AN OLD SPANISH WORD for a lodging place for travellers of respectable rank. In the late 1920s a national network of state-run hotels called Paradors was established. Many of them are converted castles, palaces or monasteries, although some have been purpose-built in strategic tourist locations. The paradors are generally well sign-posted, making them easy to find. All offer a high degree of comfort and service and have restaurants in which regional cuisine is served.

Parador de Ronda
This parador sits on the edge of the Tajo gorge, opposite Ronda's old town. Some rooms have incomparable views. (See p208.)

Parador de Carmona
Carmona's Moorish-style parador, in the palace of Pedro the Cruel, makes a relaxing base from which to explore nearby Seville. (See p206.)

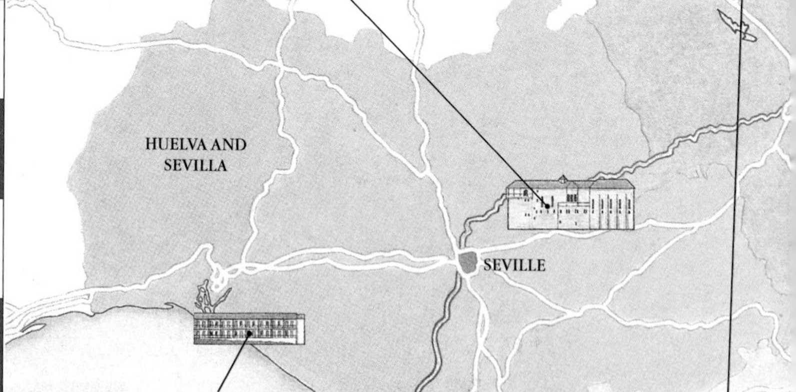

HUELVA AND
SEVILLA

SEVILLE

CADIZ AND
MALAGA

Parador de Mazagón
This purpose-built parador, in a peaceful and scenic spot near a long sandy beach, makes a convenient base for exploring the Coto Doñana. (See p206.)

**Parador de Arcos
de la Frontera**
Situated in one of the archetypal pueblos blancos (white towns) this parador has a wide terrace offering panoramic views over the river Guadalete. (See p207.)

| 0 metres | 500 |
| 0 yards | 500 |

Parador de Jaén
A re-created fortress, complete with small arched windows and vaulted chambers, this parador stands on top of a hill above the city. (See p207.)

Parador de Cazorla
A secluded mountain lodge, Cazorla's parador is set amid the dense forests of one of the principal nature reserves in Andalusia, close to the source of the Guadalquivir river. (See p206.)

Parador de Úbeda
This is one of many fine Renaissance buildings in Úbeda. It has a delightful patio fringed by slender columns. (See p207.)

CORDOBA
AND JAEN

GRANADA
AND ALMERIA

Parador de Granada
Advance booking is essential if you want to stay in this atmospheric 15th-century convent, built in the gardens of the Alhambra at the instruction of the Catholic Monarchs. (See p209.)

Parador de Mojácar
A modern white building, imitating the Cubist style of Mojácar's architecture, this parador stands by a beach and has a spacious sun terrace. (See p209.)

Choosing a Hotel

THIS CHOOSING CHART is a quick reference guide to hotels in Seville, Córdoba and Granada, and to Andalusia's best paradors. These and a selection of other hotels in Andalusia are described in detail on the following pages. Between them they offer a broad range of prices and facilities to suit all needs and pockets. For information on other types of accommodation see pages 198–201.

	Price	Number of Rooms	Family Rooms	Hotel Parking	Restaurant	Swimming Pool	Attractive Views	Quiet Location
SEVILLE CITY CENTRE *(see p205)*								
Hostal Goya	€€	20	●					■
Hotel Simón	€€€	30	●					
Hotel Baco	€€€	25	●		●			
Ciudad de Sevilla	€€€€	94	●	■	●	■		■
Taberna del Alabardero	€€€€€	7	●	■	●		●	
NH Plaza de Armas	€€€€€	262	●	■	●	■	●	
Hotel San Gil	€€€€€	60	●	■		■		■
Alfonso XIII	€€€€€	146	●	■	●	■		
Hotel Doña María	€€€€€	69	●	■		■	●	
Hotel Adriano	€€€€€	34	●	■				
CÓRDOBA *(see pp206–7)*								
Hotel Maestre	€	26		■				
Alfaros	€€€€	133	●	■	●	■		
Occidental	€€€€€	153	●	■	●	■		■
GRANADA *(see pp208–9)*								
Hotel Guadalupe	€€€	58	●	■	●		●	
Reina Cristina	€€€	43	●	■	●			
Hotel Palacio de Santa Inés	€€€€	35	●				●	
Alhambra Palace	€€€€€	126	●		●		●	■
PARADORS								
Parador de Cazorla *(see p206)*	€€€	34	●	■	●	■	●	■
Parador de Arcos de la Frontera *(see p207)*	€€€€	24	●		●		●	
Parador de Mazagón *(see p206)*	€€€€	63	●	■	●	■		■
Parador de Jaén *(see p207)*	€€€€	45	●	■	●	■		
Parador de Úbeda *(see p207)*	€€€€	36	●	■	●			
Parador de Mojácar *(see p209)*	€€€€	98	●	■	●	■		
Parador de Granada *(see p209)*	€€€€€	36	●	■	●		●	■
Parador de Carmona *(see p206)*	€€€€€	63	●	■	●	■	●	■

Price categories for a double room per night, including breakfast and tax:
€ under 50 euros
€€ 50–75 euros
€€€ 75–100 euros
€€€€ 100–125 euros
€€€€€ over 125 euros

RESTAURANT
The hotel has a restaurant on the premises serving breakfast, lunch and dinner. Non-residents are usually welcome to use the restaurant, but priority may be given to guests staying at the hotel. Breakfast is served in most of the hotels listed, but it is advisable to check before booking.

SWIMMING POOLS
Hotel pools are, with few exceptions, outdoor, and so may only be open during the summer months.

FAMILY ROOMS
Rooms for more than two people are available, or an extra bed may be put into a double room.

SEVILLE

CITY CENTRE

Hostal Goya

C/ Mateos Gago 31, 41004. **Map** 3 C2 (6 E4). **[** 95 421 11 70. **FAX** 95 456 29 88. **W** www.hostalgoyasevilla.com **Rooms**: 20. ☎ 1 ⊞ 目 €€

The popular Hostal Goya is located in the most visited part of the city. It offers basic comfort and is a good base for sightseeing (see p36).

Hotel Simón

Calle García de Vinuesa 19, 41001. **Map** 3 B2 (5 C4). **[** 95 422 66 60. **FAX** 95 456 22 41. **W** www.hotel simonsevilla.com **Rooms**: 29. ☎ 1 ⊞ 目 ≋ AE, DC, MC, V. €€€

The centrally located Hotel Simón is an 18th-century mansion built round a pleasant patio filled with ferns. The rooms vary in size and quality, and some have balconies.

Hotel Baco

Plaza Ponce de León 15, 41003. **Map** 2 E5 (6 E2). **[** 95 456 50 50. **FAX** 95 456 36 54. **W** www.baco.es **Rooms**: 25. ☎ 1 ⊞ ⊞ 目 ≋ ¶¶ ≋ AE, MC, V. €€€€

Once an old house this modern hotel has been transformed with typical Sevillian style. From the reception area, a spiral staircase leads upstairs. The quieter rooms look over small courtyards dec-orated with tiles and potted plants.

Ciudad de Sevilla

Avenida Manuel Siurot 25, 41013. **Road map** B3. **[** 95 423 05 05. **FAX** 95 423 85 39. **W** www.ac-hotels.com **Rooms**: 94. ☎ 1 ⊞ ⊞ ≋ ≋ ¶¶ P ¶¶ ≋ AE, DC, MC, V. €€€€€

Behind its old façade, this hotel, at some distance from the city centre, is wholly modern. The rooms are large and light, and there is a quaint rooftop swimming pool.

Taberna del Alabardero

C/ Zaragoza 20, 41001. **Map** 3 B1 (5 B3). **[** 954 50 27 21. **FAX** 95 456 36 66. **W** www.tabernadelalabardero. com **Rooms**: 7. ☎ ⊞ ⊞ 目 ≋ P ¶¶ ≋ AE, DC, MC, V. €€€€€

An exquisite restaurant-with-rooms occupying a 19th-century mansion. The house is built round a central courtyard illuminated by a stained-glass roof. There are cosy rooms on the top floor and five elegant private dining rooms downstairs.

NH Plaza de Armas

Marqués de Paradas s/n, 41001 Sevilla. **Map** 1 B5 (5 A1). **[** 954 90 19 92. **FAX** 954 90 12 32. **W** www. nh-hotels.com **Rooms**: 262. ☎ 1 ⊞ ⊞ ≋ ≋ P ¶¶ 目 ≋ AE, DC, MC, V. €€€€€

Situated in mid-town Seville this hotel overlooks the grounds of the 1992 World's Fair. The decoration is modern and functional and it boasts an outdoors swimming pool and sundeck.

Hotel San Gil

Calle Parras 28, 41002. **Map** 2 D3. **[** 95 490 68 11. **FAX** 95 490 69 39. **@** hsangil@arrakis.es **Rooms**: 60. ☎ 1 ⊞ ⊞ ≋ ≋ P ≋ AE, DC, MC, V. €€€€€

The Hotel San Gil is in an early 20th-century mansion, classified as one of Seville's 100 most important buildings. In its tranquil garden are palm trees. Rooms are large and beautifully furnished.

Alfonso XIII

Calle San Fernando 2, 41004. **Map** 3 C3 (6 D5). **[** 95 491 70 00. **FAX** 954 91 70 99. **W** www.westin.com **Rooms**: 146. ☎ 1 ⊞ ⊞ ≋ ≋ P ¶¶ ≋ AE, DC, MC, V. €€€€€

Seville's classic grand hotel (see p94), built in Neo-Moorish style and set among palm trees, hosts some of the city's most prestigious social events. Inside it has crystal chandeliers, paintings, statues and marble floors. Service is formal.

Hotel Doña María

Calle Don Remondo 19, 41004. **Map** 3 C2 (6 D4). **[** 95 422 49 90. **FAX** 95 421 95 46. **W** www.hdmaria. com **Rooms**: 69. ☎ 1 ⊞ ⊞ ≋ ≋ P ≋ AE, DC, MC, V. €€€€€

This hotel is in a street which runs alongside the Palacio Arzobispal, and its terrace and swimming pool overlook the Giralda. Bedrooms are decorated in a variety of styles. The rooftop bar is open to the public.

Hotel Adriano

Calle Adriano 12, 41001. **Map** 3 B2 (5 B4). **[** 95 429 38 00. **FAX** 95 422 89 46. **W** www.adrianohotel.com **Rooms**: 34. ☎ 1 ⊞ ⊞ 目 ≋ P ≋ MC, V. €€€€

The Hotel Adriano is a small, elegant hotel with lots of charm. Its location, close to the riverfront, the Giralda and Real Alcázar, make it an excellent choice for sightseers. English-speaking staff.

HUELVA AND SEVILLA

ALCALÁ DE GUADAIRA

Hotel Oromana

Sevilla. **Road map** 3B. Avda de Portugal s/n, 41500. **[** 95 568 64 00. **FAX** 95 568 64 24. **W** www.hoteloromana. com **Rooms**: 31. ☎ 1 ⊞ ⊞ ≋ ≋ P ¶¶ ≋ AE, DC, MC, V. €€€

The Oromana sits among pine trees on the edge of the pleasant town of Alcalá de Guadaira, close to Seville. The hotel goes out of its way to cater for children and the disabled. Ballroom dances are held at the weekend.

ARACENA

Sierra de Aracena

Huelva. **Road map** A3. Gran Vía 21, 21200. **[** 959 12 61 75. **FAX** 959 12 62 18. **@** hotelsierraaracena@ terra.es **Rooms**: 42. ☎ 1 ⊞ ≋ ≋ AE, DC, MC, V. €

This quiet hotel in the centre of attractive Aracena is a convenient base for a visit to the Gruta de las Maravillas (see p122). Rooms at the back overlook the castle.

Finca Buen Vino

Huelva. **Road map** A3. Los Marines, 21293. **[** 959 12 40 34. **FAX** 959 50 10 29. **W** www.fincabuenvino.com **Rooms**: 4. ☎ 1 ≋ P ¶¶ ≋ MC, V. €€€€€

This stylish villa stands on the top of a hill in the heart of a wooded nature reserve. All rooms are individually furnished and there are magnificent views. The atmosphere is informal. Cordon bleu cooking is served in the evenings.

AYAMONTE

Riu Canela

Huelva. **Road map** A4. Paseo de los Gavilanes s/n, Playa de Isla Canela, 21470. **[** 959 47 71 24. **FAX** 959 47 71 70. **W** www.riuhotels.com **Rooms**: 349. ☎ 1 ⊞ ⊞ 目 ≋ ¶¶ ≋ AE, DC, MC, V. €€€€€

The Riu Canela is more a summer holiday centre than a hotel. It has three swimming pools, one of which is for children only. It is also beside a beach, close to the Portuguese border.

For key to symbols see p201

CARMONA

Parador de Carmona

Sevilla. **Road map** B3. Calle Alcázar s/n, 41410. (95 414 10 10. **FAX** 95 414 17 12. w www.parador.es **Rooms**: 63. AE, DC, MC, V. €€€€

Originally a Moorish fortress, later the palace of the Christian King Pedro the Cruel (see pp46–7), this cliff-top parador has great views over the plains. The ancient town of Carmona makes a good base from which to explore Seville.

Casa de Carmona

Sevilla. Road map B3. Plaza de Lasso 1, 41410. (95 414 33 00. **FAX** 95 419 01 89. w www.casadecarmona. com **Rooms**: 32. AE, DC, MC, V. €€€€€

This 16th-century converted palace is decorated in a well-blended mixture of modern and period styles. It has a two-storey, porticoed patio and a delightful interior garden.

CASTILLEJA DE LA CUESTA

Hacienda de San Ygnacio

Sevilla. **Road map** B3. Calle Real 190, 41950. (95 416 92 90. **FAX** 95 416 14 37. w www.haciendasanignacio. com **Rooms**: 18. AE, DC, MC, V. €€€€

This 18th-century Andalusian farmhouse is built round a large patio dominated by tall palm trees. Close to Seville, the town of Castilleja de la Cuesta makes a relaxed base for sightseeing, away from the city.

CAZALLA DE LA SIERRA

Las Navezuelas

Sevilla. **Road map** B3. A432 km 43.5, Apartado 14, 41375. (95 488 47 64. **FAX** 95 488 45 94. w www.las navezuelas.com **Rooms**: 10. MC, V. €€

Rooms in this charming, family-run farmhouse are furnished with handworked fabrics, which gives them a homely feel. A rare opportunity to experience living in a real Andalusian cortijo (farmstead).

Hospedería La Cartuja

Sevilla. **Road map** B3. Carretera Cazalla-Constantina km 2.5, 41370. (95 488 45 16. **FAX** 95 488 47 07. w www.skill.es/cartuja **Rooms**: 12. MC, V. €€€

Art-lovers will feel right at home in this old monastery. Paintings are on display and for sale. Organic produce straight from the farm is served at dinner.

EL RÓCIO

Hotel Toruño

Huelva. **Road map** B4. Plaza Acebuchal 22, 21750. (95 944 23 23. **FAX** 95 944 23 38. w www.hoteltoruno.com **Rooms**: 30. MC, V. €€

Although modern, this hotel has a traditional patio and rooms decorated with rustic furniture. Located in the village which, in May, hosts the Romería del Rócio (see p36), for the rest of the year the area is a peaceful retreat.

MAZAGÓN

Parador de Mazagón

Huelva. **Road map** A4. Carretera San Juan de Puerto-Matalascañas km 30, 21130. (959 53 63 00. **FAX** 959 53 62 28. w www.parador.es **Rooms**: 63. AE, DC, MC, V. €€€€

A modern parador on the Huelva coast, sited between a sandy beach and a pine forest. This hotel is a good base for visiting the Parque Nacional de Doñana (see pp126–7).

SANLÚCAR LA MAYOR

Hacienda de Benazuza

Sevilla. **Road map** B3. Virgen de las Nieves s/n, 41800. (95 570 33 44. **FAX** 95 570 34 10. w www.elbullihotel.com **Rooms**: 44. AE, DC, MC, V. €€€€€€

Plenty of sumptuous Moorish and Andalusian furnishings fill this 10th-century country house on a hilltop, now a luxury hotel. Many of the rooms are suites. There are three restaurants, as well as a chapel, a game reserve and a heliport.

CORDOBA AND JAEN

BAENA

Hotel Iponuba

Nicolas Alcala 7, 14850. **Road map** D3. (957 67 00 75. **FAX** 957 69 07 02. @ Iponuba@interbook.net **Rooms**: 34. MC, V. €€

This pleasant hotel is located in the heart of Baena. The interior is decorated in a classical style and a traditional welcome is assured.

CAZORLA

Molino de la Farraga

Jaén. **Road map** E3. Camino de la Hoz s/n, 23470. (953 72 12 49. w www.molinolafarraga.com **Rooms**: 9. €€

This recently renovated 200-year-old mill near Plaza Santa María has an English botanic garden.

Parador de Cazorla

Jaén. **Road map** E3. Sierra de Cazorla s/n, 23470. (953 72 70 75. **FAX** 953 72 70 77. w www.parador.es **Rooms**: 34. AE, DC, MC, V. €€€

The forests and mountains of the Sierra de Cazorla make a wonderful setting for this modern parador, deep in a nature reserve (see p152).

CÓRDOBA

Hotel Maestre

Córdoba. **Road map** C3. C/ Romero Barros 4–6, 14003. (957 47 24 10. **FAX** 957 47 53 95. w www.hotelmaestre.com **Rooms**: 26. AE, MC, V. €

Near the Mezquita (see pp140–41) in Córdoba's town centre, this is a simple, very economically priced hotel with basic modern amenities.

Alfaros

Córdoba. **Road map** C3. Calle Alfaros 18, 14001. (957 49 19 20. **FAX** 957 49 22 10. w www.maciahoteles.com **Rooms**: 133. AE, DC, MC, V. €€€€

This hotel has a Neo-Mudéjar building has three courtyards, one with a swimming pool.

Occidental

Córdoba. **Road map** C3. Calle Poeta Alonso Bonilla 7, 14012. 957 76 74 76. FAX 957 40 04 39.
W www.occidental-hoteles.com
Rooms: 153. 1 TV 😊
P AE, DC, MC, V.
€€€€€

This modern hotel, situated in a residential suburb in the north of the city, is decorated with coffered ceilings, mirrors, plush fabrics, brass lanterns and polished wood.

JAÉN

Parador de Jaén

Jaén. **Road map** D3. Carretera Castillo Santa Catalina s/n, 23001. 953 23 00 00. FAX 953 23 09 30. W www.parador.es *Rooms: 45.* 1
TV 😊 P AE, DC, MC, V. €€€€

From this castle-parador above Jaén there are spectacular views of the city and of the Sierra Morena. The decoration recreates the feel of a castle, with dim corridors, small arched windows and huge doors with heavy bolts. Armour and tapestries add to the atmosphere.

MONTILLA

Don Gonzalo

Córdoba. **Road map** C3. Carretera Córdoba-Málaga km 47, 14550. 957 65 06 58. FAX 957 65 06 66.
Rooms: 35. 1 TV
P AE, DC, MC, V. €€

This is a comfortable and well-run roadside hotel outside a town famous for its *fino* wine. The hotel is useful as a stopover en route from Córdoba to the coast. Among the facilities is its own discotheque.

PALMA DEL RÍO

Hospedería de San Francisco

Córdoba. **Road map** C3. Avenida Pío XII 35, 14700. 957 71 01 83.
FAX 957 71 02 36.
W www.intergrouphoteles.com
Rooms: 35. 1 TV P
MC, V. €€€

Some rooms in this former Franciscan monastery, built in the 15th century, were once monks' cells (*see p134*). They are still quite basic, but have a character all of their own, with bedcovers woven by nuns and hand-painted basins. Meals are served in the cloister.

ÚBEDA

Palacio de la Rambla

Jaén. **Road map** E3. Pl del Marqués 1, 23400. 953 75 01 96. FAX 953 75 02 67. @ palaciorambla@terra.es
Rooms: 8. TV P
AE, MC, V. €€€

This 16th-century mansion is run by its aristocratic owner as a small, exclusive, central hotel. The rooms, furnished with heirlooms, enclose a Renaissance patio which is thought to be by Vandelvira.

Parador de Úbeda

Jaén. **Road map** E3. Plaza Vázquez de Molina 1, 23400. 953 75 03 45. FAX 953 75 12 59. W www.parador.es
Rooms: 36. 1 TV
AE, DC, MC, V. €€€€

Presiding over the monumental square in the centre of Úbeda, this parador is in a former aristocratic residence from the 16th century. One of the main sights of the town (*see p150*), it has a patio and walls covered in blue-and-white tiles.

CADIZ AND MALAGA

ARCOS DE LA FRONTERA

Cortijo Faín

Cádiz. **Road map** B4. Ctra de Algar km 3, 11630. 956 23 13 96 FAX 956 71 79 32. *Rooms: 11.*
1 P
DC, MC, V. €€

This whitewashed, 17th-century farmhouse stands majestically in an estate of olive trees, among which the swimming pool is hidden. The rooms are furnished with antiques and many of them have wonderful old iron or brass bedsteads.

Parador de Arcos de la Frontera

Cádiz. **Road map** B4. Plaza del Cabildo, 11630. 956 70 05 00. FAX 956 70 11 16. W www.parador.es *Rooms: 24.* TV AE, DC, MC, V. €€€€

This parador occupies a fine white mansion on the main square at the top of the town. A terrace offers spectacular views over the town and the plains below. It is a good base from which to visit Jerez de la Frontera (*see p158*) nearby.

BENAOJÁN

Molino del Santo

Málaga. **Road map** C4. Calle Barriada Estación s/n, 29370. 95 216 71 51.
FAX 95 216 7327. W www.molino delsanto.com *Rooms: 17.* 1
P AE, DC, MC, V.
€€€€

This converted water mill in the hills near Ronda is a relaxing and popular suntrap, centred on an attractive swimming pool. The owners are a useful mine of local tourist information. They also rent out mountain bikes to guests.

CASTELLAR DE LA FRONTERA

Casa Convento La Almoraima

Cádiz. **Road map** C5. Finca la Almoraima, 11350. 956 69 30 02. FAX 956 69 32 14. W www.la-almoraima.com *Rooms: 24.* 1
P AE, DC, MC, V. €€€

This house is on one of Europe's largest country estates. Built by the dukes of Medinaceli in the 17th century, it was used as a hunting lodge. It still has the atmosphere of a stately home.

GIBRALTAR

The Rock

Road map C5. 3 Europa Road. 956 77 30 00. FAX 956 77 35 13. W www.rockhotelgibraltar.com *Rooms: 104.*
1 TV P AE, DC, MC, V. €€€€€

Still trading on its old-fashioned colonial style, Gibraltar's first five-star hotel is high above the town and enjoys views across the bay.

MÁLAGA

Don Curro

Málaga. **Road map** D4. Calle Sancha de Lara 7, 29015. 95 222 72 00.
FAX 95 221 59 46.
W www.hoteldoncurro.com
Rooms: 118. 1 TV
AE, DC, MC, V. €€€

The exterior may not be attractive, but this hotel is charming inside. The owners take pride in upgrading the decor, and the hotel has a welcoming atmosphere.

For key to symbols *see p201*

MARBELLA

El Fuerte

Málaga. **Road map** C4. Avenida El Fuerte s/n, 29600. **〔** 95 286 15 00. **FAX** 95 282 44 11. **W** www.fuerte hoteles.com **Rooms**: 263. 🔧 1 🎟 📺 🍽 ⚌ ⚌ 🛗 🅿 🄿 🏊 *AE, DC, MC, V.* €€€€€

Although the first hotel in Marbella, it is one of the best in the resort. The rooms are big with great views, and it has a pool and health centre.

Marbella Club Hotel

Málaga. **Road map** C4. Bulevar Príncipe Alfonso von Hohenlohe s/n, 29600. **〔** 95 282 22 11. **FAX** 95 282 98 84. **W** www.marbellaclub.com **Rooms**: 137. 🔧 1 🎟 📺 🍽 ⚌ 🛗 🅿 🄿 🏊 *AE, DC, MC, V.* €€€€€

This exclusive, beachside complex with subtropical gardens lies between Marbella and Puerto Banús.

NERJA

Hostal Avalón

Málaga. **Road map** D4. Urbanización Punta Lara, 29780. **〔** 95 252 06 98. **FAX** 952 52 31 85 **Rooms**: 6. 🔧 1 🎟 🅿 🄿 🏊 *V.* €€

This small, friendly hotel offers clean, comfortable rooms. Most have a balcony with a sea view.

PRADO DEL REY

Cortijo Huerta Dorotea

Cádiz. **Road map** BC4. Carretera Villamartín-Ubrique km 12, 11660. **〔** 956 72 42 91. **FAX** 956 72 42 89. **Rooms**: 33. 🔧 1 🎟 📺 🍽 ⚌ 🅿 🄿 *AE, MC, V.* €€

This hotel on a hill is surrounded by olive trees. Guests stay in a room or log cabin. Horse riding is available.

EL PUERTO DE SANTA MARÍA

Monasterio San Miguel

Cádiz. **Road map** B4. Calle Larga 27, 11500. **〔** 956 54 04 40. **FAX** 986 54 26 04. **W** www.jale.com/monasterio **Rooms**: 165. 🔧 1 🎟 🍽 🛗 🅿 🄿 *AE, DC, MC, V.* €€€€€

This elegant, baroque hotel was once a monastery and is well-placed for Cádiz and Jerez de la Frontera.

RONDA

Hotel Husa Reina Victoria

Málaga. **Road map** C4. Calle Jerez 25, 29400. **〔** 95 287 12 40. **FAX** 95 287 10 75. **W** www.husa.es **Rooms**: 90. 🔧 1 🎟 📺 🍽 🛗 🅿 🄿 *AE, DC, MC, V.* €€€€

Perched on a cliff edge with spectacular views, this was once Ronda's grand hotel but the parador is now more popular.

Parador de Ronda

Málaga. **Road map** C4. Plaza España s/n, 29400. **〔** 95 287 75 00. **FAX** 95 287 81 88. **W** www.parador.es **Rooms**: 78. 🔧 1 🎟 📺 🍽 ⚌ 🛗 🅿 🄿 🏊 *AE, DC, MC, V.* €€€€

Edging up to Ronda's famous cliff, yet close to the town centre, this modern parador offers stunning views over the gorge.

El Juncal

Málaga. **Road map** C4. Carretera Rondo-El Burgo km 1, 29400. **〔** 952 16 11 70. **FAX** 952 16 11 60. **W** www.eljuncal.com **Rooms**: 11. 🔧 1 🎟 📺 🍽 🅿 🄿 🍽 ⚌ *AE, DC, MC, V.* €€€€€

Partly inspired by London's St Martin's Lane hotel, El Juncal offers state-of-the-art minimalism and luxury. The downside is its location, which is near a military college. However, there are vineyards and the owners are creating private woodlands.

SANLÚCAR DE BARRAMEDA

Hotel Los Helechos

Cádiz. **Road map** B4. Plaza Madre de Dios 9, 11540. **〔** 956 36 13 49. **FAX** 956 36 96 50. **W** www.hotellos helechos.com **Rooms**: 56. 🔧 1 🛗 🅿 🄿 🍽 *AE, DC, MC, V.* €€

Decorated with tiles and plants, Los Helechos is a stylish hideaway.

TARIFA

Hotel Hurricane

Cádiz. **Road map** B5. Carretera Nacional 340 km 7, 11380. **〔** 956 68 49 19. **FAX** 956 68 03 29. **W** www.hotelhurricane.com **Rooms**: 33. 🔧 1 🎟 🅿 🄿 🍽 *AE, DC, MC, V.* €€€€€

Tarifa is a mecca for windsurfers and the Hurricane is a temple to the sport and to physical fitness in general. An imaginative open-plan building in subtropical gardens.

TORREMOLINOS

Hotel Miami

Málaga. **Road map** D4. Calle Aladino 14, 29620. **〔** & **FAX** 95 238 52 55. **W** www.residencia-miami.com **Rooms**: 26. 🔧 1 🎟 🛗 🅿 €€

Hotel Miami offers welcome respite in the overdeveloped Torremolinos area. It has whitewashed walls, tiles, iron grilles, balconies and plant pots.

GRANADA AND ALMERIA

ALMERÍA

Torreluz IV

Almería. **Road map** F4. Plaza Flores 5, 04001. **〔** 950 23 49 99. **FAX** 950 23 47 09. **W** www.amtoreeluz.com **Rooms**: 102. 🔧 1 🎟 📺 🍽 ⚌ 🅿 🄿 *AE, DC, MC, V.* €€€€€

This is a smart city-centre hotel with a swimming pool on the roof. The management also run the adjacent and cheaper Torreluz II and III.

BUBIÓN

Villa Turística de Bubión

Granada. **Road map** E4. C/ Barrio Alto s/n, 18412. **〔** 958 76 39 09. **FAX** 958 76 39 05. **W** www.villabubion.com **Rooms**: 43. 🔧 1 🎟 📺 🅿 🄿 *AE, DC, MC, V.* €€€

This mini-village is in the style of the Alpujarras, and has flat roofs and tall chimneys. Horse-riding and guided hikes can be arranged.

DÚRCAL

La Solanilla

Granada. **Road map** E4. Apartado de Correos 34, Calle Larga 36, 18650. **〔** 958 78 05 75. **FAX** 958 78 05 75. **W** www.cortijolasolana.com **Rooms**: 4. 🔧 📺 ⚌ €€

Two renovated country houses in a valley in the mountains of Granada, with extensive grounds.

GRANADA

Hotel Guadalupe

Granada. **Road map** D4. Paseo de la Sabica s/n, 18009. 📞 *958 22 34 23.* 📠 *958 22 37 98.* 🌐 *www.hotel guadalupe.es* **Rooms**: 58. 🛏 1️⃣ 🏧 📺 ≣ 🅿 🍴 ⭐ *AE, DC, MC, V.* €€€

This friendly hotel is housed in a typically Andalusian-style building and is close to the Alhambra *(see pp186–7)*.

Reina Cristina

Granada. **Road map** D4. C/ Tablas 4, 18002. 📞 *958 25 32 11.* 📠 *958 25 57 28.* 🌐 *www.hotelreinacristina.com* **Rooms**: 60. 🛏 1️⃣ 🏧 📺 🔌 🅿 🍴 ⭐ *AE, DC, MC, V.* €€€€

An original glass-covered courtyard has been preserved in this 19th-century mansion, which was one of the last hiding places of García Lorca *(see p53)*. Rooms are small.

Hotel Palacio de Santa Inés

Granada. **Road map** D4. Cueste de Santa Inés 9, 18010. 📞 *958 22 23 62.* 📠 *958 22 24 65.* 🌐 *www.palacio santaines.com* **Rooms**: 35. 🛏 1️⃣ 🏧 📺 🔌 ≣ 🅿 ⭐ *AE, DC, MC, V.* €€€€€

Situated next to Plaza Nueva, this hotel and its surroundings will bathe you in the essence of the 16th century. It has two mudejar buildings and an ornate patio of Renaissance paintings with a fountain.

Alhambra Palace

Granada. **Road map** D4. Calle Peña Partida 2–4, 18009. 📞 *958 22 14 68.* 📠 *958 22 64 04.* 🌐 *www. h-alhambrapalace.es* **Rooms**: 126. 🛏 1️⃣ 🏧 📺 ≣ ♿ 🔌 🍴 ⭐ *AE, DC, MC, V.* €€€€€€

A gloriously kitsch mock-Moorish building occupying the same hill as the Alhambra *(see pp186–7)*. It has a superb terrace with views over one of the city's old quarters.

Parador de Granada

Granada. **Road map** D4. Calle Real de la Alhambra s/n, 18009. 📞 *958 22 14 40.* 📠 *958 22 22 64.* 🌐 *www.parador.es* **Rooms**: 36. 🛏 1️⃣ 🏧 📺 ≣ ♿ 🅿 🍴 ⭐ *AE, DC, MC, V.* €€€€€€

This elegant parador located in the gardens of the Alhambra used to be a convent. Book months in advance to ensure a room.

LOJA

La Bobadilla

Granada. **Road map** D4. Finca La Bobadilla Apartado 144, 18300. 📞 *958 32 18 61.* 📠 *958 32 18 10.* 🌐 *www.la-bobadilla.com* **Rooms**: 62. 🛏 1️⃣ 🅿 🍴 ⭐ *AE, DC, MC, V.* €€€€€

Resembling a labyrinthine Andalusian village, this luxury hotel, in its own estate, has been said to be one of the best in Europe. A variety of sports and activities is available.

MOJÁCAR

Parador de Mojácar

Almería. **Road map** F4. Avenida Mediterraneo s/n, 04638. 📞 *950 47 82 50.* 📠 *950 47 81 83.* 🌐 *www. parador.es* **Rooms**: 98. 🛏 1️⃣ 🏧 📺 ≣ 🏊 🅿 🍴 ⭐ *AE, DC, MC, V.* €€€€

The architecture of this modern parador on the Almería coast echoes that of the white cubic houses in nearby Mojácar *(see p195)*.

ORGIVA

Taray Alpujarra

Granada. **Road map** E4. Carretera A348 km 18, 18400. 📞 *958 78 45 25.* 📠 *958 78 45 31.* 🌐 *www.hotel taray.com* **Rooms**: 15. 🛏 1️⃣ 🏧 📺 ≣ 🏊 🅿 🍴 ⭐ *AE, DC, MC, V.* €€€

This hotel is set in a garden of olive and orange trees and a pond. The rooms are very large, almost small apartments. The smaller of the hotel's two restaurants is used for long lunches. The surrounding area is good walking country, and the hotel organizes horse riding.

PECHINA

Balneario de Sierra Alhamilla

Almería. **Road map** F4. Pechina, 04259. 📞 *950 31 74 13.* 📠 *950 16 02 57.* 🌐 *www. gratisweb.com/sierra-alhamilla* **Rooms**: 18. 🛏 1️⃣ 🏧 📺 🍴 ⭐ *AE, DC, MC, V.* €€

This restored, 18th-century spa hotel has Roman baths in the basement. A useful base from which to visit the city or province of Almería.

PINOS GENIL

La Bella María

Granada. **Road map** E4. Carretera Sierra Nevada km 8.2, 18191. 📞 *958 48 87 46.* 📠 *958 48 87 26.* **Rooms**: 24. 🛏 1️⃣ 🏧 📺 ♿ 🔌 🅿 🍴 ⭐ *AE, DC, MC, V.* €€

A modern, family-run hotel just outside Granada. The rooms are comfortable and airy; some are large enough to accommodate a family of four.

SAN JOSÉ

Cortijo Sotillo

Carretera San José. **Road map** F4. 📞 *950 61 11 00.* 📠 *950 61 11 05.* **Rooms**: 20. 🛏 1️⃣ 🏧 📺 ≣ ♿ 🅿 🍴 ⭐ *AE, DC, MC, V.* €€€€

This secluded, rustic retreat promises a tranquil stay. The hotel enjoys mountain views and is close to the beach. All its rooms have private terraces.

TREVÉLEZ

Hotel la Fragua

Granada. **Road map** E4. Calle San Antonio 4 18417. 📞 *958 85 86 26.* 📠 *958 85 86 14.* 🌐 *www.hotella fragua.com* **Rooms**: 24. 🛏 1️⃣ 🏧 📺 🍴 ⭐ *AE, DC, MC, V.* €

This *mesón* is located in what some say is the highest village in Spain. There are great views of the valley from the rooftop terrace.

TURRE

Finca Listonero

Almería. **Road map** F4. Cortijo Grande, 04639. 📞 *950 47 90 94.* 📠 *950 47 90 94.* 🌐 *www. fincalistonero.com* **Rooms**: 5. 🛏 1️⃣ 🏧 🏊 ♿ 🅿 🍴 ⭐ *MC, V.* €€€

This hotel is a restored farmhouse near Mojácar. Home-grown vegetables are served at meals.

El Nacimiento

Almería. **Road map** F4. Cortijo El Nacimiento, 04639. 📞 *950 52 80 90.* 🌐 *www.pagina.de/elnacimiento* **Rooms**: 5. 🛏 1️⃣ 🏧 🅿 €

This lovely bed and breakfast in a remote setting is run by a young couple who serve organic produce from their own farm.

RESTAURANTS, CAFÉS AND BARS

Sign advertising house specialities

O NE OF THE JOYS of eating out in this region is the sheer sociability of the Andalusians. Family and friends, often with children in tow, start early with tapas, and usually continue eating until after midnight. The food has a regional bias – the best restaurants have grown from taverns and tapas bars serving food based on fresh produce and home cooking. The restaurants listed on pages 216–21 have been selected for food and conviviality. Tapas bars and a glossary are listed on pages 222–3, and pages 212–15 show what to eat and drink.

The dining room of El Churrasco restaurant, Córdoba *(see p218)*

ANDALUSIAN CUISINE

T HE FOOD of Andalusia falls into two categories: coastal and inland. Five of Andalusia's eight provinces have stretches of coastline and a sixth, Seville, has a tidal river and a seaport. The cooking of the coastal regions is distinguished by a huge variety of fish and shellfish. The most famous of the many fish dishes of Andalusia is *pesca'ito frito* (fried fish).

Inland, rich stews with hams and sausages, and game, pork, lamb and chicken dishes are served. Vegetables and salads are excellent, as is Andalusia's signature dish, gazpacho, made from vine-ripened tomatoes.

Andalusia is the world's largest producer of olive oil. Its flavour is basic to the region's cooking. However, because good olive oil can be expensive, cheaper vegetable oils are used in the kitchens of many restaurants.

MEAL HOURS

I N SPAIN, breakfast, or *desayuno*, is eaten twice. The first is a light meal, often toasted bread with olive oil or butter and jam and *café con leche* (milky coffee).

A more substantial breakfast follows between 10 and 11am, perhaps in a café: a *bocadillo* or *mollete* (a sandwich or muffin) with ham, sausage or cheese; a thick slice of *tortilla de patatas* (potato omelette); or a *suizo* or *torta de aceite*, (sweet rolls). *Churros* (fried dough strips) are sold mainly from stalls. Coffee, fruit juice or beer accompany this breakfast.

By 1pm, some people will have stopped in a bar for a beer or a *copa* of wine with

Standing up, enjoying a tapa

tapas. By 1:30 or 2pm offices and business close for *la comida* (lunch), the main meal of the day, eaten between 2 and 3pm, followed by a *siesta* hour. By 5:30 or 6pm cafés, *salones de té* (tea rooms) and *pastelerías* (pastry shops) fill up for *la merienda* (tea): pastries, cakes and sandwiches with coffee, tea or juice. By 7pm tapas bars are becoming busy.

La cena (supper), is eaten from about 9pm, although some places begin service earlier for tourists. In summer people eat as late as midnight. Spaniards tend to lunch out on weekdays and dine out at weekends. Sunday lunch is usually a family affair.

HOW TO DRESS

W HILE A JACKET AND TIE are rarely required, Spanish people dress smartly, especially in city restaurants. In the beach resorts dress is casual, although shorts are frowned on at night.

READING THE MENU

T HE SPANISH FOR MENU is *la carta*. The Spanish *menú* means a fixed-price menu-of-the-day. Some finer restaurants offer a *menú de degustación*, which allows you to sample six or seven of the chef's special dishes. The day's specialities are often chalked on a board or clipped to the menu.

La carta will start with *sopas* (soups), *ensaladas* (salads), *entremeses* (hors d'oeuvres), *huevos y tortillas* (eggs and omelettes) and *verduras y legumbres* (vegetable dishes).

Bar in Calle Gerona, behind the Iglesia de Santa Catalina *(see p89)*, **Seville**

Among the vegetable, salad and egg dishes, some may be suitable for vegetarians, though some of these may contain a few pieces of ham, so ask first.

Main courses are *pescados y mariscos* (fish and shellfish) and *carnes y aves* (meat and poultry). Paella and other rice dishes often come as the first course. Follow rice with meat, or start with *serrano* ham or salad and follow with paella.

Desserts and puddings are grouped as *postres*, but fresh fruit is the preferred choice for desserts in Andalusia.

CHILDREN

CHILDREN ARE generally very welcome in restaurants, but there are seldom special facilities for them. *Ventas (see p223)* are the exception; they often have play areas.

SMOKING

FINE RESTAURANTS will have a selection of *puros* (cigars) which are offered with coffee and brandy. No-smoking areas are very rare in Spain.

WHEELCHAIR ACCESS

SINCE RESTAURANTS are rarely designed for wheelchairs, you (or hotel staff) should call to book and to discuss access to restaurant and toilets.

Stylish dining room of the exclusive Egaña Oriza, Seville *(see p217)*

WINE CHOICES

DRY FINO WINES are perfect with shell fish, *serrano* ham, olives, soups and first courses. Wines to accompany meals are usually from Ribera del Duero, Rioja, Navarra or Penedés. A tapas bar might serve Valdepeñas or La Mancha wines. *Oloroso* wines are often drunk as a digestif. *(See also What to Drink pp214–15 and The Land of Sherry pp28–9.)*

WHAT IT COSTS

THE CHEAPEST PLACES to eat are usually tapas bars and smaller, family-run establishments (*bar-restaurantes*).

A *menú del día* is offered in the majority of restaurants. It is usually three courses and priced well below choices from *la carta*.

Ordering from *la carta* in a restaurant can push your final bill way above average, especially if you choose pricey items like *ibérico* ham and fresh seafood. If you find "bargain prices" for sword-fish, hake, sole and other fish then it is probably frozen. Expect shellfish such as lobster and large prawns, and fish such as sea bass and bream, to be priced by weight.

The bill *(la cuenta)*, includes service charges and sometimes a small cover charge. Prices on the menus do not include six per cent *IVA* (VAT), which, as a rule, is added when the bill is totalled. Tipping is just that, a discretionary gratuity. The Spanish rarely tip more than five per cent, often just rounding up the the bill.

Credit cards are accepted in restaurants everywhere, but do not expect to pay by credit card in a tapas bar or café.

Relaxed ambience at the Manolo Bar in the Parque María Luisa *(see pp96–7)*, Seville

---

USING THE LISTINGS

Key to the symbols in the restaurant listings on pages 216–21.

⬜	open
⬛	closed
🍽	fixed-price menu
🏠	outdoor eating
♿	wheelchair access
👔	jacket and tie required
🚭	no-smoking section
▤	air conditioning
🍷	excellent wine list
💳	credit cards accepted
AE	American Express
MC	Mastercard
DC	Diners Club
V	Visa

Price categories for a three-course evening meal for one, including a half-bottle of house wine, cover charge, tax and service:
€ under 20 euros
€€ 20–30 euros
€€€ 30–40 euros
€€€€ over 40 euros

What to Eat in Andalusia

ANDALUSIA PRODUCES over 20 per cent of the world's olive oil *(aceite de oliva)*. It is used in the region's cooking in a huge variety of ways – to fry fish and as an ingredient in quite a few dishes, including gazpacho (cold soup). Summer fare is light: gazpacho (including a white variation called *ajo blanco*), salads and grilled fish and meat. Winter sees the preparation of hearty soups and stews *(sopa, puchero, estofado, cocido, potaje)* with sausages and pulses.

A snack of fried *churros* and hot chocolate

Tostada con Aceite
A thick slice of toasted bread, spread with olive oil, is a typical breakfast.

Jamón ibérico **(cured ham)**

Huevos rellenos **(eggs stuffed with tuna)**

Boquerones al natural **(marinated anchovies)**

Gambas al ajillo **(garlic-fried prawns)**

Albóndigas **(meatballs)**

Chorizo **(spicy garlic sausage)**

Soldaditos de pavía **(cod fish fritters)**

Salchichón **(pork sausage)**

Morcilla **(black pudding)**

Aceitunas **(olives)**

TAPAS

Tapas *(see pp222–3)* are bite-sized servings of food, which are usually offered as an accompaniment to an apéritif such as wine, beer or *fino (see p214)*. They include fish and shellfish, morsels of meat or chicken in a sauce, spicy sausages, olives and, perhaps best of all, cured Iberian ham.

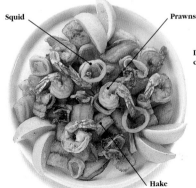

Squid
Prawns
Hake

Fritura de Pescados
Squid, fresh hake and a variety of other fish are deep fried and served as a mixed fish fry.

Fried cubes of bread
Diced cucumber
Diced pepper

Gazpacho
An archetypal Andalusian dish, this cold soup is made from ripe tomatoes, bread, garlic and olive oil. It is usually garnished with diced peppers and cucumber and fried cubes of bread.

Tortilla de Patatas
Potato is the main ingredient in this omelette, often served with beans or wild asparagus.

Rabo de Toro
Braised bull's tail in a sauce flavoured with paprika is typical of Córdoba and Seville.

Pollo al Ajillo
Chicken is sautéed in oil with lots of garlic. A touch of sherry is also added.

Mayonnaise made with olive oil

Garlic and parsley sauce

Pescado a la Sal
Whole fish is baked in a thick coating of salt. The salt is removed with the skin and the moist flesh served with sauces.

Clam

Dublin Bay prawn

Squid

Shrimp

Cazuela de Arroz con Mariscos
In this Andalusian version of paella, saffron-flavoured rice is served in a large flat dish with an assortment of fish and shellfish.

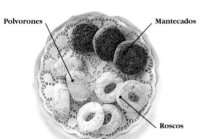

Polvorones

Mantecados

Roscos

Tocino de Cielo
This rich custard pudding looks like a piece of bacon and is usually made by nuns, thus its name, "heavenly bacon".

Mantecados, Polvorones and Roscos
Typically served at Christmas, these small cakes are flavoured with anise, sesame, almonds and cinnamon.

DESSERT FRUITS
Restaurants offer *postres* (puddings), such as *flan* (crème caramel) or *natillas* (custard), but fresh fruit is the usual dessert in Spain. Andalusia offers a wonderful choice of home-grown exotic fruits.

Figs

Orange

Galia melon

Persimmon

Pomegranate

Strawberries

What to Drink in Andalusia

ANDALUSIA IS the third largest of Spain's wine regions and produces some of the world's best-known wines; particularly sherry *(see pp28–9)*. Wine is such a large part of the culture that festivals celebrating the *vendimia* (grape harvest) are held all over the region *(see p34)*. Bars and cafés are an institution in Andalusia, and much public life takes place over morning coffee. Start the day with coffee

A jug of sangría

at the counter in a café, have sherry or beer at midday, wine with lunch, and finish lunch or dinner with coffee and a *copa* of brandy.

Autumn grape harvest or *vendimia* celebrated all over Andalusia

Fino from Jerez   **Manzanilla from Sanlúcar**   **Fino from Montilla**

WINE

ANDALUSIA PRODUCES a few young white table wines; most notably Castillo de San Diego, Marqués de la Sierra and wines from El Condado *(see p125)*. Most table wines – *tinto* (red), *blanco* (white) and *rosado* (rosé) – come from other parts of Spain. In more up-market establishments these tend to be Rioja, Ribera del Duero, Navarra and Penedés. Look for the label showing the wine's *denominación de origen* (guarantee of origin and quality). Recent vintages, or *cosecha* wines, are the least expensive; *crianza* and *reserva* wines are aged and more expensive. *Cava*, sparkling wines made by *méthode champenoise* are usually from Catalonia.

The ordinary Valdepeñas and La Mancha wines are served in simpler restaurants and tapas bars. Do not be at all surprised to see people diluting these with some *gaseosa*, a fizzy, slightly sweet lemonade. The resulting mixture is actually very refreshing.

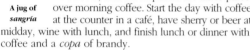

Castillo de San Diego

FINO

FINO IS ANDALUSIA'S signature drink. Ask for *un fino*, or *una copa de vino fino*. Depending on where you are, you may be served a dry, pale sherry from Jerez de la Frontera *(see p158)*, a dry Montilla-Moriles wine from Córdoba province, or a dry Manzanilla, a sherry from Sanlúcar de Barrameda *(see p158)*. You can also ask for *fino* by name: for instance, Tío Pepe, a sherry from the González Byass *bodega* in Jerez; Gran Barquero, which comes from Montilla *(see p143)*; or Solear, a Manzanilla from the Barbadillo *bodega* in Sanlúcar. Manzanilla is the favoured drink during the Feria de Abril in Seville *(see p36)*.

Fino wine is fortified, meaning that it has a higher degree of alcohol than table wines (around 15 per cent). When drunk, it should have a fresh aroma and be slightly chilled. It is usually served in a small-stemmed glass with a rim narrower than its base. (Hold it by the base, not round the middle.) However, in some rustic bars, *fino* comes in a tall, straight glass known as a *copita* or a *vasito*.

Fino is most often drunk with first courses and tapas, and its dry taste is a perfect accompaniment to dishes such as *jamón serrano* and *aceitunas aliñadas (see pp222–3)*.

BEER

SEVERAL BRANDS OF lager beers are brewed in Andalusia. These all come in bottles, though quite a few of them are available on draught, too. People often drink draught beers with tapas, especially in summer. Ask for *una caña*. One very good local beer, among the best in Spain, is Cruz Campo. Another, which may perhaps be more familiar to non-Spaniards, is San Miguel.

Una caña de cerveza

Cruz Campo in a bottle

Anise brandy (aguardiente)

Moscatel from Málaga

Lepanto coñac from Jerez

COFFEE

IN THE MORNING, the Spanish tend to drink *café con leche*, half hot milk, half coffee, often served in a glass instead of a cup. Children and insomniacs might prefer to have a *sombra* instead, prepared with just a "shadow" of coffee and lots of hot milk. Another option is a *cortado*, which is mainly coffee, with a tiny amount of milk. After dinner, you should drink *café solo*, a black espresso-style coffee, which is served in a tiny cup, though it sometimes comes in a short glass.

Café con leche

Café solo

Spanish coffee is made in espresso machines from coffee beans dark-roasted *(torrefacto)* with a little sugar to give it a special flavour.

OTHER DRINKS

HERBAL TEAS or *infusiones* can be ordered in most bars and cafés. *Poleo-menta* (mint), *manzanilla* (camomile), and *tila* (limeflower) are among the best. *Zumo de naranja natural* (freshly squeezed orange juice) is excellent but expensive and not always available. *Mosto* is grape juice. Tap water throughout Spain is safe to drink, but Andalusians are discerning about the taste of their water and buy it bottled from natural springs, such as Lanjarón *(see p181)*; it can be bought either *sin gas* (still) or *con gas* (bubbly). Fresh goat's milk is also available in most villages.

Mineral water from Lanjarón

Fresh orange juice

Camomile tea (manzanilla)

OTHER APÉRITIFS AND DIGESTIFS

ANISE BRANDY, which is often called *aguardiente*, the name for any distilled spirit, can be sweet or dry. It is drunk from breakfast *(desayuno)* to late afternoon tea *(la merienda)* and is sometimes accompanied by little cakes, especially during festivities. It is also drunk after dinner as a digestif.

Tinto de verano is a summer drink of red wine with ice and *gaseosa*. *Sangría* is a red-wine punch with fruit. With tapas, instead of *fino*, try one of the mellow apéritif wines, such as *amontillado*, *oloroso* or *palo cortado* *(see p29)*, made in Jerez and Montilla. With your dessert try a *moscatel*; the best known of these is a Málaga wine from Pedro Ximénez or muscatel grapes. Alternatively try a sweet "cream" sherry from Jerez. After dinner, have a brandy with coffee. Spanish brandy comes mainly from the sherry *bodegas* in Jerez and is called *coñac* in bars. Most *bodegas* produce at least three labels and price ranges, often displayed on shelves whose levels correspond to quality. A good middle-shelf brandy is Magno; top-shelf labels are Lepanto and Larios 1886.

If you are going on, say, to a nightclub, it is customary to switch to tall drinks – whisky with ice and water, gin and tonic or rum and soda. Rum is made on the south coast, where sugar cane is grown.

Amontillado from Jerez, an apéritif wine

HOT CHOCOLATE

Chocolate, originally from Mexico, was imported to Europe by conquistadors. *Tchocolatl*, a bitter, peppery drink made from cocoa, was drunk by the Aztec Indians during religious celebrations.

Hot chocolate

Nuns, living in the colonies, adapted it by adding sugar to the cocoa, creating a sweeter drink more acceptable to European tastes. During the 16th century, chocolate became increasingly popular. Spain had a monopoly on the export of cocoa beans and the "formula" for chocolate was a state secret for over a century. In the 1830s, the English writer, Richard Ford, described chocolate as "for the Spanish what tea is for the English". For many Spaniards this is still the case.

Indian making tchocolatl

SEVILLE

CITY CENTRE

Jamón Real

Calle Pastor Y Landero, 20–22.
[95 456 39 98. **Map** 3 B1 (5 B4).
○ noon–5pm, 8pm–1am Tue–Sun.
▤ ▯ ▣ DC, MC, V. €

Not much more than a hole-in-the-wall, this eatery offers tasty hams, olives, cheeses, honey and the country cooking of Extremadura. It is perfectly all right to *chuparse los dedos* – lick your fingers. Order a board of *ibérico* ham and sausages, or nine different cheeses.

Il Forno

Calle Trajano 44. **Map** 1 C5 (5 C1).
[95 438 09 01. ○ 1:30–5pm,
8:30pm–1:30am daily. ● Aug.
▤ ▯ ▣ MC, V. €

On offer here is a wide selection of international cuisine including Italian, Greek and Mexican. Tapas is also available at the bar along with a good selection of Spanish wines. Chic but rustic interior.

La Madraza

Calle Peris Mancheta. **Map** 2 D4.
[95 490 81 88. ○ 1–4pm,
8–midnight daily. ● Aug. ▤ ▯
▦ ▯ ▣ MC, V. €

This restaurant provides excellent fare in a stylish setting. A variety of Spanish tapas is available including *solomillo a la mostaza* (pork loin in mustard sauce), *caldreta de buey* (ox stew), *revuelto de verduras* (sautéed vegetables) and *pate casero* (homemade paté with marmalade).

Casa Robles

Calle Alvarez Quintero 58. **Map** 3 C1
(6 D3). [95 456 32 72. ○ 1–5pm,
8:30pm–1am daily. ▯●▯ ▦ ▤ ▯
▣ AE, DC, MC, V. €€€

Right in the heart of Seville, this lively place has three small dining rooms behind the tapas bar. Fish is a speciality – fried, baked or with rice. More than a dozen types of shellfish are fresh daily. The meat and tapas are good and there are *emparedados* (tiny sandwiches).

Corral del Agua

Callejón del Agua 6. **Map** 3 C2 (6 E5).
[95 422 48 41. ○ noon–4pm,
8pm–midnight Mon–Sat. ▯●▯ ▦
▣ AE, DC, MC, V. €€€

On a narrow street in the Barrio Santa Cruz, in the lee of the Reales Alcázares' gardens, this restaurant

offers the charm of dining on a cool, vine-covered patio. The menu emphasizes seasonal specialities, carefully prepared and served.

Hostería del Laurel

Plaza de los Venerables 5. **Map** 3 C2
(6 D4). [95 422 02 95. ○ 11am–
4pm, 8pm–midnight daily. ▦ ▯ ▤
▣ AE, DC, MC, V. €€

Decorated in rustic style with wooden barrels and colourful wall tiles, this restaurant and bar is reached through a labyrinth of walkways around Santa Cruz (*see pp70–71*). A fine lunch consists of *serrano* ham, fat Seville olives and *tortilla de patatas* (potato omelette).

Mesón Casa Luciano

Calle Paraíso 3. **Map** 3 B3. [95
428 46 00. ○ 1–5pm, 8:30pm–1am,
daily. ▯●▯ ▯ ▤ ▣ AE, DC, MC, V.
€€

Best *ibérico* hams hang from the wooden rafters and are a speciality at this friendly restaurant-cum-*taberna*. Charcoal-grilled beef, lamb and pork are also on the menu. The home-made custard puddings are highly recommended.

Mesón de la Infanta

Calle Dos de Mayo 26. **Map** 3 B2
(5 C5). [95 422 19 09.
○ noon–5pm, 8pm–midnight daily.
▤ ▯ ▣ MC, V. €€€

Set in a restored historic building in the heart of the lively El Arenal district, this restaurant offers an excellent choice of traditional fish and meat dishes. As well as such specialities as *pescado a la sal* (fish baked in a thick crust of salt), they are proud of their Andalusian food, including wild duck and Iberico ham. An impressively long bar runs along one side of this beautiful, high-ceilinged room with its oak beams and columns.

La Judería

Calle Cano y Cueto 13. **Map** 4 D2
(6 E4). [95 441 20 52. ○ 1–
5pm, 7:30pm–12:30am daily. ▯●▯
▤ ▯ ▣ AE, DC, MC, V. €€

A pretty restaurant in the medieval Jewish quarter, with brick arches and terracotta floors. It offers a huge range of seafood, and game in season. *Cazuela de arroz*, a rice casserole for two with lobster or prawns, is especially good.

Río Grande

Calle Betis s/n. **Map** 3 B3 (5 B5).
[95 427 83 71. ○ 1–5pm,
8pm–midnight daily. ▯●▯ ▯ ▯ ▤
▯ ▣ AE, DC, MC, V. €€

Tourists flock here because of the terrific location on the banks of the Guadalquivir and the views of the city skyline from the terrace. The gazpacho is good; the *rabo de toro* (braised bull's tail) is excellent.

Enrique Becerra

Calle Gamazo 2. **Map** 3 B1 (5 C4).
[95 421 30 49. ○ 1–5pm,
8pm–midnight Mon–Sat. ▯ ▯ ▯
AE, DC, MC, V. €€€

This plush restaurant-bar near the Ayuntamiento attracts well-heeled customers for apéritifs and meals. Besides a fine selection of fish and meat dishes, the daily specials feature Andalusian home cooking.

La Albahaca

Pl de Santa Cruz 12. **Map** 3 D2
(6 E4). [95 422 07 14.
○ noon–4pm, 8pm–midnight
Mon–Sat. ▯●▯ ▦ ▯ ▣ AE,
DC, MC, V. €€€

A 1920s mansion furnished with 17th-century antiques on the lovely Plaza Santa Cruz make this a special place for dining. The restaurant serves Basque-influenced food with a modern touch. The menu changes with the seasons.

El Burladero

Hotel Colón, Calle Canalejas 1. **Map** 3
B1 (5 B3). [954 50 55 99. ○ 1:30–
4pm, 9pm–midnight daily. ▤ ▯ ▯
AE, DC, MC, V. €€€

Dining is refined in this Seville landmark, where bullfighters change into their "suits of lights" before *corridas*. The restaurant, full of bullfighting memorabilia, is named after the *burladero*, the inner barrier in the bullring. On the menu, caviar and filet mignon keep company with traditional Seville dishes such as *puchero* (meal-in-a-pot) and bull's tail.

La Isla

Calle Arfe 25. **Map** 3 B2 (5 C4).
[95 421 26 31 or 95 421 53 76
FAX 456 2219. ○ noon–4pm,
8pm–midnight daily. ▦ ▤ ▯
▣ AE, DC, MC, V. €€€

In the heart of town, this attractive restaurant features superb seafood: turbot, bream, bass, swordfish, plus delicacies such as *percebes* (sea barnacles). Prices are steep, but quality and service are impeccable.

Habanita Bar Restaurant

Calle Golfo 3. **Map** 3 C1 (6 D3).
[60 671 64 56. ○ 1–4pm, 8pm–
midnight daily. ● Aug. ▦ ▯
▣ MC, V. €€

This popular restaurant serves Cuban fare in a warm Caribbean-style interior. Choices include pork loin with dates, exotic salads and good vegan options. Sip a tropical drink to the lulling sounds of Cuban music or sit outside and enjoy the views of an Andalusian garden.

Egaña Oriza

Calle San Fernando 41. **Map** 3 C3 (6 D5). **[** 95 422 72 11. **[** 1:30–4pm, 9pm–midnight Mon–Fri; 9pm–midnight Sat. **[📷] [🍴] [🏆] [🔖]** AE, DC, MC, V. **€€€€**

Tucked in a niche against the walls of the Alcázar Gardens, this is a light, airy and stylish restaurant. The food, created by owner-chef José María Egaña, is Basque with Andalusian accents. Fish, such as *lomo de merluza en salsa verde* (centre cut of hake in a green sauce) is a speciality. Meat dishes are excellent and the desserts are exceptional. This is undoubtedly Seville's most expensive restaurant, but worth it.

El Giraldillo

Plaza Virgen de los Reyes 2. **Map** 3 C2 (6 D4). **[** 95 421 45 25. **[** noon–midnight daily. **[🍴] [🏆] [🔖]** DC, MC, V. **€€€€**

Just a step off the plaza facing the Giralda and cathedral, but still a quiet corner for relaxed dining. Andalusian paella, fried fish and fillet of *ibérico* pork are good.

SEVILLE ENVIRONS

Jamaica

Calle Jamaica 16 (Heliópolis). **Road map** B3. **[** 95 461 12 44. **[** 1–4:30pm, 9pm–midnight Mon–Sat. **[🍴] [♿] [🏆] [🔖]** AE, DC, MC, V. **€€**

Jamaica occupies a private villa in Seville's suburb of Heliópolis. A good selection of fish and meat dishes are prepared with style and game dishes are featured in season. The wine list is also excellent.

Al-Mutamid

Calle Alfonso XI (Gran Plaza). **Road map** B3. **[** 95 492 55 04. **[** 1–5pm, 7:30pm–12:30am daily. **[🍴] [📷] [🏆] [🔖]** AE, DC, MC, V. **€€€€**

Start your meal in the *bodega* with one of the extraordinary *reserva* wines or *cavas* cellared here. In the cool, elegant restaurant, the seafood in some 30 guises is the star, but there are enough fine meat entrées to keep carnivores happy. For dessert, try a traditional Sevillian sweet, *yemas*, confected from egg yolks and sugar.

SEVILLA AND HUELVA

ALJARAQUE

Las Candelas

Huelva. **Road map** A4. Avenida de Huelva s/n, 21110. **[** 959 31 84 33. **[** 1–4:30pm, 8–11:30pm Mon–Sat. **[🍴] [♿] [🏆] [🔖]** AE, DC, MC, V. **€€**

About halfway between Huelva and the beach is this attractive restaurant with a rustic dining area with fireplace. The menu is equally divided between the fine local seafood and excellent meat dishes.

HUELVA

El Estero

Huelva. **Road map** A3. Avda Martín Alonso Pinzón 13. **[** 959 25 65 72. **[** noon–4pm, 8–11pm Mon–Fri. **[🍴] [📷] [♿] [🏆] [🔖]** AE, DC, MC, V. **€**

This is probably the best place to eat in Huelva's centre. The food is traditional local fare, with *chocos con habas* (cuttlefish and beans), *raya en pimentón* (skate with paprika), sole stuffed with oysters and *ibérico* pork fillet with herbs.

ISLA CRISTINA

Casa Rufino

Huelva. **Road map** A4. Avenida de la Playa s/n. **[** 959 33 08 10. **[** Jun–Sep & Easter: 1–4pm, 8pm–midnight daily; Oct–May: 2–4pm daily. **[●]** mid Dec–Jan. **[🍴] [📷] [🔖]** AE, DC, MC, V. **€€**

Right on the beach, Casa Rufino is popular in summer. In the *el tonteo* menu (for four), eight different fish are served in eight sauces; one is angler fish with raisin sauce.

JABUGO

Mesón Sánchez Romero Carvajal

Huelva. **Road map** A3. Carretera San Juan del Puerto s/n. **[** 959 12 10 71. **[** 10am–10pm daily. **[📷] [🏆] [🔖]** MC, V. **€**

One of Andalusia's best hams is Jabugo. Fine hams are made at Sánchez Romero Carvajal and the adjoining bar-restaurant is a good place to sample them. Besides dishes featuring ham and sausage, try the fresh *ibérico* pork dishes.

LA RÁBIDA

Hostería de la Rábida

Huelva. **Road map** A4. Paraje de la Rábida s/n. **[** 959 35 00 35. **[** 9am–11pm daily. **[🍴] [🏆] [🔖] [🔖]** MC, V. **€**

Christopher Columbus stayed at the 14th-century monastery of La Rábida beside this restaurant. With fish and seafood its speciality, it is a good place to dine.

SANLÚCAR LA MAYOR

La Alquería

Sevilla. **Road map** B3. Hacienda Benazuza, Calle Virgen de las Nieves s/n. **[** 95 570 33 44. **[** 8:30–11pm daily. **[🍴] [🏆] [🔖]** AE, DC, MC, V. **€€€€**

Only 15 minutes' drive from Seville, this beautiful country hacienda has a restaurant in what were once stables. The cuisine of Ferran Adriá is prepard by chef Rafael Moraly and strikes a good balance between innovative and simple dishes based on quality produce. His kitchen deserves its reputation for fine dishes.

CORDOBA AND JAEN

BAEZA

Juanito

Jaén. **Road map** E3. Avenida Arca del Agua s/n. **[** 953 74 00 40. **[** 1:30–4pm, 8–10:30pm daily. **[🏆] [🔖] [🔖]** DC, MC, V. **€€**

When Juanito Salcedo opened a *taberna* back in 1954, his wife Luisa provided popular home-style cooking. She still does, although the restaurant has become grander. Spinach casserole, cod dishes and partridge paté with Jaén olive oil are some of the house specialities.

Andrés de Vandelvira

Jaén. **Road map** E3. Calle San Francisco 14. **[** 953 74 81 72. **[** noon–5pm, 8:30–11pm Tue–Sat; noon–5pm Sun. **[🏆] [🔖] [🔖]** DC, MC, V. **€€€**

This restaurant in a restored 16th-century monastery, is the work of Andrés de Vandelvira, Jaén's Renaissance architect. It is furnished with antiques. Regional food includes: partridge salad, salt cod casserole, and *cardos* or cardoons, a type of artichoke, in cream sauce.

For key to symbols *see p211*

BAILÉN

Zodíaco

Jaén. **Road map** D3. Ctra Madrid–
Cádiz km 294. ▌ 953 67 10 58.
◯ 1–4pm, 8pm–11:30pm daily. ▐●▌
▐ ▤ AE, DC, MC, V. ⓔ

This is a consistently good place
to eat. In summer there are cold
soups on the menu, including *ajo
blanco* (white garlic) with white
almonds. *Revuelto* (eggs scrambled
with ham, asparagus, prawns and
elvers) and partridge are specialities.

CÓRDOBA

Federación de Peñas

Córdoba. **Road map** C3. Calle Conde
y Luque 8. ▌ 957 47 54 27. ◯ 1–
4pm, 8–11pm. ● 15 Jan–15 Feb.
▐●▌ ▦ ▐ ▤ AE, DC, MC, V. ⓔ

This cooperative restaurant, with a
patio, has inexpensive local food.
Cardos (cardoons) with clams is
an unusual dish. *Rabo de toro*
(braised bull's tail) is a speciality.

Almudaina

Córdoba. **Road map** C3. Jardines de
los Santos Mártires 1. ▌ 957 47
43 42. ◯ 12:30–4pm, 8:30–11:30pm
Mon–Sat, noon–4pm Sun. ▐●▌ ▤
▐ ▤ AE, DC, MC, V. ⓔⓔⓔ

In the 16th century this mansion
was the palace of Bishop Leopold
of Austria. There are seven dining
rooms, including a lovely brick-
walled patio. Food includes venison
and boar from the Sierra Morena.

El Churrasco

Córdoba. **Road map** C3. Calle Romero
16. ▌ 957 29 08 19. ◯ 1–4pm,
8pm–midnight daily. ● Aug, 24, 25,
31 Dec, 1 Jan. ▦ ▤ ▐ ▤ AE,
DC, MC, V. ⓔⓔⓔ

Beef steaks, tiny lamb cutlets, thick
fish steaks and fresh anchovies are
all displayed at the entrance. The
speciality is charcoal-grilled meat,
but dishes such as *salmorejo*, a thick
tomato cream served with crisp
fried aubergines, are among the
best. The terrace is typical Andalusian. The wine cellars a few doors
away, where you can sip an
apéritif, are among Spain's finest.

Taberna Pepe de la
Judería

Córdoba. **Road map** C3. Calle Romero
1. ▌ 957 20 07 44. ◯ 1:30–4pm,
8:30pm–midnight daily. ● 24 Dec
evening. ▐●▌ ▦ ▤ ▤ AE, DC,
MC, V. ⓔⓔ

This restaurant occupies the site of
a tavern which was first opened in
1930 by the original Pepe. Dining
rooms are festooned with photos
of bullfighters and other notables
who have passed through. The
gazpacho, available all year round,
and *flamenquín* (fried rolls of veal
and ham) are specialities.

El Blasón

Córdoba. **Road map** C3. Calle José
Zorilla 11. ▌ 957 48 06 25.
◯ noon–midnight daily.
● 24 Dec. ▐●▌ ▦ ▤ ▐
▤ AE, DC, MC, V. ⓔⓔⓔ

Situated near Córdoba's main
shopping area, the ground-floor
bar and café in this charming old
house is fine for light meals.
Upstairs there is a more formal
dining room. Here the cooking
features classic Cordoban recipes
but with modern, inventive touches
– for example *gazpacho de melón*.
The house wine is recommended.

Caballo Rojo

Córdoba. **Road map** C3. Calle
Cardenal Herrero 28. ▌ 957 47 53
75. ◯ 1–4:30pm, 8pm–midnight
daily. ● 24 Dec. ▐●▌ ▐ ▤ ▐
▤ AE, DC, MC, V. ⓔⓔⓔ

Just behind the Mezquita *(see
pp140–41)* is this lovely place to
dine. The menu offers traditional
foods, including many adapted from
Moorish and Sephardic dishes.
Try the lamb with honey, fish with
raisins and pine nuts, *Sefardi* salad
of wild mushrooms, asparagus,
roasted peppers, and salt cod. The
restaurant is fairly expensive but
well worth the price.

JAÉN

Casa Vicente

Jaén. **Road map** D3. Calle Francisco
Martín Mora 1. ▌ 953 23 28 16.
◯ 1–4:30pm, 9pm–midnight
Mon–Sat; 1–4:30pm Sun. ▐●▌ ▦
▐ ▤ ▤ DC, MC, V. ⓔⓔ

Located a few steps from the
cathedral, Vicente serves typical
jienense dishes – lamb stew, spinach
casserole, artichokes in sauce – in
a classic setting with a central patio.

PALMA DEL RÍO

Hospedería de San
Francisco

Córdoba. **Road map** C3. Avda Pío XII
35. ▌ 957 71 01 83. ◯ 1:30– 4pm,
8–10:30pm daily. ▤ ▐ ▤ AE, MC,
V. ⓔⓔⓔ

The food in this out-of-the-way
hostelry, a 15th-century monastery,
is exceptional and so are the
surroundings. The restaurant is
accustomed to catering for groups
of politicians and business people.

CADIZ AND
MALAGA

ANTEQUERA

La Espuela

Málaga. **Road map** D4. Calle San
Agustín, 1. ▌ 952 70 30 31.
◯ 1–4pm, 8–11:30pm daily. ▐●▌
▦ ▐ ▤ DC, MC, V. ⓔⓔ

This is probably the only restaurant
located in a bullring. Traditional
Andalusian dishes include partridge
and boar in season, and the town
speciality, *porra* (a thick gazpacho).

CÁDIZ

El Aljibe

Cádiz. **Road map** B4. Calle Plocia 25.
▌ 956 26 66 56.
◯ 12:30–5pm, 9pm–midnight daily.
▦ ▐ ▤ ▤ ▐ ▤ AE, DC,
MC, V. ⓔⓔ

Located in the old town, this
restaurant has a rustic yet elegant
bar with dining arranged over four
cosy rooms. Try the classic clams in
a parsley and garlic sauce.

Ventorrillo del Chato

Cádiz. **Road map** B4. Ctra Cádiz–
San Fernando km 684. ▌ 956 25 00
25. ◯ 1–4:30pm, 9pm–midnight
Mon–Sat. ▐ ▤ ▐ ▤ AE, DC,
MC, V. ⓔⓔⓔ

This rustic inn is over 200 years old
and claims to have catered for
Fernando VII during the Peninsular
Wars. The menu features seafood,
venison and a daily "soup spoon"
special such as *pescado a la sal*
(salted fish) or *arroz señorita* (seafood paella). The wine list includes
fino sherry from Jerez de la Frontera
and white Andalusian wine.

El Faro

Cádiz. **Road map** B4. Calle San Felix
15. ▌ 956 21 10 68. ◯ 1–4pm,
8:30pm–midnight daily. ▐●▌ ▐ ▤
▐ ▤ AE, DC, MC, V. ⓔⓔⓔ

This Cádiz classic has been serving
good food since 1966. Today's
menu is a superb blend of modern
and traditional dishes based on the
freshest of ingredients. Wooden
beams and whitewashed walls give

an atmosphere of warmth. The menu changes every day, but fish and shellfish from the Bay of Cádiz are always the star dishes. The *tortillitas de camarones* (crisp fritters of tiny shrimps) are especially recommended.

ESTEPONA

La Alborada

Málaga. **Road map** C5. Puerto Deportivo de Estepona. 🛂 95 280 20 47. 🕐 noon–4pm, 8pm–midnight Thu–Tue (Nov–Feb: Sat & Sun only). 🖪 🛗 🍴 AE, DC, MC, V. €€

This quayside eatery serves prize-winning paella and other rice dishes such as *arroz a banda* and *fideua* (pasta-paella), plus fish and steaks. Allow 30 minutes for paellas.

FUENGIROLA

Portofino

Málaga. **Road map** C4. Edificio Perla 1, Paseo Marítimo 29. 🛂 95 247 06 43. 🕐 1–3:30pm, 7–11pm Tue–Sun (closed for lunch in summer). 🖪 🍴
🛗 🍴 AE, DC, MC, V. €€

This restaurant faces the sea and is always packed. Resident foreigners love it for its good international cuisine and friendly service. The fish brochette is excellent.

JEREZ DE LA FRONTERA

La Mesa Redonda

Cádiz. **Road map** B4. Calle Manuel de la Quintana 3. 🛂 956 34 00 69. 🕐 1:30–4pm; 9–11:30pm Mon–Sat. 🌑 Sun & public hols. 🛗 🍴 🍴 🍴 AE, DC, MC, V. €€

Sherry dynasty insiders run this charming small restaurant, where the dedication to fine cooking is very much in evidence. Sample *mojama* (cured tuna) as a starter.

Gaitán

Cádiz. **Road map** B4. Calle Gaitán 3. 🛂 956 34 58 59. 🕐 1–4:30pm, 8:30–11:30pm Mon–Sat; 1–4:30pm Sun. 🍴🍴 🍴 🍴 🍴 🍴 AE, DC, MC, V. €€€

Gaitán's innovative chef combines both Basque and Andalusian influences. Turbot with mountain thyme, hake confit with roasted vegetables and laurel, and breast of chicken with *foie gras* and pine nuts, are just a few of the mouth-watering possibilities.

LOS BARRIOS

Mesón El Copo

Cádiz. **Road map** C5. Autovia Cádiz-Malaga Salida 111/112, Palmones. 🛂 956 67 77 10. 🕐 1:15–5pm, 8:30pm– midnight Mon–Sat. 🖪 🍴 AE, DC, MC, V. €€€

At El Copo, with its fish net decor and aquariums of live fish and shellfish, you will find superb seafood at competitive prices. Every day a choice of some 40 different dishes is available: from inexpensive fried anchovies to much pricier lobsters and sea bass, from sea nettles to clams and prawns. Order three or four shellfish dishes *para picar* (to share as starters). Follow with the *dorada al horno* (bream baked in a casserole with potatoes).

MÁLAGA

Marisquería Santa Paula

Málaga. **Road map** D4. Avenida de los Guindos s/n, Barriada Santa Paula. 🛂 95 223 65 57. 🕐 7:30am–midnight daily. 🍴🍴 🖪 🍴 AE, DC, MC, V. €€

One of Málaga's traditional seafood bars, Santa Paula serves a great *fritura* (mixed fish fry) and a *mariscada* (selection of shellfish). It attracts families at weekends.

Mesón Astorga

Málaga. **Road map** D4. C/ Gerona 11. 🛂 95 234 68 32. 🕐 1–4:30pm, 8pm–midnight Mon–Sat. 🖪 🛗 🍴 🍴 AE, DC, MC, V. €€

Creative flair with Málaga's superb local produce makes this restaurant popular with the local restaurant cognoscenti. Try fried aubergine drizzled with molasses, angler fish mousse, or salad of fresh tuna with sherry vinegar dressing. The tapas bar is also a lively meeting place.

MANILVA

Macues

Málaga. **Road map** C5. Puerto Deportivo de la Duquesa, local 13. 🛂 95 289 03 95. 🕐 7:30pm–12:30am Tue–Sun. 🌑 Feb. 🖪 🛗 🍴 🍴 AE, DC, MC, V. €€€

At this restaurant, with its deep, covered terrace overlooking the yacht harbour, your fish will be brought round for inspection before it is cooked. Fish baked in salt is a speciality here – priced by weight – but the meat is fine too.

MARBELLA

Santiago

Málaga. **Road map** C4. Paseo Marítimo 5. 🛂 95 277 43 39. 🕐 1–5pm, 7pm–1am daily. 🌑 Nov. 🍴🍴 🍴🖪 🛗 🍴 🍴 AE, DC, MC, V. €€€

This is probably the best place for seafood on the Costa del Sol. In 1957, Santiago Domínguez turned a beach shack into a restaurant specializing in classic Spanish dishes. On any day, there might be 40–50 fish and shellfish dishes, including paella. If meat is your thing, enjoy well-prepared suckling pig and baby lamb. An extensive *bodega* has some 120,000 *reserva* wines. The attractive dining area opens onto the beach front.

Toni Dalli

Málaga. **Road map** C4. El Oasis, Ctra Cádiz km 176. 🛂 95 277 00 35. 🕐 7:30–1am daily. 🖪 🛗 🍴
🍴 AE, DC, MC, V. €€€€

A splendiferous white palace flanked by palms, right on the beach, Toni Dalli's restaurant makes for a great night out. The food has an Italian accent and live music is sometimes provided by Toni Dalli himself. Home-made pastas, *osso buco*, meat or fish *carpaccio*, are some of the specialities.

Triana

Málaga. **Road map** C4. C/ Gloria 11. 🛂 95 283 39 33. 🕐 1:30–4pm, 8pm–midnight Tue–Sun. 🍴
🍴 AE, DC, MC, V. €€€

Right in the centre of Marbella's old town, this intimate restaurant specializes in Valencia-style rice dishes. Apart from paella, there are black rice, fish with rice on the side, *caldoso con langosta* (soupy rice with lobster), and *fideua* (a paella with pasta instead of rice).

La Hacienda

Málaga. **Road map** C4. Urbanización Hacienda Las Chapas, Ctra Cádiz km 193. 🛂 95 283 12 67. 🕐 Sep–Jun: 1–3:30pm, 8–11:30pm Wed–Sun; Jul–Aug: 8:30pm–midnight daily. 🌑 mid-Nov–mid-Dec. 🖪 🛗 🍴 🍴
AE, DC, MC, V. €€€€

Set in a gracious villa in an exclusive residential area, the restaurant has gardens with views to the sea. The kitchen, capably managed by the founder's daughter, serves excellent food – the flavours are Andalusian with French touches. Specialities are a salmon and cod *torte* with basil, guinea fowl with raisin cream and game in season.

For key to symbols *see p211*

La Meridiana

Málaga. **Road map** C4. Camino de la Cruz. [95 277 61 90 or 95 27 77 625. ○ 8pm–midnight daily ● Nov–mid-Dec. 🔲 🍴 🗐 🍷 🖂 AE, DC, MC, V. €€€€

La Meridiana, with its sleek decor, has become a Marbella classic. And so has the food. Situated in Marbella's rarefied heights, the restaurant has a canopied garden room and an adjoining patio bar. The menu features dishes such as swordfish *carpaccio*, artichokes with *foie gras*, and game in season.

MIJAS

El Castillo

Málaga. **Road map** C4. Pasaje de los Pescadores 2, Plaza de la Constitución. [95 248 53 48. ○ summer: 10am–4pm, 7pm–midnight, winter: 10am–10pm Sat–Thu. ● Fri. 🔲 🖂 DC, MC, V. €€€

This rustic-style restaurant serves up both typically Andalucían and international dishes. A flamenco show makes for a lively atmosphere on certain nights.

EL PUERTO DE SANTA MARÍA

Las Bóvedas

Cádiz. **Road map** B4. Monasterio de San Miguel, Calle Larga 27. [956 54 04 40. ○ 2–3:30pm, 9pm–midnight daily. 🍴 🖳 🗐 🍷 🖂 AE, DC, MC, V. €€€

Dine in style under the vaulted brick ceilings of what was once a cloistered monastery. There is nothing monastic about the menu, but the restaurant maintains a reverent interpretation of fine local foods, especially fish and shellfish. One dessert, named *tocino de cielo* (heavenly bacon, a kind of baked custard), is in its element here – nuns make it from egg yolks donated by nearby *bodegas*, who clarify sherry with the whites.

El Faro del Puerto

Cádiz. **Road map** B4. Avenida de Fuente-Bravia km 0.5. [956 87 09 52. ○ 1– 4:30pm, 9pm–midnight daily (Sep–Jun: closed Sun night). 🔲 🖳 🗐 🍷 🖂 AE, DC, MC, V. €€€

This restaurant has small dining rooms clustered around a sky-lighted atrium. The menu offers refined interpretations of regional dishes. Not to be missed are the desserts, especially the home-made *oloroso* sherry ice cream.

RONDA

Pedro Romero

Málaga. **Road map** C4. Calle Virgen de la Paz 18. [95 287 11 10. ○ 12:30–4pm, 8–11pm. 🍴 🖳 🗐 🖂 AE, DC, MC, V. €€€

Facing Ronda's graceful bullring, this restaurant serves well-prepared, honest country food – rabbit with thyme, braised bull's tail, beans stewed with sausages. Wood-panelled walls are covered with pictures of famous bullfighters.

SAN FERNANDO

Venta Vargas

Cádiz. **Road map** B4. Avda Puente Zuazo s/n. [956 88 16 22. ○ 1– 5pm, 8:30pm–1am Tue–Sun. 🍴 🖳 🗐 🖂 AE, DC, MC, V. €€

This popular small town eatery has lots of flamenco atmosphere. Order *raciones* of the classics – *patatas aliñadas* (potato salad), *lenguados de estero* (tiny soles from the Cádiz estuary) and *berza* (vegetable and meat stew) at midday.

SAN ROQUE

Los Remos en Villa Victoria

Cádiz. **Road map** C5. Finca Villa Victoria Carretera Nacional 351 San Roque–Gibraltar Campamento. [956 69 84 12. ○ 11:30–4pm, 8:30pm–midnight Tue–Sat, 8:30pm–midnight Sun. 🔲 🖳 🗐 🍷 🖂 AE, DC, MC, V. €€€€

Once a humble fisherman's tavern, Los Remos has now relocated to a restored mansion with Mediterranean decor. The exquisite dishes, with a focus on first-rate seafood, are created by chef Frederic Sánchez Piete. On a sampling menu of eight dishes are shrimp fritters, lobster croquettes and sea nettles.

SANLÚCAR DE BARRAMEDA

Casa Bigote

Cádiz. **Road map** B4. Bajo de Guía. [956 36 26 96. ○ 12:30–4pm, 8pm–midnight Mon–Sat. 🍴 🖳 🗐 🖂 AE, DC, MC, V. €€

At the mouth of the Guadalquivir river, this typical sailor's *taberna* is the place to sample *langostinos de Sanlúcar* (large, sweet, striped prawns) and fresh fish from the

day's catch. Baby eels, poached corvina roe and other specialities are recommended. Enjoy a glass of Manzanilla as an apéritif.

TORREMOLINOS

Casa Juan

Málaga. **Road map** D4. Calle Mar 14, La Carihuela. [95 238 41 06. ○ 1–4pm, 7:30pm–midnight Tue–Sun. ● Jan. 🔲 🍷 🖂 AE, DC, MC, V. €€

Several beach front restaurants in the La Carihuela district are equally good for fish. This is one of the most popular. Fish baked in salt and *fritura malagueña* (mixed fish fry) are favourites. Gilthead bream in salt *(dorada a la sal)* comes with three sauces and potatoes.

Frutos

Málaga. **Road map** D4. Urbanización Los Alamos; Carretera Cádiz km 228. [95 238 14 50. ○ 1–4pm, 8pm–midnight daily (Oct–Jun: closed Sun night). 🔲 🗐 🍷 🖂 AE, DC, MC, V. €€€

This "grande dame" of Costa del Sol restaurants, located between Torremolinos and Málaga, serves superb meat and fish – suckling pig, fish baked in a casserole – to a discerning clientele.

GRANADA AND ALMERIA

ALMERÍA

Rincón de Juan Pedro

Almería. **Road map** F4. C/ Federico Castro 2. [950 23 58 19. ○ 1–4pm, 8 –11pm Tue–Sat, 1–4pm Mon & Sun. 🍴 🗐 🍷 🖂 AE, DC, MC, V. €

Juan Pedro's "corner" specializes in Andalusian meat and seafood and features local dishes such as *trigo a la cortijera*, a stew with wheat berries, meat and sausage.

Club de Mar

Almería. **Road map** F4. Playa de la Almadravilla 1. [950 23 50 48. ○ 1:30 –4pm, 8:30pm–midnight daily. 🍴 🖳 🔲 🗐 🍷 🖂 AE, DC, MC, V. €€€

At this restaurant fresh fish and shellfish can be enjoyed right on the seafront. The *bullabesa* (the Spanish bouillabaisse) and *pescado a la sal* (salted fish) are specialities.

Bellavista

Almería. **Road map** F4. Urbanización Bellavista Llanos del Alquian. **958 29 71 56.** 11am–11pm Tue–Sat, 1–5pm Sun. 15 Oct–1 Nov. AE, DC, MC, V. €€€

This restaurant outside the city has top quality fish and shellfish, and is a good place to try young goat. Local dishes, such as *berza de trigo* (stew with wheat) and paella can be ordered in advance. The fine *bodega* doubles as a dining room.

ALMUÑÉCAR

Jaquy Cotobro

Granada. **Road map** D4. Paseo Cotobro Edificio Rio Playa. **958 63 18 02.** 1–4pm, 7:30–11pm Tue–Sun (summers, daily). public hols. MC, V. €€

The food here has a French touch, with specialities such as pastry with prawns and leeks, and angler fish gratin with spinach. The sea front terrace is open in summer.

BUBIÓN

Villa Turística de Bubión

Granada. **Road map** E4. Barrio Alto s/n. **958 76 39 09.** 8–11am, 1–3:30pm, 7:30–10pm, Mon–Sun. AE, DC, MC, V. €

This restaurant in the Alpujarras *(see p190)* serves typical mountain food: *plato alpujarreño* (potatoes with egg, sausages, ham and pork loin), and *choto al ajillo* (kid with garlic).

GRANADA

Don Giovanni

Granada. **Road map** D4. Avenida de Cádiz Zaidin, 65. **958 81 87 51.** noon–4:30pm, 8pm–12:30am Tue–Sun. 15 days in Aug. €

It is hard to beat Don Giovanni's prices for pizzas made in the restaurant kitchens and baked in a clay oven, and good selection of pastas, meat dishes and salads.

Carmen de San Miguel

Granada. **Road map** D4. Plaza Torres Bermejas 3, 18009. **958 22 67 23.** 1:30–4pm, 8:30–11:30pm Mon–Sat, 1:30–4pm Sun. P AE, DC, MC, V. €€€

Recommended specialities here include the seabass with aubergine and pastry of foie with mango chutney. Views of the Albaícin.

Arrayanes

Granada. **Road map** D4. Cuesta Maranas 4. **958 22 84 01.** 1–4:30pm, 7:30–11:30pm Mon, Wed–Sun. MC, V. €

Located at the foot of the Albaícin, this restaurant boasts a wonderful Moorish-style interior and some of the best Middle-Eastern and North African cuisine in Granada. Menu choices include lamb *tajin* with prunes and almonds, chicken-filled pastries and good vegetarian options. Desserts are delicious. The restaurant does not serve alcohol.

Chikito

Granada. **Road map** D4. Plaza Campillo 9, **958 22 33 64.** 1–4pm, 8–11:30pm Thu–Tue. 24 Dec evening, 25 Dec, 31 Dec evening, 1 Jan. AE, DC, MC, V. €€

This was the site of a café where the poet Lorca, composer de Falla and other artists used to meet. Though now entirely remodeled, the place maintains a rustic charm and a congenial atmosphere, which attract celebrities. Broad beans with ham and Sacromonte omelette are two specialities. Try the *piononos* (anise-scented cake).

Mirador de Morayma

Granada. **Road map** D4. Calle Pianista García Carrillo 2. **958 22 82 90.** 1:30–3:30pm, 8:30–11:30pm Mon– Sat. AE, MC, V. €€

Such a romantic location! Situated in the Albaícin *(see pp184–5)*, with views to the Alhambra, this restaurant is named after the wife of Spain's last Moorish king. The traditional dishes of Granada are the speciality, such as *remojón* (a salad of oranges and codfish) and lamb sautéed with garlic, known as *cordero albaicinero*.

Velázquez

Granada. **Road map** D4. Calle Emilio Orozco 1. **958 28 01 09.** 1–4pm, 8pm–midnight Mon–Sat. Aug. AE, DC, MC, V. €€

The ambience here is warm and elegant. The food is imaginative, with modern interpretations of such Moorish dishes as *pastela* (a meat pastry with almonds and pine nuts), savoury almond cream soup, and boned lamb shoulder with a *mozárabe* sauce with raisins.

Ruta del Veleta

Granada. **Road map** D4. Carretera Sierra Nevada 136, Cenes de la Vega. **958 48 61 34.** 1–4:30pm, 8pm–midnight daily. AE, DC, MC, V. €€€

Located 6 km (3.7 miles) from Granada on the road to the Sierra Nevada, this restaurant, which grew from a simple *mesón*, is decorated with typical Alpujarran textiles and hundreds of ceramic jugs hung from the rafters. The food is traditional – roast baby kid, broad beans with ham, asparagus with mushrooms, good seafood – but the prices are as high as the nearby mountains. A second restaurant is at Solynieve, in the ski station in the Sierra Nevada.

LOJA

La Finca

Granada. **Road map** D4. Hotel La Bobadilla, Autovía Granada–Sevilla, Exit Iznájar, 175. **958 32 18 61.** 2–4pm, 8:30–10:30pm daily. AE, DC, MC, V. €€€€

Worth a detour off the *autovía*, La Finca, although pricey, is an exceptional restaurant, a place for fine dining. The chef makes creative use of good market produce, serving fresh greens, vegetables, superb capon and pork grown on the *finca* (farm), game when in season, and seafood.

MOTRIL

Tropical

Granada. **Road map** E4. Avenida Rodríguez Acosta 23. **958 60 04 50.** 1–4pm, 8–11:30pm, Mon–Sat. AE, DC, MC, V. €€€

Both seafood, such as bass with *ajo verde* (green garlic), and meat, such as *choto a la brasa* (roast baby goat), are specialities here.

VERA

Terraza Carmona

Almería. **Road map** F4. Calle Manuel Giménez 1. **950 39 07 60.** 2–4:30pm, 9–11pm Tue–Sun. 7–21 Jan. AE, DC, MC, V. €€

The specialities here are excellent seafood and unusual regional dishes – *gurullos con conejo* (pasta with rabbit) and *guiso de pelotas* (stewed maize-flour dumplings).

For key to symbols *see p211*

Andalusia's Tapas Bars

Tapas are more than just snacks. In Andalusia, where the custom of the *tapeo* (moving from bar to bar and sampling just one dish in each) was born, they are a way of life. The word *tapa* means a cover or lid. The term is thought to come from the habit of having a few nibbles with a drink to *tapar el apetito* ("put a lid on the appetite") before a meal – or from a bartenders' practice of covering *copas* (glasses) with a saucer, or *tapa*, to keep out flies. From there it was only a small step for a chunk of sausage or cheese, or a few olives – to be placed on the saucer. After that, the free market took over, with bars producing the tastiest tapas selling the most wine. In the old days – this happens only occasionally today – tapas were served free with every glass of wine.

Some bars will offer dozens of dishes; others just three or four specialities. The list may be displayed on a board or recited at great speed by a bartender. The bill is sometimes chalked up on the bar.

Where to Eat Tapas

Even small villages have a few bars where the locals go to enjoy a *copa* and tapas. On Sundays and holidays, the favourite places are packed with whole families enjoying the fare. In Seville, certain neighbourhoods are popular for the *tapeo*. Close to the cathedral, and particularly in the Barrio Santa Cruz (see pp68–81) are clusters of lively tapas bars. Another great spot is across the river in Triana (see pp100–101) on Calle Betis and the streets radiating from it. There are lots of other tapas bars throughout the city and visitors should not feel shy about trying them. As well as the tapas bars that are listed in the directory, there are likely to be good bars attached to many of the restaurants listed on pages 216–21.

Eating Tapas

An integral part of Spain's culture, tapas are usually eaten with a drink, often with sherry (see p214). This wine is fortified – its alcohol content is higher than that of table wine, sometimes more than 15 per cent. Eating one or two tapas with a glass will enhance the taste experience and also slow down the effect of the alcohol. Some people prefer beer or table wine (see p214) with tapas, especially in summer. If you do not drink alcohol, ask for a mineral water.

You can sample tapas in bars, *tascas* and *tabernas,* and in many cafés. You can eat tapas at just one bar, but it is more customary to move from bar to bar sampling the specialities of each. Each tapa is really just a bite. You can sample two or three before dinner, or you can make a meal of them by ordering *raciones,* larger portions. Tapas *de cocina* (from the kitchen) are served from 1 to 3pm, and from 7 to 10pm.

Tapas are generally eaten standing at the bar rather than sitting at a table, for which a surcharge is often payable.

TAPAS BARS

SEVILLE

Bar El Puerto
Calle Betis s/n.
Map 3 B2 (5 B5).

Becerrita
Calle Hernando Colón 1.
Map 3 C1 (6 E4).

Casa Manolo
Calle San Jorge 16.
Map 3 A2 (5 A4).

El Bacalao
Plaza Ponce de León 15.
Map 2 E5 (6 E2).

Eslava
Calle Eslava 3–5.
Map 1 C4.

La Estrella
Calle Estrella 3.
Map 3 C1 (6 D3).

La Giralda
Calle Mateos Gago 1.
Map 3 C2 (6 E4).

La Madraza
Peris Mencheta 21.
Map 2 D4.

Levies
San Jose 15.
Map 4 D1 (6 E4).

Los Coloniales
Plaza del Cristo de Burgos
19. **Map** 6 E2.

Mariscos Emilio
Ronda de Capuchinos 2.
Map 2 E4.
Calle Génova 1. **Map** 3 B3.

Modesto
Calle Cano y Cueto.
Map 4 D2 (6 E4).

Quitapesares
Plaza Padre Jerónimo de
Córdoba 3.
Map 2 E5 (6 E2).

El Rinconcillo
Calle Gerona 2.
Map 2 D5 (6 E2).

Sol y Sombra
Calle Castilla 151 (Triana).

Las Teresas
Calle Santa Teresa 2.
Map 4 D2 (6 E4).

GRANADA

Chikito
Plaza del Campillo 9.

Las Copas
Calle Navas 19.

La Gaviota
Avda Andalucía 2, Local 1.

Los Manueles
Calle Zaragoza 2.

Meson del Trillo
Callejon del Aljibe del
Trillo 3.

CÓRDOBA

Bar Santos "La Tortilla"
Calle Magistral González
Francés 3.

El Figón
Calle Montemayor.

Taberna de Bodegas Campos
Calle de los Lineros 32.

Taberna San Miguel "Casa El Pisto"
Plaza San Miguel 1.

MÁLAGA

Antigua Casa Guardia
Alameda Principal 18.

Café de Chinitas
Pasaje de Chinitas.

Lo Güeno
Calle Marín García 11.

El Malagueto
Avenida Cánovas del
Castillo 12.

La Tasca
Calle Marín García 12.

Orellana
Calle Moreno Monroy 3.

OTHER SNACKS

BESIDES TAPAS BARS, other popular eating places are *ventas*, country or roadside restaurants; *chiringuitos* and *merenderos* are similar but are found at the beach. The *freidurías* sell fried fish, and shellfish are sold at *cocederos*. *Ventas*, some of which are old stage coach houses, offer fairly rustic dishes such as chicken or rabbit fried in lots of garlic, occasionally venison, or *potajes* (stews) of sausages, beans and pulses. Because of their locations on mountain sides and river banks, *ventas* tend to attract large crowds on Sunday outings from the cities. *Chiringuitos* used to be humble beach shacks where the fishermen's catch was served up – for example, *espetones* are fresh sardines grilled over a driftwood fire, and marvellous to taste. These days, however, the stricter regulations which now govern Andalusia's coasts have caused most to become proper (and, as an inevitable result, pricier) restaurants.

TAPAS GLOSSARY

THE SHEER range of food available as tapas can seem overwhelming to the visitor, especially if a waiter is reciting a list of them. This glossary covers most that you will encounter in Andalusia. Some common tapas are shown on pages 212–13.

HAMS AND SAUSAGES

Chorizo, morcilla, morcón, salchichón: red and black sausages in many varieties.
Jamón ibérico: salt-cured ham from small pigs fed on acorns; sometimes called *pata negra* because of their black hoofs. Very expensive.
Jamón serrano: salt-cured ham dried in mountain air.

OLIVES

Aceitunas aliñadas: home-cured olives; slightly bitter and redolent of garlic and thyme.
Alcaparrones: large, pickled caper berries.
Manzanilla, gordal: two varieties of fat Seville olives; *manzanilla* olives also come pitted and stuffed with anchovies, almonds or pimiento.

SALADS AND COLD DISHES

Campera: potato salad with chunks of tinned tuna.
Huevas: fresh fish roe, poached and dressed with oil and lemon.
Pimientos asados: salad of roasted sweet peppers.
Remojón: salad of oranges, onions, olives and codfish.
Salpicón: chopped tomatoes, peppers and onions, with a medley of shellfish, marinated overnight in vinaigrette.

SHELLFISH

Calamares: fried squid rings.
Caracoles; cabrillas: snails stewed in a herb sauce.
Cazuela Tío Diego: prawns, mushrooms and ham served in clay dishes.
Chocos con habas: cuttlefish stewed with broad beans.
Cigalas: Dublin Bay prawns, boiled in sea water.
Coquinas a la marinera: tiny clams cooked with wine, garlic and parsley.
Gambas al ajillo: peeled prawns fried with garlic.
Gambas a la plancha: grilled unpeeled prawns.
Gambas rebozadas: batter-fried prawns.
Langostinos de Sanlúcar: big striped prawns, usually cooked in their shells.
Navajas: grilled razor-shell clams; tastes a little like squid.
Puntillitas: the tiniest cuttle-fish, crisply fried.
Tigres: stuffed mussels, breaded and fried.
Tortillitas de camarones: fritters of tiny shrimp.

EGGS

Huevos a la flamenca: eggs baked with ham, asparagus, peas and tomatoes.
Huevos rellenos: eggs stuffed with tuna.
Revuelto de setas; de ajetes; de espárragos: scrambled eggs with wild mushrooms, green garlic or wild asparagus.
Tortilla de patatas: thick potato omelette.

SOUPS

Caldo: hot broth in a cup.
Gazpacho: cold soup (with ham, egg or pepper garnishes) or a drink (without garnishes).
Salmorejo: cream of tomato, sometimes with ham and egg.

VEGETABLES

Alcauciles rellenos: stuffed globe artichokes.
Berenjenas rebozadas: aubergines fried in olive oil.
Espinacas con garbanzos: stewed spinach and chick peas.
Habas con jamón: broad beans with chopped ham.

FISH

Atún encebollado: fresh tuna cooked with onions.
Boquerones al natural: fresh anchovies, marinated.
Cazón en adobo: marinated, fried cubes of shark.
Pescado en amarillo: fish braised in saffron and wine.
Pez espada a la plancha: tiny grilled swordfish steaks
Soldaditos de pavía: codfish fritters

MEAT AND POULTRY

Albóndigas: meatballs, in almond or tomato sauce.
Caldereta de cordero: stew of lamb, pepper and onion.
Estofado de ternera: veal hot-pot; often flavoured with mint.
Flamenquines: veal, ham and cheese rolls, crisply fried.
Lomo en adobo: marinated pork loin.
Menudo, callos: tripe stew.
Pajaritos: tiny birds, cooked in wine and served whole.
Pinchitos morunos: kebabs, usually of pork, with herbs.
Pollo al ajillo: chicken fried with garlic. Also with rabbit.
Pringá: chopped meat and fat from the pot, served on bread.
Punta del solomillo: grilled pork sirloin tip.
Rabo de toro: braised bull's tail in paprika-flavoured sauce.
Riñones al jerez: kidneys in a sherry sauce.
Ternera mechada: veal roast stuffed with olives and ham.

SHOPS AND MARKETS

SHOPPING IN ANDALUSIA is a highly pleasurable business, particularly if you approach it in a typically Spanish manner. Here, shopping fits in with the climate, always respects the siesta and is meant to be an unhurried, leisurely activity, punctuated with frequent coffee-breaks, tapas and afternoon tea.

Though a number of European chain stores and franchises are beginning to appear all over Spain, the towns and villages of the south are refreshingly full of shops and businesses that are unique to the area. The region is

Traditional polka-dot flamenco dress

renowned for its high-quality, traditional arts and crafts, and there is an overwhelming choice of ceramics, leather goods, marquetry, jewellery in filigree silver and sweets and biscuits.

World-famous wines can be had from the *bodegas* of Jerez, Montilla, Málaga and Sanlúcar de Barrameda. A visit to a *bodega*, an experience in itself, is the best way to become familiar with the variety of wines on offer.

Many shops still provide a charming personal service. Although few assistants speak English, most are very obliging.

One of several styles of plate made in Seville

Sales generally take place in January and July, though shops may also sometimes offer pre-Christmas discounts or start their sales in late December.

HOW TO PAY

IT IS STILL CUSTOMARY among Spaniards to pay in cash. While many shops, especially the larger stores, now accept major credit cards, few take traveller's cheques.

You are entitled to exchange goods if you can produce a receipt, although this does not apply to items bought in a sale. Large shops and department stores tend to give credit notes rather than cash refunds. It is a good idea to check the shop's policy with a sales assistant before you buy anything.

VAT EXEMPTION

VISITORS TO SPAIN who come from countries outside the European Union can claim a 16 per cent refund of sales tax (*IVA*, pronounced "eeva" in Spanish) on items bought at large department stores such as **Cortefiel** and **El Corte Inglés**. For each item that you purchase costing more than 90 euros, you need to collect a form from the store's central cash desk. You should have this stamped both as you leave Spain and on re-entering your own country. You then need to return the stamped form to the shop where the purchase was made, which, in turn, will send you a cheque for 16 per cent of the value of the articles.

Calle de las Sierpes, one of the busiest shopping streets in Seville

WHEN TO SHOP

SPANISH shops tend to close during the afternoon siesta (except for department stores and touristy souvenir shops in the large towns). Most shops open at 9:30am and close at 1:30pm. They usually reopen about 4:30pm or 5pm, and stay open until around 8pm. These times will obviously vary from shop to shop; boutiques, for example, rarely open before 10am. Times also tend to vary during summer – some shops close altogether in the afternoon heat, while others will stay open later than usual, in order to take full advantage of the large numbers of visitors.

Many shops – especially if they are in small towns – close on Saturday afternoons. This practice, however, is now gradually disappearing.

An array of fans at Díaz, Calle de las Sierpes, Seville

Stylish hats from Sombrerería Herederos de J Russi in Córdoba

SHOPPING IN SEVILLE

SEVILLE IS A CHARMING CITY in which to shop, offering the buyer a unique concoction of old-style regional crafts and good modern design.

The district that surrounds Calle Tetuán and the pedestrianized Calle de las Sierpes *(see p72)* is the place to visit for the best of Seville's old and new shops. This is a smart area of bustling streets, where you will find an eclectic range of goods. These include shoes (**Pilar Burgos** and **Pineda** are two of the best), and typically Andalusian items such as elaborate fans from **Díaz**, top-quality *cordobés* hats from **Maquedano** and some fabulous, hand-embroidered shawls from **Foronda**.

Clothes that have a distinctly Andalusian style are displayed at the designers **Victorio & Lucchino**, while stylish **Loewe** makes exquisite luggage and leather bags, clothes and accessories in striking colours.

The streets around the Plaza Nueva are full of shops such as **Adolfo Domínguez** and **Marisa Martín**, selling chic, tailored clothes; and quaint shops that sell religious objects. Among these are **Casa Rodríguez** and **Velasco**, which specialize in trimmings for church robes and religious images. For the most exquisite baby clothes, head for **Marco y Ana** and for jasmine-scented eau de toilette, stop at **Agua de Sevilla**.

Around the Barrio de Santa Cruz there are a range of interesting shops. The **Supermercado Baco** is a small grocers stocking gourmet Spanish food and wines. The Calle Hernando Colón has a few curious shops for collec-tors of everything from old children's toys to stamps, while **El Postigo** is an arts and crafts centre with a good selection of handmade items on sale.

Sevillarte, which is close to Reales Alcázares *(see pp80–81)*, and **Martián** sell attractive ceramics for both utility and decoration.

For some of Andalusia's finest ceramics, however, head for Triana *(see p100)*. Look out in particular for **Cerámica Santa Ana, Antonio Campos** and the many small workshops along the Calle Covadonga. Triana is also a good area for purchasing flamboyant flamenco outfits, while at **Juan Osete** you can buy a marvellous range of *feria* accessories.

Anyone who claims to be a serious collector of antiques must make a point of calling at **Antigüedades Angel Luis Friazza**, which specializes in classic Spanish furniture.

At **La Trinidad** glass factory Seville's famous blue glass is much cheaper than that sold in the city's gift shops.

La Trinidad, makers of Seville's characteristic blue glassware

Muebles Ceballos, situated on the busy Calle de la Feria, is one of several shops in the Seville area that specializes in traditionally made wickerwork items.

CÓRDOBA

CÓRDOBA PRESENTS plenty of options for the shopper. Perhaps the most fascinating shopping area is within the old narrow streets of the Judería *(see p136)*. Here the **Zoco Municipal** runs an interesting selection of craft workshops making Córdoban specialities such as filigree silver jewellery, hand-painted ceramics, leatherware and wonderful, award-winning painted masks. Ceramics, leatherware and woodwork can also be found at **Artesanos Cordobeses**. The area surrounding the Mezquita *(see p140)* is packed with souvenir shops, which apart from the expected tourist trinkets, sell a range of fine handicrafts. Of these, **Meryan** specializes in embossed leather goods.

At the guitar workshop of **Manuel Reyes Maldonado** you can purchase highest quality, custom-built guitars, many of which end up in the hands of internationally renowned musicians.

One of the most celebrated hat-makers in the whole of Spain is the **Sombrerería Herederos de J Russi**. You can purchase a typical, flat-topped *cordobes* hat here for a great deal less than the price that would be asked of you in either Madrid or Seville.

Manuel Reyes Maldonado in his guitar workshop in Córdoba

Marquetry in the making in a Granada workshop

GRANADA

THE CHARACTERISTICALLY cold winters ensure that shops in Granada keep a good range of smart winter clothes and shoes. **Julio Callejón** has an original collection of shoes, **Zara** stocks both menswear and womenswear, and **Cortefiel** is a quality department store specialising in clothing. With the Sierra Nevada so close by, skiwear is sold in most stores as well as in many specialist shops.

The city centre is full of surprises, among them the **Mercado Arabe**, a long gallery packed with shops that sell Moroccan-inspired clothing and accessories. **Artesania Francisco Mariscal** specializes in marquetry and mantillas.

Tienda La Victoria has a superb selection of old prints, curios and furniture; and in the streets around the Gran Vía are some grand *platerías* – smart shops selling silverware.

ANDALUSIA

IN ANDALUSIA people frequently make special trips to towns famed for one particular item, such as olive oil, wine, rugs or furniture. If you have time to explore, the whole region offers countless local, handmade specialities.

The finest virgin olive oils come from Baena *(see p143)* and Segura de la Sierra *(see p152)*. Some of the best olive oil in Sevilla province is sold in the village of Ginés. Many monasteries make and sell their own sweets and biscuits, which can be an unusual gift.

There are several *bodegas* which are worth a visit, namely those in Jerez *(see p158)*, in Sanlúcar de Barrameda *(see p158)*, in Montilla *(see p143)* and in Málaga town *(see p172)*.

Botijos – spouted ceramic drinking jugs – are a local speciality of the town of La Rambla, 30 km (19 miles) south of Córdoba. In Córdoba province, Lucena *(see p143)* is a good place to buy ceramics and wrought ironwork.

Basketware from Alhama de Granada

Ronda *(see p168)* has a few shops shops selling rustic-style furniture. In Guarromán in Jaén province, antique furniture is sold at **Trastos Viejos**, which is an old *cortijo* (farmhouse).

In Granada province, the villages of Las Alpujarras *(see p190)* are famous for *jarapas*, (rag rugs), basketwork and locally grown medicinal herbs.

Fruit and vegetable market in Vélez Blanco *(see p191)*

Just north of Granada, in the small village of Jún, **Cerámica Miguel Ruiz** collects and sells some of the finest ceramics made all over Andalusia.

Exquisite hand-embroidered shawls are sold by **Angeles Espinar** in Villamanrique de Condesa, outside Seville.

MARKETS

THE MARKETS HELD in most Andalusian towns offer a wonderful opportunity to try local food specialities, including a wide range of sausages, cheeses and cured ham.

Most markets tend to sell a little of everything. However, Seville does have a few specialized markets. These include an antiques and bric-a-brac market, which is held in Calle Feria on Thursdays.

On Sundays, Los Pájaros pet market takes place in Plaza del Alfalfa, and stamps and coins are traded at Plaza del Cabildo. All manner of bric-a-brac are sold on Charco de la Pava in La Cartuja, and a bigger *rastro* (flea market) is held in the Parque Alcosa, northeast of the centre.

The food markets in Plaza de la Encarnación and El Arenal are both very good.

Córdoba has an absorbing flea market on Saturdays and Sundays at the 16th-century, arcaded Plaza de la Corredera.

On the Costa del Sol, bric-a-brac markets and car boot sales are popular. The best of these is held on Saturday morning beside the bullring at Puerto Banús, just outside Marbella.

Pottery stall at the Plaza de la Corredera market in Córdoba

DIRECTORY

SEVILLE

Department Stores
El Corte Inglés
Pl Duque de la Victoria 10.
Map 1 C5 (5 C2).
☎ 95 422 09 31.

Fashion and Accessories
Adolfo Dominguez
Calle Sierpes 2.
Map 3 C1 (5 C2).
☎ 95 422 65 38.

El Caballo
Calle Sauceda 3.
Map 5 C2.
☎ 95 422 4448.

Loewe
Plaza Nueva 12.
Map 3 B1 (5 C3).
☎ 95 422 52 53.

Maquedano
Calle de las Sierpes 40.
Map 3 C1 (5 C3).
☎ 95 456 47 71.

Marisa Martín
C/ Argote de Molina 21.
Map 4 C1 (6 D4).
☎ 95 421 93 12.

Victorio & Lucchino
Plaza Nueva 10.
Map 3 B1 (5 C3).
☎ 95 450 26 60.

Zara
Calle Jose de Velilla 2–4.
Map 3 B1 (5 C2).
☎ 95 456 00 96.

Children's Clothes
Marco y Ana
Calle Cuna 24.
Map 4 C1 (6 D3).
☎ 95 421 30 38.

Shoes
Calzados Mayo
Plaza del Alfalfa 2.
Map 3 C1 (6 D3).
☎ 95 422 55 55.

Pilar Burgos
La Campana 3 .
Map 3 B1 (5 C2).
☎ 95 422 68 45.

Pineda
Plaza Nueva 12.
Map 3 B1 (5 C3).
☎ 95 456 42 49.

Flamenco
Díaz
Calle de las Sierpes 71.
Map 3 C1 (5 C3).
☎ 95 422 81 02.

Foronda
Calle de las Sierpes 67.
Map 3 C1 (5 C3).
☎ 95 422 17 27.

Juan Osete
Calle Castilla 12.
Map 3 A1.
☎ 95 434 33 31.

Perfume
Agua de Sevilla
Plaza Nueva 9.
Map 3 B1 (5 C3).
☎ 95 421 31 45.

Religious Objects
Casa Rodríguez
Calle Francos 35.
Map 3 C1 (6 D3).
☎ 95 422 78 42.

Velasco
Calle Chapineros 4
(off Calle Francos).
Map 3 C1 (6 D3).
☎ 95 422 60 38.

Arts and Crafts
Antonio Campos
Calle Alfarería 22,
Triana.
Map 3 A2.
☎ 95 434 33 04.

Cerámica Santa Ana
Calle San Jorge 31,
Triana. **Map** 3 A2 (5 A4).
☎ 95 433 81 76.

Martián
Calle de las Sierpes 74.
Map 3 C1 (5 C3).
☎ 95 421 34 13.

Muebles Ceballos
Calle de la Feria 49
(near Calle de Relator).
Map 2 D4.
☎ 95 490 17 56.

El Postigo
Calle Arfe s/n.
Map 3 B2 (5 C4).
☎ 95 456 00 13.

Sevillarte
Calle Vida 13.
Map 3 C2 (6 D5).
☎ 95 421 03 91.

La Trinidad
Avda de Miraflores 18–20
(off Ronda de Capuchinos).
Map 2 F4.
☎ 95 435 31 00.

Art and Antiques
Antigüedades Angel
Luis Friazza
Calle Zaragoza 48.
Map 3 B1 (5 B3).
☎ 95 422 35 67.

Food and Wine
Hornos San Bernado
Marques de Parada 51.
Map 3 B1 (5 B3).
☎ 95 421 09 26.

Hornos de San
Buenaventura
Calle Carlos Cañal 28.
Map 3 B1 (5 B3).
☎ 95 422 33 72.

Supermercado Baco
Calle Cuna 4.
Map 3 C1 (6 D2).
☎ 95 421 66 73.

El Torno
Plaza del Cabildo s/n.
Map 3 C2 (5 C4).
☎ 95 421 91 90.

CÓRDOBA

Fashion
Mango
Avda Gran Capitán 14–16.

Arts and Crafts
Artesanos Cordobeses
Judios, s/n (Zoco).
☎ 957 20 40 33.

Manuel Reyes
Maldonado
Calle Armas 4.
☎ 957 47 91 16.

Meryan
Calleja de las Flores 2.
☎ 957 47 59 02.

Sombrerería Herederos
de J Russi
Calle Gondomar 4.
☎ 957 47 10 88.

Zoco Municipal
Calle Judíos s/n.
☎ 957 29 05 75.

GRANADA

**Fashion, Shoes
and Accessories**
Adolfo Dominguez
Calle Alhondigas 5.
☎ 958 52 31 32.

Cortefiel
Gran Vía de Colón 1.
☎ 958 22 93 99.

Julio Callejón
Calle Mesones 36.
☎ 958 25 87 74.

Zara
Calle Recogidas 8.

Arts and Crafts
Artesania Beas
Santa Rosalia 20.
☎ 958 12 00 34.

Artesania Francisco
Mariscal
Calle Alcaiceria 2–11.
☎ 958 22 30 11.

Mercado Arabe
La Alcaicería.

Antiques and Gifts
Antiqudades Gonzalo
Reyes
Meson Placeta de
Cauchiles 1.
☎ 958 52 32 74.

Food and Wine
Flor y Nata
Avda Constitucion 13.
☎ 958 27 23 45.

ANDALUSIA

Angeles Espinar
Calle Pascual Márquez 8,
Villamanrique de
Condesa, Sevilla.
☎ 95 575 56 20.

Cerámica Miguel Ruiz
Camino Viejo de Jún s/n,
Jún, Granada.
☎ 958 41 40 77.

Trastos Viejos
Autovía E5 km 280,
Aldea de los Rios,
Guarromán, Jaén.
☎ 953 61 51 26.

What to Buy in Andalusia

Filigree silver bracelet

THE STRONG AND VIBRANT CULTURE of Andalusia is reflected in the items available in the region's markets and shops. Andalusia has a long tradition of arts and crafts, so its towns and villages produce a surprising range of unique, often exquisite, hand-made goods. Many towns have specialities; for example, Granada is famous for marquetry and Moorish-style painted ceramics; Seville for fans and *mantillas*; Jerez, Montilla and Málaga for their renowned wines; while Córdoba specializes in filigree silver, leather work and guitars.

Traditional glazed earthenware pots from Úbeda (see pp150–51) in the province of Jaén

THE CERAMICS OF ANDALUSIA

The rich, terracotta soil of Andalusia has been utilized for centuries in the creation of practical and decorative ceramics. The variety encompasses simple earthenware cooking dishes *(cazuelas)*, drinking jugs *(botijos)*, pots *(tinajas)*, decorative painted tiles *(azulejos)*, and kitchen and tableware. You can buy them from workshops or, more cheaply, from local markets.

Ceramic plate painted in traditional colours

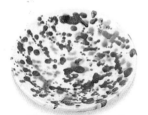

Plate from Ronda spattered in blue and green

Bowl from Córdoba in a traditional design

Replicas of 18th-century tiles from Triana (see p100)

Leather Goods
Leather goods such as bags and belts can be bought all over Andalusia. Embossed leather, however, is a speciality of the city of Córdoba (see pp136–42).

Rugs
Andalusian rug-making skills have developed over centuries. The most famous rug-making area is in the Alpujarras (see pp190–91), where rugs are made in various fibres, including cotton and wool, and in colour schemes in which earth colours and blues predominate.

Inlaid Boxes
Marquetry is produced in Granada (see pp182–8). Craftsmen make furniture, boxes, and other items inlaid with ivory and coloured woods in Moorish designs.

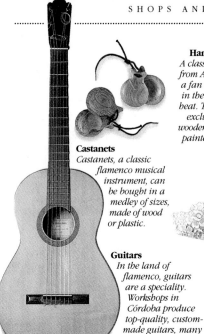

Castanets
Castanets, a classic flamenco musical instrument, can be bought in a medley of sizes, made of wood or plastic.

Handmade Fans
A classic souvenir from Andalusia, a fan is useful in the searing heat. The most exclusive are wooden, carved and painted by hand.

Guitars
In the land of flamenco, guitars are a speciality. Workshops in Córdoba produce top-quality, custom-made guitars, many of which are destined for famous guitarists.

Mantillas
A mantilla is a headdress of lace draped over a large and ornate comb which is crafted from tortoiseshell or made in plastic.

THE FLAVOURS OF ANDALUSIA

Andalusian gastronomy reflects locally grown produce. An astonishing range of olive oils is available, and the region's grapes are made into sherry vinegars, as well as some of Spain's most distinctive wines *(see p214)*. Almonds are used to make delicious sweets, such as *turrón*, a type of nougat.

Olive oil from the provinces of Córdoba and Sevilla

Sherry wine vinegars produced by sherry *bodegas*

Yemas, sweets produced by nuns in the Convento de San Leandro *(see p75)*

Marmalade from the Convento de Santa Paula *(see p88)* in Seville

HERBS AND SPICES

Almost 800 years of Moorish occupation in Andalusia left a distinctive mark on the region's cuisine. Many dishes are flavoured with fragrant spices once imported from the East, such as cumin, coriander, paprika, and strands of saffron. Markets are the best place to buy exotic spices and locally grown herbs, which are sold loose by weight.

Saffron threads

Pimentón (paprika)	**Coriander seeds**	**Cumin seeds**

ENTERTAINMENT IN ANDALUSIA

I N ANDALUSIA life takes place on the streets. The *paseo*, *tapeo* and dressing up for a night on the town are all an integral part of a day. Southern Spain is also a land of *fiestas* and *ferias (see pp36–7)*, and at certain times of the year a constant stream of music, singing and excited voices fills the air.

With temperatures soaring to 45° C (113° F), summer days are orga-nized around enjoying the cool of the

Poster for dance festival at Itálica

night. Evenings out begin late and go on until dawn; many of the cultural events and concerts start at around midnight.

Seville sets the pace for the whole region and the stylish *sevillanos* are fiercely proud of their beautiful city and of their reputation as all-night revellers. A thriving centre for art, fashion and flamenco, Seville is also an excellent place to see bullfights and to watch or participate in sports.

Flamenco guitarist playing at a festival in Teatro de la Maestranza, Seville

PRACTICAL INFORMATION

E VENTS are normally advert-ised on posters all around town, especially in Seville. *El Giraldillo* is a monthly listings magazine featuring everything from the arts to bars, clubs and sporting activities. On Fridays, the *Diario 16*, a national news-paper, publishes a regional listings supplement. Granada has its own monthly listings magazine, which is called *Guía de Ocio. (See also p245.)*

BOOKING TICKETS

I T IS USUALLY POSSIBLE to book tickets in advance for major sports events, opera, concerts and festivals. Your hotel or nearest tourist information office should have details on

where to purchase them. Football is always immen-sely popular, so ensure that you start queueing early for tickets to import-ant matches. Bear in mind that even major events are often set up hurriedly, so that customers have little advance warning.

FLAMENCO

F LAMENCO embraces a broad spectrum, and in Seville it can be found in all its expressions. The *tablaos* (flamenco bars) in the Barrio de Santa Cruz *(see p68)* are aimed at tourists and yet they still provide high quality per-formances. Soul-stirring outbursts of song known as *cante jondo* are sung in the gypsy bars of Triana, while in Calle Salado there are bars where the public can dance *sevillanas*, upbeat folk dances popular with, and danced by, virtually everyone in Andalusia. **El Patio Sevillano** and **La Carbonería** are *tablaos* with traditional Andalusian patios.

One of the best-known flamenco venues in the city of Granada is in the gypsy caves of Sacromonte *(see p185)* on the city outskirts.

Flamenco festivals and competitions are held fre-quently, all over Andalusia *(see pp32–4)*. Among these is the prestigious Festival de la Guitarra in Córdoba, which also features classical guitarists, and the **Bienal de Arte Flamenco** festival

held in Seville. In Córdoba, **El Cardenal** is a bar and restaurant that hosts flamenco shows at night. The craft market **La Posada del Potro** also puts on live flamenco shows occasionally.

THEATRE

M AKING A VISIT to the theatre in Andalusia and mixing with the perfectly groomed *andaluces* decked out in their finery is a true occasion.

In Seville, the **Teatro de la Maestranza** *(see p66)* and the **Teatro Lope de Vega** *(see p95)* are the leading places for a grand evening out. On Isla de la Cartuja *(see p102)*, the open-air stage **El Auditorio** and the **Teatro Central** are also fine venues for theatre.

In May, sometimes running on into early June, the Festival Internacional de Teatro y Danza *(see p36)* is held at the **Teatro de la Maestranza** in Seville.

Córdoba also boasts its own highly respected season of theatre at the **Gran Teatro**.

Gran Teatro, Córdoba, one of the city's leading venues for theatre

Rosario Flores, the famous Andalusian singing star, performing at one of her concerts

OPERA AND CLASSICAL MUSIC

SEVILLE, THE SETTING of Bizet's *Carmen* and Rossini's *The Barber of Seville*, is a city of opera lovers. Most operas, including those by prestigious international companies, are performed either in the Post-Modern setting of **El Auditorio** on Isla de la Cartuja *(see p102)* or at the elegant **Teatro de la Maestranza** *(see p66)*.

Classical music is also performed at the **Teatro Lope de Vega** *(see p95)*, at the old **Conservatorio Superior de Música Manuel Castillo** and at the cathedral *(see pp76–7)*.

Several classical music festivals are held in Andalusia *(see pp32–4)*. Among them, Sevilla en Otoño provides a rich and varied musical programme from October to February. In June and July, Granada hosts the Festival Internacional de Música y Danza *(see p33)*, one of the most prestigious events in Andalusia, when concerts are held against the backdrop of the Generalife *(see p188)*.

FOLK

OCCASIONALLY, lively groups of minstrels with lutes and mandolins, known as *la tuna*, perform in Andalusia. In Seville on the eve of the feast of the Inmaculada Concepción *(see p35)*, 8th December, *la tuna* play and sing in honour of the Virgin in front of her statue at Plaza del Triunfo *(see p78)*.

ROCK, POP AND JAZZ

FEW INTERNATIONAL rock stars make it to Seville, as Madrid and Barcelona monopolize the market. Large concerts are sometimes held at **Estadio Ramón Sánchez Pijuán**, or at the open-air El Auditorio on Isla de la Cartuja. However, there are plans to hold more international concerts in Seville in the future.

Some of Spain's most popular groups are from Andalusia, particularly those in the flamenco pop genre, for example Ketama or Rosario Flores.

International jazz festivals *(see p34)* are held in Seville and Granada. In Seville, bars featuring live jazz nights include **Sur Café Bar** and **La Buena Estrella**. The **Naima Café** is a themed jazz bar where jazz cds and t-shirts can be purchased.

La tuna, traditional singers in Santa Cruz, Seville

NIGHTLIFE

THE NIGHTLIFE of Seville offers an endless array of possibilities. Timing, however, is of the essence. The early meeting bars are typically traditional-style cafés or tapas bars, while the late bars have a completely different decor, ambience, music and clientele.

Virtually all nightclubs offer their customers free entrance. Seville's Plaza del Alfalfa overflows with youthful revellers, while the Calle Reina Mercedes near the university is a favourite haunt of the city's students. Calle Mateos Gago, and particularly **Bar Giralda**, round the corner from the Giralda *(see p76)*, is packed on Friday and Saturday nights. Calle Betis, along the Triana side of the river, has numerous bars, restaurants and nightclubs. Some of Seville's clubs are only just getting going at 3am. Head off to **Catedral** late, for a club with a novel ecclesiastical theme.

In Granada, one of the great social hubs is the area around the cathedral. **Cunini** is a wonderful place in which to enjoy wine, champagne and oysters. After dinner, Paseo de los Tristes, overlooked by the Alhambra *(see pp186–7)*, offers bohemian bars with music and a warm, arty ambience.

In Córdoba, the *tapeo (see p222)* is the dominant element in the city's nightlife. **Soul Chicken** is open for breakfast and has DJs performing at night. The Judería *(see p136)* is an attractive area for enjoyable drinking.

A display of flamenco dancing in a bar in Seville

Real Escuela Andaluza de Arte Ecuestre, Jerez de la Frontera

BULLFIGHTING

THE MAESTRANZA bullring in Seville is mythical among fans of bullfighting and some of the most important bullfights in Spain are held here during the Feria de Abril *(see p36)*. Most towns in Andalusia have their own bullrings; Ronda, Córdoba and Granada are among the other famous venues.

Generally, the bull-fighting season runs from April to October. Booking tickets in advance is essential if the matadors are well known, and advisable if you want to be seated in the shade *(sombra)*. It may be easier to get tickets for *novilladas*, fights involving matadors who are not yet fully qualified. Tickets are sold at the *taquilla* (booking office) at the bullring.

SPECTATOR SPORTS

FOOTBALL IS hugely popular. Seville has two rival teams, FC Sevilla, who are based at the **Estadio Ramón Sánchez Pizjuán** and Betis, who play at the **Estadio Manuel Ruiz de Lopera**. Matches are played on Sunday afternoons from September to May. Also very popular, particularly in Seville, is basketball *(baloncesto)*. The main Seville team is the Caja de San Fernando, which often competes against international teams at **Complejo Deportivo San Pablo**.

Tile for Seville's Betis football club

GOLF

GOLF IS A MAJOR sport in Andalusia and a spectacular range of courses is available on the Costa del Sol *(see p174)*. Seville and Jerez both also have a few excellent courses. Green fees range from 20 to 90 euros a round. Only the few most exclusive clubs require membership. Advance booking is advisable at Easter and in the autumn.

EQUESTRIAN SPORTS

THE HORSE IS an integral part of life in Andalusia, as is demonstrated during Seville's Feria de Abril *(see p36)*. The undoubted equestrian capital of Andalusia, however, is Jerez de la Frontera *(see p158)*. The Feria del Caballo (International Horse Week) *(see p32)* is held here in May, while horses form an important part of the local *fiestas* celebrated in September and October. Dancing horses perform in spectacular shows at the **Real Escuela Andaluza de Arte Ecuestre** *(see p158)*. Andalusians also have a great interest in horse-racing. A day at the races is considered to be quite a chic occasion.

Horse-trekking is a splendid way in which to get to know the often rugged countryside of Andalusia. Several riding schools, among them **Hípica Puerta Príncipe**, offer lessons in the area around Seville.

WATER SPORTS

WATER-SPORTS facilities are available at most resorts along the coast. Tarifa has ideal conditions for windsurfing. In Seville, windsurfing, canoeing and rowing on the Río Guadalquivir are popular. East of the city is the **Guadalpark**, an outdoor swimming pool complex open from June to September.

SKIING

THE SIERRA NEVADA *(see p189)* is the southernmost skiing region in Europe. **Solynieve**, its only resort, has the facilities to accommodate up to 30,000 skiers. The season starts late – mid to late December – but may run on until May.

In 1996, **Solynieve** played host to the World Ski Championships, thereby raising the profile of the Sierra Nevada as a skiing holiday destination.

Skiers enjoying the Solynieve ski resort in the Sierra Nevada

DIRECTORY

FLAMENCO

Seville
Bienal de Arte Flamenco
(festival held every other year: 1996, 1998, etc.)
(95 459 28 70.

Café Sol Cantante
Calle Sol 5.
Map 2 E5 (6 E2).
(95 422 51 65.

La Carbonería
Calle Levies 18.
Map 4 D1 (6 E4).
(95 421 44 60.

Los Gallos
Plaza de Santa Cruz 11.
Map 4 D2 (6 E4).
(95 421 69 81.

El Patio Sevillano
Paseo de Cristóbal Colón 11. **Map** 3 B2 (5 C5).
(95 421 41 20.

Granada
La Reina Mora
Mirador de San Cristóbal, Carretera Murcia.
(958 27 82 28.

Córdoba
Mesón Flamenco La Bulería
Calle Pedro López 3.
(957 48 38 39.

El Cardenal
Calle Torrijos 10.
(957 48 33 20.

La Posada del Potro
Plaza del Potro.
(957 45 80 01.

THEATRE

Seville
El Auditorio
Camino del Descubrimiento s/n, Isla de la Cartuja.
Map 1 B4.
(95 446 75 38.

Teatro Alameda
Calle Crédito 13.
Map 2 D4.
(95 490 01 64.

Teatro Central
Avenida José Gálvez, Isla de la Cartuja.
Map 1 C2.
(95 503 72 00.

Teatro Lope de Vega
Avenida María Luisa s/n.
Map 3 C3.
(95 459 08 67.
w www.andalunet.com

Teatro de la Maestranza
Paseo de Colón 22.
Map 3 B2 (5 C5).
(95 422 65 73.

Córdoba
Gran Teatro
Avenida Gran Capitán 3.
(957 48 02 37.

OPERA AND CLASSICAL MUSIC

Seville
El Auditorio
Camino del Descubrimiento s/n, Isla de la Cartuja.
Map 1 B4.
(95 446 75 38.

Conservatorio Superior de Música Manuel Castillo
Calle Banos 48.
Map 1 C5 (5 B1).
(95 491 56 30.

Teatro Lope de Vega
Avenida María Luisa s/n.
Map 3 C3.
(95 459 08 67.

Teatro de la Maestranza
Paseo de Cristóbal Colón 22.
Map 3 B2 (5 C5).
(95 422 65 73.

Córdoba
Conservatorio Superior de Música
C/ Angel de Saavedra 1.
(957 47 66 61.

ROCK, POP AND JAZZ

Seville
La Buena Estrella
Calle Trajano 51.
Map 1 C5 (5 C1).
(95 434 23 64.

Naima Café
Calle Trajano 47.
Map 1 C5 (5 C1).
(95 438 24 85.

Sur Café Bar
Carlos Canal 5.
Map 3 B1 (5 C3).
(95 456 11 91.

NIGHTLIFE

Seville
Bar Antigüedades
Calle Argote de Molina.
Map 3 C1 (6 D4).

Bar Giralda
Calle Mateos Gago 2.
Map 3 C2 (6 E4).

Catedral
Calle Cuesta del Rosario.
Map 3 B1 (5 C3).

Granada
Cunini
Plaza de Pescadería 14.
(958 26 75 87.

Granada 10
Calle de Cárcel Baja 10.
(958 22 41 26.

Córdoba
Cafetería Gaudí
Avda Gran Capitán 22.
(957 48 57 62.

Soul Chicken
Calle Alfonso XIII 3.
(957 49 15 80.

BULLFIGHTING

Seville
Plaza de Toros de la Maestranza
Paseo de Cristóbal Colón 12. **Map** 3 B2 (5 B4).
(95 422 35 06.

Granada
Plaza de Toros
Avenida Doctor Oloriz 25.
(958 27 24 51.

Córdoba
Plaza de Toros
Avda de Gran Vía Parque.
(957 45 60 81.

SPECTATOR SPORTS

Estadio Manuel Ruiz de Lopera (Real Betis)
Avenida Heliópolis s/n, Seville.
(95 461 03 40.

Estadio Ramón Sánchez Pizjuán (Sevilla FC)
Avenida Eduardo Dato s/n, Seville. **Map** 4 F2.
(95 453 53 53.

Complejo Deportivo San Pablo
Avda Kansas City, Seville.
(95 426 08 81.

GOLF

Seville
Real Club de Golf de Seville
Ctra Sevilla–Utrera km 3, Montequinto.
(95 412 43 01.

Costa del Sol
Club de Golf Valderrama
Ctra Cádiz–Málaga km 132, Sotogrande.
(956 79 12 00.

Mijas Golf Internacional
Camino Viejo de Coin 35, Mijas Costa.
(95 247 68 43.

Golf La Dama de Noche
Carretera Istan, Río Verde, Nueva Andalucía.
(95 281 81 50.

EQUESTRIAN SPORTS

Seville
Hípica Puerta Príncipe
Ctra Sevilla-Utrera km 11.5.
(607 60 73 19.

Hipódromo Real Club Pineda
Avenida de Jerez s/n.
(95 461 14 00.

Cádiz - Jerez
Real Escuela Andaluza de Arte Ecuestre
Avenida Duque de Abrantes s/n.
(956 31 96 35.

WATER SPORTS

Guadalpark
Polígono Aeropuerto. Sevilla-Este.
(95 451 66 22.

SKIING

Solynieve
Sierra Nevada (Granada).
(958 48 00 11 (info); 958 24 91 11 (booking).

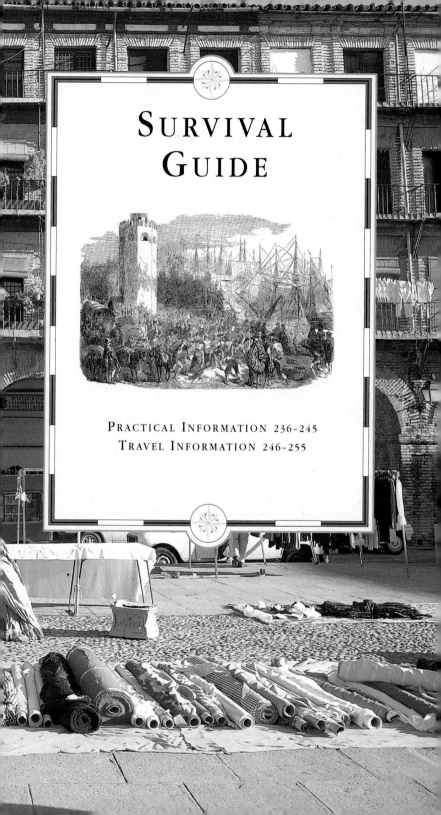

SURVIVAL
GUIDE

PRACTICAL INFORMATION

THE ECONOMY of Andalusia is heavily dependent on tourism. The rich variety of natural attractions and its cultural heritage draw visitors to the area throughout the year. Many have even settled in this evocative region, home of all things quintessentially Spanish: rich terracotta landscapes, olive groves, flamenco dancing, and *corridas* (bullfights).

Junta de Andalucía
tourist office logo

Events such as Expo '92 in Seville, the 500th anniversary of Columbus, the Sierra Nevada Ski Championships, and the cultural tours created for the Legado Andalusi in 1995 have led to an increase in the number of tourist facilities and an improved infrastructure. The Junta de Andalucía has tourist offices across the region, offering a wealth of helpful brochures, maps and leaflets.

Try not to do too much at once, but savour the particular delights of one or two places. Adjust to the slower pace and, in summer, do your sightseeing early in the day before the heat becomes unbearable.

Tickets for Hospital de los Venerables, Seville *(see p79)*

Leaflets on Andalusian culture, published by Junta de Andalucía

TOURIST INFORMATION

MOST OF THE major cities of Andalusia have several Oficinas de Turismo (tourist offices). Turespaña provides tourist information on Spain at a national level, while offices run by the Junta de Andalucía cover Andalusia as a region. Local tourist offices, found also in small towns, usually have details only of their environs.

Most tourist offices are well organized, offering brochures covering monuments, trips, emergency services and places to stay, among other services. They have a range of leaflets listing local festivals and can also offer suggestions on nightlife, theatres and flamenco shows. If you require more detailed information on sports, exhibitions, and concerts, check the listings in local papers *(see p245)*.

If you wish to hire a tour guide while staying in a major city, the tourist office will be able to direct you to a number of multilingual agencies.

El Legado Andalusi ("The Legacy of Andalus"), a project organized in 1995, highlights Andalusia's Moorish heritage through exhibitions and self-guided cultural tours. These are accompanied by leaflets and a guidebook.

ADMISSION CHARGES

SOME MONUMENTS and museums offer free entry to Spanish residents and members of the European Union. Others charge a moderate fee (children up to 12 years pay half price). Large groups may be offered a 50 per cent discount on tickets. Payments must be made in cash and not by credit card.

OPENING HOURS

HOURS KEPT BY monuments and museums can vary considerably, so it is always best to check them before your visit. From October until March, most museums open between 9:30 and 10am and close for the siesta at 1:30 or 2pm. They open again from

Foreign visitors on a guided tour of Seville

◁ **Plaza de la Corredera market, Córdoba**

Flamenco street performers entertaining visitors outside a bar

around 4:30pm and then close at 6 or 8pm. Most close on Sunday afternoons. However, during the tourist season many museums stay open all day.

Most churches open only for Mass, but in small towns a caretaker will often let visitors in between religious services.

VISITING CHURCHES

M ASS IS HELD every hour on Sundays, and at about 7–9pm on weekdays. In most churches, tourists are welcome in the church during a service as long as they are quiet.

Dress codes are not as strict as in other Catholic countries, but avoid skimpy shorts and bare arms. There is usually no admission charge, although a donation may be expected.

ETIQUETTE

T HE OPEN, FRIENDLY character of the Spanish means that strangers usually greet each other with a ¡Hola!, ¡Buenos días!, or ¡Buenas tardes! on meeting in doorways or lifts – and even when passing on the street in small towns. It is also considered polite for people who know each other to shake hands each time they meet, and for women to kiss each other on both cheeks.

Smoking is not allowed in cinemas, lifts or on public transport, but elsewhere non-smoking areas are rare.

Spaniards rarely drink alcohol without nibbles until after dinner. It is not thought polite to share the price of a round of drinks except with people you know very well.

While totally accepted on the Costa del Sol, topless sunbathing is frowned upon in many small coastal places.

TIPPING

O WING TO THE RISING COST of living, tipping tends to be an issue of discretion in Spain. A service charge (servicio) is usually included (see p211) in checks, but it is common to tip up to 10 per cent in addition and to give small change to taxi drivers, cinema ushers, and doormen.

COMPLAINTS BOOK

I F YOU ARE NOT HAPPY with a service, particularly in a restaurant or hotel, you are entitled to ask for the Libro de Reclamaciones. This is an official complaints book at the disposal of customers, which

Sign indicating the establishment has a Libro de Reclamaciones

is inspected periodically by the local authorities. Only use it for very unsatisfactory affairs, or threaten to use it if you suspect you are being cheated.

TOILETS

P UBLIC TOILETS are scarce. However, there is a bar on virtually every corner which is legally bound to allow you to use their toilets. Nevertheless some bars do so reluctantly, if no purchase has been made. A "D" on the door stands for Damas (ladies), and a "C" indicates Caballeros (men).

Keep small change handy – because if the toilets are not coin-operated (newer buildings only), it is usual to leave some small change for the attendant.

Foreign student relaxing by a fountain in Seville

IMMIGRATION AND CUSTOMS

VISITORS FROM the European Union (EU), the US and New Zealand do not need a visa for stays of up to 90 days. If your visit is for more than three months, you will need to apply to your Spanish Consulate for a permit *(visado)*. Citizens of Canada and Australia need a visa regardless of length of stay. Always check visa requirements before travelling.

On arrival, it is not necessary to register with the local police, but hotels will take your passport details. Vaccinations are not needed.

A sales tax *(IVA)* refund system is available in large department stores *(see p224)*, applicable to all except members of the EU.

EMBASSIES AND CONSULATES

IN THE EVENT of losing your passport or needing legal advice or other help, contact your national embassy or consulate. Most towns have volunteer interpreters, found at local police stations *(see p240)*. On the Costa del Sol, the Foreigners' Department of the Ayuntamiento (Departamento de Extranjeros) can help.

USEFUL ADDRESSES

Australian Embassy
Plaza del Descubridor Diego de Orgaz, 3, 2nd floor, 28003.
(91 441 60 25.

British Consulate
Calle Mauricio Moro Pareto 2, Málaga.
(95 235 23 00.
W www.ukinspain.com

Canadian Embassy
Calle Nunez de Balboa 35, 3rd floor, 28001 Madrid.
(91 423 32 50.
W www.canada-es.org

US Embassy
Calle Serrano 75, Madrid.
(91 587 22 00.
W www.embusa.es

DISABLED TRAVELLERS

MODERN BUILDINGS generally have adequate provision for the disabled, with lifts, ramps and special toilet facilities. However, owing to their construction, entry to certain historical monuments may be restricted. Local tourist offices, or the monument staff, can provide information about wheelchair access.

Two UK charities, **RADAR** and **Holiday Care Service** provide travel information for the disabled. **Servi-COCEMFE** in Madrid advises on hotels that are suitably equipped for disabled travellers *(see p201)*.

STUDENT INFORMATION

SEVILLE, GRANADA and Córdoba attract large numbers of students, many of whom come to Andalusia to learn Spanish. Most large towns have a **Centro de Documentación e Información Juvenil** which provides information for students and young people. A valid International Student Identification Card (ISIC card) entitles you to some price reductions, including museum entrance fees and travel.

SPECIALIST HOLIDAYS

THERE IS AMPLE opportunity to study Spanish language and culture in Andalusia. The universities of Seville *(see p94)* and **Granada** run various courses throughout the year and there are also several private organizations. Contact **AEEA** (Asociación Empresarial de Escuelas de Español para

Horse-riding in the Granada countryside

STREET SIGNS IN ANDALUSIA

Many of the streets of Andalusia's towns are adorned with beautiful street signs. They are usually made of white tiles with a painted border, often displaying the emblem of the town or province. For example, the Calle Barrio Alto sign features a pomegranate *(granada)*, the historical emblem of the city of Granada.

Colourful street signs, found all over Andalusia

Extranjeros de Andalucía) or the **Instituto Cervantes** (Spanish Institute) for a list of Spanish language courses.

For details on leisure activities including cookery, salsa and flamenco contact **Instituto Internacional Gibralfaro**. There is also plenty on offer for the nature lover and for golf, horse-riding and water sport enthusiasts *(see p232)*. More information on alternative and special interest holidays can be found at Spanish tourist offices *(see p237)*.

ELECTRICAL ADAPTORS

THE CURRENT IN SPAIN is 220v-AC with two-pin, round-pronged plugs. Adaptors can be found in many hypermarkets, supermarkets and also some electrical stores. If you can, take one with you to be on the safe side. Most hotels and *pensiones* have electric points for hair dryers and shavers in all the bedrooms. Many now use the key/card system for switching on the electricity supply in rooms.

ADDRESSES

IN SPEECH, on maps and in written information, the Spaniards often drop the *Calle* in street names, so that Calle Mateos Gago becomes Mateos Gago. Other terms, such as *Plaza, Callejón, Carretera* and *Avenida*, do not change.

In addresses, a *s/n (sin número)* after the street name indicates that the building has no number. Outside towns, an address may say "Carretera Córdoba–Málaga km 47" – the sight is on the highway near to the kilometre sign.

SPANISH TIME

SPAIN IS ONE HOUR AHEAD of Greenwich Mean Time (GMT) and British Summer Time. The time difference between Seville and other cities is: London -1 hour, New York -6, Perth +7, Auckland +12, Tokyo +8. These figures may vary for brief periods in spring and autumn when clock changes are not synchronized.

The 24-hour clock is used in listings and for official purposes but not in speech. The morning (am) is referred to as *por la mañana* and the afternoon (pm), *por la tarde*. Afternoon does not start at midday, but rather after siesta time, at around 4 or 5pm.

CONVERSION CHART

Imperial to Metric
1 inch = 2.54 centimetres
1 foot = 30 centimetres
1 mile = 1.6 kilometres
1 ounce = 28 grams
1 pound = 454 grams
1 pint = 0.6 litres
1 gallon = 4.6 litres

Metric to Imperial
1 centimetre = 0.4 inches
1 metre = 3 feet, 3 inches
1 kilometre = 0.6 miles
1 gram = 0.04 ounces
1 kilogram = 2.2 pounds
1 litre = 1.8 pints

Personal Security and Health

Mounted police officers from the *Policía Nacional*

ANDALUSIA IS, BY AND LARGE, a safe place for visitors. Women travelling alone tend not to be hassled, but may have to put up with so-called compliments from men of all ages. Pickpockets and bag-snatchers, however, are very common, especially in Seville, so it is best to be cautious around popular tourist spots and on crowded buses. Try to avoid carrying valuable items and, if possible, wear a money belt. If you become ill during your stay, go to the nearest pharmacy, where someone should be able to advise you. Organize your travel insurance before leaving for Spain as it is difficult to obtain and more expensive once there.

Officer of the *Policía Nacional*

PROTECTING YOUR PROPERTY

PICKPOCKETS ARE COMMON in crowded areas, especially outside monuments and at markets. Be particularly wary of people asking you the time, as they are probably trying to distract you while someone else attempts to snatch your bag or wallet. Also, if you have a scooter, make sure that it is securely chained, especially in Seville and Málaga.

Use traveller's cheques or Eurocheques rather than cash, and carry a photocopy of your passport, leaving the original in the hotel safe. If you have a car, do not leave valuables in view and try to leave it in a security-controlled car park.

In the event of being robbed or attacked, try to report the incident to the police (*poner una denuncia*) as soon as possible (at least within 24 hours). This is extremely important if you wish to obtain a statement (*denuncia*) to make an insurance claim.

PERSONAL SAFETY

THE ABUNDANCE of street-life means that you will rarely find yourself alone or in a position to be harassed. However, women may be intimidated by men passing comment as they walk by, or even following them. This pastime, known as *piropo*, is common and not meant as a serious threat.

There are no particularly notorious areas of Seville to be avoided. Just act streetwise: do not use maps late at night and try to look like you know where you're going.

When visiting the Sacromonte caves in Granada to see gypsy families perform flamenco (*see p185*), it is a good idea to go in a group and keep an eye on your belongings.

Make sure that you take official taxis displaying a licence number and avoid public transport at night if alone. Any cab driver touting for business is likely to be illegal.

Marked car of the *Policía Nacional*

***Policía Local* patrol car, mainly seen in small towns**

POLICE

THERE ARE BASICALLY three types of police in Spain – the *Guardia Civil*, the *Policía Nacional* and the *Policía Local*. When approaching the police remember that it is illegal to be without ID.

Out of the main towns you will usually encounter the green-uniformed *Guardia Civil*. They patrol the country highways and, although they have a mean reputation, they will help if your car breaks down (*see p253*).

The *Policía Nacional*, who wear a dark blue uniform, are the best to turn to, especially when reporting a crime. They have many different responsibilities, including dealing with visitors' permits and documentation. In the bigger cities the *Policía Nacional* also guard many important establishments, such as government buildings, embassies and barracks.

The *Policía Local* take care of the day-to-day policing of small towns and villages.

EMERGENCY NUMBERS

First Aid
Seville (112.
Córdoba (112.
Granada (112.

Police
(112.

Traffic Police
Seville (95 462 11 11.
Córdoba (957 20 30 33.
Granada (958 15 36 00.

Pharmacies

For minor complaints, visit a pharmacy *(farmacia)*, where pharmacists are highly trained. They dispense a wide range of medication over the counter, including antibiotics.

Farmacias have a green or red neon cross outside, usually flashing, and are found in most villages and towns. They keep the same hours as most other shops (9:30am–1:30pm and 4–8pm). At least one will be *de guardia*

Spanish pharmacy signs

– ready to dispatch out of hours, at night and on Sunday. The opening rota is posted on the door of all *farmacias* and you will also be able to find it listed in local newspapers.

Medical Treatment

If in need of urgent medical assistance, go to the nearest *Urgencias* – the emergency ward of a hospital or clinic.

All the cities have several hospitals each, while the Costa del Sol has a hospital situated on the main coastal highway (N340) just east of Marbella. Most hospitals have volunteer interpreters who speak English and occasionally also other languages.

A Red Cross ambulance

The Cruz Roja (Red Cross) has an extensive network throughout Spain and runs an ambulance service.

Members of the European Union (EU) and visitors from Iceland are entitled to free or reduced-cost emergency treatment by the state medical services, but not from the private sector. If travelling from Britain, pick up form E111 from the post office or a travel clinic before you leave. Fill the form in there and have it stamped, as it is of no use unless stamped. When seeking medical help, you need to take the form to the local clinic or hospital where you are receiving treatment. It entitles you to the same cover as nationals. Do not part with the original, but hand over a photocopy instead.

If you have private travel insurance, make sure you have your policy on you when requesting medical assistance. Depending on the insurance company, you may be expected to pay for treatment and be reimbursed at a later date.

Health Precautions

Beware of the sun, particularly from May to October when temperatures can reach up to 45° C (113° F). Try to avoid walking in the midday sun and stay in the shade whenever possible. Drink plenty of bottled mineral water.

It is advisable to wear sunglasses and a hat when you are out sightseeing. When in the countryside, you may see signs showing a bull or saying *Toro bravo* (fighting bull). These signs should be taken seriously as these bulls are extremely dangerous animals and by no means should be approached.

Legal Assistance

If you are involved in an incident which requires a lawyer, ask your Embassy or Consulate *(see p238)* for the name of a reputable one. However, do not expect all lawyers to speak English. Police stations can sometimes provide volunteer interpreters *(intérpretes)* to help visitors from other countries. Otherwise it may be necessary to hire an interpreter to state your case clearly. *Traductores Oficiales* or *Jurados* are qualified to undertake most types of legal or official work.

DIRECTORY

Lost Property

Seville
Oficina de Objetos Perdidos, Almansa 21. **Map** 4 D3.
[95 421 50 64.

Córdoba
Comisaria de Policia, Avenida Doctor Fleming, 2.
[957 59 45 00.

Granada
Ayuntamiento, Plaza del Carmen 5.
[958 24 81 00.

Lost Cards and Traveller's Cheques

American Express
[902 37 56 37.

Diners Club
[901 10 10 11.

MasterCard (Access)
[900 97 12 31 *(toll free)*.

Travelex
[900 94 89 71 *(toll free)*.

VISA
[900 99 12 16 *(toll free)*.

Medical Treatment

Cruz Roja
Hospital Victoria Eugenia, Avenida de la Cruz Roja, Seville.
Map 2 E4. [95 435 14 00.

Hospital Costa del Sol
Carretera Nacional 340 km 187, Marbella, Málaga.
[95 282 82 50.

Hospital General
Avenida de las Fuerzas Armadas, Granada.
[95 802 00 00.

Hospital Nuestra Señora de Valme
Carretera de Cádiz, Seville.
[95 501 50 00.

Hospital Reina Sofia
Avenida Menéndez Pidal s/n, Córdoba.
[95 701 00 00.

Legal Assistance

Asociación Profesional de Traductores e Intérpretes
C/Recoletos 5, 28001 Madrid.
[91 541 07 23.

Banking and Local Currency

CHANGING MONEY IN SPAIN can often be quite time-consuming. Finding exchange facilities is not a problem, however. There are usually one or two banks even in small towns (but not necessarily in villages). Other options for changing traveller's cheques and currency include *casas de cambio*, hotels and travel agents. Alternatively, credit cards and Eurocheques are widely accepted in larger shops, hotels and restaurants.

You can take any amount of foreign currency into Spain, but sums worth over 6,000 euros should be declared at customs when you enter the country.

CHANGING MONEY

YOU CAN CHANGE money and cash traveller's cheques at *casas de cambio* (bureaux de change), banks and *cajas de ahorros* (building societies). Travel agents and hotels also change money. Málaga airport has 24-hour exchange facilities and Seville airport has a bank open at the usual times.

It is better to take enough euros for your initial needs before travelling, and to shop around for the best rates at your leisure after you arrive. Hotels and travel agents do not give good exchange rates and commissions charged on foreign currency transactions also vary. They are higher than average at the airports.

It is compulsory to show your passport or driver's licence when changing money or traveller's cheques.

USING BANKS

IT USUALLY REQUIRES a lot of patience when using banks in Andalusia. You will generally find that there are very few bank clerks who are attending the public and that queues can be endless. In larger banks you may find that some staff speak English, but only a few words.

In some banks you must fill in a few forms at the *cambio* (exchange desk) before going to the *caja* (cash desk) to queue up for your money. It is best to choose one of the bigger banks, such as the BBVA (Banco Bilbao Vizcaya Argentaria) or the Banco Central Hispano. These banks will have branches throughout Andalusia and you often have to queue just once to receive your money.

To enter a bank you will have to ring a bell then the teller will open the door for you from behind the counter. Alternatively, many banks now have electronically operated double doors. First you must press the button to open the outer door. Once inside, wait until you see the green light (which comes on when the outer door closes) and the second door will then open automatically.

BBVA

Logo for BBVA, the Banco Bilbao Vizcaya Argentaria

BANKING HOURS

BANKS IN ANDALUSIA are open for business from 8:30am to 2pm Monday to Friday but only from 8:30am to 1pm on Saturdays during the winter. From May to September they do not open on Saturdays.

Banks are never open on public holidays (*see p35*) and during a town's annual *feria* week (*see pp36–7*) the banks will open for just three hours from 9am to noon. This is to allow the staff to join in the general merrymaking.

CREDIT CARDS

CREDIT CARDS such as VISA, American Express and Mastercard (Access) are widely accepted all over Spain. Some establishments may require identification such as a passport or driving licence before accepting the transaction. Major banks will give cash on credit cards, and if your card is linked to your home bank account, you can also use it with your PIN number to withdraw money straight from cash machines. Instructions are given on the display in several languages.

Standard bank cards that bear the Cirrus and Maestro logos can also be used widely across Andalusia to withdraw money from cash machines or, as at home, as swipe cards to purchase goods.

TRAVELLER'S CHEQUES

MOST TYPES of traveller's cheques are accepted in Spanish banks. It is probably best to choose US dollars or pounds sterling, but most currencies are acceptable. All banks charge a commission for cashing traveller's cheques. However, American Express offices do not charge any commission on their own cheques.

If you wish to cash cheques larger than 3,000 euros, you must give the bank 24 hours' notice. Also if you draw more than 600 euros on traveller's cheques, you will probably be asked to produce the purchase certificate.

DIRECTORY

FOREIGN BANKS

Banco Halifax Hispania
Martin Villa, 3, 41003 Seville.
📞 95-450 04 40.

Barclays Bank
Reyes Católicos, 6, 41001 Seville.
📞 95-421 60 49.

Citibank
Avenida República Argentina, 24, 41011 Seville.
📞 95-499 04 60.

Lloyds TSB
Plaza Nueva, 8, 41001 Seville.
📞 95-450 15 46.

THE EURO

INTRODUCTION OF the single European currency, the euro, took place in 12 of the 15 member states of the EU. Austria, Belgium, Finland, France, Germany, Greece, Ireland, Italy, Luxembourg, The Netherlands, Portugal and Spain have joined the new currency; the UK, Denmark and Sweden stayed out, with an option to review the decision. The euro was introduced on 1 January 1999, but only for banking purposes. Notes and coins came into circulation on 1 January 2002. A transition period has allowed euros and pesetas to be used simultaneously, with national notes and coins being phased out by March 2002. All euro notes and coins can be used anywhere within the participating member states.

Bank Notes

Euro bank notes have seven denominations. The 5-euro note (grey in colour) is the smallest, followed by the 10-euro note (pink), 20-euro note (blue), 50-euro note (orange), 100-euro note (green), 200-euro note (yellow) and 500-euro note (purple). All notes show the 12 stars of the European Union.

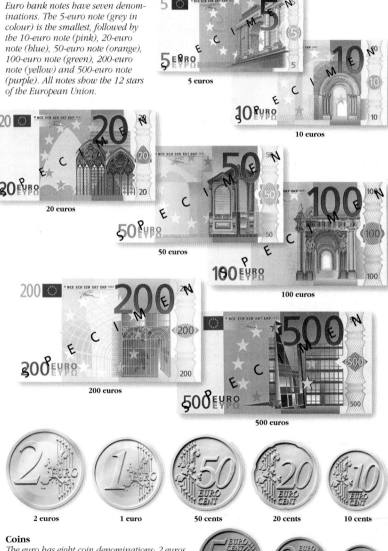

5 euros

10 euros

20 euros

50 euros

100 euros

200 euros

500 euros

2 euros

1 euro

50 cents

20 cents

10 cents

Coins

The euro has eight coin denominations: 2 euros and 1 euro (silver and gold); 50 cents, 20 cents and 10 cents (gold); and 5 cents, 2 cents and 1 cent (bronze). The reverse (number) side of euros are the same in all Euro-zone countries, but the front is different in each state.

5 cents

2 cents

1 cent

Communications

Post office (correos) sign

THE TELEPHONE SYSTEM in Spain is run by Telefónica. It is efficient, but one of the most expensive in Europe. Most lines abroad are good and there are plenty of public telephones. In recent years, Spain has also built up internet and electronic communications.

Spain's postal service is notoriously inefficient but letters posted at central post offices will not take too long. Radio and television are very popular and there are many local radio stations. Regional newspapers have also gained popularity in Andalusia.

TELEPHONING IN ANDALUSIA

SPANIARDS LOVE to talk, so there are plenty of phone booths (cabinas telefónicas) on the streets, and most bars have public phones. There are also public telephone offices (locutorios), where you make a call and pay for it afterwards, and also private bureaux with both phone and fax facilities.

Public phones use coins and phonecards (tarjetas telefónicas). Cabinas are often positioned in pairs on the streets, one accepting coins

Logo of Spanish telecom system, Telefónica

and one phonecards. You can buy phonecards from all tobacconists (estancos) and newsstands. They are priced according to their value in call units.

It is easiest to make long-distance calls (conferencias interurbanas) at locutorios. A

Telefónica's modern, blue and green-coloured public telephones

call made from a cabina telefónica or locutorio costs 35 per cent more than from a private phone. In a bar the cost can be prohibitive, since many bars install phone meters and some charge very high rates. Calls from hotel telephones are also more expensive. Calling abroad is cheapest between 10pm and 8am daily.

USING A COIN AND CARD TELEPHONE

1 Lift the receiver, wait for dialling tone and for the display to show *"Inserte monedas o tarjeta"*.

2 Insert either coins (monedas), pressing the button to the right of the slot if there is one, or a card (tarjeta).

3 Key in the number (Spanish phones prefer you to pause between digits).

4 As you press the digits, the number you are dialling will show on the display. You will also be able to see how much money or units are left and when to insert more coins.

5 When your call is finished, replace the receiver. A phonecard then re-emerges automatically. Any excess coins inserted will also be returned.

Spanish phonecard

USING A PUBLIC TELEPHONE

MOST OF the new public phone booths have a visual display to guide users. Illustrated instructions on how to use the phone, and lists of local and national dialling codes, are posted up in most booths in cities and centres of tourism. Some phones are designed so that users may change the language of the instructions by pressing a button with a flag symbol.

Expect some public phones in streets to be out of order. If you call from an open booth, watch your purse, wallet and bags as you are an obvious target for pickpockets.

SENDING LETTERS

THE SPANISH POSTAL SERVICE is rightly known as slow and unreliable. Services between major cities are fairly efficient,

Distinctive yellow Spanish postbox *(buzón)*

Standard issue stamps

but mail to or from smaller towns can be very slow. Postcards sent abroad can take more than a month to arrive, particularly in the summer. Letters posted at a central post office will usually arrive in reasonable time, but be aware that post-boxes *(buzones)* may not be emptied for days, even in large towns and cities.

If you need to send important or urgent mail use the *certificado* (registered) and *urgente* (express) mail. It should arrive anywhere in Spain on the following day and in towns elsewhere in Europe in three to five days.

Buy stamps *(sellos)* at post offices and *estancos* (state-run tobacconists), displaying a distinctive yellow and red sign. Main post offices open 8am–9pm Monday to Friday, 9am–7pm Saturday; local post offices 9am–2pm Monday to Friday, 9am–1pm Saturday.

POSTE RESTANTE

IN MOST LARGE TOWNS a *poste restante* service is available. A letter should be addressed to the relevant person, *"Lista de Correos"*, the town name and region. Letters are kept at the town's main post office from where they can be collected. A passport or other form of identification is needed but there is no collection fee.

REACHING THE RIGHT NUMBER

• When dialling within a city, province or to another province, dial the entire number – the province is indicated by the initial numbers: Seville & Málaga 95, Córdoba 957, Cádiz 956, Granada 958, Huelva 959, Jaén 953, Almería 950 .
• International calls: dial 00, wait for tone, dial country and area codes and number.
• Telefonica directory enquiries are on 11818.

• International directory enquiries are on 025.
• Operator assistance for calls to Europe and North Africa is on 1008. For the rest of the world, dial 1005. If you want to know the cost, ask the operator beforehand.
• To connect directly with the operator in your country dial 900 followed by 990061 (Australia); 990015 (Canada); 990011 (USA); or 990044 for the United Kingdom.

TV AND RADIO

THERE ARE TWO state channels in Spain, TVE1 and TVE2, plus stations Antena 3 and Telecinco (5). In addition, Andalusia has its own TV channels: Canal Sur and Canal 2 Andalucia. Canal Plus is a cable television company showing films, sport and documentaries. Subtitled foreign films are listed in TV listings by the letters V.O. *(Versión Original)*.

Canal Sur, the local broadcasting station

The best radio news programmes are broadcast on Radio Nacional de España. BBC World Service frequencies and listings can be found in its monthly *Worldwide* magazine for English language listening.

A selection of national and regional Spanish newspapers

NEWSPAPERS AND MAGAZINES

THE MOST IMPORTANT national papers are *El País* (which prints an Andalusian version daily and is linked to the

Socialist Government), *ABC* (conservative), and *El Mundo* (independent). Local papers such as *Ideal* in Granada, the Córdoba *Diario* or the Málaga *Sur,* have more extensive listings of local cultural and sporting activities. An English version of *Sur* is distributed free in Málaga on Fridays. The local listings magazines are the *Giraldillo* in Seville and the *Guía del Ocio* in Granada *(see p230). La Tribuna,* Córdoba's weekly free sheet, publishes useful practical information.

TRAVEL INFORMATION

ANDALUSIA is well served by a wide range of transport. Each year sees the arrival of thousands of charter and scheduled flights, mostly from European countries, though some are from the USA. Most flights from beyond Europe stop in Madrid or Barcelona before arriving at Andalusia's busiest airport, Málaga. Located only a few miles from Morocco, Málaga serves as a gateway to Africa. Seville airport also caters to international flights. Seville has good rail links, and the AVE high-speed train

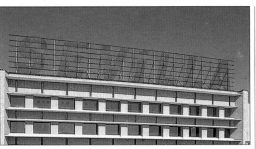

Iberia Airlines aircraft

between Seville and major cities – such as Córdoba and Madrid – will often be quicker than flying (if you include checking-in time). There are coaches from northern Europe and regional services throughout Andalusia. Ferries sail from Plymouth and Portsmouth to Santander and Bilbao; from here it is around a ten-hour drive to Andalusia. However, driving is not recommended in summer when there is a mass exodus from Madrid to the Costa del Sol and the number of hire cars on the roads is at its greatest.

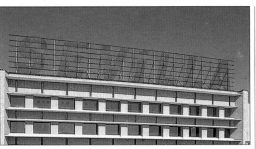

Seville Airport, conveniently situated just outside the city

ARRIVING BY AIR

MOST OF EUROPE'S major airlines, as well as some Middle Eastern and American lines, run scheduled flights to Málaga, Andalusia's main airport. The majority of air traffic, however, is made up of cheap charter flights, which bring in thousands of holiday-makers at all hours of the day and night. While charter flights are inexpensive, over-booking can be a problem in summer and flights are often subject to long delays. Seville airport is much less busy and is convenient for travellers staying inland.

PACKAGE HOLIDAYS

ALMOST ALL package deals to Andalusia focus on beach holidays. However, one or two tour operators also offer city breaks. Some offer a tour of a number of cities, starting in Málaga (you can fly there from a choice of UK airports), then following an itinerary,

travelling by coach, along the Costa del Sol, to Seville, Córdoba, Granada and Cádiz.

SEVILLE AIRPORT

SEVILLE AIRPORT is useful for travellers who are staying away from the coast. Located just 4 km (2.5 miles) out of the city centre, on the NIV road to Córdoba and Madrid, it is modern and very convenient.

There are scheduled flights daily to and from London, Paris and Frankfurt. Charter flights also operate out of Seville, but only at certain times of the year. As well as cities, such as Madrid, Barcelona and Santiago de Compostela, the internal destinations include Palma de Mallorca and Tenerife. **Vueling Airlines** offers low-cost internal flights.

Iberia Airlines ticket machine

Airport services include gift shops, a café and a ticket machine for purchasing internal Iberia flight tickets. *Los Amarillos* runs a regular bus service to and from the airport between 6:15am and 11pm. Taxis to the city centre are also available and cost 17–20 euros.

MÁLAGA AIRPORT

THE BUSY AIRPORT at Málaga receives around 10 million passengers a year, and has links to about 120 international destinations. Eighty per cent of international traffic is chartered flights, mostly from the UK. The airport is busy all year round, but particularly so from June to September. If you are intent on travelling to Málaga by charter, be sure to book well in advance. Obtaining scheduled flights is easier; they are available from **British Airways**, **Iberia**, **Easyjet**, **Ryanair**, **Spanair** and Vueling.

The airport terminal at Málaga is vast. Electronic buggies can be ordered, and there are electronic walkways too. Airport facilities include gift shops, jewellers, photographic stores, a pharmacy and a multi-denominational chapel.

There are plenty of car hire facilities, but it is advisable to book well in advance. The *tren de* cercanías (see p248) runs into Málaga and to the Costa del Sol as far as Fuengirola, every 20 minutes from 6am to 11pm.

By car it takes 20 minutes into Málaga. Taxis are available 24 hours a day, with tariffs beside the rank. The No. 19 bus, which runs every 30 minutes from 6:30am to midnight, also goes into Málaga.

Logo for Iberia Airlines

GRANADA AIRPORT

GRANADA'S AIRPORT is 17 km (10.5 miles) southeast of the city on the main road to Málaga. There are plans to expand the flight network but at present the airport caters for internal flights only. Facilities are also fairly limited: there is a newsagent and a gift shop, a café and a restaurant. There are regular flights to Palma de Mallorca, Tenerife and Las Palmas, as well as to major Spanish cities – Barcelona,

Madrid and Valencia. The airport opens from 8:30am to 8:30pm and there are car hire facilities in the terminal.

GIBRALTAR AIRPORT

THIS AIRPORT, located on the famous British rock, can be a useful arrival point for people visiting the west of Andalusia. Flights are operated exclusively by **GB Airways** from Britain (Gatwick, Heathrow and Manchester) and North Africa. The airport itself is small and manageable, but has few amenities.

AIRPORT CAR HIRE

THE MAJOR AIRPORTS are well served with international car hire companies such as **AVIS**, **Hertz** and **Europcar**, as well as local companies. **Holiday Autos** is a budget option, best booked online. Hire your car prior to your visit during high-season.

Many UK travel agents are able to organize fly-drive deals. These usually offer discounts on car hire arranged from abroad before travelling.

USEFUL NUMBERS

British Airways
Aeropuerto de Málaga.
📞 95 204 82 36.

Easyjet
📞 90 229 99 92.

GB Airways
Cloister Building, Irish Town, Gibraltar.
📞 9567 79300.

Iberia
Avenida Buhaira 8, Seville.
Map 3 C2 (5 C5).
📞 90 240 05 00.

Ryanair
📞 807 220 022.

Spanair
📞 90 292 91 91.

Vueling Airlines
📞 90 233 39 33.

Airport Information
Seville 📞 95 444 90 00.
Málaga 📞 95 204 84 84.
Granada 📞 958 24 52 00.

Car Hire
Avis W www.avis.es
Europcar W www.europcar.es
Hertz W www.hertz.com
Holiday Autos W www.holidayautos.co.uk

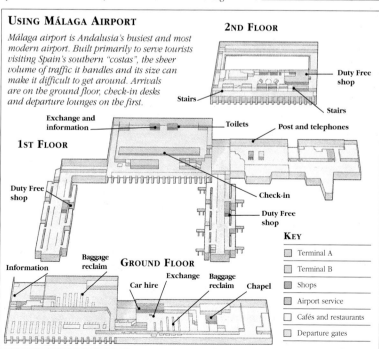

USING MÁLAGA AIRPORT

Málaga airport is Andalusia's busiest and most modern airport. Built primarily to serve tourists visiting Spain's southern "costas", the sheer volume of traffic it handles and its size can make it difficult to get around. Arrivals are on the ground floor, check-in desks and departure lounges on the first.

2ND FLOOR

Duty Free shop

Stairs

Stairs

Exchange and information

Toilets

Post and telephones

1ST FLOOR

Duty Free shop

Check-in

Duty Free shop

KEY

Terminal A

Terminal B

Shops

Airport service

Cafés and restaurants

Departure gates

Information

Baggage reclaim

GROUND FLOOR

Car hire

Exchange

Baggage reclaim

Chapel

Travelling by Train

Owing to the natural bottleneck of the Pyrenees, train connections between Spain and the rest of Europe are a little restricted. **Iberail**, however, a subsidiary of Spain's national network, RENFE, runs a service which links Madrid and Barcelona to France, Italy, Austria and Switzerland. **RENFE** offers routes throughout the country, on a variety of trains, and at a high level of service. The high-speed AVE *(Tren de Alta Velocidad Española)* linking Seville, Córdoba and Madrid has cut down journey times by almost half, and is extremely efficient.

AVE high-speed trains at Estación de Santa Justa, Seville

ARRIVING BY TRAIN

Trains coming from other European countries to Spain terminate in either Madrid or Barcelona. From Barcelona it is nine hours to Seville; from Madrid it takes around three hours travelling by AVE.

Andalusia's most important station is Santa Justa *(see p250)* in Seville. It has connections with major Andalusian towns and with Barcelona and Madrid (including 11 AVE high-speed trains running daily).

European and American rail passes, including EurRail and Inter-Rail, are accepted on the RENFE network, subject to the usual conditions. However, on certain trains you may find a supplement is payable.

TRAIN TRAVEL IN SPAIN

The train network in Spain is very extensive and there are services designed to suit every pocket. Travelling on the AVE is expensive, but fast. There is also a money-back guarantee that the train will reach its destination no more than five minutes late.

Other long distance services, known as *largo recorrido*, are divided into *diurnos* (daytime) and *nocturnos* (night-time). *Intercity* is the name given to standard daytime trains. *Talgos* are slightly more luxurious and more expensive. Night trains include *Expresos* and *Talgo cama (cama* means bed). *Regionales* run daytime from

city to city within a limited area. *Cercanías* are commuter trains running from large towns to their surrounding suburbs, towns and villages.

BOOKINGS AND RESERVATIONS

It is advisable to book long-distance journeys in advance, essential if you travel on public holidays *(días festivos)* or long weekends *(puentes)*. You can book a ticket from a station up to 60 days in advance and to collect it up to 24 hours before travelling. It can also be sent to your hotel *(servicio a domicilio)*. Tickets for *regionales* cannot be booked in advance. Most staff are helpful, although few speak English. RENFE agents in travel agencies are often more willing to discuss the available options.

TICKETS

Train travel in Spain is fairly reasonably priced. *Largo recorrido* and *regionales* have first and second class *(primera/segunda clase)*. The pricing for AVE trains and the Talgo 200 from Málaga to Madrid is worked out on a class system – *turista* (low), *preferente* (medium) and *club* (high) – and also by how busy trains are at certain times – *valle* (low), *plano* (middle) and *punta* (high). Thus, the most expensive tickets are *club punta* and the cheapest are *turista valle*. The tickets on Spanish trains always show a number for your seat (or bed

AL ANDALUS EXPRESO

The Al Andalus Expreso is a luxurious and evocative way to see Andalusia in style. This magnificent train is Spain's version of the Orient Express. Pulling 14 original carriages, all built between 1900–30, the Al Andalus provides the splendour of turn-of-the-century travel accompanied by all the comforts of modern-day living.

Short, leisurely paced journeys around the cities of Andalusia operate from April to October. On each trip, visits are scheduled to Seville, Córdoba, Jerez, Granada and Ronda.

Al Andalus Expreso, interior

Spain's Principal RENFE Network

Spain's Rail Network operates a wide variety of services. Study a RENFE brochure or train timetable before you buy your ticket.

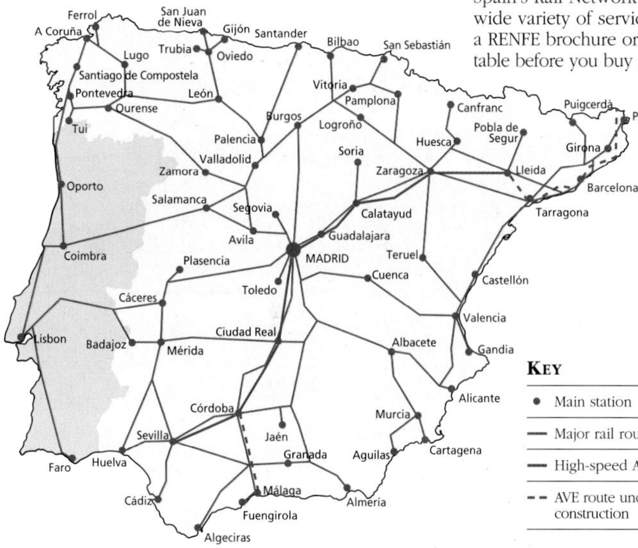

Key

- Main station
- Major rail route
- High-speed AVE route
- AVE route under construction

on sleepers). Tickets for long journeys are sold at main line stations, at the RENFE offices and some *cercanías* stations. Credit cards are accepted at the main stations, but not at the smaller or *cercanías* stations. You can change the date of a ticket twice, but you pay an extra 10–15 per cent. If further changes are then required, the ticket is reissued at full fare.

Tickets for Cercanías and Regional Trains

On regional lines and on *cercanías* you can buy a ticket, or *bono*, covering ten journeys, which offers a saving of about 40 per cent of the standard price. When entering a station, you pass the *bono* through a slot in the automatic barrier leading to the platform.

Using a Ticket Machine

Ticket machines for *cercanías* and regional lines are easy to use. A green flashing light guides you through the instructions printed on the front of the machine until you complete them and your ticket is dispatched.

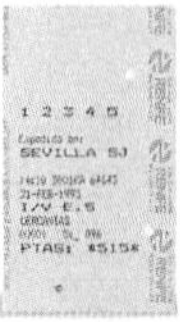

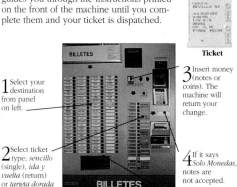

Ticket

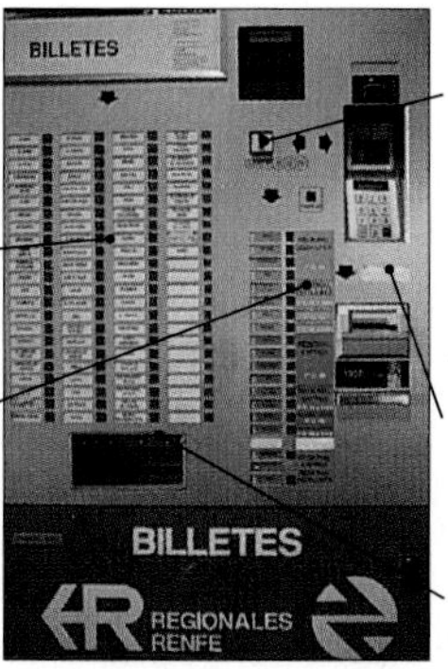

1 Select your destination from panel on left.

2 Select ticket type; *sencillo* (single), *ida y vuelta* (return) or *tarjeta dorada* (for pensioners).

3 Insert money (notes or coins). The machine will return your change.

4 If it says *Solo Monedas*, notes are not accepted.

5 Take your ticket.

Timetables

The punctuality rating of trains in Andalusia is quite high, particularly for the AVE. Brochures with prices and timetables are distributed free and are easy to follow. Information for *labor-ables* (weekdays) and *sábados, domingos y festivos* (Saturdays, Sundays and public holidays) is at the bottom of the timetable.

Useful Numbers

Booking Agents for RENFE
90 224 02 02. *www.renfe.es*

Seville
Calle Zaragoza 1.
Map 5 C2.
95 422 61 60.

Córdoba
Ronda de los Tejares 11.
957 47 78 35.

Granada
Reyes Católicos 30.
958 22 97 77.

Málaga
Calle Trinidad Grund 2.
95 221 81 91.

Iberail
Estación de Santa Justa, Avenida Kansas City s/n, Seville. **Map** 4 F1.
90 230 36 06.

Al Andalus Expreso
91 570 16 21.

The ultra-modern façade of Seville's Santa Justa railway station, built in 1992

SEVILLE, SANTA JUSTA

MODERN and user-friendly, Santa Justa is one of Andalusia's most recent landmarks. Even when busy, it seems spacious and safe, though visitors should look out for pickpockets during the summer months.

It is an easy station to use and all trains and platforms are visible through huge windows in the centre of the building.

Near the ticket office there are large notices featuring timetables for AVE and other long-distance train services. Self-service ticket machines are available for regional journeys and journeys by *cercanías (see pp248–9)*.

Electronic departures board at Santa Justa railway station

Ticket counter at Santa Justa railway station

The station has a large self-service restaurant-cum-café, gift shops, newsstands, cashpoint machines and money-changing facilities. For lost property, make your way to the office marked *Atención al Cliente*. At the front of the station you will find a large taxi rank and a spacious car park. The station is open from 4am to midnight and, though it is located in a slightly drab suburb, it is only about five minutes by car or bus from the city centre.

RENFE

RENFE logo

CÓRDOBA

CÓRDOBA HAS A GRAND, new station which opened in October 1994. Located in the northwest of the city, it is just a few minutes by car or taxi to the city centre. Like Santa Justa it is large, efficiently run and easy to find one's way around. Trains run to Madrid, Málaga, Barcelona, Seville, Jaén and Bilbao. The AVE to Madrid takes just 2 hours; to Seville 45 minutes. The station is well served with cafés, shops and ticket offices. Lockers for storing luggage are available.

GRANADA

SMALL AND PROVINCIAL, the station in Granada is more fitting to a village than a city. It is housed in an old building and has few amenities. There is a small café-cum-restaurant and a taxi rank outside. Most trains that pass through are regional or *cercanías* but long-distance trains do run to Madrid, Seville, the Costa Blanca, Barcelona, Almería, Córdoba and Málaga.

Exterior of Granada station

MÁLAGA

THE STATION IN MALAGA is quite small and is only busy at times when trains are due to set off or arrive. Connected by a *cercanías* to the coast as far as Fuengirola, it is convenient for visitors to the Costa del Sol. Trains also leave regularly for Madrid, Barcelona, Seville, Córdoba and Cádiz. There is a taxi rank outside.

TRAIN STATIONS

Seville, Santa Justa
Avenida Kansas City. **Map** 2 F5 & 4 F1.

Granada
Avenida Andalusia s/n.

Córdoba
Glorieta de las Tres Culturas.

Málaga
Explanada de la Estación s/n.

Rail Enquiries
📞 902 24 02 02
🖥 www.renfe.es

Travelling by Coach

THE MAJOR COACH LINKS between Andalusia and the rest of Europe are with France, Holland, Belgium, Switzerland and Austria. Within the region itself, coach travel is very popular and has improved enormously in recent years. Most coaches now have air-conditioning, a video, bar and WC. Travelling by coach in Andalusia is very economical and thanks to the recent improvement in roads, it can be quick and enjoyable. However, around the many holidays in the Spanish festive calendar, travelling can be difficult: coach stations tend to be overcrowded, coaches slow to depart and the roads busy.

Regional coach operated by the Alsina Graells company

ARRIVING BY COACH

THE MAJOR COACH STATIONS in Andalusia are in Seville, Granada, Córdoba and Málaga. However, some individual companies have a policy of avoiding central coach stations for departures and arrivals, particularly in Granada where there are a number of different companies in operation.

Coaches run frequently between major cities and towns and can sometimes provide the only way of getting to and from small villages. Travelling on these routes will certainly give you an experience of the region's local colour.

SEVILLE

SEVILLE'S main coach station is located in the centre of town at the Plaza de Armas. It is a modern, user-friendly building with an information desk and shopping mall. From here the Alsa coach company operates routes to destinations all over Spain as well as to France and Switzerland.

CÓRDOBA

THE MAIN COACH STATION in Córdoba is run by the Alsina Graells coach company. It is small and basic, comprising just a small waiting area with a café and a newsstand. Coaches depart regularly from

this point for Granada, Murcia, Almería, Málaga, Algeciras, Cádiz and Seville.

GRANADA

IN GRANADA, coach travellers may be confused by the choice of coach companies, each of which deals with a variety of different destinations. The largest is Alsina Graells Sur, and its station is what is normally referred to as the central coach station. Dirty and overcrowded, it is not an attractive place to linger, and it is advisable to buy your ticket in advance and turn up at the coach station a few minutes before departure. This

coach station offers routes all over Murcia and Andalusia. Coaches for Madrid leave from outside the main train station in Avenida Andaluces.

MÁLAGA

MÁLAGA COACH STATION is located in the centre of town. From here you can take coaches daily to a variety of locations all over Spain including Madrid, Barcelona, Valencia and Alicante, as well as the eight provincial capitals of Andalusia. Julia Tours and Lineabus operate coaches to Belgium, Holland, Switzerland and Germany from Málaga. Eurolines and Iberbus operate lines to the United Kingdom via Madrid and Paris.

COACH STATIONS

Seville
Estación Plaza de Armas
Plaza de Armas. **Map** 1 B5 & 5 A2.
[95 490 80 40.
Prado de San Sebastian Estación
(for all destinations within Andalusia)
[95 441 71 11.

Córdoba
Terminal Alsina Graells
Glorieta de las Tres Culturas.
[957 40 40 40.

Granada
Terminal Alsina Graells Sur
Carretera de Jaen, Granada.
[958 18 54 80.

Málaga
Estación de Autobuses
Paseo de los Tilos.
[95 235 00 61.

The main departure hall of Plaza de Armas coach station in Seville

Driving in Andalusia

Logo of a leading chain of petrol stations

MANY OF THE MAIN ROADS and motorways in Andalusia are new and in very good condition. However, as a result of the rapid expansion of the road network in recent years, some road maps are out of date, so be sure to buy one that was published recently. You should also bear in mind that the number of accidents on Spanish roads is the second highest in Europe. Always drive with caution, but particularly in July and August when the roads are packed with holiday-makers who do not know the area. When visiting towns and villages, it is generally best to park away from the centre and then walk in.

Typically narrow Andalusian street blocked by a parked car

ARRIVING BY CAR

VISITORS DRIVING vehicles from other countries need no special documentation in Spain. You should just make sure you have all the relevant papers from your country of origin: your driving licence, vehicle registration document and insurance. Your insurance company should be able to arrange an overseas extension of your car insurance. To hire a car in Spain you need show only a current driving licence.

When driving from Britain, if you have an old-style green licence you will also need to purchase an International Driving Permit. Obtain these from the RAC or the AA.

Most Spanish motorways are well equipped with an SOS network of telephones, which provide instant access to the emergency services. Ask for *auxilio en carretera.*

RULES OF THE ROAD

IN SPAIN PEOPLE DRIVE on the right, so you must give way to the right. At roundabouts, you should give way to cars already on the roundabout – but be extremely careful when on a roundabout yourself, do not expect oncoming cars to stop. Some will disregard you and drive straight on.

The speed limits are 50 kmh (30mph) in built-up areas; 90–100 kmh (55–60 mph) outside them and 120 kph (75 mph) on motorways. Seat belts are compulsory both in the back

and front; motor cyclists must wear crash helmets. Drivers must always carry a warning triangle and can be fined by the traffic police for not being equipped with a first-aid kit.

ROAD SIGNS

THE STANDARD EUROPEAN road signs are used on the roads in Andalusia. However, signposting is often confusing and inconsistent, so you need to be especially attentive when navigating in or out of cities. When leaving a town, scan the road for direction signs to other towns. Some are rather small and easily missed.

If you find yourself on the wrong road so that you need to change direction, look for signs which say *Cambio de Sentido.* They generally lead to bridges or underpasses where you can turn round.

LOCAL DRIVERS

MANY DRIVERS in Andalusia ignore road signs and most speed up at amber traffic lights instead of stopping.

It is common for drivers to close right up to the tail of the

ROAD SIGNS IN ANDALUSIA

Look out for the following road signs: *Peligro,* indicating danger, *Obras,* meaning roadworks ahead, *Ceda el Paso,* showing that you should give way and *Cuidado,* advising caution.

A road sign showing major routes at a crossroads

Overhead sign indicating the road is a motorway

Be alert to the fact that bulls may be on the road

Warning of the likelihood of snow or ice

car in front to signal that they want to overtake. Vehicles overtaking may signal with an arm for you to let them pass.

Indicators are not necessarily used by Spainsh drivers, so be alert and try to anticipate the movements of nearby vehicles.

MOTORWAYS

IN ANDALUSIA almost all the motorways are toll-free; they are called *autovías* and they are often revamped preexisting routes. An *autopista* (toll motorway), the A4 (*Autopista Mare Nostrum*) connects Seville and Cádiz.

As you approach the *autopista,* drive into one of the lanes to the booths, move up when a green light shows, and take the ticket which is given. You pay when you leave the *autopista* for the distance you have travelled, so take care not to lose your ticket.

DRIVING IN THE COUNTRYSIDE

ONLY HEAD OFF the major "N" roads *(rutas nacionales)* if you are not in any hurry. The "N" roads are usually very good, but some of the minor roads in Andalusia wind and climb, and their surfaces will often be in poor condition. In addition, although diversions may be marked, when you take them you may find they are inadequately or confusingly signposted. You could add hours to a journey by taking a minor road.

BUYING PETROL

MORE THAN HALF of the petrol stations in Andalusia still have attendants, although this is changing. There are many petrol stations out of town, and the larger ones tend to remain open 24 hours a day.

At self-service stations you generally have to pay for the petrol before it is dispatched. S*uper* (four-star), *gasoil* (diesel), and *sin plomo* (unleaded) are usually available. Credit cards are widely accepted.

DRIVING IN TOWN

DRIVING IN THE TOWNS and cities of Andalusia can be difficult. The centres of Seville (in particular around Santa Cruz) and Córdoba (near the Mezquita) have streets that are narrow, labyrinthine and hard to negotiate in a car.

When this is coupled with the fast, often inconsiderate driving of the residents, it can be stressful to drive in town. If you arrive by car, you are advised to garage it and use public transport until you are familiar with the area.

PARKING

AS LONG AS you avoid the narrow streets of Barrio Santa Cruz, the parking situation in Seville is usually not too bad. There are no official areas with parking meters (known as *zonas azules* in other parts of Spain), but quite a few convenient underground car parks.

In some streets or squares, however, there are parking attendants. They operate unofficially but most of them are honest. For a tip they will help you into a space and then watch your car until you return.

It is very difficult to park in Córdoba centre, but you may find space in the underground car park beside the Mezquita.

Granada is reasonably well provided with parking spaces

Self-styled parking attendant

and with indoor car parks. The charge for parking is around one euro an hour.

CYCLING

SPAIN IS NOT a cycle-friendly country. There are no cycle lanes in Andalusia's cities and cars tend to treat cyclists as a nuisance. A certain amount of sexual harassment also tends to afflict female cyclists. The traffic in the cities is usually too fast and chaotic to make for enjoyable or safe cycling, so it is generally best to stick to excursions into the country on mountain bikes.

DIRECTORY

BREAKDOWN SERVICES

ADA
(900 10 01 42.

Europ Assistance
(91 597 21 25.

RACE
(affiliated to the RAC in the UK)
(91 593 33 33.

CITY CAR HIRE

Avis
Seville (954 42 61 56.
Córdoba (957 40 14 45.
Granada (958 25 23 58.

Hertz
Seville (954 41 70 09.
Córdoba (957 40 20 60.
Granada (958 20 44 54.
Malaga (952 24 10 17.

Driving in the Sierra Nevada along one of the highest roads in Europe

Getting Around on Foot and by Bus

MANY OF ANDALUSIA'S TOWNS and villages have small, historic centres, characterized by narrow streets and tiny squares. Walking is an excellent and practical way of getting around the sights, especially as entry by car is restricted to residents only in parts of many towns. For the same reason, city buses are generally not much good for travelling between monuments, but they are useful to get to shopping areas or from your hotel into the centre of town. Buses are very cheap, clean and safe, and generally only crowded at rush hours.

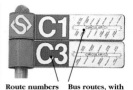

Route numbers **Bus routes, with**
for *circulares* **stops shown**

Orange, singledecker Tussam city bus, operating in Seville

WALKING

IN MANY ANDALUSIAN TOWNS, major sights are often only a short walk from where you are likely to be staying – at most just a short bus or taxi ride away.

In Seville, the tourist offices have a brochure, *Paseando por Sevilla* (strolling around Seville), which lists the city's interesting

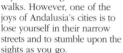

Red signal for wait; green for walk with care

walks. However, one of the joys of Andalusia's cities is to lose yourself in their narrow streets and to stumble upon the sights as you go.

There are plenty of organized walking groups which make excursions into the countryside. Look them up in the listings magazine *Giraldillo (see p245)* under *Deportes* (Sports).

The evening *paseo*, or stroll, is an institution. Groups of friends, couples and families dress up and take to the streets to shop, drink coffee, and see and be seen, before stopping off for dinner at around 10pm.

CROSSING ROADS

DRIVERS IN SPAIN tend not to respect pedestrians, even where pedestrians have the right of way. It is very rare for a driver to stop at zebra crossings. Crossings with pedestrian signals often have only a flashing amber light showing to oncoming drivers, even when the signal pedestrians see shows a green man; it is advisable to be very cautious when crossing if you can see any traffic approaching.

CITY BUSES

BUSES IN SPAIN are all single-decker. Get on at the front and either pay the driver, show your travel card or punch your *bonobus* (ticket) in the machine at the front of the bus. When alighting, press the button to request your stop and, if the bus is crowded, remember to give yourself plenty of time to get off at the side exit.

Seville's air-conditioned buses are controlled mainly by **Autobuses Urbanos Tussam** and are orange, or red and black (new buses). The useful lines for visitors are the *circulares*, numbered C1 to C4, which run around the city centre. Buses run from 6am on weekdays and Saturdays (from 7am on Sundays and public holidays), until 11:30pm in winter and 12:30am in summer. After these times, night buses take over, running on the hour until 2am.

A great way to see the major sights in Seville is by **Sevirama City Tour**, an open-topped double-decker bus. It goes from the Torre del Oro *(see p67)* or Plaza de España *(see p96)*.

The buses are less useful in Granada, as most of the sights are in pedestrian areas. Bus No. 2 runs from the centre of the city to the Alhambra.

In Córdoba the centre of town is again geared towards pedestrians. The No. 12 takes passengers from the Mezquita area to the newer, commercial centre of the city.

CITY BUS COMPANIES

Autobuses Urbanos Tussam
Avda de Andalucia II, Seville. **Map** 4 D3.
📞 902 45 99 54. W www.tussam.es

Sevirama City Tour
Paseo de las Delicias 1, Seville.
Map 3 C3. 📞 954 56 06 93.

Sevillanos **enjoying the Spanish national institution of the** *paseo*

Horse-Drawn Carriages

There is no better way to soak up the ambience of Andalusia's fine cities than from the seat of an old-fashioned, horse-drawn carriage. The official tariffs are usually posted by the places where the drivers wait in line with their carriages; for example near the Giralda *(see p76)* in Seville or the Mezquita *(see pp140–41)* in Córdoba. The price is usually a few thousand pesetas, although you will find that the drivers are sometimes willing to negotiate a cheaper fare. The carriages can seat up to four passengers.

Horse-drawn carriage by the cathedral in Seville

Tickets and Travel Cards

IN SEVILLE, a *billete sencillo* or *univiaje* (single ticket) can be purchased on the buses. Make sure, however, that you have enough small change, as a driver who cannot change a large note may ask you to get off at the next stop.

A *bonobus* ticket, valid for ten journeys, is good value at half of the price of ten single tickets. A *bonobus con derecho a transbordo* is similar, but it allows you to switch buses to continue a journey, as long as you do so within an hour. It is slightly more expensive.

Also good value, if you make more than five bus journeys in a day, is a *tarjeta turística* (a three- or seven-day tourist bus pass), which gives you unlimited bus travel. This can be bought from Tussam kiosks, newsstands and tobacconists.

For visitors staying longer in Seville, a *bono mensual* (a one-month pass) is good value. To buy one you need a photocard, which you can get made up at the Tussam central office.

Taxis

SPANISH TOWNS and cities are generously supplied with taxis, so there is not usually a problem finding one, day or night. Taxis are always white and have a logo on the doors, which diplays their official number. Drivers rarely speak any English, so learn enough Spanish to explain where you are going and to negotiate the fare. The meter marks up the basic fare; however, supplements may be added for *tarifa nocturna* (night-time driving), *maletas* (luggage), or *días festivos* (public holidays). If in doubt of the correct price, ask for the *tarifas* (tariff list).

Standard, white Seville taxi, with its logo and official number

Taxi Booking Numbers

Seville
℡ 95 458 00 00.

Córdoba
℡ 957 76 44 44.

Granada
℡ 958 28 06 54.

Metro

THE CONSTRUCTION of a new metro system for the city of Seville is now underway. The system, designed to aid transport between the outer areas of Seville and the city centre, will consist of four metro lines. The first of these, Line 1, is scheduled to open in December 2006. The lines will provide easy access to bus and train stations and will include a line to the airport (Line 4). However, because of the labyrinth of protected Roman ruins under the city, along with the unstable foundations of many of Seville's historic buildings, only key stations in the city centre will be serviced by the new metro.

Using a Ticket Stamping Machine

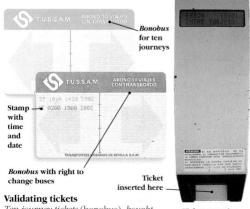

Bonobus for ten journeys

Stamp with time and date

Bonobus with right to change buses

Ticket inserted here

Ticket-stamping machine

Validating tickets

Ten journey tickets (bonobus), *bought in advance, are valid when stamped.*

General Index

Acknowledgments

DORLING KINDERSLEY would like to thank the following people whose contributions and assistance have made this book possible.

MAIN CONTRIBUTORS

DAVID BAIRD, resident in Andalusia from 1971 to 1995, has written many articles and books on Spain, including *Inside Andalusia*.

MARTIN SYMINGTON is a travel journalist and author who has written extensively on Spain. He is a regular contributor to *The Daily Telegraph* and also worked on the *Eyewitness Travel Guide to Great Britain*.

NIGEL TISDALL, contributor to the *Eyewitness Travel Guide to France,* is the author of many travel publications, including the *Insight Pocket Guide to Seville*.

ADDITIONAL CONTRIBUTORS

Louise Cook, Josefina Fernández, Adam Hopkins, Nick Inman, Janet Mendel, Steve Miller, Javier Gómez Morata, Clara Villanueva.

ADDITIONAL ILLUSTRATIONS

Richard Bonson, Louise Boulton, Brian Cracker, Roy Flooks, Jared Gilbey, Paul Guest, Christian Hook, Mike Lake, Maltings Partnership, John Woodcock.

ADDITIONAL CARTOGRAPHY

James Anderson, DK Cartography.

DESIGN AND EDITORIAL ASSISTANCE

Pilar Ayerbe, Eugenia Blandino, Greta Britton, Maggie Crowley, Cathy Day, Karen Fitzpatrick, Tim Hollis, Colin Loughrey, Francesca Machiavelli, Susan Mennell, Michael Osborne, Olivia Shepherd.

INDEX

Hilary Bird.

ADDITIONAL PHOTOGRAPHY

Patrick Llewelyn-Davies, David Murray, Martin Norris, Clive Streeter.

PHOTOGRAPHIC AND ARTWORK REFERENCE

Concha Moreno at Aeropuerto Málaga; Fanny de Carranza at the Area de Cultura del Ayuntamiento, Málaga; Tere González at Oficina de Turismo, Ayuntamiento, Cádiz; and staff at Castillo San Marcos, El Puerto de Santa María, Itálica, Seville cathedral and the Museo Bellas Artes, Seville.

SPECIAL ASSISTANCE

DORLING KINDERSLEY would like to thank all the regional and local tourist offices, *ayuntamientos* and *diputaciones* in Andalusia for their valuable help, and especially the Oficina de Turismo de Sevilla de Junta de Andalucía and other departments of the Junta de Andalucía. Particular thanks also to: Javier Morata, Jose Luis de Andrés de Colsa and Isidoro González-Adalid Cabezas at Acanto Arquitectura y Urbanismo, Madrid; Juan Fernández at Aguilar for his helpful comments; Robert op de Beek at Alvear, Montilla; Francisco Benavent at Fundación Andaluza de Flamenco, Jerez de la Frontera; staff at the Locutorio, Granada; Paul Montegrifo; Amanda Corbett at Patronato Provincial de Turismo de Sevilla; José Pérez de Ayala at the Parque Nacional de Doñana; Gabinete de Prensa, RENFE, Sevilla; Graham Hines and Rachel Taylor at the Sherry Institute of Spain, London; Dr David Stone; Joaquín Sendra at Turismo Andaluz SA; *6 Toros 6* magazine, Madrid.

PHOTOGRAPHY PERMISSIONS

THE PUBLISHER would like to thank all those who gave permission to photograph at various *ayuntamientos*, cathedrals, churches, galleries, hotels, museums, restaurants, shops, transport services and other establishments too numerous to thank individually.

PICTURE CREDITS

t = top; tl = top left; tc = top centre; tr = top right; cla = centre left above; ca = centre above; cra = centre right above; cl = centre left; c = centre; cr = centre right; clb = centre left below; cb = centre below; crb = centre right below; bl = bottom left; b = bottom; bc = bottom centre; br = bottom right; d = detail.

Every effort has been made to trace the copyright holders and we apologize in advance for any unintentional omissions. We would be pleased to insert the appropriate acknowledgments in any subsequent edition of this publication.

Works of art have been reproduced with the permission of the following copyright holders: © DACS London 1996: 52clb, 53ca; © PATRIMONIO NACIONAL MADRID: 43br, 46cl, 46cb, 47ca, 50bl.

Photos taken with the assistance of AL-ANDALUS, IBERRAIL SA, Madrid: 248b; CASA-MUSEO FG LORCA, Fuentevaqueros, Granada: 195b; TEATRO DE LA MAESTRANZA, Seville: 230t; CANAL SUR, Sevilla: 245cr.

The publisher would like to thank the following individuals, companies and picture libraries for permission to reproduce their photographs:

AISA ARCHIVO ICONOGRÁFICO, Barcelona: 4t, 21b, 21cr, *Juanita Cruz*, A Beltrane (1934) 24bl (d); Biblioteca Nacional Madrid/Museo Universal, *La Spange de C Davillier*, Gustavo Doré 26cl (d); 39t, 40tl, 40c, 40br, 41cr, 42ca; Cathedral, Seville, *San Isidoro y San Leandro*, Ignacio de Ries (17th century) 43crb; Universidad de Barcelona, *La Corte de Abderramán*, Dionisio Baixeres (1885) 44cr–45cl; 45tc, 45bl, 46bl, 46br, 47bl, 48bl; Museo Naval Madrid, *Retrato de Magallanes*, 48br; 50cl; Casón del Buen Retiro, *La Rendición de Bailén*, J Casado del Alisal (1864) 51t; Greenwich Museum, *Battle of Trafalgar*, G Chamberg 51ca (d); 50cr–51cl, 53br, 117bl; Museo-Casa de los Tiros, *Gitanos Bailando el Vito*, Anonymous 185br (d); Algar 42bl, 44clb; Servicio Histórico Nacional, *Alfonso XII*, R de Madrazo 51br (d); 53ca; © DACS 1996 Museo Nacional del Teatro, Almagro, Ciudad Real, poster "Yerma" (FG Lorca) by José Caballero y Juan Antonio Morales (1934) 53cb; D Baird 34b, 37c; Bevilacqua 43bl, 47c; JD Dallet 40clb; Dulevant 48clb; J Lorman 31tc; M Ángeles Sánchez 36t; Sevillano 37t; ARENAS FOTOGRAFÍA ARTÍSTICA, Seville: 47cr, 116cl, Monasterio de la Rábida, Huelva, *Partida de Colón*, Manuel Cabral Bejarano 123b (d).

LLA BELLE AURORE, Steve Davey & Juliet Coombe: 17c, 244clb; BRIDGEMAN ART LIBRARY/INDEX: *The Life and Times of Don Quixote y Saavedra* (1608), Biblioteca Universidad Barcelona 49bl.

CEPHAS: Mick Rock 18tr, 28tr, 28cl, 29cr, 29br, 155; Roy Stedall 29tr; CNES, 1987 DISTRIBUTION SPOT IMAGE: 11t; BRUCE COLEMAN: Hans Reinhard 19crb; Konrad Wothe 153crb; DEE CONWAY: 27ca, 27cr; GIANCARLO COSTA, MILAN: 25bc (d), 39b; JD DALLET, MÁLAGA: 16bl, 30tl, 30clb, 30br, 33b, 34t, 126tl, 142cr, 154, 198t; AGENCIA EFE, MADRID: 54clb, 54b, 55b, 55crb; EQUIPO 28, SEVILLE: 27tl; EUROPA PRESS REPORTAJES: 55br; MARY EVANS PICTURE LIBRARY: 9 (inset), 26tl, 57 (inset), 67b, 94b, 115 (inset), 169b (d), 235 (inset).

THE ROLAND GRANT ARCHIVE: *"For a Few Dollars More"*, United Artists 194t; GIRAUDON, PARIS: 40cr; Flammarion-Giraudon 41c; JOSÉ M GUTIERRÉZ GUILLÉN, SEVILLE: 82; ROBERT HARDING PICTURE LIBRARY: Sheila Terry 47br, 56–57; HULTON DEUTSCH: 52cr–53cl, AM/Keystone 55tl, 163b.

IBERIA ARCHIVES: 246t; INCAFO ARCHIVO FOTOGRÁFICO, MADRID: 153t, 153ca; A Camoyán 153cra, 153cb; JL Glez Grande 153cla; Candy Lopesino/Juan Hidalgo 153clb; JL Muñoz 153b; INDEX, BARCELONA: 41cb, 42br, 44cla, 44bl, 44br, 45cb, 50tl, 50br, 51crb, 51clb (d), 51bl, 187cra; Image/Index 52tl, Private Collection, *Sucesos de Casaviejas*, Saenz Tejada 53tl, 197 (inset); Iranzo 42clb; THE IMAGE BANK: © Chasan 59b; Stockphotos inc © Terry Williams 176; IMAGES: 4b, 14, 18b, 19tl, 19bl, 30tr, 32b; AGE Fotostock, 11b, 15t, 24tr, 24clb, 25c, 26br, 29cl, 35t, 35b, 36b, 133t, 153c, 214tr, 232t; Horizon/Michele Paggetta 24c–25c; courtesy ISLA MAGICA: 102tl, 102b.

PABLO JULIÁ, SEVILLE: 231b.

ANTHONY KING: 19tr.

LIFE FILE PHOTOGRAPHIC LIBRARY/Emma Lee 28tl, 144bl; JOSÉ LUCAS, SEVILLE: 230c, 232cl; NEIL LUKAS: 126cb, 126b.

ARXIU MAS, BARCELONA: 24br; Museo Taurino, Madrid, poster for a bullfight featuring Rodolfo Gaona, H Colmenero 25bl; 43tc, 44tl, 46tl, 46c, 46cr–47cl; Museo América, Madrid, *View of Seville*, Sánchez Coello 48cr–49cl; © Patrimonio Nacional Madrid 43br, 46cl, 46cb, 47ca; MAGNUM/Jean Gaumy 55cb.

NHPA: Vicente Garcia Canseco 127 ca; NATURPRESS, MADRID: Jose Luis G Grande 127b; Francisco Márquez 19br; NETWORK PHOTOGRAPHERS:

29tl; Rapho/Hans Silvester 32c.

ORONOZ ARCHIVO FOTOGRÁFICO, MADRID: Private Collection, *La Feria* (Seville), J Domínguez Bécquer (1855) 8–9; 24ca, Private Collection *Reyes Presidiendo a una Corrida de Toros* (1862), Anonymous 25br, Banco Urquijo *Cartel Anunciador Feria de Sevilla* (1903), J Aranda 32t, 36c, 40b, 41tl, 41tc, 41cl, 41crb, 41br, 42tl, 43tl; María Novella Church, Florence, *Detail of Averroes*, Andrea Bonainti 45tl; 45crb, 45br, 47tl; Diputación de Granada, *Salida de Boabdil de la Alhambra*, Manuel Gómez Moreno 47clb; 48tl, 48cla; Museo del Prado, *Cristo Crucificado*, Diego Velázquez 49c (d); Museo de Prado, *Expulsión de los Moriscos*, Vicent Carducho 49cb (d); Musée du Louvre, Paris, *Joven Mendigo*, Bartolomé Murillo 49br (d); © Patrimonio Nacional Madrid, Palacio Real, Riofrio, Segovia, *Carlos III Vestido de Cazador*, F Liani 50bl; © DACS London 1996, Sternberg Palace, Prague, *Self-Portrait*, Pablo Picasso 52clb; Private Collection, Madrid, *Soldados del Ejército Español en la Guerra de Cuba* 52br; 53crb, 53bl, 54tl, 55tc, 70bl, 81b, 139t, 140c; 86t; Private Collection, Madrid, *Patio Andaluz*, Garcia Rodríguez 142cl; 160tl; Museo de Bellas Artes, Cádiz, *San Bruno en Éxtasis*, Zurbarán 160tr; 185bl, 215br.

EDUARDO PAEZ, GRANADA: *Porte de la Justice*, Baron de Taylor 38; PAISAJES ESPAÑOLES, MADRID: 87t; JOSE M PEREZ DE AYALA, DOÑANA: 126tr, 126cl, 127t, 127ca; PICTURES: 37b; PRISMA, BARCELONA: 49tl, 131b; Museo Lázaro Galdiano, Madrid, *Lope de Vega*, F Pacheco 134b; 137t; *Vista desde el Puerto* Nicolás Chapny (1884) 175t; 231t, 232b; Ferreras 238b, Hans Lohr 157b; Anna N 166c; Sonsoles Prada 41bl.

M ÁNGELES SÁNCHEZ, MADRID: 228tr, 228tc; TONY STONE IMAGES: Robert Everts 80cla. 6 TOROS 6, MADRID: 25crb.

VISIONS OF ANDALUCÍA SLIDE LIBRARY, MÁLAGA: M Almarza 19cr; Michelle Chaplow 17br; 26cr–27cl, 158b, 249b; A Navarro 34cl.

PETER WILSON: 1, 2–3, 33t, 59cb, 141t, 166t, 166b, 171t.

Front endpaper: all commissioned photography except JD DALLET, MÁLAGA: bc; THE IMAGE BANK: Stockphotos inc © Terry Williams br; JOSE M GUTIERREZ GUILLÉN, SEVILLE: tc.

JACKET: Front - CEPHAS PICTURE LIBRARY: Mick Rock clb; COVER: main image; DK PICTURE LIBRARY: cr; Neil Lukas bc. Back - DK PICTURE LIBRARY: Linda Whitwam t; POWERSTOCK PHOTOLIBRARY: Walter Bibikow br. Spine - COVER.

DORLING KINDERSLEY SPECIAL EDITIONS

DORLING KINDERSLEY books can be purchased in bulk quantities at discounted prices for use in promotions or as premiums. We are also able to offer special editions and personalized jackets, corporate imprints, and excerpts from all of our books, tailored specifically to meet your own needs.

To find out more, please contact: (in the United Kingdom) Sarah.Burgess@dk.com or Special Sales, Dorling Kindersley Limited, 80 Strand, London WC2R 0RL; (in the United States) Special Markets Department, DK Publishing, Inc., 375 Hudson Street, New York, NY 10014.

Phrase Book

IN EMERGENCY

Help!	¡Socorro!	soh-**koh**-roh
Stop!	¡Pare!	**pah**-reh
Call a doctor!	¡Llame a un médico!	**yah**-meh ah **oon meh**-dee-koh
Call an ambulance!	¡Llame a una ambulancia!	**yah**-meh ah **oonah** ahm-boo-**lahn**-thee-ah
Call the police!	¡Llame a la policía!	**yah**-meh ah lah poh-lee-**thee**-ah
Call the fire brigade!	¡Llame a los bomberos!	**yah**-meh ah lohs bohm-**beh**-rohs
Where is the nearest telephone?	¿Dónde está el teléfono más próximo?	**dohn**-deh ehs-**tah** ehl teh-**leh**-foh-noh mahs **prohx**-ee-moh
Where is the nearest hospital?	¿Dónde está el hospital más próximo?	**dohn**-deh ehs-**tah** ehl ohs-pee-**tahl** mahs **prohx**-ee-moh

COMMUNICATION ESSENTIALS

Yes	Sí	see
No	No	noh
Please	Por favor	pohr fah-**vohr**
Thank you	Gracias	**grah**-thee-ahs
Excuse me	Perdone	pehr-**doh**-neh
Hello	Hola	**oh**-lah
Goodbye	Adiós	ah-dee-**ohs**
Good night	Buenas noches	**bweh**-nahs **noh**-chehs
Morning	La mañana	lah mah-**nyah**-nah
Afternoon	La tarde	lah **tahr**-deh
Evening	La tarde	lah **tahr**-deh
Yesterday	Ayer	ah-**yehr**
Today	Hoy	oy
Tomorrow	Mañana	mah-**nya**-nah
Here	Aquí	ah-**kee**
There	Allí	ah-**yee**
What?	¿Qué?	keh
When?	¿Cuándo?	**kwahn**-doh
Why?	¿Por qué?	pohr-**keh**
Where?	¿Dónde?	**dohn**-deh

USEFUL PHRASES

How are you?	¿Cómo está usted?	**koh**-moh ehs-**tah** oos-**tehd**
Very well, thank you.	Muy bien, gracias.	mwee **byehn grah**-thee-ahs
Pleased to meet you.	Encantado de conocerle.	ehn-kahn-**tah**-doh deh koh-noh-**thehr**-leh
See you soon.	Hasta pronto.	ahs-tah **prohn**-toh
That's fine.	Está bien.	ehs-**tah** bee-**yehn**
Where is/are . . .?	¿Dónde está/están . . .?	**dohn**-deh ehs-**tah**/ehs-**tahn**
How far is it to . . .?	¿Cuántos metros/ kilómetros hay de aquí a . . .?	**kwahn**-tohs **meh**-trohs/kee-**loh**-meh-trohs **eye** deh ah-**kee** ah
Which way to . . .?	¿Por dónde se va a . . .?	pohr **dohn**-deh seh vah ah
Do you speak English?	¿Habla inglés?	**ah**-blah een-**glehs**
I don't understand	No comprendo	noh kohm-**prehn**-doh
Could you speak slowly please?	¿Puede hablar más despacio por favor?	pweh-deh ah-**blahr** mahs dehs-pah-thee-oh pohr fah-**vohr**
I'm sorry.	Lo siento.	loh see-**ehn**-toh

USEFUL WORDS

big	grande	**grahn**-deh
small	pequeño	peh-**keh**-nyoh
hot	caliente	kah-lee-**ehn**-teh
cold	frío	**free**-oh
good	bueno	**bweh**-noh
bad	malo	**mah**-loh
enough	bastante	bahs-**tahn**-teh
well	bien	bee-**yehn**
open	abierto	ah-bee-**ehr**-toh
closed	cerrado	eeth-key-**ehr**-dah
left	izquierda	deh-**reh**-chah
right	derecha	toh-doh **rehk**-toh
straight on	todo recto	**thehr**-kah
near	cerca	**leh**-hohs
far	lejos	ah-**ree**-bah
up	arriba	ah-**bah**-hoh
down	abajo	tehm-**prah**-noh
early	temprano	

late	tarde	**tahr**-deh
entrance	entrada	ehn-**trah**-dah
exit	salida	sah-**lee**-dah
toilet	lavabos, servicios	lah-**vah**-bohs, sehr-**vee**-thee-ohs
more	más	mahs
less	menos	**meh**-nohs

SHOPPING

How much does this cost?	¿Cuánto cuesta esto?	**kwahn**-toh **kwehs**-tah **ehs**-toh
I would like . . .	Me gustaría . . .	meh goos-tah-**ree**-ah
Do you have?	¿Tienen?	tee-**yeh**-nehn
I'm just looking.	Sólo estoy mirando, gracias.	**soh**-loh ehs-**toy** mee-**rahn**-doh **grah**-thee-ahs
Do you take credit cards?	¿Aceptan tarjetas de crédito?	ah-**thehp**-tahn tahr-**heh**-tahs deh **kreh**-dee-toh
What time do you open?	¿A qué hora abren?	ah **keh** oh-rah **ah**-brehn
What time do you close?	¿A qué hora cierran?	ah keh oh-rah thee-**yehr**-rahn
This one.	Este	**ehs**-teh
That one.	Ese	**eh**-seh
expensive	caro	**kahr**-oh
cheap	barato	bah-**rah**-toh
size, clothes	talla	**tah**-yah
size, shoes	número	**noo**-mehr-oh
white	blanco	**blahn**-koh
black	negro	**neh**-groh
red	rojo	**roh**-hoh
yellow	amarillo	ah-mah-**ree**-yoh
green	verde	**vehr**-deh
blue	azul	ah-**thool**
antique shop	la tienda de antigüedades	lah tee-**yehn**-dah deh ahn-tee-gweh-**dah**-dehs
bakery	la panadería	lah pah-nah-deh-**ree**-ah
bank	el banco	ehl **bahn**-koh
book shop	la librería	lah lee-breh-**ree**-ah
butcher	la carnicería	lah kahr-nee-theh-**ree**-ah
cake shop	la pastelería	lah pahs-teh-leh-**ree**-ah
chemist	la farmacia	lah fahr-**mah**-thee-ah
fishmonger	la pescadería	lah pehs-kah-deh-**ree**-ah
greengrocer	la frutería	lah froo-teh-**ree**-ah
grocery	la tienda de comestibles	lah tee-**yehn**-dah deh koh-mehs-**tee**-blehs
hairdresser	la peluquería	lah peh-loo-keh-**ree**-ah
market	el mercado	ehl mehr-**kah**-doh
newsagent	el kiosko de prensa	ehl kee-**yohs**-koh deh **prehn**-sah
post office	la oficina de correos	lah oh-fee-**thee**-nah deh kohr-**reh**-ohs
shoe shop	la zapatería	lah thah-pah-teh-**ree**-ah
supermarket	el supermercado	ehl soo-pehr-mehr-**kah**-doh
tobacconist	el estanco	ehl ehs-**tahn**-koh
travel agent	la agencia de viajes	lah ah-**hehn**-thee-ah deh vee-**ah**-hehs

SIGHTSEEING

art gallery	el museo de arte	ehl moo-**seh**-oh deh **ahr**-teh
cathedral	la catedral	lah kah-teh-**drahl**
church	la iglesia la basílica	lah ee-**gleh**-see-yah lah bah-**see**-lee-kah
garden	el jardín	ehl hahr-**deen**
library	la biblioteca	lah bee-blee-yoh-**teh**-kah
museum	el museo	ehl moo-**seh**-oh
tourist information office	la oficina de información turística	lah oh-fee-**thee**-nah deh een-fohr-mah-thee-**yohn** too-**rees**-tee-kah
town hall	el ayuntamiento	ehl ah-yoon-tah-mee-**yehn**-toh
closed for holiday	cerrado por vacaciones	thehr-**rah**-doh pohr vah-kah-thee-**yoh**-nehs
bus station	la estación de autobuses	lah ehs-tah-thee-**yohn** deh owtoh-**boo**-sehs
railway station	la estación de trenes	lah ehs-tah-thee-**yohn** deh **treh**-nehs

STAYING IN A HOTEL

Do you have a vacant room?	¿Tiene una habitación libre?	tee-**yeh**-neh **oo**-nah ah-bee-tah-thee-**yohn** lee-breh
double room	habitación doble	ah-bee-tah-thee-**yohn** doh-bleh
with double bed	con cama de matrimonio	kohn **kah**-mah deh mah-tree-**moh**-nee-oh
twin room	habitación con dos camas	ah-bee-tah-thee-**yohn** kohn dohs **kah**-mahs
single room	habitación individual	ah-bee-tah-thee-**yohn** een-dee-vee-doo-**ahl**
room with a bath	habitación con baño,	ah-bee-tah-thee-**yohn** kohn bah-nyoh
shower	ducha	**doo**-chah
porter	el botones	ehl boh-**toh**-nehs
key	la llave	lah **yah**-veh
I have a reservation.	Tengo una habitación reservada.	tehn-goh **oo**-na ah-bee-tah-thee-**yohn** reh-sehr-**vah**-dah

EATING OUT

Have you got a table for ...?	¿Tienen mesa para ...?	tee-**yeh**-nehn meh-sah pah-**rah**
I want to reserve a table.	Quiero reservar una mesa.	kee-yeh-roh reh-sehr-**vahr** **oo**-nah **meh**-sah
The bill please.	La cuenta por favor.	lah **kwehn**-tah pohr fah-**vohr**
I am a vegetarian	Soy vegetariano/a	soy beh-heh-tah-ree-**yah**-no/na
Waitress/ waiter	Camarera/ camarero	kah-mah-**reh**-rah kah-mah-**reh**-roh
menu	la carta	lah **kahr**-tah
fixed-price menu	menú del día	meh-**noo** dehl **dee**-ah
wine list	la carta de vinos	lah **kahr**-tah deh **bee**-nohs
glass	un vaso	oon **vah**-soh
bottle	una botella	oo-nah boh-**teh**-yah
knife	un cuchillo	oon koo-**chee**-yoh
fork	un tenedor	oon teh-neh-**dohr**
spoon	una cuchara	oo-nah koo-**chah**-rah
breakfast	el desayuno	ehl deh-sah-**yoo**-noh
lunch	la comida el almuerzo	lah koh-**mee**-dah ehl ahl-**mwehr**-thoh
dinner	la cena	lah **theh**-nah
main course	el primer plato	ehl pree-**mehr plah**-toh
starters	los entremeses	lohs ehn-treh-**meh**-sehs
dish of the day	el plato del día	ehl **plah**-toh dehl **dee**-ah
coffee	el café	ehl kah-**feh**
rare	poco hecho	**poh**-koh **eh**-choh
medium	medio hecho	**meh**-dee-yoh **eh**-choh
well done	muy hecho	mwee **eh**-choh

MENU DECODER

al horno	ahl **ohr**-noh	baked
asado	ah-**sah**-doh	roast
el aceite	ah-**theh**-ee-teh	oil
las aceitunas	ah-theh-**toon**-ahs	olives
el agua mineral	**ah**-gwa mee-neh-**rahl**	mineral water
el ajo	**ah**-hoh	garlic
el arroz	ahr-**rohth**	rice
el azúcar	ah-**thoo**-kahr	sugar
la carne	**kahr**-neh	meat
la cebolla	theh-**boh**-yah	onion
la cerveza	thehr-**veh**-thah	beer
el cerdo	**thehr**-doh	pork
el chocolate	choh-koh-**lah**-teh	cho....
el chorizo	choh-**ree**-thoh	...sage
el cordero	kohr-**deh**-roh	.....
el fiambre	fee-**ahm**-breh	cold meat
frito	**free**-toh	fried
la fruta	**froo**-...	fruit
los frutos secos	fr... **seh**-kohs	nuts
las gambas	...bahs	prawns
el helado	...**lah**-doh	ice cream
el huevo	oo-**eh**-voh	egg
el jamón	hah-**mohn** sehr-**rah**-noh	cured ham

el jerez	heh-**rehz**	sherry
la langosta	lahn-**gohs**-tah	lobster
la leche	**leh**-cheh	milk
el limón	lee-**mohn**	lemon
la limonada	lee-moh-**nah**-dah	lemonade
la mantequilla	mahn-teh-**keh**-yah	butter
la manzana	mahn-**thah**-nah	apple
los mariscos	mah-**rees**-kohs	seafood
la menestra	meh-**nehs**-trah	vegetable stew
la naranja	nah-**rahn**-hah	orange
el pan	**pahn**	bread
el pastel	pahs-**tehl**	cake
las patatas	pah-**tah**-tahs	potatoes
el pescado	pehs-**kah**-doh	fish
la pimienta	pee-mee-**yehn**-tah	pepper
el plátano	**plah**-tah-noh	banana
el pollo	**poh**-yoh	chicken
el postre	**pohs**-treh	dessert
el queso	**keh**-soh	cheese
la sal	sahl	salt
las salchichas	sahl-**chee**-chahs	sausages
la salsa	**sahl**-sah	sauce
seco	**seh**-koh	dry
el solomillo	soh-loh-**mee**-yoh	sirloin
la sopa	**soh**-pah	soup
la tarta	**tahr**-tah	pie/cake
el té	teh	tea
la ternera	tehr-**neh**-rah	beef
las tostadas	tohs-**tah**-dahs	toast
el vinagre	bee-**nah**-greh	vinegar
el vino blanco	**bee**-noh **blahn**-koh	white wine
el vino rosado	**bee**-noh roh-**sah**-doh	rosé wine
el vino tinto	**bee**-noh **teen**-toh	red wine

NUMBERS

0	cero	**theh**-roh
1	uno	**oo**-noh
2	dos	dohs
3	tres	trehs
4	cuatro	**kwa**-troh
5	cinco	**theen**-koh
6	seis	says
7	siete	see-**yeh**-teh
8	ocho	**oh**-choh
9	nueve	**nweh**-veh
10	diez	dee-**yehz**
11	once	**ohn**-theh
12	doce	**doh**-theh
13	trece	**treh**-theh
14	catorce	kah-**tohr**-theh
15	quince	**keen**-theh
16	dieciséis	dee-eh-thee-**seh-ees**
17	diecisiete	dee-eh-thee-see-**yeh**-teh
18	dieciocho	dee-eh-thee-**oh**-choh
19	diecinueve	dee-eh-thee-**nweh**-veh
20	veinte	**beh**-yeen-teh
21	veintiuno	beh-yeen-tee-**oo**-noh
22	veintidós	beh-yeen-tee-**dohs**
30	treinta	**treh**-yeen-tah
31	treinta y uno	treh-yeen-tah ee **oo**-noh
40	cuarenta	kwah-**reh**...
50	cincuenta	theen-**k**...
60	sesenta	seh...
70	setenta	...**h**-tah
80	ochenta	...**chehn**-tah
90	noventa	noh-**behn**-tah
100	cien	thee-**yehn**
101	ciento uno	thee-**yehn**-toh **oo**-noh
102	ciento dos	thee-**yehn**-toh **dohs**
200	doscientos	dohs-thee-**yehn**-tohs
500	quinientos	khee-nee-**yehn**-tohs
700	setecientos	seh-teh-thee-**yehn**-tohs
900	novecientos	noh-veh-thee-**yehn**-tohs
1,000	mil	meel
1,001	mil uno	**meel oo**-noh

TIME

one minute	un minuto	oon mee-**noo**-toh
one hour	una hora	**oo**-na **oh**-rah
half an hour	media hora	**meh**-dee-a **oh**-rah
Monday	lunes	**loo**-nehs
Tuesday	martes	**mahr**-tehs
Wednesday	miércoles	mee-**ehr**-koh-lehs
Thursday	jueves	**hweh**-vehs
Friday	viernes	bee-**yehr**-nehs
Saturday	sábado	**sah**-bah-doh
Sunday	domingo	doh-**meen**-goh

EYEWITNESS TRAVEL INSURANCE

FOR PEACE OF MIND ABROAD,
WE'VE GOT IT COVERED

 DK INSURANCE PROVIDES YOU
WITH QUALITY WORLDWIDE
INSURANCE COVER

For an instant quote
go to **www.dk.com/travel-insurance**

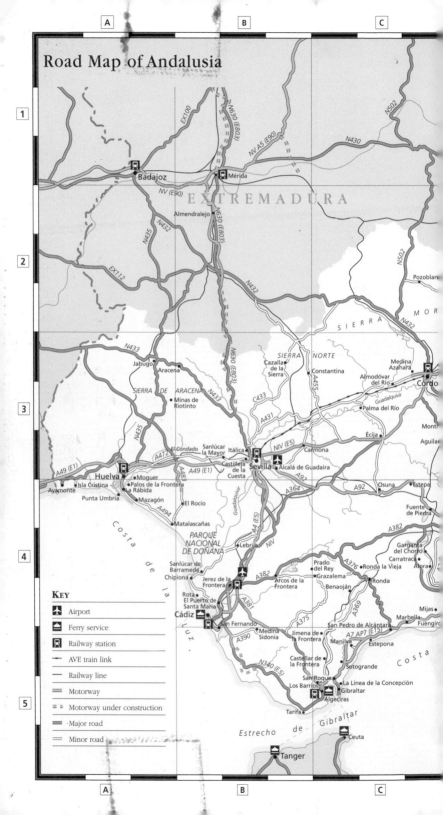